SECOND EDITION

FINANCIAL MARKET RATES AND FLOWS

JAMES C. VAN HORNE

Stanford University

PRENTICE-HALL, INC., *Englewood Cliffs, NJ   07632*

Library of Congress Cataloging in Publication Data

VAN HORNE, JAMES C.
  Financial market rates and flows.

  Bibliography: p.
  Includes index.
  1. Interest rates. 2. Flow of funds. 2. Capital
market. I. Title.
HB539.V338 1984   332.8   83-13959
ISBN 0-13-316414-4

Editorial/production supervision and interior design: Maureen Wilson
Cover design: Marvin R. Warshaw/Design
Manufacturing buyer: Ed O'Dougherty

Printed in the United States of America

10 9 8 7 6 5 4 3 2

ISBN 0-13-316414-4

PRENTICE-HALL INTERNATIONAL, INC., *London*
PRENTICE-HALL OF AUSTRALIA PTY. LIMITED, *Sydney*
EDITORA PRENTICE-HALL DO BRASIL, LTDA., *Rio de Janeiro*
PRENTICE-HALL CANADA INC., *Toronto*
PRENTICE-HALL OF INDIA PRIVATE LIMITED, *New Delhi*
PRENTICE-HALL OF JAPAN, INC., *Tokyo*
PRENTICE-HALL OF SOUTHEAST ASIA PTE. LTD., *Singapore*
WHITEHALL BOOKS LIMITED, *Wellington, New Zealand*

CONTENTS

PREFACE

The purpose of the second edition of *Financial Market Rates and Flows* remains to provide a conceptual understanding of the function of financial markets, of the flow of funds, of levels of interest rates, and of interest-rate differentials. The latter are due to differences in maturity, coupon rate, default risk, call feature, sinking fund, and taxability; the effect of each is examined in detail. Throughout there is an emphasis on market efficiency and on the effect that any imperfections may have on market returns. Another factor, the social allocation of capital, affects both interest rates and financial flows; the effect here is examined in the last chapter.

A second purpose of the book is to evaluate a rich body of empirical evidence as it bears on the various theories that are considered. The focus, then, is not only on the theoretical foundations for interest rates, but on the real world conditions that affect these rates and differentials between rates on various instruments. Our principle concern is with fixed-income securities, though in Chapter 11 securities convertible into common stock are studied.

The theory of interest rates, the types and variety of instruments available in the market, and the institutional environment in which markets equilibrate all have changed rather dramatically since the first edition of this book. This edition attempts to capture these changes. As a result, there have been a large number of improvements. Chapter 4, *Inflation and*

Returns, is new, and it reflects the important—and often less than pre-dictable—impact of inflation on promised and real returns. Chapter 5, *The Term Structure of Interest Rates*, has been substantially revised in keeping with new theoretical and empirical developments. Chapter 6, *Coupon Rate Effect and Immunization*, is largely new, and Chapter 7, *Interest Rate Futures*, is entirely new.

A number of significant changes occur in Chapter 8, *The Default Risk Structure of Interest Rates*, particularly with respect to the cyclical behavior of risk premiums and market segmentation. Chapter 9, *The Call Feature and Sinking Fund Provision*, is new for the most part. Chapter 10, *The Influence of Taxes*, has been materially changed to incorporate changing tax laws and new empirical evidence and conceptual developments. Chapter 11, *Convertible Securities*, is entirely new; the valuation of this hybrid instrument is explored in several ways, including the option pricing model. Chapter 12, *The Social Allocation of Capital*, has been revised to reflect changing regulations and tax laws, as well as to introduce a new section on tax-exempt financing of private projects. In addition to these changes, pertinent improvements and updatings are made in the first three chapters, which serve as a foundation for the subsequent development of the book.

Financial Market Rates and Flows can be used as a foundation text or as a supplement for courses in money and capital markets, money and banking, monetary policy, investments, and financial institutions. In addition, it is useful to those in the financial community, in business, and in government who are concerned with investing in or issuing fixed-income securities and with the flow of funds through financial markets.

JAMES C. VAN HORNE

Palo Alto, California

1

THE FUNCTION OF
FINANCIAL MARKETS

In this book, the underlying structure of financial markets is examined, as is the price mechanism, which brings about a balance between supply and demand. Our purpose is not to describe specific money or capital markets or the institutions involved in these markets; this information is available elsewhere.[1] Rather, this book provides a basis for understanding and analyzing interest rates and funds movements in financial markets. The instruments studied are financial assets. Unlike real, or tangible, assets, a *financial* asset is a paper claim on some other economic unit. It does not provide its owner with the physical services that a real asset does. Instead, financial assets are held as a store of value and for the return that they are expected to provide. The holding of these assets, with the exception of equity securities, indicates neither direct nor indirect ownership of real assets in the economy.

---

[1]S. Kerry Cooper and Donald Fraser, *The Financial Marketplace* (Reading, Mass.: Addison-Wesley Publishing Co., Inc., 1982); Murray E. Polakoff et al., *Financial Institutions and Markets*, 2nd ed. (Boston: Houghton Mifflin Co., 1981); J. O. Light and William L. White, *The Financial System* (Homewood, Ill.: Richard D. Irwin, 1979); Roland I. Robinson and Dwayne Wrightsman, *Financial Markets: The Accumulation and Allocation of Wealth* (New York: McGraw-Hill Book Company, 1980); David S. Kidwell and Richard L. Peterson, *Financial Institutions, Markets, and Money* (Hinsdale, Ill.: The Dryden Press, 1981).

SAVINGS-INVESTMENT FOUNDATION

Financial assets exist in an economy because the savings of various economic units (current income less current expenditures) during a period of time differ from their investment in real assets. In this regard, an economic unit can be (1) a household or partnership, (2) a nonprofit organization, (3) a corporation (financial or nonfinancial), or (4) a government (federal, state, or local). There are a number of reasons why economic units invest more than they save or save more than they invest over an interval of time. These include the present income of the economic unit, expected future income, costs of goods and services, personal tastes, age, health, education, family composition, and current interest rates, as well as a number of other reasons.

The productive resources in any society, such as land, machines, buildings, natural resources, and workers, are limited. These resources may all be devoted to producing goods and services for current consumption; or a part of them may go toward things that will enhance the nation's ability to produce, and hence consume, in the future. This process might involve the production of machinery, the exploration for iron ore, or the training of workers in new technology. Capital formation can be defined as any investment that increases the productive capacity of society. If resources are fully employed, the only way to make such investments is to refrain from current consumption. If resources are less than fully employed, however, it is possible to have capital formation without necessarily foregoing current consumption.

In a broad sense, capital formation involves not only investment in tangible assets, such as buildings, equipment, and inventories, but also intangible investments in such things as education, training, health, and labor mobility—all of which enhance productivity. For our purposes in studying financial flows, however, we will use a narrower definition and restrict our attention to investments in tangible or real assets. Investment in human capital will be treated as consumption, not because it does not contribute to increased productivity, but because data on it are imprecise for purposes of quantifying financial flows.

Assume for the moment a closed economy in which there are no foreign transactions. If savings equal investment for all economic units in that economy over all periods of time, there would be no external financing and no financial assets. In other words, each economic unit would be self-sufficient; current expenditures and investment in real assets would be paid for out of current income. A financial asset is created only when the investment of an economic unit in real assets exceeds its savings, and it finances this excess by borrowing, issuing equity securities, or issuing money (if the economic unit happens to be a monetary institution).[2] Of course, for an economic unit to finance, another economic unit or other units in the economy must be willing to lend. This interaction of the borrower with the lender determines interest rates. For identification, economic units whose current savings exceed their investment in real assets are called *savings-surplus units*. Economic units whose investment in real assets exceeds their current savings are labeled *savings-deficit units*.[3] In the economy as a whole, funds are provided by the savings-surplus units to the savings-deficit units. This exchange of funds is evidenced by pieces of paper representing financial assets to the holders and financial liabilities to the issuers.

If an economic unit holds existing financial assets, it is able to cover the excess of its investments in real assets over savings by means other than issuing financial liabilities. It simply can sell some of the financial assets it holds. Thus, as long as an economic unit holds financial assets, it does not have to increase its financial liabilities by an amount equal to its excess of investment over savings. The purchase and sale of existing financial assets occur in the *secondary market*. Transactions in this market do not increase the total stock of financial assets outstanding. It is possible, although unlikely, for a substantial number of savings-deficit units to exist in an economy over a period of time and for little change to occur in the total financial assets outstanding. For this to happen, however, savings-deficit units must have sufficient financial assets to cover the excess of their investment in real assets over savings and, of course, must be willing to sell these assets.

EFFICIENCY OF FINANCIAL MARKETS

The purpose of financial markets is to allocate savings efficiently in an economy to ultimate users, either for investment in real assets or for consumption. In this section, we regard financial markets in a broad sense as including all institutions and procedures for bringing buyers and sellers of financial instruments together, no matter what the nature of the financial instrument. If those economic units which saved were the same as those which engaged in capital formation, an economy could prosper without financial markets. In modern economies, however, the units in the economic sector most responsible for capital formation—nonfinancial

[2]A financial asset may be created for the purpose of financing consumption in excess of current income. Although it is possible for investment in real assets for a period to be zero, that investment would still exceed the negative savings of the economic unit.

[3]These labels correspond to those given by Raymond W. Goldsmith, *The Flow of Capital Funds in the Postwar Economy* (New York: National Bureau of Economic Research, 1965).

corporations—invest in real assets in an amount in excess of their total savings. The household sector, on the other hand, has total savings in excess of total investment. Therefore, a balance is *not* achieved. The more diverse the pattern of desired savings and investment among economic units, the greater the need for efficient financial markets to channel savings to ultimate users. Their job is to allocate savings from savings-surplus economic units to savings-deficit units so that the highest level of want satisfaction can be achieved. These parties should be brought together, either directly or indirectly, at the least possible cost and with the least inconvenience.

Stages of Efficiency

Efficient financial markets are essential to assure adequate capital formation and economic growth in a modern economy. To appreciate this statement, imagine an economy without financial assets other than money.[4] In such an economy, each economic unit could invest in real assets only to the extent that it saved. Without financial assets, then, an economic unit would be greatly constrained in its investment behavior. If it wanted to invest in real assets, it would have to save to do so. If the amount required for investment were large in relation to current savings, the economic unit simply would have to postpone investment until it had accumulated sufficient savings. Moreover, these savings would have to be accumulated as money balances, there being no alternatives. Because of the absence of financing, many worthwhile investment opportunities would have to be postponed or abandoned by economic units lacking sufficient savings.[5]

In such a system, savings in the economy would not be channeled to the most promising investment opportunities; accordingly, capital would be less than optimally allocated. Those economic units that lacked promising investment opportunities would have no alternative except to accumulate money balances. Likewise, economic units with very promising opportunities might not be able to accumulate sufficient savings rapidly enough to undertake the projects. Consequently, inferior investments might be undertaken by some economic units, while very promising investment opportunities would be postponed or abandoned by others. Capital is misallocated in such a system, and total investment tends to be low relative to what it might be with financial assets. In this situation, growth in the

[4]In a barter economy, without money or financial assets, each economic unit must be in balance with respect to savings and investment. It must invest in real assets in an amount equal to its savings. No economic unit could invest more than it saved.

[5]The development of this section draws on John G. Gurley and Edward S. Shaw, *Money in a Theory of Finance* (Washington, D.C.: The Brookings Institution, 1960).

economy is restrained, if not stagnant, and the level of want satisfaction is far from optimal.

The discussion above has been confined to the private sector of the economy. With money, however, the federal government is able to finance its purchases of goods and services by issuing money. If the federal government increases the supply of money in keeping with increases in the demand for money by other economic units, purchases of goods and services by the government increase. To the extent that the federal government centralizes investment and channels it into promising opportunities, capital formation in the economy is efficient. However, if the government is a cumbersome bureaucracy that is unresponsive to market conditions, government decisions are unlikely to result in efficient capital formation.

We turn now to the situation where there are financial assets as well as money in the economy, but no financial institutions. With financial assets, investment in real assets by an economic unit is no longer constrained by the amount of its savings. If the economic unit wants to invest more than it saves, it can do so by reducing the amount of its money balances, by selling financial assets, or by increasing its financial liabilities. When an economic unit increases its financial liabilities, it issues a *primary security*. For this to be done, however, another economic unit or other units in the economy must be willing to purchase it. In a developing economy, these transactions between borrower and lender usually take the form of direct loans. The ability of economic units to finance an excess of investment over savings greatly improves the allocation of savings in a society. Many of the problems cited earlier are eliminated. Individual economic units no longer need to postpone promising investment opportunities for lack of accumulated savings. Moreover, savings-surplus units have an outlet for their savings other than money balances—an outlet that provides an expected return. With financial assets in the form of direct loans the overall level of want satisfaction in the economy is higher than it would be otherwise.

Still there are degrees of efficiency. A system of direct loans may not be sufficient to assemble and "package" large blocks of savings for investment in large projects. To the extent that a single savings-surplus economic unit cannot service the capital needs of a savings-deficit unit, the latter must turn to additional savings-surplus units. If the need for funds is large, users may have considerable difficulty in locating pockets of available savings and in negotiating multiple loans. For one thing, their information network is limited. Consequently, there is a need to bring together ultimate savers and investors in a more efficient manner than through direct loans between the two parties.

To service this need, various loan brokers may come into existence to find savers and bring them together with economic units needing funds. Because brokers are specialists who are continually in the business of matching the need for funds with the supply, they are usually able to perform more efficiently and at a lower cost than are the individual economic units themselves. One improvement is that they are able to divide a primary security of a certain amount into smaller amounts more compatible with the preferences of savings-surplus economic units. As a result, savers are able to hold their savings in a diversified portfolio of primary securities; this feature encourages savers to invest in financial assets. The resulting increased attractiveness of primary securities improves the flow of savings from savers to users of funds. In addition to performing the brokerage function involved in selling securities, investment bankers may underwrite an issue of primary securities. By underwriting, investment bankers bear the risk of selling the issue. They buy the primary securities from the borrower and resell them to savers. Since they pay the borrower for the security issue, the latter does not bear the risk of not being able to sell the securities. This guaranteed purchase makes it easier than otherwise for savings-deficit economic units to finance their excess of investment in real assets over savings.

Another innovation that enhances the efficiency of the flow of savings in an economy is the development of *secondary markets*, where existing securities can be either bought or sold. With a viable secondary market, a savings-surplus economic unit achieves flexibility when it purchases a primary security. Should it need to sell the security in the future, it will be able to do so because the security is marketable. The existence of secondary markets encourages more risk-taking on the part of savings-surplus economic units. If, in the future, they want to invest more than they save, they know that they will be able to sell financial assets as one means of covering the excess. This flexibility encourages savings-surplus economic units to make their savings available to others rather than to hold them as money balances. In addition, the secondary market gives valuable pricing information to the primary market. The prices and yields reflected in this market provide a rational basis for borrowing and lending decisions in the primary market and for pricing new loans.

All of the innovations discussed in this section contribute to the efficiency of the flow of savings from ultimate savers to ultimate users through primary securities. As a result, capital allocation is more efficient: Savings are more readily channeled to the most promising investments.

The Role of Financial Intermediaries

Up until now, we have considered only the direct flow of savings from savers to users. However, the flow can be indirect if there are financial intermediaries in the economy. Financial intermediaries include such institutions as commercial banks, savings banks, savings and loan associations, life insurance companies, mutual funds, and pension and profit-sharing funds. These intermediaries purchase primary securities and, in turn, issue their own securities. Thus, they come between ultimate borrowers and ultimate lenders. In essence, they transform direct claims—primary securities—into indirect claims—*indirect securities*—which differ in form from direct claims. For example, the primary security that a savings and loan association purchases is a mortgage; the indirect claim issued is a savings account or certificate of deposit. A life insurance company, on the other hand, purchases mortgages and bonds and issues life insurance policies.

Financial intermediaries transform funds in such a way as to make them more attractive. On one hand, the indirect security issued to ultimate lenders is more attractive than is a direct, or primary, security. In particular, these indirect claims are well suited to the small saver. On the other hand, the ultimate borrower is able to sell its primary securities to a financial intermediary on more attractive terms than it could if the securities were sold directly to ultimate lenders. Financial intermediaries provide a variety of services and economies that make the transformation of claims attractive.

1. *Transaction costs.* Because financial intermediaries are continually in the business of purchasing primary securities and selling indirect securities, economies of scale not available to the borrower or to the individual saver are possible. As a result, transactions costs and costs associated with locating potential borrowers and savers are lowered.

2. *Information production.* The financial intermediary is able to develop information on the ultimate borrower in a more efficient manner than the saver. Moreover, the intermediary may be able to reduce the moral hazard problem of unreliable information. Another possible advantage is that intermediaries can protect the confidentiality of information.

3. *Divisibility and flexibility.* A financial intermediary is able to pool the savings of many individual savers to purchase primary securities of varying sizes. In particular, the intermediary is able to tap small pockets of savings for ultimate investment in real assets. The offering of indirect securities of varying denomination makes financial intermediaries more attractive to the saver. Moreover, borrowers have more flexibility in dealing with a financial intermediary than with a large number of lenders and are able to obtain terms better suited to their needs.

4. *Diversification and risk.* By purchasing a number of different primary securities, the financial intermediary is able to spread risk. If these securities are less than perfectly correlated with each other, the intermediary is able to reduce the risk associated with fluctuations in

value of principal. The benefits of reduced risk are passed on to the indirect security holders. As a result, the indirect security provides a higher degree of liquidity to the saver than does a like commitment to a single primary security. To the extent individuals are unable, because of size or other reasons, to achieve adequate diversification on their own, the financial intermediation process is beneficial.

5. *Maturity*. A financial intermediary is able to transform a primary security of a certain maturity into indirect securities of different maturities. As a result, the maturities on the primary and the indirect securities may be more attractive to the ultimate borrower and lender than they would be if the loan were direct.

6. *Expertise and convenience*. The financial intermediary is an expert in making purchases of primary securities and in so doing eliminates the inconvenience to the saver of making direct purchases. For example, not many individuals are familiar with the intricacies of making a mortgage loan; they have neither the time nor the inclination to learn. For the most part, they are happy to let savings and loan associations, commercial banks, savings banks, and life insurance companies engage in this type of lending and to purchase the indirect securities of these intermediaries. The financial intermediary is also an expert in dealing with ultimate savers—an expertise lacking in most borrowers.

Financial intermediaries tailor the denomination and type of indirect securities they issue to the desires of savers. Their purpose, of course, is to make a profit by purchasing primary securities yielding more than the return they must pay on the indirect securities issued and on operations. In so doing, they must channel funds from the ultimate lender to the ultimate borrower at a lower cost or with more convenience or both than is possible through a direct purchase of primary securities by the ultimate lender. Otherwise, they have no reason to exist.

To illustrate this notion, suppose that without financial intermediaries the rate of interest to a borrower would be 14 percent. In addition, the borrower must incur the indirect costs of searching for lenders and arranging for the loan. Suppose that these costs approximate 1 percent per annum. Therefore, the effective cost of borrowing via the direct loan is 15 percent. The rate of interest to the lender, of course, is 14 percent. However, search costs are incurred by the lender. In addition, the amount of the funds the lender has available may not correspond to the amount that the potential borrower wishes to obtain. As a result, it may be necessary to pool the funds of several potential lenders, and this involves time and energy. Also, there is the cost of administering the loan and attending to the numerous details involved. The amount that some individuals are required to lend may be so great, relative to their total financial assets, that it precludes adequate diversification. Such lenders must be compensated for the greater risk. Finally, the lumpiness of the loan may result in pockets of unusable funds. For example, an individual may have $2,700 to lend, but the loan amount is only $2,500. As a result, there is an idle $200.

Suppose that all of these costs correspond to an annual interest rate of 6 percent. When this is deducted from the gross interest rate of 14 percent, the "net" interest rate to the lender becomes 8 percent. Thus, we have the following:

Borrower:	
Total cost to borrower	15 percent
Less search costs	1 percent
Interest rate charged	14 percent
Lender:	
Gross interest rate received	14 percent
Less costs of search, administration, pooling, and diversification constraints	6 percent
Net interest return	8 percent

Therefore, the differential between the total cost to the borrower and the net return to the lender is 15 percent less 8 percent, which equals 7 percent.

Suppose now that financial intermediation is possible, and that a deposit-type intermediary stands ready to accept longer-term deposits at a 10 percent rate with no inconvenience to the saver. The intermediary also will lend to the borrower in question at a 13 percent rate. The 3 percent spread between the two rates covers the expenses of the intermediary and provides it with a profit. We see then that the ultimate borrower is able to borrow at a lower effective rate—13 percent as opposed to 15 percent. Moreover, the net return to the lender is higher—10 percent as opposed to 8 percent. The spread between the effective borrowing and lending rates has been narrowed from 7 percent to 3 percent. This is possible for all of the reasons stated above. As a result, the presence of financial intermediaries is beneficial both to ultimate borrowers and to ultimate lenders.

Thus, financial intermediaries tend to make financial markets more efficient. By transforming primary securities into indirect securities, they lower the cost to the ultimate borrower and provide a security better suited to the ultimate lender. The yield differential, as represented by the difference in yield between the borrower's cost and the net yield to the saver on an equivalent loan, is narrowed by their presence. In our example, it is narrowed from a 15–8 percent spread to a 13–10 percent spread. One of the marks of efficient financial markets is that when opportunities for profit exist or arise, financial intermediaries and other financial innovations come into being to exploit the opportunity. By entering the market, they tend to narrow the differential, as defined above. Thus, they facilitate the movement of savings from ultimate savers to ultimate borrowers at a lower cost and with less inconvenience. The result is that a higher proportion of income tends to be saved in a society, and interest costs to borrowers tend to be lower than they would be in the absence of these intermediaries. The development of financial intermediaries has been an important factor contributing to capital formation and the growth of the economy. In turn, this has contributed to a higher level of want satisfaction.

With the introduction of financial intermediaries, we have four main sectors in an economy: households, nonfinancial business firms, governments, and financial institutions. These four sectors form a matrix of claims against one another. This matrix is illustrated in Fig. 1-1, which shows hypothetical balance sheets for each sector. Financial assets of each sector include money as well as primary securities. Households, of course, are

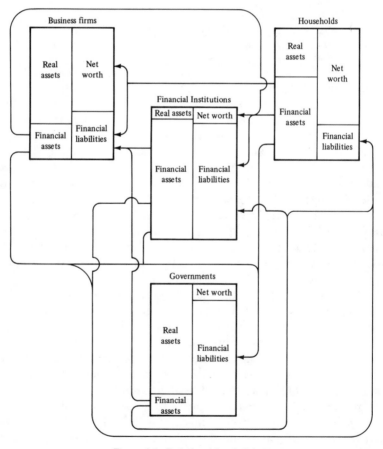

Figure 1-1. Relationship of claims.

the ultimate owners of all business enterprises, whether they are nonfinancial corporations or private financial institutions. The figure illustrates the distinct role of financial intermediaries. Their assets are predominantly financial assets; they hold a relatively small amount of real assets. On the right-hand side of the balance sheet, financial liabilities are predominant. Financial institutions, then, are engaged in transforming direct claims into indirect claims that have a wider appeal. The relationships of financial to real assets and of financial liabilities to net worth distinguish them from other economic units.

The more varied the vehicles by which savings can flow from ultimate savers to ultimate users of funds, the more efficient the financial markets of an economy usually are. The more developed the financial markets, the greater the choices of the saver in putting savings to work and the greater the financing opportunities available to the borrower. The utility of both is increased. With efficient financial markets, then, there can be sharp differences between the pattern of savings and the pattern of investment for economic units in the economy. The result is a higher level of capital formation, growth, and want satisfaction. Individual economic units are not confined either to holding their savings in money balances or to investing them in real assets. Their alternatives are many; each contributes to the efficient channeling of funds from ultimate savers to users.

The Implications of Savings

Having outlined the reason for financial assets in an economy and traced through the efficiency of financial markets, we now consider the implications of savings, individually and collectively, for economic units. Recall that savings represent current income less current consumption.

For the *individual*, savings represent expenditures foregone out of current income, and they may be the result of a number of acts. One of the most familiar is spending less than one's discretionary income, with the difference going into a savings account. The buildup in a savings account, in itself, does not represent an act of savings but, rather, is the result of it. Other aspects of savings for the individual are less familiar. For example, savings may be the result of repayment of principal in a mortgage payment. Another means by which net worth may be increased is through contributions, either voluntary or involuntary, to a pension or profit-sharing plan or both. In addition, an individual may save through the payment of a premium on a life insurance policy.

For the *corporation, net* savings represent earnings retained during the period being studied—that is, profits after taxes and after the payment of dividends on preferred and common stock. *Gross* savings for corporations include capital-consumption allowances (mainly depreciation) in addition to retained earnings. Finally, savings for a *government* unit represent a budget surplus, and dissavings a budget deficit.

For a given period of time, the total uses of funds by an economic unit must equal its total sources. Thus,[6]

$$RA + MT + L + E = S + D + IM + B + IE \qquad (1\text{-}1)$$

where RA = gross change in real assets
$\quad MT$ = change in money held
$\quad\ L$ = lending (change in fixed-income securities held)
$\quad\ E$ = equity investment (change in equity securities held)
$\quad\ S$ = net savings
$\quad\ D$ = capital-consumption allowance
$\quad IM$ = issuance of money
$\quad\ B$ = borrowing
$\quad IE$ = issuance of equity securities

All the symbols represent net flows over a period of time, and they can be positive or negative. Depending upon the type of economic unit involved, however, some of the variables may not be applicable. As only monetary institutions can issue money, IM is applicable only to the central bank and commercial banks. Similarly, only corporations can issue equity securities, so IE applies only to them. For the economic unit, the total uses of funds on the left side of the equation must equal total sources on the right side.

For purposes of financial-market analysis, net savings for the economic unit usually are defined as[7]

$$S = (MT + L + E) - (IM + B + IE) + (RA - D) \qquad (1\text{-}2)$$

| gross savings through financial assets | financing | net savings through real assets |

net savings through financial assets

---

[6]This equation is a modification of an equation developed by Goldsmith in *The Flow of Capital Funds in the Postwar Economy*, p. 59. For simplicity, we assume a closed economy with no foreign transactions.

[7]Again, this equation is a modification of Goldsmith, *The Flow of Capital Funds in the Postwar Economy*.

For the economy as a whole, *ex post* savings for a given period of time must equal *ex post* investment in real assets for that period. Consequently,

$$\sum_j S = \sum_j (RA - D) \qquad (1\text{-}3)$$

where j is the jth economic unit in the economy and the capital Greek sigma is the summation of all of these units. Thus, changes in financial assets for a period cancel out when summed for all economic units in the economy.

$$\sum_j (MT + L + E) - \sum_j (IM + B + IE) = 0 \qquad (1\text{-}4)$$

As a result, savings for the economy as a whole must correspond to the increase in net real assets in that economy. There is no such thing as savings through financial assets for the economy as a whole. However, individual economic units can save through financial assets, and this is the process we wish to study. The fact that financial assets wash out when they are totaled for all economic units in the economy is a recognizable identity. It is the interaction between the issuers of financial claims and the potential holders of those claims that is important. Also, we must recognize that desired or *ex ante* savings for the economy as a whole need not equal *ex ante* investment. The equilibrating process has implications not only for interest rates in general but for the interactions among individual economic units.

LIQUIDITY AND FINANCIAL MARKETS

All financial instruments have a common denominator in that they are expressed in terms of money—the accepted medium of exchange. Thus, financial flows occur in terms of money. Money, the most liquid of assets, is the measure against which various types of financial instruments are compared as to their degree of substitution. In this regard, *liquidity* may be defined as the ability to realize value in money. As such, it has two dimensions: (1) the length of time and transaction cost required to convert the asset into money, and (2) the certainty of the price realized. The latter represents the stability of the ratio of exchange between the asset and money—in other words, the degree of fluctuation in market price. The two factors are interrelated. If an asset must be converted into money in a very short period of time, there may be more uncertainty as to the price realized than if there were a reasonable time period in which to sell the asset.

Financial markets tend to be efficient relative to other markets. As the good involved is a claim, evidenced by a piece of paper, it is transportable at little cost and is not subject to physical deterioration. Moreover, it can be defined and classified easily. For most financial markets, information is readily available, and geographical boundaries are not a great problem. By their very nature, then, financial markets are fairly efficient when compared with the full spectrum of markets.

Frequently, these markets are classified according to the final maturity of the particular instrument involved. On one hand, *money* markets usually are regarded as including financial assets that are short term, are highly marketable, and, accordingly, possess low risk and a high degree of liquidity. These assets are traded in highly impersonal markets, where funds move on the basis of price and risk alone. Thus, a short-term loan negotiated between a corporation and a bank is not considered a money-market instrument. Examples of money markets include the markets for short-term government securities, bankers' acceptances, and commercial paper. *Capital* markets, on the other hand, include instruments with longer terms to maturity. These markets are somewhat more diverse than money markets. Examples include markets for government, corporate, and municipal bonds; corporate stocks; and mortgages. The maturity boundary that divides the money and capital markets is rather arbitrary. Some regard it as one year, while others maintain that it is five years. Because the foundation for their existence is the same, we have not concerned ourselves in this chapter with the breakdown between the two markets.

FINANCIAL FLOWS AND INTEREST RATES

In studying financial markets, we are interested in the flow of savings from ultimate savers to ultimate users. These flows can be analyzed with *flow-of-funds* data. Flow of funds is a system of social accounting that enables one to evaluate savings flows among various sectors in the economy. This system and its usefulness are examined in Chapter 2. The actual allocation, or channeling, of savings in an economy is accomplished primarily through interest rates. Presumably, economic units with the most promising investment opportunities will pay more for the use of funds on a risk-adjusted return basis than those with less promising opportunities. To the extent that the former bid funds away from the latter, savings tend to be channeled to the most efficient uses. Interest rates adjust continually to bring changing supply and demand in each market into balance. The movement toward equilibrium occurs not only in an individual financial market but also across financial markets. The role of interest rates in the equilibrating process is studied in Chapter 3.

The important influence of inflation expectations on interest rates is explored in Chapter 4. One can view the market equilibration process in terms of real rates of return, as opposed to nominal returns. Subsequent chapters are devoted to an analysis of relative interest rates and returns for various financial instruments. In Chapters 5 through 10, we investigate reasons for differences in the level of interest rates among fixed-income securities. These differences are called *yield differentials*. In each case, the theoretical reasons for a yield differential are considered first, followed by an examination of relevant empirical evidence. In Chapter 5, we see how the length of time to maturity affects the yield. Known as the *term structure of interest rates,* this topic is qualified in Chapter 6 for the effect of differences in coupon rates, which, in turn, affect the duration of a financial instrument. The investment in coupon-bearing bonds, as opposed to pure discount bonds, involves reinvestment risk, a risk that can be partially immunized through judicious bond selection. Reducing risk exposure also may be accomplished through interest rate futures markets. These markets, their use, and the relationship of futures rates to the forward rates embodied in the term structure of interest rates are explored in Chapter 7.

In Chapter 8, the effect of differences in default risk on interest rates is analyzed. Chapter 9 is devoted to the effects of a call feature and of a sinking fund on the value of a financial instrument. The presence of a call provision usually results in the possibility that the actual maturity of a security will be less than the stated maturity. A sinking fund provides for the periodic retirement of a security, and it also affects the security's valuation. In Chapter 10, the effect of taxes on the interest rates we observe in the marketplace is explored. If market equilibrium occurs in terms of after-tax rates of return, the impact of whether or not interest income is taxed, the differential tax on interest and capital gains, and estate tax consideration have important influences on relative interest rates.

A convertible security has some of the features of a fixed-income security, as well as an option to purchase common stock. The valuation of this hybrid instrument is investigated in Chapter 11. While allocation of savings in an economy occurs primarily through interest rates, it is affected also by institutional imperfections and by government restrictions. The effects of various institutional imperfections are taken up in Chapters 5 through 11, as they bear on a particular problem. The effect of government restrictions is addressed in Chapter 12; here we consider attempts by the government to socially allocate capital in an economy and/or to lower the interest-rate cost for certain borrowers. The various methods for socially allocating capital are presented and are analyzed as to their effectiveness and cost.

SUMMARY

A financial asset is a claim against some economic unit in an economy. It is held for the return it provides and as a store of value—reasons that differentiate it from a real asset. Financial assets and markets exist because during a period of time some economic units save more than they invest in real assets, while other economic units invest more than they save. To cover an excess of investment over savings for a period, an economic unit can reduce its holdings of existing financial assets, increase its financial liabilities, or undertake some combination of the two. When it increases its financial liabilities, a new financial instrument is created in the economy. The existence of financial markets permits investment for economic units to differ from their savings.

The purpose of financial markets is to allocate efficiently savings in an economy to ultimate users of funds. For the economy as a whole, *ex post* investment must equal *ex post* savings. However, this is not true for individual economic units; they can have considerable divergence between savings and investment for a particular period of time. The more vibrant the financial markets in an economy, the more efficient the allocation of savings to the most promising investment opportunities, and the greater the capital formation in that economy. A number of innovations make financial markets efficient. Among the most important are financial intermediaries. A financial intermediary transforms the direct claim of the ultimate borrower into an indirect claim, which is sold to ultimate lenders. Intermediaries channel savings from ultimate savers to ultimate borrowers at a lower cost and with less inconvenience than is possible on a direct basis.

All financial flows occur in terms of money, the most liquid of assets. Liquidity may be defined as the ability to realize value in money. Generally, financial markets are efficient relative to other markets. In the chapters that follow, we shall investigate in depth both the flow of savings and the price mechanism—namely, interest rates—which bring about a balance between supply and demand in the various financial markets. Our concern is with both the level of interest rates and the differentials between interest rates for different financial instruments.

SELECTED REFERENCES

Benston, George J., and Clifford W. Smith, Jr., "A Transactions Cost Approach to the Theory of Financial Intermediation," *Journal of Finance*, 31 (May 1976): 215–32.

Campbell, Tim S., and William A. Kracaw, "Information Production, Market Signalling, and the Theory of Financial Intermediation," *Journal of Finance*, 35 (September 1980): 863–82.

Cooper, S. Kerry, and Donald R. Fraser, *The Financial Marketplace*. Reading, Mass.: Addison-Wesley Publishing Co., Inc., 1982.

Dougall, Herbert E., and Jack E. Gaumnitz, *Capital Markets and Institutions*, 4th ed. Englewood Cliffs, N.J.: Prentice-Hall, Inc., 1980.

Goldsmith, Raymond W., *Financial Institutions*. New York: Random House, Inc., 1968.

———— , *The National Balance Sheet of the United States*. Chicago: University of Chicago Press, 1982.

Gurley, John G., and Edward S. Shaw, *Money in a Theory of Finance*. Washington, D.C.: The Brookings Institution, 1960.

Kaufman, George G., *The U.S. Financial System*. 2nd ed. Englewood Cliffs, N.J.: Prentice-Hall Publishing Co., Inc. 1983.

Leland, Hayne E., and David H. Pyle, "Informational Asymmetries, Financial Structure, and Financial Intermediation," *Journal of Finance,* 32 (May 1977): 371–88.

Light, J. O., and William L. White, *The Financial System*. Homewood, Ill.: Richard D. Irwin, 1979.

Moore, Basil J., *An Introduction to the Theory of Finance,* Chapters 1, 3, and 4. New York: The Free Press, 1968.

Polakoff, Murray E., et al., *Financial Institutions and Markets*, 2nd ed. Boston: Houghton Mifflin Company, 1981.

Pyle, David H., "On the Theory of Financial Intermediation," *Journal of Finance,* 26 (June 1971): 737–47.

Ritter, Lawrence S., and William L. Silber, *Principles of Money, Banking and Financial Markets,* 4th ed. New York: Basic Books, Inc., 1983.

Robinson, Roland I., and Dwayne Wrightsman, *Financial Markets: The Accumulation and Allocation of Wealth*. 2nd ed. New York: McGraw-Hill Book Co., 1980.

Wood, John H., "Financial Intermediaries and Monetary Control: An Example," *Journal of Monetary Economics,* 8 (September 1981): 145–64.

2

THE FLOW-OF-FUNDS SYSTEM

An indispensable tool of financial-market analysts is the flow-of-funds framework. This framework enables them to analyze the movement of savings through the economy in a highly structured, consistent, and comprehensive manner. Analysts are able not only to evaluate the complex interdependence of financial claims throughout the economy, but also to identify various pressure points in the system. The insight gained from studying these pressure points is valuable when it comes to analyzing possible changes in market rates of interest. In addition, the flow-of-funds framework makes possible an analysis of the interaction between the financial and the real segments of the economy. Such analysis was not possible before flow-of-funds data were available.

The flow of funds is a system of social accounting. Its foundation was Morris A. Copeland's celebrated work in 1952.[1] The Board of Governors of the Federal Reserve System first began to publish data on the flow of

---

[1]Morris A. Copeland, *A Study of Moneyflows in the United States* (New York: National Bureau of Economic Research, 1955).

funds in 1955[2] and published a revised and quarterly presentation of data in 1959.[3] Since 1959, quarterly data have been published regularly by the Federal Reserve System. Flow-of-funds accounts are a companion to national-income accounts. Whereas the national-income accounting system deals with goods and services, or the real side of the economy, flow-of-funds data provide information on the financial side. For example, national-income accounts provide data on the amount of savings, but they give no information on how savings are used. The process by which funds flow from savings to investment is omitted. One must turn to flow-of-funds data to obtain this information. In this chapter, we discuss the structure of the flow-of-funds accounting system, examine the interrelationship of sources and uses of funds for various sectors in the economy, and, finally, investigate the uses of this information.

THE STRUCTURE OF THE SYSTEM

Flow-of-funds data for an economy are derived for a specific period of time by (1) preparing source-of-funds and use-of-funds statements for each sector in the economy, (2) totaling the source and uses for all sectors, and (3) presenting the information in a flow-of-funds matrix for the entire economy.[4] The time span studied usually is either a quarter of a year or a full year.

Sectoring

The starting point in any flow-of-funds accounting system is the division of the economy into a workable number of sectors; the idea is to lump together those economic units with similar behavior. Because funds movements through sectors are being analyzed, economic units in a sector must be relatively homogeneous decision-making units if the analysis is to be meaningful. For this reason, sectors are defined along institutional lines according to the similarity of their asset and liability structures. The number of sectors used depends upon the purpose of the analysis, the availability of data, and the cost involved in collecting the data. The max-

[2]*Flow of Funds in the United States, 1939–1953* (Washington, D.C.: Board of Governors of the Federal Reserve System, 1955).

[3]See "A Quarterly Presentation of Flow of Funds and Savings," *Federal Reserve Bulletin, 45* (August, 1959), 828–59.

[4]See Lawrence S. Ritter, *The Flow of Funds Accounts: A Framework for Financial Analysis* (New York: Institute of Finance, New York University, 1968) for an exposition on the preparation of a flow-of-funds system of social accounting.

imum possible number of sectors, of course, is the total number of economic units in the economy; in the United States, this would be around 100 million. The minimum number is two, for there can be no flow of funds with only one sector—the economy as a whole.

If there are too few sectors, significant relationships among various groups of economic units are likely to be hidden. On the other hand, if there are too many sectors, the analysis of the interaction among sectors becomes very cumbersome. Here, the problem is that important relationships, although not hidden, may be overlooked. Needless to say, the number of sectors finally employed usually represents a compromise. In the sectoring of the economy, it is absolutely necessary that all economic units be included. Moreover, if foreign transactions are considered, a sector must be included for the rest of the world.

The four main sectors used in the U.S. flow-of-funds system are households, governments, business enterprises, and financial institutions. For reporting purposes, the Federal Reserve has subdivided some of these sectors, breaking them down into the following categories:

1. Households, personal trusts, and nonprofit organizations.
2. Nonfinancial business (subsectors: farm; nonfarm; noncorporate; and corporate).
3. Governments (subsectors: state and local governments; U. S. government; federally sponsored credit agencies; and mortgage pools).
4. Banking system (subsectors: monetary authorities; and commercial banks).
5. Nonbank finance (subsectors: savings and loan associations; mutual savings banks; credit unions; life insurance companies; private pension funds; state and local government retirement funds; other insurance; finance companies; real estate investment trusts; open-end investment companies; money market funds; and security brokers and dealers).
6. Rest of the world.

The last sector comprises all residents and governments outside the United States. Essentially, it serves to net together all external inflows and outflows so that the flow-of-funds system can be brought into balance. As the Federal Reserve is the principal source of flow-of-funds data, the analyst must settle for this breakdown of the economy.

Source and Use Statements

Once the economy has been divided into sectors, the next step is to prepare a source-and-use-of-funds statement for each sector. The starting point here is a balance sheet for each sector at the beginning of the period being studied.

SECTOR A JANUARY 1, 19__	
Assets	*Liabilities and Net Worth*
Money	Financial Liabilities
Other financial assets	
Real assets _____	Net worth _____
Total assets ======	Total liabilities and net worth ======

Most of the assets in the above balance sheet are reported at their market values. It is important to recognize that the presence of financial assets on the balance sheet for one sector means that financial liabilities of the same amount appear on the balance sheets of other sectors in the economy. In other words, financial assets represent claims against someone else and consequently must be shown as a liability on that party's balance sheet. In contrast, real assets appear on only one balance sheet, namely that of the owner.

Also, we must recognize that financial assets and liabilities among economic units in a particular sector are netted out. The financial asset figure for the sector includes only claims against economic units in other sectors. By the same token, the financial liability figure includes only claims held by economic units in other sectors against economic units in the sector being studied. As long as at least one economic unit in a sector holds a financial claim against another economic unit in that sector, the financial asset figure and the financial liability figure shown on the balance sheet for the sector will be less than the sum of financial assets and the sum of financial liabilities for all economic units in that sector. This statement does not hold for real assets, however. Because a real asset appears on the balance sheet only of the economic unit which owns it, the real asset figure shown on the balance sheet for a sector is the sum of real assets for all economic units in the sector.

By definition, a balance sheet shows the stocks of assets, liabilities, and net worth of a sector at a moment in time. By taking the change which occurs in stocks between two balance sheets at different points in time, expressed as Δ, we obtain the net flows for the sector over the time span. These net flows can be expressed in a source-and-use-of-funds statement for the sector.

SECTOR A
SOURCES AND USES OF FUNDS, 19___

Uses		Sources	
Δ Money		Δ Financial liabilities	
Δ Other financial assets		Δ Net worth	_____
Δ Real assets	_____		
Δ Total assets	═══════	Δ Total liabilities and net worth	═══════

For the period, the net change in total assets for a sector must equal the net change in total liabilities and net worth. The change in net worth represents savings for the period—that is, the difference between current income and current expenditures. Positive savings imply an increase in total assets, a decrease in total liabilities, or both. A savings-deficit sector, with investment in real assets greater than its savings, must reduce its money holdings, sell other financial assets, increase its liabilities, or perform some combination of these actions. Conversely, a savings-surplus sector must show an increase in its holdings of financial assets (including money), a reduction in its financial liabilities, or some combination.

The Preparation of a Matrix and Its Use

Once source-and-use-of-funds statements have been prepared for all sectors, these statements can be combined into a matrix for the entire economy. A hypothetical example of such a matrix is shown in Table 2-1. In the table, a closed economy consisting of four sectors—households, business firms, financial institutions, and governments—is assumed. We see the matrix forms an interlocking system of flow of funds for the period. For each sector, the total uses of funds equal the total sources. Because the system is self-contained, the total uses of funds for all sectors must equal the total sources for these sectors. More important, total savings for all sectors during the period must equal the total increase in real assets for that period. Likewise, the total change in financial assets, including money, must equal the total change in financial liabilities. Again, we see that financial assets and financial liabilities cancel each other for the economy as a whole.

The value of the matrix is that it allows analysis of the flow of funds through various sectors of the economy in a manner similar to that of an input-output analysis. For the individual sector, savings need not equal investment in real assets, and the change in financial assets need not equal the change in financial liabilities. For example, business firms represent a

Table 2-1. Matrix of Flow of Funds of Entire Economy 19___

	HOUSEHOLDS		BUSINESS FIRMS		FINANCIAL INSTITUTIONS		GOVERNMENTS		ALL SECTORS	
	U	S	U	S	U	S	U	S	U	S
Net worth (savings)		101		77		4		−3		179
Real assets (investments)	82		96		1				179	
Money	2		2			5	1		5	5
Other financial assets	37		18		60		17		132	
Financial liabilities		20		39		52		21		132
	121	121	116	116	61	61	18	18	316	316

savings-deficit sector in Table 2-1. For this sector, the excess of investment in real assets over savings was financed by an increase in financial liabilities in excess of the increase in financial assets. The existence of this rather large savings-deficit sector means that there must be one or more savings-surplus sectors in the economy for the period being studied. When we analyze the matrix, we see that households, the sector primarily responsible for financing the business sector on a net basis, is the largest savings-surplus sector. In addition, however, financial institutions are a savings-surplus sector, although the excess of savings over investment for this sector is small. This sector acts almost entirely as a financial intermediary; it increases its financial assets by issuing financial liabilities to finance the increase in financial assets. Because the sector contains commercial banks and the monetary authorities, it provides money to other sectors in the economy. The $5 source of money for this sector represents an increase in demand deposits and currency held by the public and governments as claims against commercial banks and the monetary authorities. Therefore, the total increase in money held by households, business firms, and governments must equal the increase in money-balance claims against the financial institutions sector.

The last sector in our example, governments, is a savings-deficit sector. This means that, collectively, federal, state, and local governments ran a budget deficit for the period. Although governments made substantial expenditures for real assets, their expenditures are not shown because of the lack of reliable estimates. Unfortunately, then, this rather important effect must be omitted from any analysis. A budget deficit for the governments sector must be financed by an increase in financial liabilities in excess of the increase in financial assets. The matrix in Table 2-1 illustrates the fundamental aspects of flow of funds in an economy over a period of time.

The example is kept purposely simple, with only four sectors in the economy.

It is important to recognize that certain information is destroyed in the final presentation of the results. As mentioned earlier, the change in financial assets and liabilities for a sector reflects changes that occur only with other sectors. No information is given about financial transactions among economic units in a given sector. Financial claims among these economic units simply cancel out. As a result, we do not know how much net financing occurs within the sector. The need for this information decreases, of course, as the number of sectors used in the flow-of-funds system increases. With aggregation of economic units into a sector, no information is given about the distribution of investment-savings behavior for economic units in that sector. Only the total for all economic units is reported.

Another problem is that the flow of funds for a period represents the net rather than the gross flow between two points in time. For example, the change in financial assets for a sector is simply beginning financial assets less ending financial assets. During the period, there may have been numerous changes in claims against economic units in other sectors. However, no information is given about the magnitude of these changes. For example, financial institutions may purchase $140 billion in mortgages over the period, while principal payments on existing mortgages held and the sale of existing mortgages amounts to $80 billion. The net change in mortgages reported in flow-of-funds data for the financial institutions sector is $60 billion. Although it may be revealing to know the gross funds flow over time, we are constrained to the information available—namely, the net flow between the two dates. This problem, however, occurs in any source-and-use-of-funds analysis. Although all flows are netted, financial assets and liabilities for single transaction categories are not netted out. For example, a household may borrow to purchase a house. In this case, the assets and liability are not netted; both are shown. These shortcomings, together with the problem of appropriate sectoring of the economy discussed previously, should be recognized when interpreting the published data. In certain cases, they may have an important influence upon the conclusions reached.

FEDERAL RESERVE FLOW-OF-FUNDS DATA

The basic source of data on the flow of funds is the Federal Reserve System. Quarterly, the Flow-of-Funds Section of the Division of Research and Statistics compiles extensive data on net funds flows. This publication is available upon request. It contains information that allows one to construct a matrix of the flow-of-funds accounts.

An example of the type of information provided by the Federal Reserve is shown in Table 2-2. Here the household sector is illustrated. The gross savings for this sector are shown in row 11. For 1981, they were $440.7 billion and for the first quarter of 1982, $449.7 billion, on an annual basis. These figures should be compared with capital expenditures, line 13, to determine whether or not the sector was a savings-surplus or a savings-deficit sector. We see that it was a substantial savings-surplus sector. The difference between gross savings and capital expenditures should be reflected in a buildup of financial assets, line 18, less the net increase in financial liabilities, line 38.

Thus, for the first quarter of 1982, we see that gross savings of $449.7 billion (row 11), less capital expenditures of $326.3 billion (row 13), is $123.4 billion. The buildup in financial assets of $291.2 billion (row 18), less the net increase in financial liabilities of $75.8 billion (row 38), equals $215.4 billion, which is shown in row 17 and labeled *net financial investment*. Obviously, $123.4 billion does not equal $215.4 billion; there is a discrepancy. This discrepancy of $92 billion is reflected in row 49. Although the flow of funds is an interlocking accounting system, which should balance in principle, unfortunately discrepancies occur. These are due to inconsistencies in timing, valuation, classification, coverage, and statistical errors in data collection. As a result, we must work with this shortcoming and allow for errors and discrepancies in balancing.

With the information in Table 2-2, together with that for other sectors, we are able to construct a matrix of actual funds flows for a period of time. This construction is illustrated in Table 2-3 for the first quarter of 1982. As reflected here, households were the most important savings-surplus sector, while the U. S. government was a substantial savings-deficit sector. Nonfinancial business also was a modest savings-deficit sector, with capital expenditures exceeding gross savings. This pattern is typical, although the federal deficit is extremely large and the business deficit extremely small by historical standards. For the period under review, the federal government was the dominant user of savings in the United States. In the table, we see that financial institutions were primarily conduits for savings; that is, the direct impact of their activities on the real economy was relatively unimportant. However, substantial savings flows occurred through them.

Because of foreign transactions, the foreign sector account is necessary. In this sector, all foreign economic units are lumped together. The sector records transactions only between economic units in foreign countries and economic units in the United States. For example, a transaction between a business firm in France and one in West Germany would not be shown. In the last column, the all sectors summary, the items for the various sectors are added together. In this regard, we know that gross savings should equal the investment in real assets, and that the increase

Table 2-2. Flow of Funds for the Household Sector, 1977–82 (billions of dollars)

SEASONALLY ADJUSTED ANNUAL RATES

	1977	1978	1979	1980	1981	1980 IV	1981 I	1981 II	1981 III	1981 IV	1982 I		
Households, Personal Trusts, and Nonprofit Organizations													
1538.0	1721.7	1943.8	2160.2	2404.1	2256.2	2319.8	2368.5	2441.7	2486.5	2511.3	Personal income	1
226.5	258.8	302.0	338.5	388.2	359.2	372.0	382.9	399.8	398.0	398.3	− Personal taxes and nontaxes	2
1311.5	1462.9	1641.7	1821.7	2016.0	1897.0	1947.8	1985.6	2042.0	2088.5	2113.0	= Disposable personal income	3
1237.5	1386.6	1555.6	1720.4	1908.4	1799.4	1858.9	1879.0	1935.1	1960.5	1997.7	− Personal outlays	4
74.1	76.3	86.2	101.3	107.6	97.6	88.9	106.6	106.9	128.0	115.3	= Personal saving, NIA basis	5
22.5	27.9	24.4	35.3	37.4	28.1	25.4	45.8	46.5	32.0	30.2	+ Credits from government insurance	6
.6	.7	.9	1.7	2.7	2.2	4.2	1.6	2.0	3.0	1.6	+ Capital gains dividends	7
50.2	56.3	52.4	33.8	34.4	37.7	48.2	32.0	36.1	21.3	26.5	+ Net durables in consumption	8
147.5	161.2	163.9	172.0	182.1	165.6	166.7	186.0	191.5	184.2	173.6	= Net savings	9
162.0	182.1	205.3	230.8	258.6	241.4	247.8	255.3	262.0	269.2	276.1	+ Capital consumption	10
309.5	343.3	369.2	402.9	440.7	407.1	414.5	441.3	453.5	453.4	449.7	= Gross saving	11
344.4	386.5	419.5	482.5	537.0	495.0	499.0	505.7	579.7	563.7	541.7	Gross investment	12
265.4	302.9	326.1	313.1	335.8	322.4	344.9	337.3	339.5	321.4	326.3	Capital expend. net of sales	13
80.7	97.1	106.6	93.8	96.2	91.6	99.0	102.4	95.7	87.2	82.0	Residential construction	14
178.8	199.3	212.3	211.9	232.0	223.3	238.3	227.3	236.2	226.4	236.5	Consumer durable goods	15
5.9	6.5	7.2	7.4	7.6	7.5	7.5	7.6	7.7	7.7	7.8	Nonprofit plant and equip.	16
78.9	83.6	93.4	169.5	201.2	172.6	154.2	168.4	240.2	242.3	215.4	Net financial investment	17
221.3	251.9	265.8	279.5	307.7	302.4	275.6	304.9	347.7	302.9	291.2	Net acq. of financial assets	18
161.1	186.8	221.3	198.9	242.5	239.7	221.1	242.5	281.7	224.6	218.2	Dep. + cr. mkt. instr. (1)	19
129.0	129.1	136.8	171.4	199.3	208.8	213.7	165.6	189.0	229.1	208.4	Deposits	20
21.3	22.2	23.2	10.9	21.9	−3.3	57.5	2.3	−7.6	35.5	12.2	Checkable dep. + curr.	21
95.1	63.6	62.3	81.2	40.6	102.3	29.8	−2.0	18.7	116.0	109.4	Small time + svgs. dep.	22
12.5	36.4	16.9	50.0	29.3	121.7	−22.0	105.3	40.5	−6.7	50.4	Large time deposits	23
.2	6.9	34.4	29.2	107.5	−11.9	148.4	59.9	137.3	84.3	36.4	Money market fund shrs	24

25	Credit mkt. instruments	32.1	57.6	84.5	27.6	43.2	30.9	7.4	77.0	92.8	-4.4	9.9
26	U.S. govt. securities	16.9	30.7	51.8	20.5	30.6	13.7	-8.3	55.7	96.8	-21.6	4.6
27	St. + local obligations	-1.5	1.8	2.4	3.0	14.9	10.0	24.6	14.8	7.9	12.5	11.3
28	Corporate + fgn. bonds	-3.8	-2.9	10.3	3.6	-10.4	2.8	-1.4	-19.0	-21.5	.3	-10.0
29	Mortgages	10.8	11.7	12.4	8.1	7.7	10.3	6.5	9.0	9.0	6.5	5.4
30	Open-market paper	9.8	16.3	7.5	-7.6	.3	-5.8	-13.9	16.5	.6	-2.0	-1.6
31	Mutual fund shares	.4	-.5	-.6	4.4	7.8	.1	11.0	7.7	4.0	8.6	15.0
32	Other corporate equities	-4.8	-5.2	-16.2	-6.3	-39.0	-5.4	-26.5	-39.7	-52.4	-37.5	-32.3
33	Life insurance reserves	11.5	12.0	12.5	11.5	10.1	11.4	11.5	12.3	12.3	4.1	13.0
34	Pension fund reserves	54.6	61.8	54.3	77.5	87.9	66.6	67.5	91.9	99.2	92.8	81.8
35	Net inv. in noncorp. bus.	-7.6	-12.2	-13.4	-18.3	-11.7	-22.4	-19.4	-18.0	-6.9	-2.3	-11.2
36	Security credit	-1.0	2.6	.6	4.1	3.6	4.3	3.9	1.6	3.1	5.8	-.2
37	Miscellaneous assets	6.9	6.6	7.2	7.7	6.6	8.0	6.4	6.5	6.7	6.8	6.9
38	Net increase in liabilities	142.4	168.3	172.4	110.1	106.5	129.8	121.4	136.5	107.5	60.5	75.8
39	Credit market instruments	139.1	164.3	170.6	101.7	103.6	114.2	119.7	128.9	110.3	55.4	86.2
40	Home mortgages	93.0	107.6	114.6	83.4	65.3	83.8	78.2	78.3	64.3	40.5	56.9
41	Other mortgages	1.1	1.3	1.5	1.5	1.4	1.5	1.4	1.4	1.4	1.4	1.4
42	Installment cons. credit	34.9	41.9	39.2	1.4	19.9	12.7	23.4	24.1	26.6	5.5	8.4
43	Other consumer credit	5.3	5.7	7.1	.9	5.4	-1.6	3.5	8.0	7.4	2.7	2.2
44	Bank loans n.e.c.	2.5	4.1	1.8	5.6	.7	11.1	1.8	8.5	-2.6	-4.7	9.6
45	Other loans	2.3	3.8	6.4	8.9	10.8	6.7	11.4	8.6	13.2	10.0	7.8
46	Security credit	1.3	1.3	-1.2	5.0	.2	12.4	-1.3	4.7	-5.4	2.7	-12.6
47	Trade debt	1.1	1.5	1.6	2.1	1.5	2.0	1.8	1.6	1.4	1.1	.9
48	Miscellaneous	.9	1.1	1.3	1.2	1.3	1.2	1.3	1.3	1.3	1.3	1.3
49	Discrepancy	-34.9	-43.3	-50.3	-79.6	-96.4	-87.9	-84.5	-64.4	-126.3	-110.3	-91.9

Source: *Flow of Funds Accounts, 1st Quarter, 1982* (Washington, D.C.: Federal Reserve System).

Table 2-3. *Matrix of Flow of Funds, First Quarter, 1982, Seasonally Adjusted Annual Rate (billions of dollars)*

ASSETS AND LIABILITIES	HOUSE-HOLDS U	HOUSE-HOLDS S	NON-FINANCIAL BUSINESS U	NON-FINANCIAL BUSINESS S	STATE AND LOCAL GOVERNMENT U	STATE AND LOCAL GOVERNMENT S	U.S. GOVERNMENT AND FEDERALLY SPONSORED AGENCIES U	U.S. GOVERNMENT AND FEDERALLY SPONSORED AGENCIES S	MONETARY AUTHORITIES U	MONETARY AUTHORITIES S	COMMERCIAL BANKS U	COMMERCIAL BANKS S	NON-BANK FINANCE U	NON-BANK FINANCE S	FOREIGN U	FOREIGN S	ALL SECTORS U	ALL SECTORS S
1. Gross savings		449.7		294.3		10.8		-122.1		0.5		15.1		-2.1		5.0		651.2
2. Capital expenditures	326.3		297.4		1.0						11.8		1.5				637.0	
3. Net financial investments (5–6)	215.4			58.2	1.0			121.4	0.5		4.1			3.2		26.3	11.9	
4. Gross investment (2 and 3)	541.7		239.2		1.0		-121.4		0.5		15.9		-1.7		-26.3		648.9	
5. Financial assets increase	291.2		48.7		28.6		17.3		1.9		202.9		245.0		23.9		859.5	
6. Financial liabilities increase		75.8		106.9		27.6		138.7		1.4		198.8		248.2		50.2		847.6
7. Sector discrepancy (1–4)	92.0		55.1		9.8			0.7				0.8		0.4	21.3			2.3

Source: *Flow of Funds, 1st Quarter, 1982* (Washington, D.C.: Board of Governors of the Federal Reserve System, May 1982).

in financial assets should equal the increase in financial liabilities. Because of discrepancies, however, this does not occur, although there is almost a balance for the period.

Credit Flows

In addition to the information provided on ultimate sources and uses of funds, the Federal Reserve provides a wealth of information on the specific financial instruments through which savings flow. The information is of particular interest to capital market analysts. It tells them what sectors finance with what types of instruments and what sectors hold these instruments. In order to illustrate the usefulness of this information, we examine three sectors in more detail—households; nonfinancial corporate business; and nonbank finance. The information for households is in Table 2-2, whereas the data for the other two sectors are shown in Tables 2-4 and 2-5, respectively.

For households, we find that mortgages and consumer credit (rows 40–43)—in that order—represent the largest single increase in financial liabilities. Turning to Table 2-5, we can see that the nonbank finance sector usually is a large acquirer of home mortgages (row 13). This is largely accounted for by savings and loan associations, a subsector in this category. The nonbank finance sector also is typically the most important provider of consumer credit. Here credit unions and finance companies are the most important subsectors.

The principal means of financing corporations (Table 2-4) are bank loans (row 49), followed by bonds (row 44), mortgages (row 45), and commercial paper (row 50). Returning to Table 2-5, we see that nonbank financial institutions are large investors in corporate bonds (row 12), as well as mortgages (row 13) and commercial paper (row 15, under *other loans*). The principal subsectors are: life insurance companies, pension funds, and state and local government employee retirement funds for corporate bonds; life insurance companies and state and local government employee retirement funds for mortgages; and money market mutual funds for commercial paper. Finally, nonbank financial institutions form the principal sector involved with investing in corporate equities (row 8). Whereas the household sector liquidated corporate equities on a net basis for the period under review (line 32 of table 2-2), the nonbank finance sector absorbed an amount *in excess of the net amount issued by corporations.* The principal subsectors involved are private pension funds and state and local government retirement funds. The pattern of net liquidation by the household sector and net accumulation by the nonbank finance sector has existed for a number of years. Increasingly, through these intermediaries,

Table 2-4. Flow of Funds for Nonfinancial Corporate Business, 1977–82 (billions of dollars)

SEASONALLY ADJUSTED ANNUAL RATES

Nonfinancial Corporate Business, Excluding Farms

	1977	1978	1979	1980	1981	1980 IV	1981 I	1981 II	1981 III	1981 IV	1982 I		
Profits before tax	153.1	173.8	192.8	183.3	184.2	190.9	202.6	181.5	186.8	166.0	127.0	Profits before tax	1
− Profit tax accruals	59.2	67.1	69.5	62.9	58.7	65.7	67.9	57.6	59.4	50.1	31.4	− Profit tax accruals	2
− Domestic net dividends	41.6	46.2	52.3	58.8	66.3	60.7	62.6	65.0	68.0	69.4	70.0	− Domestic net dividends	3
= Domestic undist. profits	52.3	60.6	71.0	61.7	59.2	64.6	72.1	58.8	59.4	46.5	25.7	= Domestic undist. profits	4
+ Capital consumption adj.	−11.1	−12.1	−13.7	−14.0	−9.9	−14.2	−11.0	−10.6	−9.3	−8.5	−5.5	+ Capital consumption adj.	5
+ Depreciation charges, NIPA	115.2	128.1	145.6	163.7	184.0	170.7	174.7	181.2	187.1	193.2	196.8	+ Depreciation charges, NIPA	6
+ Earnings rec. from abroad	9.8	10.3	15.2	18.6	16.1	18.2	15.9	16.5	15.7	16.2	13.8	+ Earnings rec. from abroad	7
= U. S. internal funds, book	166.3	186.8	218.1	230.0	249.5	239.2	251.7	245.9	252.9	247.4	230.8	= U. S. internal funds, book	8
+ Fgn. earnings ret. abroad	5.7	9.4	15.1	12.5	8.1	9.5	9.5	6.3	8.8	7.8	6.0	+ Fgn. earnings ret. abroad	9
+ Inv. valuation adjustment	−15.8	−24.3	−42.6	−45.7	−27.7	−48.4	−39.2	−24.0	−25.3	−22.3	−10.1	+ Inv. valuation adjustment	10
= Total internal funds + IVA	156.1	171.9	190.6	196.8	229.9	200.3	222.0	228.2	236.4	232.9	226.7	= Total internal funds + IVA	11
Gross investment	120.4	142.4	164.5	152.4	177.6	148.5	195.2	167.1	173.7	174.6	171.6	Gross investment	12
Capital expenditures (1)	174.1	199.2	220.9	216.9	258.7	224.3	231.6	265.4	281.8	256.1	228.4	Capital expenditures (1)	13
Fixed investment	153.1	177.4	202.6	212.7	239.1	222.6	232.4	235.1	244.2	244.9	254.7	Fixed investment	14
Plant and equipment	149.4	175.0	202.0	212.6	239.9	216.8	229.4	236.7	246.9	246.7	254.1	Plant and equipment	15
Home construction	2.1	.6	−.6	−1.0	−1.9	5.0	1.5	−2.7	−3.7	−2.8	−.3	Home construction	16
Multifamily residential	1.6	1.8	1.2	1.1	1.1	.8	1.4	1.1	1.0	1.0	.9	Multifamily residential	17
Inventory change + IVA	18.5	19.9	13.5	−2.3	13.3	−13.0	5.4	21.8	22.5	3.7	−35.3	Inventory change + IVA	18
Mineral rts. from U. S. govt.	2.5	2.0	4.7	6.5	6.2	14.7	−6.1	8.5	15.1	7.5	9.0	Mineral rts. from U. S. govt.	19
Net financial investment	−53.7	−56.9	−56.4	−64.5	−81.1	−75.8	−36.4	−98.3	−108.1	−81.5	−56.8	Net financial investment	20
Net acq. of financial assets	54.4	91.7	119.7	74.9	66.1	118.2	68.5	85.4	64.0	46.4	40.6	Net acq. of financial assets	21
Liquid assets	4.7	10.9	17.7	13.1	12.9	1.7	21.7	14.1	1.0	14.8	18.2	Liquid assets	22
Demand dep. and currency	1.6	4.8	5.3	2.3	2.5	−5.6	5.2	2.6	−4.3	6.5	.6	Demand dep. and currency	23
Time deposits	4.8	2.0	4.7	1.7	5.2	.7	12.2	4.1	7.8	−3.2	1.1	Time deposits	24
Security RP's	1.2	5.5	2.6	6.6	*	5.5	7.4	−4.5	−11.6	8.7	9.4	Security RP's	25
Foreign deposits	1.3	2.0	1.5	.9	−.6	4.9	10.2	−7.8	−5.0	*	.3	Foreign deposits	26
U. S. govt. securities	−4.1	−3.7	−.4	−2.1	1.8	−2.6	−15.1	14.3	5.9	2.2	4.1	U. S. govt. securities	27

SEASONALLY ADJUSTED ANNUAL RATES

#		C1	C2	C3	C4	C5	C6	C7	C8	C9	C10	C11
28	State + local obligations	*	.2	*	-.2	*	.2	-.1	.1	*	–	*
29	Commercial paper	-.1	.2	3.9	3.9	4.0	-1.4	1.9	5.3	8.3	.6	2.9
30	Consumer credit	.8	1.0	2.9	1.6	1.8	1.7	4.8	3.9	-.8	-.6	-.1
31	Trade credit	31.1	58.1	70.1	33.2	32.7	78.7	25.6	33.6	49.5	21.9	10.5
32	Miscellaneous assets	17.8	21.6	29.0	27.0	18.7	36.1	16.4	33.8	14.3	10.3	12.0
33	Foreign dir. invest.	11.5	15.7	23.7	18.2	6.6	25.5	4.0	20.9	7.5	-5.8	3.6
34	Equity, etc.	5.1	4.4	4.7	1.2	-4.8	11.9	-12.1	7.8	-1.6	-13.5	-4.0
35	Retained earnings	6.4	11.3	19.0	17.0	11.5	13.6	16.1	13.1	9.1	7.7	7.6
36	Insurance receivables	4.4	5.6	5.5	4.8	4.9	4.8	4.8	4.9	4.9	5.0	5.0
37	Equity in sponsored ags.	.1	*	.1	*	–	*	*	*	*	*	–
38	Other	1.8	.3	-.3	3.9	7.2	5.7	7.6	8.1	1.9	11.2	3.4
39	Net increase in liabilities	108.1	148.5	176.1	139.3	147.2	194.0	105.0	183.7	172.1	128.0	97.4
40	Net funds raised in mkts.	84.6	93.2	104.8	106.1	107.3	134.3	70.4	145.3	121.3	92.2	117.7
41	Net new equity issues	2.7	-.1	-7.8	12.9	-11.5	25.0	5.2	-3.4	-24.6	-23.0	-5.3
42	Debt instruments	81.9	93.3	112.6	93.2	118.7	109.3	65.2	148.7	145.9	115.2	123.0
43	Tax-exempt bonds (3)	4.8	3.7	3.6	2.5	3.9	3.4	2.6	6.4	3.1	3.5	4.9
44	Corporate bonds (2)	21.0	20.1	21.2	30.4	20.2	18.8	23.5	22.0	13.0	22.2	24.2
45	Mortgages	19.7	22.1	22.6	20.7	21.5	27.0	24.8	26.5	18.0	16.6	15.4
46	Home mortgages	1.7	.5	-.5	-.8	-1.6	4.0	1.2	-2.2	-3.0	-2.3	-.3
47	Multifamily	2.3	2.9	2.4	2.7	1.6	2.7	1.3	2.4	1.2	1.3	1.6
48	Commercial	15.7	18.7	20.6	18.8	21.5	20.2	22.3	26.3	19.8	17.5	14.0
49	Bank loans n.e.c.	20.8	30.3	43.9	29.3	46.4	56.6	1.9	58.0	70.7	54.8	58.8
50	Commercial paper	1.6	2.7	9.0	4.9	14.7	-7.6	9.1	16.5	29.8	3.4	21.6
51	Acceptances	.6	1.2	1.0	.8	2.2	-1.0	4.8	-1.5	1.0	4.8	-.3
52	Finance company loans	13.5	11.5	10.2	3.1	8.7	10.7	-1.9	19.1	8.5	9.0	-2.7
53	U. S. government loans	*	1.7	1.2	1.5	1.2	1.5	.5	1.5	1.9	.9	1.1
54	Profit taxes payable	-1.3	3.4	*	-6.7	-7.6	-4.5	1.2	-7.6	-7.0	-16.8	-50.5
55	Trade debt	21.1	44.0	59.5	29.1	28.8	55.9	23.4	30.7	41.2	19.8	16.2
56	Fgn. direct invest. in U. S.	3.7	7.9	11.9	10.9	18.7	8.2	9.9	15.4	16.5	32.8	14.0
57	Equity, etc.	2.1	5.3	7.9	4.7	14.1	2.8	5.8	10.7	12.5	27.4	8.4
58	Retained earnings	1.6	2.6	4.0	6.2	4.6	5.5	4.1	4.7	4.1	5.4	5.6
59	Discrepancy	35.7	29.5	26.2	44.5	52.2	51.9	26.8	61.1	62.7	58.3	55.1

Source: *Flow of Funds Accounts, 1st Quarter, 1982* (Washington, D.C.: Federal Reserve System, May, 1982).

Table 2-5. Flow of Funds for Private Nonbank Financial Institutions, 1977–82 (billions of dollars)

SEASONALLY ADJUSTED ANNUAL RATES

	1977	1978	1979	1980	1981	1980 IV	1981 I	1981 II	1981 III	1981 IV	1982 I		
												Current surplus	1
	10.7	12.7	13.0	10.0	.3	9.3	.9	2.7	.6	-3.2	-2.1	Current surplus	1
	2.2	2.2	3.0	3.9	6.2	4.9	6.8	4.9	5.4	7.5	1.5	Physical investment	2
				Private Nonbank Financial Institutions – Total									
	193.6	203.5	211.6	224.2	294.9	223.2	323.5	273.3	316.5	266.4	245.0	Net acq. of financial assets	3
	1.0	3.2	3.1	3.7	2.5	4.7	-5.1	7.1	5.7	2.3	-2.8	Demand deposits and currency	4
	3.9	8.4	4.1	12.8	23.4	13.3	26.9	6.9	37.2	22.8	-14.2	Time and savings deposits	5
	3.0	2.7	4.6	3.2	13.8	7.1	1.6	14.2	14.7	24.9	14.3	Security RP's	6
	*	.5	4.6	1.7	12.1	-7.6	15.9	13.7	11.6	7.1	17.7	Foreign deposits	7
	7.3	4.5	10.6	17.7	22.4	25.5	28.0	24.9	22.4	14.5	25.6	Corporate equities	8
	173.3	173.6	171.3	170.6	202.7	155.7	250.5	184.1	201.8	174.5	192.9	Credit market instruments	9
	22.1	18.2	21.2	48.5	58.2	36.9	92.8	4.2	38.8	96.9	116.1	U. S. government securities	10
	13.5	15.2	10.9	10.2	5.3	5.7	5.9	7.7	1.2	6.3	11.1	State + local obligations	11
	36.2	33.0	21.6	29.2	30.7	13.3	12.4	42.8	28.2	39.3	22.3	Corporate + foreign bonds	12
	69.5	69.2	61.5	43.9	28.1	57.3	51.4	39.9	16.6	4.7	16.4	Mortgages	13
	16.1	19.0	21.7	10.0	15.5	15.6	21.7	14.6	26.0	-.5	6.4	Consumer credit	14
	15.8	19.0	34.5	28.9	65.1	27.0	66.3	75.0	91.1	27.9	20.7	Other loans	15
	1.0	1.8	-1.1	5.1	-.5	12.0	-2.2	4.1	-5.7	1.7	-10.8	Security credit	16
	1.3	1.5	1.9	1.8	2.0	1.8	1.9	1.9	2.0	2.1	2.2	Trade credit	17
	2.8	7.4	12.4	7.7	16.4	10.6	6.0	16.3	26.7	16.5	20.3	Miscellaneous assets	18

SEASONALLY ADJUSTED ANNUAL RATES

SEASONALLY ADJUSTED ANNUAL RATES

Private Nonbank Financial Institutions – Total

	1977	1978	1979	1980	1981	1980 IV	1981 I	1981 II	1981 III	1981 IV	1982 I	
Net increase in liabilities	184.2	192.8	200.7	217.3	300.9	216.9	326.4	274.3	323.3	279.5	248.2	19
Time and savings deposits	69.9	59.1	45.6	55.3	23.4	71.4	37.9	8.2	5.2	42.2	59.1	20
Money market fund shares	.2	6.9	34.4	29.2	107.5	−11.9	148.4	59.9	137.3	84.3	36.4	21
Security RP's (s + 1)	1.9	2.1	.5	2.1	3.0	7.5	−1.3	9.5	−8.8	12.8	−1.1	22
Insurance + pension reserves	59.5	66.6	58.7	80.2	87.8	71.3	75.2	94.8	92.3	88.9	90.2	23
Corporate equity issues (1)	2.0	.7	1.2	5.8	7.9	1.2	10.8	7.6	3.9	9.0	15.7	24
Credit market instruments	24.3	31.0	26.9	10.4	27.7	14.9	20.7	50.6	51.6	−12.1	8.1	25
Corporate bonds	8.9	6.8	5.7	5.6	−2.0	2.8	−5.6	−.1	−5.2	2.8	−3.9	26
Mortgage loans in process	3.1	.8	−1.2	−.8	−2.4	3.8	−2.7	−1.5	−4.3	−1.2	1.7	27
Other mortgages	*	.1	*	−.1	−.5	−.4	−.3	−1.3	*	−.5	–	28
Bank loans n.e.c.	−.3	2.8	−.4	−.5	2.5	−3.7	4.2	5.1	−.1	.7	12.7	29
Open-market paper	8.4	7.9	13.6	−.9	13.9	−1.4	16.6	20.9	29.4	−11.2	−13.9	30
Fed. home loan bank loans	4.3	12.5	9.2	7.1	16.2	13.8	8.5	27.5	31.7	−2.8	11.6	31
Security credit	.9	.2	−.2	4.9	8.2	19.0	6.0	6.6	1.8	18.4	.4	32
Profit taxes payable	.7	1.4	2.3	3.1	−2.3	3.1	−2.1	−2.3	−2.1	−2.5	−2.4	33
Miscellaneous liabilities	24.8	24.7	31.4	26.2	37.7	40.4	30.7	39.5	42.3	38.4	41.6	34
Discrepancy	−.8	−.4	−.9	−.9	*	−1.9	−3.0	−1.2	2.1	2.3	−.5	35

Source: *Flow of Funds Accounts, 1st Quarter, 1982* (Washington, D.C.: Federal Reserve System, May 1982).

individuals are becoming *indirect* rather then *direct owners* of common stocks.

The analysis of the interlocking nature of financial claims can be extended to all of the sectors and subsectors included in the information provided by the Federal Reserve. We have illustrated such an analysis for only three sectors. A more penetrating analysis would involve the tracing of each financial liability to find out what sectors had acquired it as a financial asset. While flow-of-funds data will not permit analysis of the behavior of individual economic units or small groups of economic units, it does enable one to evaluate economic units which are reasonably homogeneous in their behavior, as well as to trace the interaction of the financial system and the real system of the economy in a systematic and consistent manner. It tells the financial-market analyst how various sectors financed the excess of their investment in real assets over savings and how these sectors changed their holdings of financial assets. The flow-of-funds framework provides a structured, interlocking means by which to analyze what has happened in the capital markets. The interrelation of sources and uses among sectors enables the analyst to trace the movement of funds through various sectors of the economy for the period of time under review.

Given the breakdown of financial assets and liabilities provided by the Federal Reserve, a fairly detailed analysis of certain types of financial instruments and markets is possible. While data are individually presented for longer-term capital instruments, money-market instruments—such as Treasury bills, commercial paper, bankers' acceptances, and negotiable certificates of deposit—are scattered among several broader categories. As a result, we are unable to trace through supply and demand patterns for a specific money market instrument. For a capital market instrument, however, we are able to evaluate which sectors are important in the market and the magnitude of their purchases. When this analysis is extended over time, one is able to evaluate the degree of pressure in the various markets. Pressure arises whenever a traditional source of financing curtails its investment in the financial instrument. The curtailment of investment should be related to the savings and investment in real assets for the sector involved. Thus, a study of the behavior of individual sectors with respect to investment in financial assets and issuance of financial liabilities over time is useful in determining the impact of that sector on the capital markets.

OTHER FLOW-OF-FUNDS INFORMATION

In addition to the Federal Reserve, various private organizations provide useful data on the source and use of funds. Among these organizations are Bankers Trust Company, Salomon Brothers, and the Life Insurance Association of America, which publish information on the "final" sources and uses of funds according to the institutions providing the funds and the instrument in which the funds are used. This information differs from that provided by the Federal Reserve in that a flow-of-funds matrix for the entire economy cannot be constructed. The ultimate sources and uses of funds by sectors are not shown—only the final sources and uses. Although the former is sometimes implied, it is difficult to evaluate savings-surplus and savings-deficit sectors on the basis of the information provided. The users shown may or may not be the ultimate investors in real assets. By the same token, the suppliers of funds may or may not be ultimate savers. Where financial institutions are the suppliers, for the most part they are not the ultimate savers. Thus, only a portion of the flow-of-funds matrix of the entire economy is revealed. Still, these sources provide considerable in-depth information about the major sources and uses of funds for the various capital and credit markets.

So far we have considered only *ex post* data, whether they be flow-of-funds or source-and-use statements. Although these data are valuable in appraising past trends and in forming expectations of the future, we often need forecasts of the future involving *ex ante* estimates. We now turn to this aspect.

FORECASTS OF FUTURE FLOWS OF FUNDS

In addition to flows that have actually occurred, estimates of future funds flows are important in financial-market analysis. These estimates indicate likely strains in the system and the resulting pressure on interest rates. In this way, analysts are able to get a better feel for desired demand and supply and for the change in interest rates necessary to bring about a balance between the two. They are interested both in the expected absolute change in interest rates for a particular market and in the change relative to changes in interest rates in other markets. Bankers Trust Company and Salomon Brothers, as well as certain others, make forecasts of future flows of funds. In the preparation of these forecasts, independent estimates are made of the expected need for funds, classified according to the type of financial instrument, and of the expected funds available for investment by various financial institutions and by individuals.

Once independent estimates of supply and demand have been made, one benefit of the forecast comes in analyzing how supply and demand will come into balance. We know, of course, that on an *ex post* basis supply must equal demand. The first step is simply to match the independently prepared estimates to determine the size and direction of any imbalance. This imbalance indicates pressures that are likely to develop. Knowing these pressures, the analyst is able to estimate in an approximate way the change in market interest rates necessary to bring about a balance in supply and demand. For example, suppose the need for mortgage funds is estimated to be $130 billion in the forthcoming year, but the supply of funds into this market is estimated at only $105 billion. As a result of this imbalance, there would likely be upward pressure on interest rates in order to bring about a balance between supply and demand for mortgages.

By analyzing imbalances across capital markets, analysts can estimate whether interest rates in one segment of the financial markets are likely to rise or fall relative to interest rates in other segments. In this way, analysts may be able to forecast relative changes in interest rates. However, one must be careful not to lose sight of the interrelated nature of financial markets. Supply-and-demand forces in one market are not independent of those in other markets. Therefore, interest-rate changes in the various markets cannot be estimated independently. Only if there are market imperfections such that the market for one financial instrument is partially segmented from those of others will such relative forecasts hold promise.

In the published forecasts, a balance is always shown between estimated sources of funds and estimated uses. In other words, adjustments are made until a balance is achieved. Consequently, certain valuable information is not available to the reader—namely, the independent estimates of supply and demand by the forecasters and the resulting *ex ante* gap. However, a residual category is shown, and this category gives us some information about any imbalance between supply and demand. To illustrate, an example of a source-and-use-of-funds statement, prepared by Salomon Brothers, is shown in Table 2-6. Historical sources and uses and also a forecast for 1982 are shown.

In the table, the residual—which consists mostly of households—is shown in the next-to-last row. In a certain sense, this residual can be regarded as a balancing factor in the forecast (last column) and can be used to judge the strains in particular markets. The larger the residual, the more "gap" there is for individuals to fill and the higher interest rates would be expected to go in order to bring about a balance between supply and demand. In our example, the large residuals existing in 1979 and forecast for 1982 would suggest a rise in interest rates. This was the case during the latter part of 1979. In 1981 interest rates rose through most of the year and remained high through the first half of 1982. Similar experiences have been recorded in the past, when the portion of total funds supplied by the residual was relatively large. Still, other factors affect interest rates and the correlation is far from perfect. While analysts may be able to use the estimate of the residual as a basis for forecasting overall interest rates, the accuracy of such forecasts varies considerably over time. The usefulness of residual analysis heightens for specific financial markets, such as municipal securities and mortgages, where tax and institutional imperfections play an important role in the determination of interest rates relative to rates in other markets.

Table 2-6. Salomon Brothers' Summary of Supply and Demand for Credit (billions of dollars)

	Annual Net Increases in Amounts Outstanding						
	1976	1977	1978	1979	1980	1981ᵉ	1982ᵖ
Net Demand							
Privately Held Mortgages	70.5	108.0	116.0	105.0	70.9	72.2	71.7
Corporate & Foreign Bonds	39.1	39.1	31.8	36.1	37.9	27.4	28.8
Subtotal Long-Term Private	109.6	147.1	147.8	141.1	108.8	99.6	100.5
Short-Term Business Borrowing	14.1	49.0	76.0	91.4	55.0	127.1	142.1
Short-Term Other Borrowing	40.7	50.7	65.5	52.8	20.7	47.0	59.7
Subtotal Short-Term Private	54.8	99.7	141.5	144.2	75.7	174.1	201.8
Privately Held Federal Debt	73.0	74.5	81.7	77.4	118.0	113.5	135.4
Tax-Exempt Notes and Bonds	17.6	28.9	32.5	27.7	33.0	31.0	30.7
Subtotal Government Debt	90.6	103.4	114.2	105.1	151.0	144.5	166.1
Total Net Demand for Credit	**255.0**	**350.2**	**403.5**	**390.4**	**335.5**	**418.2**	**468.4**
Net Supply							
Thrift Institutions	70.5	82.0	73.5	55.9	57.9	39.7	41.1
Insurance, Pensions, Endowments	49.0	68.1	73.2	63.6	75.4	70.8	76.7
Investment Companies	2.9	7.0	6.4	25.5	22.5	69.4	64.0
Other Nonbank Finance	12.9	13.4	18.9	26.4	16.6	33.3	41.4
Subtotal Nonbank Finance	135.3	170.6	172.0	171.3	172.3	213.2	223.1
Commercial Banks	60.8	84.1	105.9	103.9	83.3	115.0	126.8
Business Corporations	9.0	−2.3	−0.9	8.3	3.7	6.8	7.7
State & Local Government	4.0	13.3	11.1	9.5	7.3	11.0	8.2
Foreign ·	19.6	47.2	58.8	8.9	37.9	17.9	16.0
Subtotal	228.7	312.9	346.9	301.9	304.5	363.9	381.8
Residual (mostly household direct)	26.3	37.3	56.6	88.5	31.0	54.3	86.6
Total Net Supply of Credit	**255.0**	**350.2**	**403.5**	**390.4**	**335.5**	**418.2**	**468.4**

Source: Salomon Brothers Inc., *1982 Prospects for Financial Markets*. Reprinted by permission.

A forecast of sources and uses of funds differs from a forecast of the flow of funds for the entire economy. Whereas the former takes account of the final sources and uses of funds for various financial instruments, a flow-of-funds forecast takes account of the source and use of funds for each sector of the economy. Because a simultaneous balance must be reached for each sector and across all sectors, a flow-of-funds forecast forces a tighter analysis than does a forecast of sources and uses. The idea of having to force projections into the flow-of-funds framework may cause analysts to be less conservative in their final estimates. To achieve a balance which satisfies the interlocking structure of the flow of funds, analysts must sometimes make fairly extreme estimates. These estimates, however, may well be warranted by the conditions projected. A less rigorous framework encourages the tendency to project only moderate changes and not to predict extreme changes and turning points. The flow-of-funds matrix forces the use of estimates that are consistent and in keeping with the initial assumptions. Therefore, they may tend to be more realistic.

The flow-of-funds framework and the source-and-use-of-funds statement, which we have examined, provide a basis for analyzing financial markets. By comparing estimates of supply and demand, analysts obtain insight into the likely strains in the system. Given these likely strains, it is possible to interpret their effect upon interest rates. Within either of these frameworks, the analysis of interest rates is likely to be far more rigorous, consistent, and comprehensive than it is if estimates are made on a market-by-market basis.

SUMMARY

The flow of funds is a system of social accounting that permits financial-market analysts to evaluate the flow of savings through various sectors of the economy. A sector consists of a grouping of economic units that are relatively homogeneous in their behavior. By combining source-and-use-of-funds statements for all sectors, we may obtain a matrix for the entire economy. This matrix shows the interlocking nature of financial assets and liabilities among various sectors. It enables us to analyze savings-deficit sectors and the means by which they finance the excess of their investment in real assets over savings, together with the behavior of savings-surplus sectors and the way they invest in financial assets. Subject to certain limitations, the flow-of-funds data give the financial-market analyst rich insights. By tracing through the sources of funds for investment in a particular financial instrument, one gains information about strains in the financial system and about interest rates.

In addition to the Federal Reserve flow-of-funds data, various source and use statements are published by several private organizations. However, these data do not show the interaction between the real and the financial segments of the economy. They are concerned only with the final supply and demand for funds. Nevertheless, source and use statements provide detailed information on financial markets and are very valuable to the financial-market analyst.

Analysts gain insight not only from a study of flows that have occurred in the past, but also from forecasts of the future. Here, independent forecasts should be made of the demand for and the supply of funds. If there is an imbalance, analysts study the change in interest rates necessary to bring about a balance. In the published forecasts, there usually is a residual category for individuals and other investors. The amount of the residual tends to vary directly with the level of interest rates in financial markets.

Consequently, the residual is useful in estimating future interest rates if the forecast supply-and-demand figures prove to be accurate.

SELECTED REFERENCE

Cohen, J., "Copeland's Moneyflows after Twenty-Five Years: A Survey," *Journal of Economic Literature,* Vol. 2 (March 1972): 1–25.

Copeland, Morris A., *A Study of Moneyflows in the United States.* New York: National Bureau of Economic Research, 1955.

The Flow-of-Funds Approach to Social Accounting. New York: National Bureau of Economic Research, 1962.

Freund, William C., and Edward D. Zinbarg, "Application of Flow of Funds to Interest-Rate Forecasting," *Journal of Finance,* 18 (May 1963): 231–48.

Goldsmith, Raymond W., *Capital Market Analysis and the Financial Accounts of the Nation.* Morristown, N.J.: General Learning Press, 1972.

_____ , *The Flow of Capital Funds in the Postwar Economy,* Chapter 2. New York: National Bureau of Economic Research, 1965.

Ibbotson, Roger G., and Carol L. Fall, "The United States Market Wealth Portfolio," *Journal of Portfolio Management,* 6 (Fall 1981): 17–27.

Introduction to the Flow of Funds. Washington, D.C.: Board of Governors of the Federal Reserve System, February, 1975.

Polakoff, Murray E., et al., *Financial Institutions and Markets,* 2nd ed., Chapters 2 and 25. Boston: Houghton Mifflin Company, 1981.

"A Quarterly Presentation of Flow of Funds and Savings," *Federal Reserve Bulletin,* 45 (August 1959): 828–59.

Ritter, Lawrence S., *The Flow of Funds Accounts: A Framework for Financial Analysis.* New York: Institute of Finance, New York University, 1968.

Taylor, Stephen, "Uses of Flow-of-Funds Accounts in the Federal Reserve System," *Journal of Finance,* 18 (May 1963): 249–58.

3

FOUNDATIONS FOR
INTEREST RATES

As we showed in Chapter 1, the function of financial markets is to facilitate the flow of savings from savings-surplus economic units to savings-deficit ones. The allocation of these savings occurs primarily on the basis of price, expressed by interest rates. Economic units in need of funds must outbid others for their use, holding risk constant. Although the allocation process is affected by capital rationing and government restrictions, interest rates are the primary mechanism whereby supply and demand are brought into balance for a particular financial instrument across financial markets. Those economic units willing to pay the highest interest rate for the use of funds, holding risk constant, are the ones entitled to their use. If rationality prevails, the economic units bidding the highest prices are the ones with the most promising investment opportunities. As a result, savings are allocated to the most efficient uses, and capital formation and want satisfaction in the economy tend to be maximized. In this chapter, we analyze how the price mechanism works to bring the supply of a financial instrument into balance with its demand. In subsequent chapters, the focus is on explaining relative returns or return differentials among various financial instruments.

DEFINITION OF YIELD

Before we proceed, a brief discussion of the measurement of yields is in order. The yield on a financial instrument is the discount rate that equates the present value of expected cash inflows to the investor with the current market price of the security. If these inflows are assumed to occur at the end of the year, the yield can be determined by solving the following equation for r:

$$P_0 = \frac{C_1}{(1+r)} + \frac{C_2}{(1+r)^2} + \cdots + \frac{C_n}{(1+r)^n} \tag{3-1}$$

where P_0 is the current market price of the instrument
C_t is the expected cash inflow to the investor in period t
n is the final period in which a cash inflow is expected
r is the yield to maturity for which we solve

Depending upon the security being analyzed, C_t may be interest payments, repayment of principal, or dividend payments.

If interest or dividends are paid more than once a year, Eq. (3-1) is modified to

$$P_0 = \frac{C_1}{\left(1+\dfrac{r}{m}\right)} + \frac{C_2}{\left(1+\dfrac{r}{m}\right)^2} + \frac{C_3}{\left(1+\dfrac{r}{m}\right)^3} + \cdots + \frac{C_n}{\left(1+\dfrac{r}{m}\right)^{mn}} \tag{3-2}$$

where m is the number of times in the year interest is compounded. If interest is paid semiannually on a bond with $1,000 face value, 10 years to final maturity, a coupon rate of 12 percent, and a current market price per bond of $900, Eq. (3-2) becomes

$$\$900 = \frac{\$60}{\left(1+\dfrac{r}{2}\right)} + \frac{\$60}{\left(1+\dfrac{r}{2}\right)^2} + \frac{\$60}{\left(1+\dfrac{r}{2}\right)^3}$$

$$+ \cdots + \frac{\$60}{\left(1+\dfrac{r}{2}\right)^{20}} + \frac{\$1,000}{\left(1+\dfrac{r}{2}\right)^{20}} \tag{3-3}$$

To solve for r, we can use a bond-value table. Given any three of the four factors mentioned above (coupon rate, final maturity, present market price, and yield to maturity), we are able to determine the fourth from these tables. In addition, a number of calculators are programmed to solve for yield to maturity as well as for the market price, given the other three inputs. Using either method, the yield to maturity, or r in Eq. (3-3), is found to be 13.88 percent.

Were the market price $1,100, so that the bond traded at a premium instead of a discount, the yield to maturity—substituting $1,100 for $900 in Eq. (3-3)—would be 10.37 percent. On the basis of these calculations, several observations are in order: (1) When a bond's market price is less than its face value of $1,000 so that it sells at a discount, the yield to maturity exceeds the coupon rate; (2) when a bond sells at a premium, its yield to maturity is less than the coupon rate; and (3) when market price equals face value, the yield to maturity equals the coupon rate.

The yield to maturity, as calculated above, may differ from the holding-period yield on that security if the security is sold prior to maturity. The holding-period yield is the rate of discount that equates the present value of cash inflows (interest payments or dividends) plus the present value of terminal value at the end of the holding period with the price paid for the security. For example, suppose a share of stock were bought for $50 on a net basis and sold three years later for $70 net. Moreover, assume that the stock paid a $3 cash dividend at the end of each year. The holding-period yield, or annual return, would then be found by solving the following equation for r:

$$\$50 = \frac{\$3}{(1+r)} + \frac{\$3}{(1+r)^2} + \frac{\$3}{(1+r)^3} + \frac{\$70}{(1+r)^3} \tag{3-4}$$

Here, r is found to be 17.27 percent. In the ensuing discussion, both yield to maturity and holding-period yield will be considered. They facilitate the comparison of returns for different financial instruments. While commonly used because of their general natures, both measures have certain drawbacks. These drawbacks relate primarily to oversimplification and will become apparent as we explore the meaning of return in depth. For now, however, they will suffice.

THE INTEREST RATE IN AN EXCHANGE ECONOMY

Interest rates in financial markets are determined by a complex interaction of supply and demand forces. In order to understand these forces we will simplify the problem by looking at it in varying degrees of abstraction. Essentially, we will focus on the choice of individual economic units between consumption and investment. In market equilibrium, of course, there must be a balance between investment and savings, or forgoing of consumption. We begin by looking at the consumption-savings phenomenon for the individual and then move on to consider the equilibrating process among individuals. We assume initially a world of certainty and analyze the determination of the rate of interest in such a world—namely, the riskless rate. Following this presentation, we will consider the determination of interest rates when risk exists.

The Individual Choice

Consider an individual with a two-point time horizon—now and 1 year from now. Moreover, suppose the individual is concerned only with a single commodity—call it corn. While the example could be extended to a "basket" of consumption commodities, for ease of comprehension we simplify and consider only one commodity. The initial question is: What is the individual's preference for present consumption vis à vis future consumption? This can be visualized with the help of Fig. 3-1. Along the horizontal axis we have *present consumption*, whereas along the vertical we have consumption at time 1, or *future consumption*. The curves depict the individual's tradeoff between present and future consumption and are called *indifference curves*. Along a curve, an individual is indifferent with regard to present or future consumption. To part with present consumption, that is, to save, the individual must be promised increasing amounts of future consumption, C_1. Each curve upward and to the right represents a higher level of satisfaction or utility. The object then is to strive for the highest indifference curve, because it represents the highest level of present and future want satisfaction. The indifference curves give us the *preference function* of the individual.

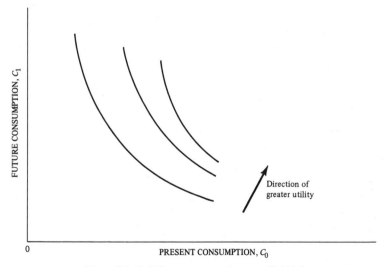

Figure 3-1. Indifference curves for an individual.

Imagine now a situation where individuals can produce corn, but there is no exchange—that is, they cannot exchange the commodity they produce for something else or for corn in the future. The corn just harvested can either be consumed now or saved for the next planting. Suppose that the production opportunity situation for the individual is depicted by the curve $X'X$ in Fig. 3-2. Point X on the horizontal axis represents the individual's present endowment of corn—the harvest just past; it can be entirely consumed and nothing saved for next year's planting. In that case, consumption at time 1 will be zero. Alternatively, part or all of the present endowment can be saved as seed corn for next year's planting. In our world of certainty we know the yield of corn at time 1, given an amount of seed corn held over at time 0. If all corn is held over as seed corn, consumption at time 1 will be X'. The $X'X$ curve shows the combinations of present and future consumption that are possible. Starting with the present endowment of X, note that each increment of corn saved for seed increases future consumption but at a decreasing rate. In other words, production increases but at a diminishing rate as more seed is planted in a given plot of land.

The optimum present consumption and hence the savings of the individual is represented by the point of tangency of the production opportunity curve with the highest indifference curve. This is depicted in Fig. 3-2 by X^*. Given this equilibrium point, the individual would consume C_0^* of corn presently and withhold $X - C_0^*$ for seed. This would result in future production and consumption of C_1^*.

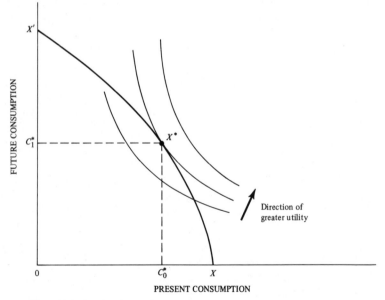

Figure 3-2. Production and consumption optimum without exchange.

Optimum with Exchange

What happens if there exists the possibility of exchange? By exchange we mean opportunities for the exchange of present and future claims to consumption—in this case to corn—with other economic units. In general, this possibility allows the individual economic unit to obtain a higher level of present and future want satisfaction.[1] Suppose that the market exchange opportunities are depicted by the diagonal lines shown in Fig. 3-3. The slope of these lines describes the exchange ratio between present and future consumption. The graph shows that to obtain a number of units of present consumption, it is necessary to give up an even greater number of units of future consumption. This implies a preference in the market for present consumption vis-à-vis future consumption. The ratio of

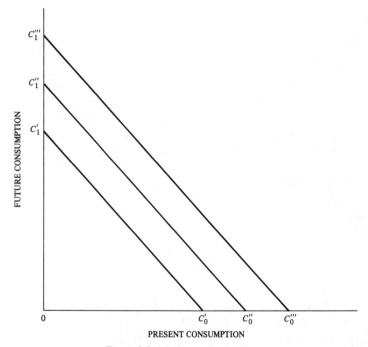

Figure 3-3. Market exchange lines.

[1]The approach presented was formulated many years ago by Irving Fisher, *The Theory of Interest* (New York: The Macmillan Co., 1930). For analyses of Fisher's work, which place it in perspective with respect to the theory of interest rates, see Joseph W. Conard, *An Introduction to the Theory of Interest* (Berkeley: University of California Press, 1959), Chapter IV; and Friederich A. Lutz, *The Theory of Interest* (Dordrecht, Holland: D. Reidel Publishing Co., 1967), Chapter 7.

exchange for the first line and, because they are parallel, for all other lines, is

$$\frac{C_1'}{C_0'} = 1 + r \tag{3-5}$$

Thus, r represents the rate of interest for the sacrifice of current consumption for future consumption. At this rate, trading in the market is possible between present and future consumption claims. While the interest rate is positive in this case, it need not be. Time preferences could favor future consumption vis-à-vis present consumption. In this case, the slope of the lines in Fig. 3-3 would be less than 45 degrees and a negative interest rate would prevail.

Each line in the figure represents a level of endowment of present and future consumption. The further upward and to the right, the higher the level of endowment. The endowment can be thought of as a constraint, in that it limits the opportunities for consumption. If the initial endowment in present consumption were C_0'', for example, only opportunities along the line $C_0''C_1''$ would be possible. If C_0'' were consumed now, nothing would be exchanged for future consumption. At the other extreme, all of C_0'' could be exchanged for C_1'' of future consumption. Any combination between these two extremes is possible and connotes some exchange of present consumption for future consumption at an exchange ratio of $1 + r$. This corresponds to *lending*. In contrast, if one's endowment were entirely in a claim to future consumption, any exchange of future for present consumption would occur at an exchange ratio of $1/(1+r)$. This corresponds to *borrowing*. Thus, the initial endowment can be in terms of present consumption claims, future consumption claims, or, as is likely, some combination of the two.

Combined Effect

Whereas we have analyzed separately the productive optimum, in the absence of exchange, and the exchange of present and future consumption claims (borrowing–lending), in the absence of production opportunities, we wish now to consider both simultaneously. For the individual economic unit, the derivation of production and consumption optimums can be pictured by the example in Fig. 3-4. The productive opportunity set is denoted by the curve $X'X$, as it was in Fig. 3-2. However, in this case the production optimum is not determined by the point of tangency of the production opportunity curve with the highest indifference

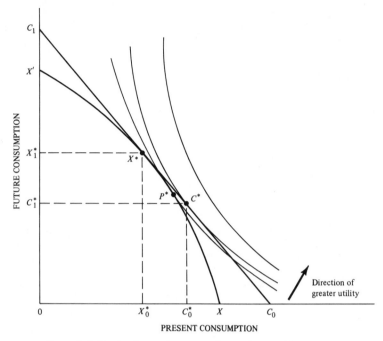

Figure 3-4. Production and consumption optimum with exchange.

curve. The situation is altered by the possibility of exchange. Optimal behavior by the individual is determined by the point of tangency between the production opportunity curve and the highest market exchange line. We see that this is point X^* in Fig. 3-4.

Having determined a production optimum, individuals then would undertake borrowing or lending along the market exchange line $C_1 - C_0$ until a point of tangency with the highest indifference curve was reached. We see in the figure that this is at point C^*, which is below and to the right of X^*, the production optimum. This means that individuals would exchange future consumption claims for present ones. In other words, individuals would borrow. If the point of tangency were above X^* and to the left, individuals would have to lend to obtain an optimal balancing of present and future consumption claims.

To recapitulate, the individual should seek the productive opportunity along curve $X'X$ where a point of tangency exists between this curve and the highest market exchange ratio line. This is point X^*, and it implies that $X - X_0^*$ units of corn (along the horizontal axis) will be withheld as seed corn. It also implies X_1^* of future production, on the vertical axis. Given a productive optimum of X^*, the individual then would borrow against his future production in order to obtain the highest level of present and future want satisfaction. This is attained at C^*. It represents borrowing in the sense of giving up $X_1^* - C_1^*$ of claim to future consumption (vertical axis) for $C_0^* - X_0^*$ of additional present consumption (horizontal axis). Thus, the individual would move upward and to the left along line $X'X$ to point X^* and then downward and to the right along line $C_1 C_0$ until point C^* was reached.

Note that the overall level of want satisfaction of C^* with production *and* exchange opportunities is higher than that obtained with production opportunities alone. The latter optimum would occur at P^*, where the productive opportunity curve is tangent with an indifference curve. With exchange opportunities, a higher level of want satisfaction is usually possible.

Also, we should emphasize that with production *and* exchange opportunities, determination of the production optimum, point X^* in Fig. 3-4, is independent of the individual's utility preferences. This is illustrated in Fig. 3-5, where we draw another set of indifference curves. The lower set of indifference curves depicts borrowing to obtain C^*, whereas the upper set depicts lending to obtain C^{**}. In both cases, determination of

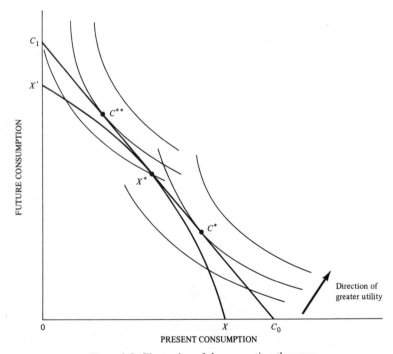

Figure 3-5. Illustration of the separation theorem.

the productive optimum is distinct from the utility preferences of the individual. Put another way, the individual's utility preferences can change but this will not affect the production optimum. This condition is known as the *separation theorem*. It derives from our underlying assumption that the individual can both borrow and lend at the market rate r. Under such circumstances the intertemporal production decision is based solely on the point of tangency of the productive opportunity curve with the highest market exchange line.

Market Equilibrium

Up until now we have assumed a given value for the slope of the market exchange line—that is, the rate of interest. In effect, the individual has been viewed as a price taker with the exchange ratio as the price. However, the market is comprised of many individuals and the equilibrium rate of interest is determined by their interaction. In order to borrow, for example, there must be one or more individuals who are willing to lend at an agreed-upon exchange ratio. To illustrate, suppose that the production-consumption optimum for individual 1 is that shown in Fig. 3-4. In the figure the individual is seen to want to exchange $X_1^* - C_1^*$ in future consumption claims for $C_0^* - X_0^*$ of present consumption.

Suppose that the market is comprised of only one other individual, whose productive-consumptive equilibrium is illustrated in Fig. 3-6. The slope of the market exchange line is the same as that in Fig. 3-4. The productive optimum for this individual is X^* and, given his or her utility preference, this individual would strive to lend $X_0^* - C_0^*$ of present consumption claims for $C_1^* - X_1^*$ of future consumption claims. However, the amount the second individual desires to lend at the prevailing rate of interest is less than that which the first individual desires to borrow. This creates a disequilibrium situation.

The forces in this situation work in the direction of a higher rate of interest—thus, there is a greater slope to the market exchange line. With a greater slope, the second individual's productive optimum will be downward and to the right. This is depicted in the lower panel of Fig. 3-7. Instead of X^* being the optimum production opportunity, given a market exchange line of $C_1 C_0$, the optimum becomes X^{**} with a market exchange line of $C_1' C_0'$. Moreover, the individual is able to attain a higher indifference curve in lending owing to the greater slope of the market exchange line. The import of all this is that at the new rate of interest the individual is willing to lend more than before, $X_0^{**} - C_0^{**}$ as opposed to $X_0^* - C_1^*$.

The shift in slope of the market exchange line also affects the behavior of the first individual. His or her production optimum also shifts downward and to the right, as shown in the upper panel of Fig. 3-7. Moreover, the

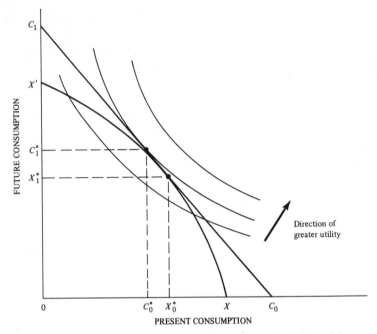

Figure 3-6. Production and consumption optimum for individual 2.

higher rate of interest results in this individual being able to achieve only a lower indifference curve. The overall effect is a dramatic lessening in his or her desire to borrow for current consumption, $C_0^{**} - X_0^{**}$ as opposed to $C_0^* - X_0^*$ before. In fact, the first individual wishes to borrow much less than the second individual desires to lend at the higher interest rate. Therefore, a lower rate of interest is in order. The interest rate, or slope of the market exchange line, will continue to adjust until the amount the first individual wishes to borrow equals the amount the second individual desires to lend.

Obviously, the "market" is comprised of more than two individuals. However, the equilibrating process works in the way illustrated when we have multiple economic units. As the rate of interest changes, some individuals will want to borrow more or less, while others will want to lend less or more. In fact, as the interest rate rises, some economic units previously wanting to borrow will want to lend; as the interest rate declines, some economic units will wish to borrow although they wanted to lend before. This can be visualized by shifting the slope of the market exchange lines in Fig. 3-7. Market equilibrium is achieved when desired lending equals desired borrowing across all economic units. In the context of Chapter 1, lending corresponds to saving, or the refraining from current con-

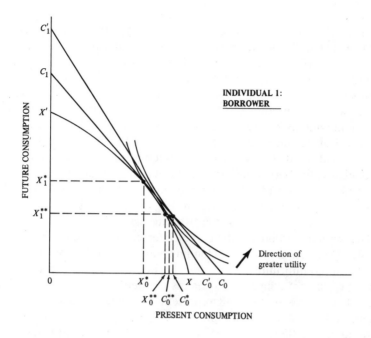

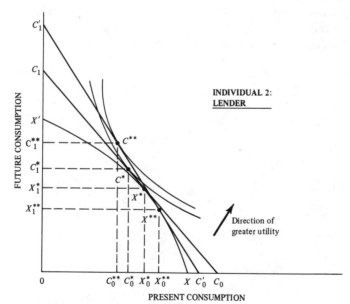

Figure 3-7. Illustration of upward shift in the interest rate.

sumption, whereas borrowing corresponds to investment, or dissavings.

Market equilibrium then is determined by the forces of supply and demand for current consumption claims vis-à-vis future claims. This is depicted in Fig. 3-8. The lending curve represents an aggregation of the amounts of desired lending for all economic units at various interest rates. In other words, any point on the curve represents the horizontal sum of different individuals' desired lending at the particular interest rate involved. In terms of our example in the lower panel of Fig. 3-7, the desired loans of the individual at the two different rates were $X_0^* - C_0^*$ and $X_0^{**} - C_0^{**}$. Similarly, the borrowing curve represents an aggregation of the amounts of desired borrowing for all economic units at various interest rates. (In the example in the upper panel of Fig. 3-7, desired borrowings are $C_0^* - X_0^*$ and $C_0^{**} - X_0^{**}$ for the two interest rates.)

The lending and borrowing curves intersect at the equilibrium rate of interest, r^*. At this rate, desired lending equals desired borrowing and the market is in equilibrium. Recall that the rate of interest is a measure of the price of current consumption claims in relation to future consumption claims. The curves in Fig. 3-8 represent an aggregation of production-consumption optimums for all individuals under varying interest rates, as illustrated in Fig. 3-7 and earlier figures. Thus, the equilibrium market rate of interest embodies the desired lending and borrowing behavior of all economic units according to their productive opportunity sets and their utility preferences. Shifts in these factors will cause shifts in desired lending or borrowing and in the equilibrium rate of interest.

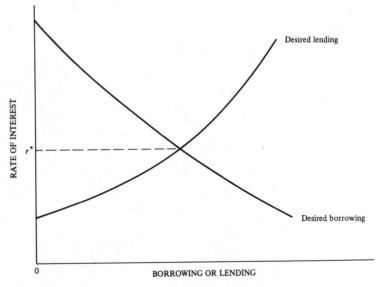

Figure 3-8. Market equilibrium.

What we have described is a *neoclassical loanable funds theory* of market equilibrium. Savings, or forgoing immediate consumption, are the source of loanable funds, and investments are the use of funds. The market rate of interest changes in order to bring about equilibrium when aggregate desired lending and/or borrowing in Fig. 3-8 change. In a sense, the loanable funds theory allows for a full equilibrium analysis of an economy and of its financial market. When all forces are in equilibrium, the interest rate is automatically determined.

At the beginning of this section, we invoked the assumption of certainty with respect to the future. As a result, our problem was reduced to showing the determination of the riskless rate of interest. Assuming no transaction costs or other market impediments, this then became the rate at which all individual economic units could either borrow or lend. When we leave the world of certainty, necessarily we must consider risk. In the remainder of this chapter and in the appendix, we present an overall framework for determining interest rates under conditions of risk. In subsequent chapters, we extend this analysis to consider the factors that give rise to risk and their impact on market rates of interest. In other words, we proceed from the general to the specific.

INTEREST RATES IN A WORLD WITH RISK

When we leave the riskless world assumed in the previous section, the determination of interest rates is altered. With risk, for example, we can and do have multiple financial instruments. This contrasts with the previous section, where there was but one financial instrument—a riskless contract between the borrower and lender. This contract bore an interest rate that was the same for all such contracts in the market. Stated in another way, only one rate of interest prevailed, the risk-free rate. In a world characterized by risk, different interest rates occur. This is the topic we wish to study.

Behavior of Individual Economic Units

Interest rates in risky financial markets cannot be analyzed in isolation. They are dependent not only upon interest rates in other financial markets but also upon the real sector of the economy and upon consumption. All these factors interact to determine an equilibrium structure of interest rates. In this section we study the behavior of individual economic units in choosing assets and issuing financial liabilities. An understanding of this behavior allows us later to examine how economic units interact to determine interest rates in the economy.

As recalled from Chapter 2, the balance sheet for an economic unit at any moment is

Assets	Liabilities and Net Worth
Money	Financial liabilities
	1
Other financial assets	2
1	.
2	.
.	.
.	n
.	
n	
Real assets	
1	
2	
.	
.	Net worth
.	
n	

It is assumed that the economic unit adjusts its balance sheet toward a desired, or preferred, mix of assets and liabilities in keeping with changes in interest rates, investment opportunities, wealth, and other factors. It may increase its total asset holdings only if its net worth increases, it issues additional financial liabilities, or both. In turn, a change in net worth can be the result of two occurrences: (1) current expenditures less than or more than current income, and (2) capital gains or losses on financial assets and liabilities and on real assets over the period.

Consumption clearly represents an alternative to holding assets or issuing financial liabilities and, accordingly, influences the desired totals in the balance sheet for the economic unit. A household, for example, has several choices to make in the allocation of its wealth and income. To purchase a house, it may have to save, by consuming less than its income, until it has accumulated sufficient funds for a downpayment. The alternative to purchasing a house in this case would be increased consumption. If the household were already consuming less than its current income, the alternative might be increasing its financial assets. A household must decide not only on the proportion of income to save, but also on where these savings are to be employed—that is, what type of asset is to be increased (money, other financial assets, or real assets) or what type of financial liability is to be paid off. A business corporation, on the other hand, may purchase a piece of capital equipment by retaining its earnings, by reducing its financial assets, or by increasing its financial liabilities.

These examples are sufficient to illustrate the complexities that face the individual economic unit in determining the total amount and composition of financial assets it holds and the amount and composition of financial liabilities it issues. How does the individual economic unit adjust its holdings of assets, its financial liabilities, and its consumption to achieve a preferred position? It does so on the basis of maximizing total utility. At a moment in time, the economic unit increases its financial liabilities to finance its holding of money, other financial assets, and real assets as long as it can increase its total utility by doing so. Over time the economic unit can increase or decrease its marginal propensity to consume. Changes in net worth affect and are affected by consumption, the holdings of various assets, and the financial liabilities issued. Thus, all of these factors are interdependent with respect to the utility preferences of an economic unit and its behavior.

Utility for Financial Assets

Assuming that economic units attempt to maximize their total utility, we must consider now the utility derived from holding various assets and from issuing financial liabilities. This consideration is fundamental to understanding how economic units in an economy interact to determine interest rates. For financial assets other than money, we assume that the preferences of economic units are based upon a two-parameter utility function; these parameters are (1) the expected return from the instrument and (2) the risk involved in holding it.[2] If the future were known, no risk would be involved in holding a financial asset. The income stream would be certain. Because utility is associated positively with return, all economic units would try to maximize their total return from the holding of financial assets by investing in that financial asset which promised the greatest return. With certainty about the future and perfect capital markets, however, arbitrage would assure that every financial asset yielded no more than the risk-free rate, as determined in the previous section.

When the future is *not* known, the utility function of an economic unit is more complex. The economic unit must consider the range of possible returns. To reduce the problem to manageable proportions, we assume that individuals are able to summarize their beliefs about the probability

---

[2]For a justification of this approach, see James Tobin, "Liquidity Preference as Behavior Towards Risk," *Review of Economic Studies*, XXV (February 1958): 65–86.

distribution of possible returns from a financial asset or portfolio of financial assets in terms of two parameters of the distribution. These parameters are the expected value and the standard deviation of the distribution.

The *expected value* of the probability distribution is calculated by

$$\overline{R} = \sum_{x=1}^{n} R_x P_x \tag{3-6}$$

where $\overline{R}$ is the expected value, R_x is the return for the xth possibility, P_x is the probability of occurrence of that return, n is the total number of possibilities, and the capital Greek sigma denotes the sum of possible returns 1 through n. It is assumed that investors associate risk with the dispersion of the probability distribution. The greater the dispersion, the more risky the financial asset, and vice versa. The conventional measure of dispersion of a probability distribution is the *standard deviation*, which is calculated by

$$\sigma = \sqrt{\sum_{x=1}^{n} (R_x - \overline{R})^2 \, P_x} \tag{3-7}$$

Equation (3-7) gives the standard deviation only for a single financial asset. However, an economic unit usually has more than one investment opportunity available. Rather than evaluate the expected value of return and the standard deviation for a single financial asset, one must evaluate them for a portfolio of financial assets. It is implied that economic units maximize the utility arising from holding a portfolio of financial assets. The expected value of return for a portfolio is simply the sum of the expected values of return for the financial assets making up the portfolio, Eq. (3-6). The standard deviation, however, is not the sum of the individual standard deviations, but

$$\sigma = \sqrt{\sum_{j=1}^{m} \sum_{k=1}^{m} A_j A_k r_{jk} \sigma_j \sigma_k} \tag{3-8}$$

where m is the total number of financial assets under consideration, A_j is the proportion of total funds invested in financial asset j, A_k is the proportion invested in financial asset k, r_{jk} is the expected correlation between returns for financial assets j and k, σ_j is the standard deviation about the expected value of return for financial asset j, and σ_k is the standard deviation for financial asset k. These standard deviations are calculated with Eq. (3-7).

The value of a correlation coefficient, r_{jk}, always lies in the range -1 to $+1$. A correlation coefficient of 1.00 indicates that an increase in the return for one financial asset is always associated with a proportional increase in the return for the other financial asset, and similarly for decreases. A correlation coefficient of -1.00 indicates that an increase in the return for one financial asset is always associated with a proportional decrease in the return for the other financial asset, and vice versa. A zero coefficient indicates an absence of correlation, so that the returns of the securities vary independently of each other.

To illustrate the determination of the standard deviation for a portfolio using Eq. (3-8), consider a financial asset for which the expected value of annual return is 16 percent, with a standard deviation of 15 percent. Suppose further that another financial asset has an expected value of annual return of 14 percent and a standard deviation of 12 percent, and that the expected correlation between the two financial assets is 0.40. By investing equal portions in each of the financial assets, the expected value of return for the portfolio would be

$$R_p = 16\%(.5) + 14\%(.5) = 15\% \qquad (3\text{-}9)$$

This contrasts with a 16 percent return when the portfolio is comprised entirely of the first financial asset. However, the standard deviation for the probability distribution of possible returns for the new portfolio is

$$\sigma_p = [(.5)^2(1.00)(.15)^2 + (2)(.5)(.5)(.4)(.15)(.12)$$
$$+ (.5)^2(1.00)(.12)^2]^{1/2} = 11.3\% \qquad (3\text{-}10)$$

From Eq. (3-8) we know that the covariance between the two financial assets must be counted twice. Therefore, we multiply the covariance by 2, when $j = 1$ and $k = 1$ for financial asset 1 and square the proportion invested (.5), as well as standard deviation (.15). The correlation coefficient, of course, is 1.00. The same thing applies to financial asset 2 when $j = 2$ and $k = 2$. The important principle to grasp is that as long as the correlation coefficient between two financial assets is less than 1.00, the standard deviation of the portfolio will be less than the weighted average of the two individual standard deviations.

The example suggests that by diversifying its holdings to include financial assets with less than perfect positive correlation among themselves, the risk-averse economic unit is able to reduce the dispersion of the probability distribution of possible returns relative to the expected value of return for that distribution. In other words, the risk will be less, compared to the expected return. Whereas the standard deviations for two financial assets were 15 and 12 percent, respectively, the standard deviation for the portfolio is only 11.3 percent.

It is evident from Eq. (3-8) that the dispersion of the probability distribution for a portfolio could be reduced to zero if financial assets with negative correlation could be found. The objective of diversification, however, is not to reduce dispersion per se but to obtain the best combination of expected value of return and standard deviation.[3]

The individual economic unit is assumed to have a preference function with respect to the expected value of return and risk from holding a portfolio of financial assets. In other words, it is assumed to make optimal portfolio decisions on the basis of these two parameters. If an economic unit is averse to risk and associates risk with divergence from expected return, its utility schedule may be similar to that shown in Fig. 3-9. The expected value of return is plotted on the vertical axis, while the standard deviation is along the horizontal. As before, the curves are known as

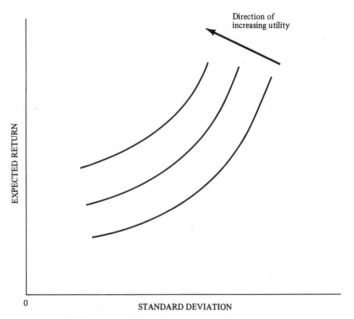

Figure 3-9. Hypothetical indifference curves.

[3]For a much more detailed analysis of diversification, see, among others, William F. Sharpe, *Investments* 2nd ed. (Englewood Cliffs, N.J.: Prentice-Hall, Inc., 1981); John Lintner, "Security Prices, Risk and Maximal Gains for Diversification," *Journal of Finance*, 20 (December 1965), 587–615; and Franco Modigliani and Gerald A. Pogue, "An Introduction to Risk and Return," *Financial Analysts Journal* 30 (March–April 1974). All of the work along this line is an outgrowth of the classic work of Harry M. Markowitz, *Portfolio Selection: Efficient Diversification of Investments* (New York: John Wiley & Sons, Inc., 1959).

indifference curves; in this case the individual is indifferent between any combination of expected value of return and standard deviation on a particular curve. In other words, a curve is defined by those combinations of expected return and standard deviation that result in a fixed level of expected utility.[4] The greater the slope of the indifference curves, the more averse the investor is to risk. As we move upward and to the left in Fig. 3-9, each successive curve represents a higher level of expected utility.

Individuals will want to hold that portfolio of financial assets that places them on the highest indifference curve, choosing it from the opportunity set of available portfolios. An example of an opportunity set, based upon the subjective probability beliefs of an individual economic unit, is shown in Fig. 3-10. This opportunity set reflects all possible portfolios of securities as envisioned by the individual. The dark line at the top of the set is the line of efficient combinations, or the efficient frontier. It depicts the tradeoff between risk and expected value of return. According to the Markowitz mean-variance maxim, an economic unit should seek a portfolio of securities that lies on the efficient frontier.[5] A portfolio is not

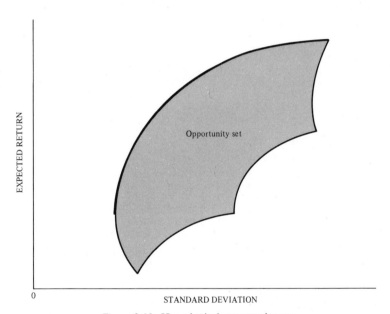

Figure 3-10. Hypothetical opportunity set.

[4]For further discussion and proof that indifference curves for a risk-averse investor are concave, see Eugene F. Fama and Merton H. Miller, *The Theory of Finance* (New York: Holt, Rinehart and Winston, 1972), pp. 226–8.

[5]Markowitz, *Portfolio Selection: Efficient Diversification of Investments* (New York: John Wiley & Sons, Inc., 1959), Chapters 7 and 8.

efficient if there is another portfolio with a higher expected value of return and a lower standard deviation, a higher expected value and the same standard deviation, or the same expected value but a lower standard deviation. If an economic unit's portfolio is not efficient, the unit can increase the expected value of return without increasing the risk, decrease the risk without decreasing the expected value of return, or obtain some combination of increased expected value and decreased risk by switching to a portfolio on the efficient frontier.

As can be seen, the efficient frontier is determined on the basis of dominance. Portfolios of securities tend to dominate individual securities because of the reduction in risk obtainable through diversification. As discussed before, this reduction is evident when one explores the implications of Eq. (3-8). The objective of the economic unit is to choose the best portfolio from those that lie on the efficient frontier. The portfolio with the maximum utility is the one at the point of tangency of the opportunity set with the highest indifference curve. This tangency is illustrated in Fig. 3-11, and the portfolio represented by the point of tangency is the optimal one for an economic unit with those expectations and utility function.[6]

Presence of Risk-Free Security

If a risk-free security exists that yields a certain future return, the process of portfolio selection described above must be modified. Suppose for now that the economic unit is able not only to lend at the risk-free rate, but to borrow at it as well. To determine the optimal portfolio under these conditions, we first draw a line from the risk-free rate, i (on the expected return axis), through its point of tangency with the opportunity set of portfolio returns, as illustrated in Fig. 3-12. This line then becomes the new efficient frontier. Note that only one portfolio of risky financial assets—namely, m—would be considered. In other words, this portfolio now dominates all others, including those on the efficient frontier of the opportunity set.

Any point on the straight line tells us the proportion of the risky portfolio, m, and the proportion of loans or borrowings at the risk-free rate. To the left of point m the economic unit would hold both the risk-free security and portfolio m. To the right, it would hold only portfolio m and would borrow funds, in addition to initial investment funds, in order to invest further in it. The farther to the right in the figure, the greater the borrowing will be.

[6]For a more sophisticated and mathematical discussion of the point of tangency, see Fama and Miller, *Theory of Finance*, pp. 223–6 and 243–50. For ease of understanding, we have purposely kept the presentation graphical.

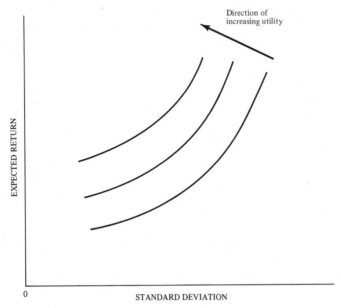

Figure 3-11. Selection of optimal portfolio.

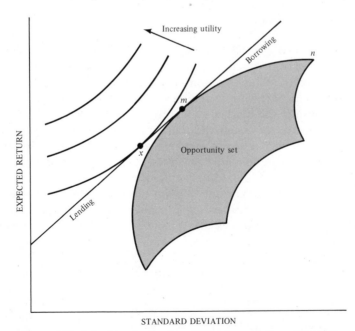

Figure 3-12. Selection of optimal portfolio when risk-free asset exists.

Overall expected return $= (w)$ (expected return on risky portfolio) $+ (1-w)$ (risk-free rate)

where w is the proportion of total wealth invested in portfolio m and $1-w$ is the proportion invested in the risk-free asset. If lending is involved, w is less than 1.0; if borrowing occurred, it is greater than 1.0. The overall standard deviation is simply w times the standard deviation of the risky portfolio. No account is taken of the risk-free asset because its standard deviation is zero.

The optimal investment policy is determined by the point of tangency between the straight line in Fig. 3-12 and the highest indifference curve. As shown in the figure, this point is portfolio x and it consists of an investment in both the risk-free financial asset and the risky portfolio, m.

The theory underlying this notion could be developed in much more detail. For example, if homogeneous expectations are assumed on the part of all economic units, one can determine the expected rate of return for an individual financial asset, given the risk-free rate and the incremental riskiness of that financial asset with respect to an efficiently diversified portfolio of financial assets. Development of this line of thought, known as the *capital asset pricing model*, is well advanced in literature and is available elsewhere.[7] Rather than the single-factor, capital asset pricing model, which explains returns according to the degree of undiversifiable risk, multiple factors may be involved in the return generating process. The *arbitrage pricing theory* suggests that the market equilibrating mechanism is driven by individuals eliminating arbitrage profits across multiple factors, one of which is undiversifiable risk. Discussion of the implications of this theory also is available elsewhere.[8] Our focus in this chapter is somewhat broader in sketching a theory of general equilibrium in financial and other markets. While this approach does not provide much in the way of predictive ability (owing to the generality involved), it does afford an overall insight into the market equilibrating process.

In this regard, we assume that all economic units select portfolios of financial assets in such a way as to maximize their expected utility. In turn, utility preferences are assumed to be formulated on the basis of the expected value and the standard deviation of the probability distribution of possible returns. It is important to point out that we allow for heterogeneous expectations on the part of individual economic units. As we will discuss in the latter part of this chapter and in the appendix, heterogeneous

[7]See, for example, Sharpe, *Investments*; James C. Van Horne, *Financial Management and Policy*, 6th ed. (Englewood Cliffs, N.J.: Prentice-Hall, Inc., 1983), Chapter 3; and numerous other books and articles dealing with the topic.

[8]Stephen A. Ross, "The Arbitrage Theory of Capital Asset Pricing," *Journal of Economic Theory*, 13 (December 1976): 341–60; and Richard Roll and Stephen A. Ross, "An Empirical Investigation of the Arbitrage Pricing Theory," *Journal of Finance*, 35 (December 1980): 1073–1103.

expectations, together with differences in utility preferences among economic units, have a major bearing upon the structure of interest rates.

Utility for Financial Liabilities

We assume also that the issuance of financial liabilities can be analyzed on the basis of a two-parameter utility function. Because an economic unit must pay the return on a financial liability, it would have a negative utility for doing so, all other things the same. Consequently, $\partial U/\partial e < 0$, where e is the expected value of return on the financial liability. If an economic unit is a risk averter, it would prefer less variance to more variance, holding constant the expected value of return, so $\partial U/\partial v < 0$, where v is the standard deviation for the financial liability. For the risk seeker, $\partial U/\partial v > 0$. For a financial liability, variance pertains to the dispersion of the probability distribution of possible future market prices. For fixed-income financial liabilities, the issuer knows with certainty its contractual obligation to meet interest and principal payments. After issuance, however, the instrument fluctuates in market price because of changes in the overall level of interest rates and because of changes in perceived risk by investors.

Utility for Other Assets

In the previous discussion, we considered the effect of holding financial assets and issuing financial liabilities on the utility of an economic unit. We now must consider the utility arising from the holding of other assets. Because our primary interest is in financial instruments, however, our examination necessarily will be brief. Afterward, the maximization of utility for an economic unit in its holdings of assets, in its issuance of financial liabilities, and in its consumption will be considered. Having established these building blocks, we will deal in the remainder of the chapter and in the appendix with how economic units interact to determine interest rates in an economy.

Because money is a medium of exchange and other financial assets are not, it was not included in our previous discussion. If it were not for money, of course, trading would have to be done on the basis of exchanging one good for another. Such a barter system allows little or no store of purchasing power, no common unit of account in which different goods can be expressed, and little divisibility. Because of these obvious inefficiencies, money has come to serve as the accepted medium of exchange in acquiring goods and services. In addition, it serves as the unit of account, or common denominator, in the pricing of goods and services. For example, a good or service does not have to be priced in terms of so many units of other goods and services. It can be priced in terms of units of money. Although money additionally serves as a store of value, other assets, of course, also serve this function.

Keynes has identified three motives for holding money—the transactions motive, the precautionary motive, and the speculative motive.[9] The transactions motive is the desire to hold money to pay for goods and services. This need tends to rise with the level of income and expenditures of an economic unit. The precautionary motive for holding money involves maintaining a cushion, or buffer, to meet unexpected contingencies. The more predictable the money needs of an economic unit, the less precautionary balances are needed. If an economic unit is able to borrow on short notice to meet emergency money drains, the need for this balance is also reduced. The last motive, the speculative one, means holding money to take advantage of expected changes in security prices. When interest rates are expected to rise and security prices to fall, this motive would suggest that the economic unit should hold money until the rise in interest rates ceases, in order to avoid a loss in security value. When interest rates are expected to fall, money may be invested in securities; the economic unit will benefit by any subsequent fall in interest rates and rise in security prices.

The marginal utility for holding money can be related to these three motives, and it is assumed that economic units formulate utility preferences for money on these bases. The expected value of return for holding paper money is zero. However, no risk is involved, for the future price is known. To be sure, there may be an opportunity loss in the form of eroded purchasing power. However, there is no dispersion of the probability distribution of possible monetary returns; X dollars of paper money held today will be worth X dollars tomorrow.

Unlike financial assets, real assets are held for the physical services they provide the owner. These assets may be productive, such as a machine tool, or may be designed to satisfy the wants of economic units, such as a house or a consumer durable. Real assets are tangible; they cannot be produced instantaneously but only over time. The marginal utility arising from owning a real asset must be related to the services it provides. In the case of a productive asset, it usually is related to the marginal profitability of another unit of input. In analyzing profitability one must take account of the interdependence of inputs in the production function. It is the partial derivative of profitability with respect to the asset that is important. The marginal utility of consumer durables and dwellings is much more difficult

---

[9]John Maynard Keynes, *The General Theory of Employment Interest and Money* (New York: Harcourt, Brace & World, Inc., 1936), pp. 170–4.

to measure. Here, marginal utility must be related to the want satisfaction the asset provides the owner.

The holding of certain real assets can be explained in terms of the overall portfolio of the owner. Business firms, on the one hand, hold capital assets for the return they are expected to provide. Households, on the other hand, do not appear to acquire consumer durables on the basis of portfolio considerations. However, the acquisition of a home has portfolio implications, for generally it is the largest asset holding of the household. Although the model developed in this chapter implies an independence of the utility function for real assets from that for financial assets, the holding of certain real assets can be explained in terms of an expected return-risk tradeoff for the economic unit as a whole. In these cases, the interdependence of real and financial assets must be recognized in the final determination of an optimal portfolio.

MARKET EQUILIBRIUM

The amount of money, financial assets, and real assets held, the amount of financial liabilities issued, and consumption are determined by an economic unit on the basis of maximizing its total utility, subject to net worth and income constraints. In equilibrium, the marginal utility derived from holding each asset is the same. *Marginal utility* is defined as the change in total utility that accompanies an increase of $1 in a particular asset. Thus, the marginal utility derived from the last dollar increase in financial asset 1 must equal the marginal utility derived from the last dollar increase in money, in financial assets 2, 3, and n and in real assets 1, 2, . . ., n. In equilibrium, the following equation holds:

$$\frac{MU \text{ money}}{P \text{ money}} = \frac{MU \ FA_1}{PFA_1} = \frac{MU \ FA_2}{PFA_2} = \frac{MU \ FA_n}{PFA_n}$$

$$= \frac{MU \ RA_1}{PRA_1} = \frac{MU \ RA_2}{PRA_2} = \frac{MU \ RA_n}{PRA_n} \qquad (3\text{-}11)$$

Here MU stands for marginal utility, P for price per unit, FA_n for financial asset n, and RA_n for real asset n. In other words, maximum satisfaction occurs at the point at which the marginal utility of a dollar's worth of money equals the marginal utility of a dollar's worth of financial asset n and the marginal utility of a dollar's worth of the other assets held. If this equation is not satisfied, an economic unit can increase its total utility by shifting from an asset with a lower ratio of marginal utility to price to one with a higher ratio. By such shifting, equilibrium will eventually be achieved, where the ratios of marginal utility to price are all equal to some constant

λ. If the price of money is 1, $\lambda = $ MU money/1, or the marginal utility of money.

For simplicity in analysis, we hold constant the effect of consumption by considering the balance sheet of an economic unit at only a moment in time. Over time, of course, an economic unit can have current expenditures. Then, in equilibrium, the marginal utility derived from a dollar's worth of current expenditures must equal that derived from a dollar's worth of each asset held. In other words, consumption competes with the holding of assets in the maximization of total utility. This implies that the marginal utility of savings (current income less current expenditures) must be evaluated in relation to the satisfaction derived from the assets into which savings are put. To facilitate later analysis, however, we hold constant the effect of savings and consumption and assume that an economic unit will not sell assets, use money, or issue financial liabilities for consumption.

Financial liabilities represent a negative marginal utility to the issuer. An economic unit does not issue a financial liability for its own sake, but rather to acquire assets. As long as the positive marginal utility from an additional dollar's worth of assets exceeds in absolute magnitude the negative marginal utility from the issuance of an additional dollar of financial liabilities, the economic unit will issue financial liabilities. In equilibrium, the negative marginal utility per dollar's worth of each financial liability should be the same. Moreover, the ratio of marginal utility to price for each financial liability should equal the ratio of marginal utility to price for each asset (if we ignore the sign of the ratio). For the risk averter, we would expect the negative ratio of marginal utility to price to increase at an increasing rate as a financial liability is increased beyond some point. This occurrence is a result not only of the utility preferences of the economic unit, but also of possible increases in the interest rate as more financial liabilities are issued. Because of the decreasing positive ratio of marginal utility to price for acquiring additional assets and the increasing negative ratio of marginal utility to price for issuing financial liabilities, an equilibrium will be achieved for the individual economic unit.

Maximizing Utility for the Economic Unit

At any moment in time, the holding of financial assets and the issuance of financial liabilities are constrained by the net worth of the individual economic unit.

$$
\begin{aligned}
M + FA_1 P_{FA1} &+ FA_2 P_{FA2} \\
&+ \ldots + FA_n P_{FAn} + RA_1 P_{RA1} + RA_2 P_{RA2} \\
&+ \ldots + RA_n P_{RAn} - FL_1 P_{FL1} - FL_2 P_{FL2} \\
&- \ldots - FL_n P_{FLn} = NW
\end{aligned} \tag{3-12}
$$

where FA$_n$ is the quantity of financial asset n, $P_{\text{FA}n}$ is the price per unit of that asset, FL$_n$ is the quantity of liability n, and $P_{\text{FL}n}$ is the price per unit of that financial liability. The individual economic unit will try to maximize its total utility by changing its asset holdings and liabilities issued, subject to its net worth constraint. Its objective function is

$$\text{Max } X = U\ (M,\ X,\ R,\ Y) \tag{3-13}$$

subject to

$$M + \sum_i P_i x_i + \sum_k P_k r_k - \sum_j P_j y_j = \text{NW} \tag{3-14}$$

where X = a column vector of x_i, where x_i is the quantity of the ith financial asset

P_i = price per unit of the ith financial asset

R = a column vector of r_k, where r_k is the quantity of the kth real asset

P_k = price per unit of the kth real asset

Y = a column vector of y_j, where y_j is the quantity of the jth financial liability

P_j = price per unit of the jth financial liability

Recall that the utility to an economic unit of holding financial assets and issuing financial liabilities was assumed to be based upon the expected value and standard deviation of the probability distributions of possible returns. Each economic unit forms expectations about possible returns from all feasible portfolios of financial assets and all feasible combinations of financial liabilities. We recognize, however, that an economic unit is limited in the number of financial assets it can consider at one time. It simply is unable to form expectations about the universe of financial assets available to it for investment; consequently, the number of feasible portfolios is restricted. Once the optimal portfolio of financial assets and the optimal combination of financial liabilities are determined by an economic unit, it then increases or decreases them to maximize its total utility, in keeping with Eqs. (3-13) and (3-14).

In summary, the individual economic unit maximizes its utility according to Eq. (3-13) by varying M, X, R, and Y, subject to the net worth constraint. In equilibrium, the marginal utility per dollar of money equals the marginal utility per dollar of the optimal financial-asset portfolio, which, in turn, equals the marginal utility per dollar of real assets held. In addition, the negative marginal utility per dollar of the optimal combination of financial liabilities must equal the ratio for the assets (if we ignore the sign). If it were less, an economic unit could increase its total utility by increasing its financial liabilities and increasing its holdings of assets.

The Action of All Economic Units

The action of all economic units in an economy maximizing their utility according to Eq. (3-13) determines market prices for real and financial assets in that economy. Whereas prices in Eq. (3-14) are assumed to be given for the individual economic unit, they are not given for economic units collectively. These economic units act to maximize their individual utilities, and in doing so, they determine market prices and interest rates in the economy. For the economy as a whole, financial assets equal financial liabilities. Accordingly, market prices must adjust so that in equilibrium there is no excess demand or excess supply.

The equilibrium structure of financial-asset prices and interest rates is the result of a complex blending of the expectations, net worths, incomes, and utility functions of all economic units in an economy. This structure is affected by the utility preferences of economic units regarding money, real assets, financial assets, and financial liabilities. For example, an increase in the marginal utility of all economic units toward holding real assets would lead, *ceteris paribus*, to a greater aggregate demand for real assets, higher prices for these assets, a lower aggregate demand for financial assets, and a greater aggregate supply of financial liabilities. For equilibrium to be achieved, prices of financial instruments would have to decline and interest rates rise.

Equilibrium in financial markets requires that the total quantity of a financial instrument demanded equal the total quantity an economic unit desires to issue. The relative influence of an economic unit on market price depends on its net worth, its utility preferences, its expectations, and its existing holds of assets and liabilities. On the supply side of the market, the quantity of a particular financial liability that an economic unit desires to issue also depends on these factors. In a modern economy, most economic units exert at least some influence on interest rates. Differing expectations, net worths, and utility functions of economic units, however, make determination of equilibrium prices of financial instruments in an economy an extremely complex process involving the interaction of all economic units in the economy. Perhaps the key element in this process is expectations. On the basis of expectations as to return, variance, and covariance, different financial instruments are perceived differently by different economic units. Economic units in need of funds must compete for them on the basis of the expected return paid. (Actually, the need for funds and the expected return paid are determined simultaneously.) Through the interaction of the various economic units, interest rates are determined and savings are allocated in the economy. Because of the mathematical complexity of the process, it is examined in detail in the appendix to this chapter.

SUMMARY

Savings in an economy are allocated primarily through interest rates. The *yield* on a financial instrument is the discount rate that equates the present value of expected future cash inflows, including the redemption price, with the current market price. The yield to maturity on an instrument differs from its *holding-period yield* in that the latter encompasses both the cash inflows and the capital gain or loss for the holding period.

In a riskless world, individuals maximize their utility by first seeking a productive optimum between *current* consumption claims and *future* consumption claims. This optimum occurs at the point of tangency between their production opportunity curve and the market exchange line. Individuals then move up (lend) or down (borrow) the line until a point of tangency is reached with the highest indifference curve. At this point, present and future want satisfaction is maximized. When all economic units behave in this manner, the slope of the market exchange line, which represents the interest rate, shifts until the amount of desired lending equals the amount of desired borrowing at the particular interest rate involved. Thus the equilibrium rate of interest embraces the productive opportunity sets and utility preferences of all economic units.

In a risky world, there is not one but many interest rates. A general equilibrium framework is necessary to understand their determination. The individual economic unit continually adjusts its asset holdings and liabilities toward a preferred mix of assets, liabilities, and consumption. At the preferred mix, the wealth and income of the unit are allocated optimally. The economic unit adjusts its mix to maximize its total utility. In equilibrium, the marginal utilities of each dollar of money, each dollar of each financial asset, and each dollar of each real asset are the same. These ratios are equal also to the negative marginal utility of each dollar of each financial liability (if we ignore the sign).

The utility preferences for holding financial assets and issuing financial liabilities are assumed to be based upon the expected value and the dispersion of the probability distribution of possible returns. In either case, it is the portfolio of assets or liabilities that is important, for an economic unit can reduce dispersion of its portfolio through diversification. The behavior of risk averters and risk seekers with respect to an optimal portfolio was examined. Individual economic units maximize their total utility arising from holding money, financial assets, and real assets; from issuing financial liabilities; and from consuming, subject to wealth and income constraints. The behavior of all economic units in a closed economy maximizing their total utility in this manner determines interest rates on financial instruments in that economy. In equilibrium, the total amount of financial assets demanded must equal the total amount supplied; there can be no excess demand or excess supply in financial markets. Interest rates adjust to clear these markets and are the result of a complex interaction of all economic units in the economy.

APPENDIX:
THE EQUILIBRIUM PRICES
OF FINANCIAL ASSETS

The purpose of this appendix is to develop a model of financial-asset prices in a closed economy. We begin by assuming that at a moment in time an individual economic unit may hold money, financial assets, and real assets. In addition, it may issue a variety of financial liabilities to finance its holding of assets. Consider a simplified situation with only one financial asset—a fixed-income security—in which an individual economic unit may invest and with only one type of financial liability which it may issue—also a fixed-income security. The asset and the liability are assumed to have a zero coupon rate with interest expressed as a discount. Moreover, we assume no transaction costs, no short sales, and no taxation. The economic unit will attempt to maximize its total utility arising from holding money, the financial asset, and real assets, and from issuing the financial liability. The amounts to the various assets are constrained by the net worth of the economic unit at time t plus the amount of the financial liability it issues.[1] The relationship for the individual economic unit may be expressed as

$$\max Z = U(M, x, R, y) + \lambda(N - M - P_x x - R + P_y y) \quad (3A\text{-}1)$$

where M = money, expressed in units of \$1, and assumed to
  be nonnegative[2]
  x = quantity of the financial asset held at time t
  P_x = price of the financial asset at time t
  R = market value of real assets held at time t, expressed
  in units of one dollar, and assumed to be nonnegative
  y = quantity of the issued financial liability at time t
  P_y = price of the financial liability at time t
  N = net worth of economic unit at time t, expressed in
  units of one dollar
  λ = a Lagrangian multiplier

It is evident from Eq. (3A-1) that the individual economic unit will increase

---

[1] The net worth of an individual economic unit is assumed to be constant. We assume that it will not sell assets, use money, or borrow to consume.

[2] We assume that the economic unit analyzed is not able to issue money.

its financial liability to finance its holdings of money, the financial asset, and real assets as long as it can increase its total utility by doing so. Assuming no short sales, so that $x \geq 0$ and $y \geq 0$, the equilibrium conditions for the financial asset and liability are

$$\frac{\partial U}{\partial x} - \lambda P_x \leq 0, \qquad x \geq 0, \qquad x\left[\frac{\partial U}{\partial x} - \lambda P_x\right] = 0 \qquad \text{(3A-2)}$$

$$\frac{\partial U}{\partial y} + \lambda P_y \leq 0, \qquad y \geq 0, \qquad y\left[\frac{\partial U}{\partial y} + \lambda P_y\right] = 0 \qquad \text{(3A-3)}$$

We assume a one-period horizon and that the future price of the financial asset and the future price of the financial liability at time $t + 1$ are subjective random variables.[3] We also assume that the individual economic unit knows the mean and variance of the probability distributions. Thus, the value of the financial asset to rule at time $t + 1$ is a random variable with a mean of

$$E = \bar{\rho}_x x \qquad \text{(3A-4)}$$

and a variance of

$$V = \sigma_x^2 x^2 \qquad \text{(3A-5)}$$

where $\bar{\rho}_x$ is the mean of the probability distribution of possible prices one period hence, σ_x^2 is the variance, and x is the quantity of the asset held.

Similarly, the value of the financial liability to rule at time $t + 1$ is also a random variable with a mean of

$$e = \bar{\rho}_y y \qquad \text{(3A-6)}$$

and a variance of

$$\upsilon = \sigma_y^2 y^2 \qquad \text{(3A-7)}$$

where $\bar{\rho}_y$ is the mean of the probability distribution, σ_y^2 is the variance, and y is the quantity of the liability issued.

We assume that individual economic units may be analyzed as though their utilities with respect to holding and issuing a financial asset and a liability were governed by the mean and variance of the respective prob-

[3]For similar approaches, see G. O. Bierwag and M. A. Grove, "On Capital Assets Prices: Comment," *Journal of Finance*, 20 (March 1965): 89–93; and J. R. Hicks, "Liquidity," *The Economic Journal*, LXXII (December, 1963): 795, 798–802.

ability distributions. We also assume that the price of money and the prices of real assets at time $t + 1$ are known with certainty and that these prices are the same as those that prevailed at time t. Thus, we consider only a subset of prices of financial assets and liabilities within which equilibrium can occur. Moreover, we assume that the prices of the financial asset and the financial liability are stochastically independent.

Under conditions (3A-4) through (3A-7), Eqs. (3A-2) and (3A-3) become

$$\frac{\partial U}{\partial E}\frac{\partial E}{\partial x} + \frac{\partial U}{\partial V}\frac{\partial V}{\partial x} - \lambda P_x \le 0, \qquad x \ge 0,$$

$$x\left[\frac{\partial U}{\partial E}\frac{\partial E}{\partial x} + \frac{\partial U}{\partial V}\frac{\partial V}{\partial x} - \lambda P_x\right] = 0$$

(3A-8)

or

$$\frac{\partial U}{\partial E}\bar{P}_x + \frac{\partial U}{\partial V}2x\sigma_x^2 - \lambda P_x \le 0, \qquad x \ge 0,$$

$$x\left[\frac{\partial U}{\partial E}\bar{P}_x + \frac{\partial U}{\partial V}2x\sigma_x^2 - \lambda P_x\right] = 0$$

and

$$\frac{\partial U}{\partial e}\frac{\partial e}{\partial y} + \frac{\partial U}{\partial v}\frac{\partial v}{\partial y} + \lambda P_y \le 0, \qquad y \ge 0,$$

$$y\left[\frac{\partial U}{\partial e}\frac{\partial e}{\partial y} + \frac{\partial U}{\partial v}\frac{\partial v}{\partial y} + \lambda P_y\right] = 0$$

(3A-9)

or

$$\frac{\partial U}{\partial e}\bar{P}_y + \frac{\partial U}{\partial v}2y\sigma_y^2 + \lambda P_y \le 0, \qquad y \ge 0,$$

$$y\left[\frac{\partial U}{\partial e}\bar{P}_y + \frac{\partial U}{\partial V}2y\sigma_y^2 + \lambda P_y\right] = 0$$

The equilibrium quantity of the financial asset held is

$$x = \max\left\{\left.\frac{-\dfrac{\partial U}{\partial E}\bar{p}_x + \lambda P_x}{2\dfrac{\partial U}{\partial v}}\right/ \sigma_x^2, 0\right\}$$

$$= \max\left\{\left.\left(k\frac{\partial U}{\partial E}\bar{p}_x - k\lambda P_x\right)\right/ \sigma_x^2, 0\right\} \tag{3A-10}$$

where $k = -[1/2(\partial U/\partial V)]$ or a measure of risk aversion.

For the risk averter who associates risk with variance, $\partial U/\partial V$ will be negative and k positive; for the risk seeker, $\partial U/\partial V$ will be positive and k negative. We assume, of course, that $\partial U/\partial E > 0$.

For the issuance of a financial liability, the equilibrium quantity is

$$y = \max\left\{\left.\frac{-\dfrac{\partial U}{\partial E}\bar{p}_y - \lambda P_y}{2\dfrac{\partial U}{\partial v}}\right/ \sigma_y^2, 0\right\}$$

$$= \max\left\{\left.\left(l\frac{\partial U}{\partial E}\bar{p}_y + l\lambda P_x\right)\right/ \sigma_y^2, 0\right\} \tag{3A-11}$$

where $l = -[1/2(\partial U/\partial v)]$, or a measure of risk aversion for the issuance of the financial liability. For the issuer, we assume $\partial U/\partial e < 0$.

Market Equilibrium: Two Economic Units

In a closed economy of two economic units, if unit b is to issue a financial liability, unit a must invest in it. In market equilibrium, $x_a = y_b$, the amount of the financial asset demanded by a must equal the amount that b desires to issue. Thus,

$$\max\left\{\frac{k\dfrac{\partial U}{\partial E}\bar{p}_{xa} - k\lambda_a P}{\sigma_{xa}^2}, 0\right\} = \max\left\{\frac{l\dfrac{\partial U}{\partial e}\bar{p}_{yb} + l\lambda_b P}{\sigma_{yb}^2}, 0\right\} \tag{3A-12}$$

If both x_a and y_b are greater than zero, the equilibrium price at time t of the financial asset is

$$
P = \frac{k\left(\dfrac{\partial U}{\partial E}\right)\left(\dfrac{\bar{p}_{xa}}{\sigma_{xa}^2}\right) - \left(l\dfrac{\partial U}{\partial e}\right)\left(\dfrac{\bar{p}_{yb}}{\sigma_{yb}^2}\right)}{\dfrac{k\lambda_a}{\sigma_{xa}^2} + \dfrac{l\lambda_b}{\sigma_{yb}^2}}
\tag{3A-13}
$$

Equation (3A-13) suggests that the equilibrium price of the financial asset is a balancing of the expectations, net worths, and utility functions of the economic units involved. If both a and b are risk averters, an assumption we continue throughout this section, the price of the financial asset will vary directly, ceteris paribus, with the means of the probability distributions of prices that a and b expect at time t to prevail at time $t+1$.

The direction of the variation with the variances of the probability distributions will depend upon the relative marginal utilities of units a and b. When $(\partial U/\partial E)\bar{p}_{xa}/\lambda_a = (\partial U/\partial e)\bar{p}_{yb}/\lambda_b$, price does not vary with either the variance of a's probability distribution, σ_{xa}^2, or that of b's, σ_{yb}^2. When $(\partial U/\partial E)\bar{p}_{xa}/\lambda_a < (\partial U/\partial e)\bar{p}_{yb}/\lambda_b$, price varies directly with σ_{xa}^2 and inversely with σ_{yb}^2. Finally, when $(\partial U/\partial E)\bar{p}_{xa}/\lambda_a > (\partial U/\partial e)\bar{p}_{yb}/\lambda_b$, price varies inversely with σ_{xa}^2 and directly with σ_{yb}^2.

If expectations are homogeneous, so that the probability distributions of a and b are the same, Eq. (3A-13) becomes

$$
P = \frac{\bar{p}\left(k\dfrac{\partial U}{\partial E} - l\dfrac{\partial U}{\partial e}\right)}{k\lambda_a + l\lambda_b}
\tag{3A-14}
$$

For the actual price at time t to equal the mean of the probability distribution of prices expected by a and b at time t to prevail at time $t+1$, $[k(\partial U/\partial E) - l(\partial U/\partial e)]$ must equal $(k\lambda_a + l\lambda_b)$. If $\partial U/\partial E$ and $-\partial U/\partial e$ are less than λ_a and λ_b, respectively, P, the actual price at time t, will be less than $\bar{p}$, the mean of the probability distribution.

Market Equilibrium: Multiple Financial Assets

Clearly, it is inappropriate to consider an economy of only one financial asset and two economic units. An individual economic unit may both invest in and issue a variety of financial assets and liabilities.

Thus, Eq. (3A-1) must be expanded as follows:[4]

$$\max Z = U(M, X, R, Y) + \lambda \left(N - M - \sum_i P_i x_i - R + \sum_j P_j y_j\right) \quad \text{(3A-15)}$$

where X = a column vector of x_i, where x_i is the quantity of
the ith financial asset

P_i = price of the ith financial asset at time t

Y = a column vector of y_j, where y_j is the quantity of
the jth financial liability

P_j = price of the jth financial liability at time t

For the individual economic unit in equilibrium,

$$\frac{\partial U}{\partial x_i} - \lambda P_i \leq 0, \qquad x_i \geq 0,$$

$$x_i \left[\frac{\partial U}{\partial x_i} - \lambda P_i\right] = 0 \qquad (i = 11,\ldots,mn) \quad \text{(3A-16)}$$

$$\frac{\partial U}{\partial y_j} + \lambda P_j \leq 0, \, y_j \geq 0,$$

$$y_j \left[\frac{\partial U}{\partial y_j} + \lambda P_j\right] = 0 \qquad (j = 1,\ldots,n) \quad \text{(3A-17)}$$

where mn is security n issued by the mth economic unit in the economy. We assume that individual economic units do not issue financial liabilities to themselves. As before, the utilities of holding financial assets and issuing financial liabilities are assumed to be functions of the mean and variance of the probability distributions of prices expected by the economic unit at time t to prevail at time $t+1$. The value of an individual's entire portfolio of financial asset expected at time t to rule at time $t+1$ is a random variable with a mean of

$$E = \sum_{i=11}^{mn} \bar{p}_i x_i \qquad \text{(3A-18)}$$

---

[4]Again, we assume that R for each economic unit in the economy is nonnegative. However, M for certain units now may be negative. The monetary authorities and commercial banks are assumed to be able to issue money, while all other economic units cannot.

where $\bar{p}_i$ is the mean of the probability distribution of prices of the ith financial asset expected to prevail at time $t+1$. The variance of the random variable is

$$V = \sum_{i=11}^{mn} \sum_{q=11}^{mn} x_i x_q \sigma_{iq} \qquad \text{(3A-19)}$$

where σ_{iq} is the covariance between the price of financial asset i expected at time t to prevail at time $t+1$ and the price of financial asset q expected at time t to prevail at time $t+1$.

In equilibrium, Equation (3A-17) becomes

$$\left[\frac{\sigma U}{\partial E} \bar{p}_i + \frac{\partial U}{\partial V} 2 \sum_{q=11}^{mn} x_q \sigma_{qi} - \lambda P_i \right] \leq 0, \qquad x_i \geq 0,$$

$$x_i \left[\frac{\partial U}{\partial E} \bar{p}_i + \frac{\partial U}{\partial V} 2 \sum_{q=11}^{mn} x_q \sigma_{qi} - \lambda P_i \right] = 0 \qquad (i=11,\ldots,mn) \qquad \text{(3A-20)}$$

Assuming $\partial U / \partial V < 0$, this equation becomes

$$\left[\sum_{q=11}^{mn} x_q \sigma_{qi} - k \left(\frac{\partial U}{\partial E} \bar{p}_i - \lambda P_i \right) \right] \geq 0, \qquad x_i \geq 0,$$

$$x_i \left[\sum_{q=11}^{mn} x_q \sigma_{qi} - k \left(\frac{\partial U}{\partial E} \bar{p}_i - \lambda P_i \right) \right] = 0 \qquad (i=11,\ldots,mn) \qquad \text{(3A-21)}$$

In matrix notation, condition (3A-21) becomes[5]

$$X \geq 0 \leq CX - k \left(\frac{\partial U}{\partial E} \theta - \lambda \Phi \right) \qquad \text{(3A-22)}$$

where C is the matrix of variances and covariances, X is a column vector of the quantities of financial assets $(x_{11},\ldots,x_{mn})$, where x_{mn} is security n issued by the mth economic unit, θ is a column vector of the means of the probability distributions of prices expected at time t to prevail at time $t+1$ for these financial assets $(\bar{p}_{11},\ldots,\bar{p}_{mn})$, and Φ is a column vector of their actual prices at time t, $(P_{11},\ldots,P_{mn})$. The equilibrium vector X for the individual economic unit may be expressed as

$$X = C^{-1} k \left(\frac{\partial U}{\partial E} \theta - \lambda \Phi \right) + C^{-1} \varepsilon \qquad \text{(3A-23)}$$

where $X \geq 0 \leq \varepsilon$ and C^{-1} is an inverse matrix.

[5] We shall follow the notational convention that triplets of the form $[a \geq 0, b \geq 0, ab = 0]$ are represented as $[a \geq 0 \leq b]$.

In addition to investing in financial assets, the individual economic unit may issue a number of different financial liabilities.[6] As with financial assets, the risk averter will issue less of a particular financial liability as its contribution to the total variance of its financial liabilities increases. Assuming $\partial U/\partial v < 0$, the equilibrium vector Y of financial liabilities for the economic unit is

$$Y = T^{-1} l \left(\frac{\partial U}{\partial e} \Psi + \lambda \Phi \right) + T^{-1} \delta \qquad (3A\text{-}24)$$

where $Y \geq 0 \leq \delta$; and T^{-1} is an inverse matrix of variances and covariances; Y is a column vector of the quantities of financial liabilities $(y_{1m}, ..., y_{nm})$, where y_{nm} is the quantity of security n issued by economic unit m; Ψ is a column vector of the means of the probability distributions of prices expected at time t to prevail at time $t+1$ for the financial liabilities; and Φ is a column vector of their actual prices at time t.

Equilibrium in the market requires that the total quantity of a financial asset demanded equal the quantity of the financial liability an economic unit desires to issue. If X and Y are greater than or equal to zero.

$$\sum_{f=1}^{m} X_f = W \qquad (3A\text{-}25)$$

where f is the economic unit investing in a financial asset and W is a column vector of financial liabilities for economic units 1 through m (ordered such that the Y column vector of financial liabilities for economic unit 1 is followed by the Y column for unit 2, and so on all the way through unit m). Substituting Eqs. (3A-23) and (3A-24) into (3A-25), we obtain[7]

$$\sum_{f=1}^{m} C_f^{-1} k_f \left(\frac{\partial U}{\partial E_f} \theta_f - \lambda_f \Phi \right) = T^{-1} l \left(\frac{\partial U}{\partial e} \Psi + \lambda \Phi \right) \qquad (3A\text{-}26)$$

The vector Φ of equilibrium prices of financial assets in the market is

$$\Phi = \frac{\displaystyle\sum_{f=1}^{m} C_f^{-1} k_f \frac{\partial U}{\partial E_f} \theta_f - T^{-1} l \frac{\partial U}{\partial e} \Psi}{\displaystyle\sum_{f=1}^{m} C_f^{-1} k_f \lambda_f + T^{-1} l \lambda} \qquad (3A\text{-}27)$$

---

[6]Again, we assume that individual economic units do not issue themselves financial liabilities.

[7]For the right-hand side of the equation, we assume the ordering mentioned earlier, namely, that the Y column vector, or $T^{-1} l[(\partial U/\partial e)\Psi + \lambda \Phi]$, for unit 1 is followed by the Y column vector for unit 2, and so on through unit m.

According to this equation, the price of a financial asset in the market is an intricate blending of the expectations, net worths, and utility functions of all economic units in an economy. The relative influence of an investor on market price varies according to his net worth, his utility functions, his probability distributions of prices expected at time t to prevail at time $t+1$, the covariances for the financial asset under consideration, and his probability distributions and covariances for all other financial assets and for all financial liabilities he may issue. Because expectations, net worths, and utility functions of the different economic units in the economy differ, determination of the equilibrium price of a financial asset is an extremely complex process.

SELECTED REFERENCES

Bierwag, G. O., and M. A. Grove, "On Capital Asset Prices: Comment," *Journal of Finance*, 20 (March 1965): 89–93.

Fama, Eugene F., and Merton H. Miller, *The Theory of Finance*. New York: Holt, Rinehart and Winston, 1972.

Fisher, Irving, *The Theory of Interest*. New York: The Macmillan Co., 1930.

Hirshleifer, J., *Investment, Interest and Capital*. Englewood Cliffs, N.J.: Prentice-Hall, Inc., 1970.

Keynes, John Maynard, *The General Theory of Employment Interest and Money*. New York: Harcourt, Brace & World, Inc., 1936.

Lintner, John, "Security Prices, Risk and Maximal Gains from Diversification," *Journal of Finance*, 20 (December 1965): 587–615.

Lutz, Friedrich A., *The Theory of Interest*. Dordrecht, Holland: D. Reidel Publishing Co., 1967.

Markowitz, Harry M., *Portfolio Selection: Efficient Diversification of Investments*. New York: John Wiley & Sons, Inc., 1959.

Ross, Stephen A., "The Arbitrage Theory of Capital Asset Pricing," *Journal of Economic Theory*," 13 (December 1976): 341–60.

Sharpe, William F., *Investments*. 2nd ed. Englewood Cliffs, N.J.: Prentice-Hall, Inc., 1981.

Tinic, Seha M., and Richard R. West, *Investing in Securities: An Efficient Markets Approach*. Reading, Mass.: Addison-Wesley Publishing Co., Inc., 1979.

Van Horne, James C., *Financial Management and Policy*, 6th ed., Chapters 2 and 3. Englewood Cliffs, N.J.: Prentice-Hall, Inc., 1983.

4

INFLATION AND RETURNS

The consideration of interest rates in the financial market must be expanded to include the effect of inflation on returns. Because interest and principal payments are expressed in terms of money and because the monetary standard changes over time, the *real rate of return* to the holder of a financial asset can differ from its money, or *nominal return*. From the previous chapter we know that the return from a security is the rate of discount, which equates the present value of the stream of interest and principal payments—including the selling price—with the purchase price. For the nominal return, the cash flows received are in current dollars at the time of receipt. They have not been adjusted for inflation.

With inflation, these dollars will be worth less in purchasing power than were the dollars put out at the time the security was bought. As a result, the *real rate of return* on the security will be less than the nominal return. To illustrate, suppose the expected nominal return on a security to be held 5 years is 15 percent and that expectations are realized. If the rate of inflation over the period turns out to be 10 percent per annum, the real rate of return is less than the nominal return. In this case, the real return is approximately 5 percent. The real return, then, is simply the return realized when dollars received in the future are placed on the same purchasing-power basis as the dollars put out to buy the security.

THE HISTORICAL RECORD IN BRIEF

The relationship between inflation and interest rates has varied over time. Prior to World War II, the relationship, if any, was obscure. In fact, it was difficult to suggest that inflation expectations had any systematic effect on interest rates from the 1860s to World War II.[1] Since World War II, a relationship of sorts has emerged, in which interest rates are a positive function of inflation. Figure 4-1 depicts long- and short-term interest rates, together with the annual rate of inflation in the post–World War II period. Several things are apparent from the figure. First of all, there has been an upward trend in all three series, in accord with the idea of inflation having an influence. However, actual inflation is more volatile than either of the two interest rates. The important thing in financial asset

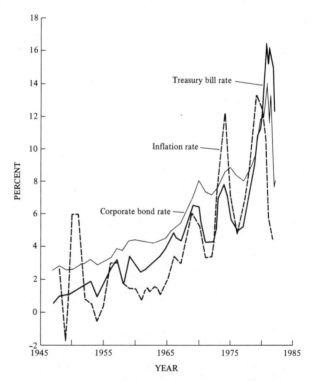

Figure 4-1. Three-month Treasury bill rate, Aaa corporate bond rate, and inflation (consumer price index), 1947–1982.

[1]See Lawrence H. Summers, "The Non-Adjustment of Nominal Interest Rates: A Study of the Fisher Effect," Working Paper, National Bureau of Economic Research, January 1982.

valuation is expected future inflation, and this is not always the same as present actual inflation. Finally, we see in the figure that short-term rates are more volatile than long-term rates.

In perhaps the most extensive study of actual nominal and real returns, Roger G. Ibbotson and Rex. A. Sinquefield analyzed Treasury bills, long-term government bonds, long-term corporate bonds, and common stocks over the period 1926–1981.[2] The authors found that over the entire period, Treasury bills provided a zero real return compounded annually. In other words, on the average, the nominal return matched inflation. Of course, for the taxable investor, the real after-tax return was negative. Other average before-tax returns, compounded annually, were:

	Inflation-Adjusted Average Return	Nominal Average Return	Standard Deviation of Nominal Returns
Treasury Bills	0.0%	3.0%	3.1%
Long-term Government Bonds	0.0	3.0	5.7
Long-term Corporate Bonds	0.5	3.6	5.6
Common Stocks	5.9	9.1	21.9
Small Stocks	8.8	12.1	37.3

The small stocks reported are comprised of the lowest quintile of stocks on the New York Stock Exchange, ranked by the amount of market capitalization.

Year-to-year and month-to-month differences in real and nominal returns occurred for each of the categories of securities reported above. As evidenced by the standard deviation column, the fluctuations were smallest for Treasury bills and largest for small stocks, all of which is in keeping with the notion of risk and return. Moreover, the patterns of annual nominal and real returns changed over the period 1926–1981. To illustrate, Fig. 4-2 shows such returns for Treasury bills. We see that from 1931 to around 1953, nominal returns were low and relatively stable. This was due to the depression, the pegging of interest rates by the Federal Reserve and Treasury during World War II and up to the Treasury–Federal Reserve Accord in 1951, and the Korean War, where again the government tried to keep interest rates low. During the period 1931–1953, inflation fluctuated, so there was considerable variability in real rates of return. In contrast, the period 1954–1981 was characterized by considerable fluctuation and increase in nominal returns, while real returns were more stable. With the

[2]Roger G. Ibbotson and Rex A. Sinquefield, *Stocks, Bonds, Bills, and Inflation* (Charlottesville, Va: Financial Analysts Research Foundation, 1982).

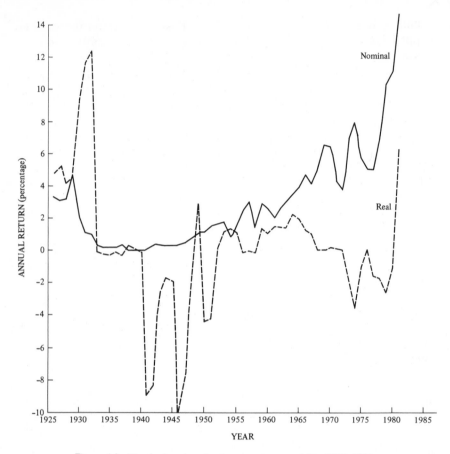

Figure 4-2. Nominal and real returns on treasury bills, 1926–1981.

exception of 1981—which will be discussed later—there was a reasonably close tracking of short-term interest rates with inflation, whereas there was not in the earlier period.

In a subsequent section, we summarize the results of a number of empirical studies that bear on the question of the response of interest rates and returns to unexpected changes in inflation. Our purpose here is to present general background information, so that we have some historical perspective as we explore certain concepts regarding inflation and returns. We now turn to these concepts.

THE NATURE OF INFLATION PREMIUMS

The difference between the nominal return and the real return is known as an *inflation premium*. While the actual inflation premium realized for a holding period is straightforward, the expected inflation premium is more complicated. In a loanable funds framework, both the supply and the demand functions for funds are affected by inflation expectations.[3] The supply of and demand for loanable funds can be expressed as:

$$S = S(r, \alpha, X)$$
$$D = D(r, \alpha, Y) \qquad (4\text{-}1)$$
$$S = D$$

where S and D are the supply and demand for funds, r is the nominal rate of interest, α is the expected rate of inflation, X is the vector of other factors influencing supply, and Y is the vector of other factors affecting demand. Other factors include such things as the expected returns on other assets, real economic activity variables, and wealth.

When supply and demand are equated in the market equilibrium process described in Chapter 3, both the nominal interest rate, r, and the supply of loanable funds are determined. The difference here is that we assume a given level of expected price inflation, designated by α, which was not an explicit variable in Chapter 3. Given this level, the market equilibrium is shown in the upper panel of Fig. 4-3. The intersection of the curves for supply (lenders) and demand (borrowers) determines the nominal interest rate, r, and the quantity of loanable funds outstanding, Q.

Suppose now that there is an unexpected increase in the rate of inflation to a new and higher level, denoted by α'. As shown in the bottom panel of Fig. 4-3, the supply curve shifts upward and to the left. Because of the increased inflation, lenders, or suppliers of loanable funds, demand a higher nominal rate of interest. On the other hand, borrowers are willing to pay a higher nominal return and the demand curve shifts upward and to the right.[4] The intersection of the new supply and demand curves determine the new equilibrium rate of interest, r', and the new quantity of loans outstanding, Q'.

In this illustration, the increase in expected inflation, $\alpha' - \alpha$, leads to an increase in the nominal interest rate, $r' - r$, and to a decrease in the quantity of loans outstanding, $Q - Q'$. While an unanticipated increase in inflation would be expected to increase nominal interest rates by some amount, whether the quantity of loans outstanding increases or decreases depends on the reaction of the supply and demand curves in the figure to unexpected changes in inflation, holding constant other factors. Moreover, the shift in nominal interest rate, $r' - r$, may or may not equal the change

---

[3]For further discussion of this framework, see Benjamin M. Friedman, "Who Puts the Inflation Premium into Nominal Interest Rates?" *Journal of Finance*, 33 (June 1978): 833–45.

[4]Throughout, we abstract from the issue of default risk by assuming all borrowers have the same degree of default risk.

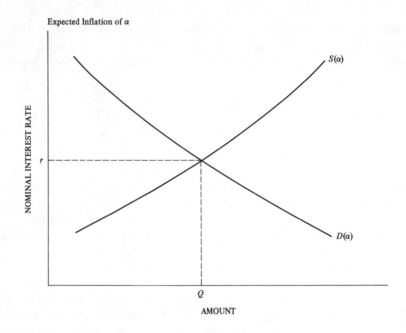

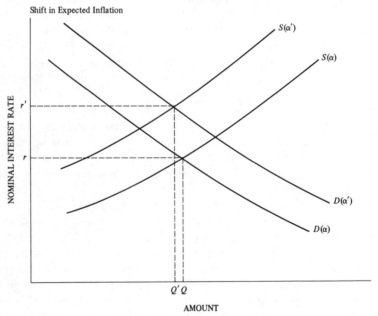

Figure 4-3. The supply and demand for loanable funds.

in inflation, $\alpha' - \alpha$. Let us focus now on the response of interest rates to unexpected changes in inflation, bearing in mind the overall equilibrium process of supply and demand for loanable funds in the face of inflation.

The Fisher Effect

Many years ago, Irving Fisher expressed the nominal rate of interest on a bond as the sum of the real rate and the rate of price change expected to occur over the life of the instrument. More formally, the nominal rate, r, is

$$1 + r = (1 + R)(1 + \alpha)$$
$$r = R + \alpha + R\alpha \tag{4-2}$$

where R is the real rate and α is the rate of inflation per annum expected to prevail over the life of the instrument.[5] Where inflation is only moderate, the cross-product term, $R\alpha$, is small and is usually ignored in the formulation. As a result, we have

$$r = R + \alpha \tag{4-3}$$

Traditionally, this formulation is known as the *Fisher effect*. It states merely that the nominal rate of interest embodies in it an inflation premium sufficient to compensate lenders for the expected loss of purchasing power associated with the receipt of future dollars. Put another way, lenders require a nominal rate of interest sufficiently high for them to earn an expected real rate of interest. In turn, the real rate required is a function of productive returns on real assets in our society plus a risk premium commensurate with risk of the borrower. The Fisher effect implies that if expected inflation rises by 1 percent, the nominal interest rate will rise by 1 percent as well. In other words, the effect is one-to-one. If r and α are the nominal rate and the expected inflation rate now and r' and α' are those which prevail after a change in expected inflation, the Fisher effect suggests that

$$r' - r = \alpha' - \alpha \tag{4-4}$$

According to this expression, the nominal rate of interest fully adjusts to changes in expected inflation; that is, the relationship of changes in nominal interest rates to changes in expected inflation is one-to-one. Fi-

---

[5]Irving Fisher, "Appreciation and Interest," *Publications of the American Economic Association*, 11 (August 1896): 1–100.

nancial markets would equilibrate in terms of expected real rates of return. Holding risk constant, economic units would be indifferent between investing in a real asset or a financial asset, for both would provide the same expected return after adjusting for inflation.

Money, Inflation, and Interest Rates

When changes in monetary policy are incorporated into the analysis, the effect of lags in adjustment becomes an important factor in determining the impact of inflation expectations on interest rates. The monetarist view, as espoused by Milton Friedman, suggests that the initial impact of an expansion of the money supply is to lower nominal interest rates.[6] This decline in interest rates is known as the *liquidity effect*. It occurs because a drop in interest rates is necessary to bring the demand for liquidity in balance with the supply. Over time, however, economic units will purchase additional assets with their excess cash balances. Also, the lower interest rate will stimulate capital expenditures on the part of business and others. This is known as the *income effect*.

It is argued then that the expansion of money has very little initial effect on income and prices. However, over time the increase in demand for assets will cause both income and prices to rise. Whereas initially real income may rise above its normal rate of growth, eventually its growth rate is said to return to that which is considered normal. At that point, the expansion of money is reflected entirely in a rise in prices.

With the increase in prices, the inflation premium rises, causing nominal interest rates to rise. In final equilibrium, it is argued that the nominal rate rises by exactly the amount of the increase in the inflation rate. In other words, the Fisher effect is entirely realized. Implied is that the increase in prices and income has no effect on the real rate of interest in final equilibrium.

If nominal rates behave in the manner described, the time sequence can be illustrated by the graph in Fig. 4-4.[7] The initial real rate of interest is R and the initial rate of inflation is $I_0 - R$. As a result, the initial nominal rate is $R + (I_0 - R) = I_0$. At time 1 on the horizontal axis, an expansion of

[6]Milton Friedman, "Factors Affecting the Level of Interest Rates," in *Conference on Savings and Residential Financing* (Chicago: U.S. Savings and Loan League, 1968). See also William E. Gibson, "Interest Rates and Monetary Policy," *Journal of Political Economy*, 78 (May–June 1970): 431–55; Phillip Cagan, *The Channels of Monetary Effects on Interest Rates* (New York: Columbia University Press, 1972); Frank G. Steindl, "Price Expectations and Interest Rates," *Journal of Money, Credit and Banking*, 5 (November 1973): 939–49; and Michael R. Darby, "The Financial and Tax Effects of Monetary Policy on Interest Rates," *Economic Inquiry*, 13 (June 1975): 266–76. For empirical testing of the issue, see G. J. Santoni and Courtenay C. Stone, "What Really Happened to Interest Rates?: A Longer Run Analysis," *Review of the Federal Reserve Bank of St. Louis*, 63 (November 1981): 3–14.

[7]This figure is based on Darby, "Financial and Tax Effects," p. 270.

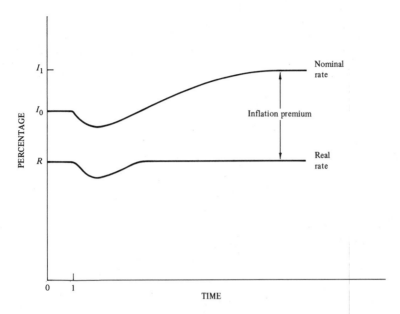

Figure 4-4. Change in nominal rate with monetary expansion.

money takes place. The initial liquidity effect of this money expansion is reflected in a decrease in the nominal rate of interest as well as in the real rate. As new inflation occurs with the increased spending by economic units, however, the nominal rate of interest rises. Moreover, the real rate is said to rise to where it was before. In final equilibrium, the nominal rate rises by the full amount of the increase in the rate of inflation. This inflation increase is represented by $I_1 - I_0$, and the new rate of inflation is $I_1 - R$. In other words, there is a one-for-one relationship between the change in inflation and the change in the nominal interest rate.

Leaving aside for now the question of whether this relationship holds, it is clear that a lagged effect may cause problems in empirical testing. Unless the nominal and real rates are measured at final equilibrium, there will be a bias in studying the effect of inflation on nominal interest rates. In a period marked by frequent changes in monetary policy, the measurement problems will pose great difficulty if this model of behavior holds.

NOMINAL INTEREST RATES AND INFLATION THEORETICALLY

The question of whether the relationship between changes in nominal interest rates and changes in expected inflation is one-to-one is a subject of considerable controversy, both theoretically and empirically. On a theoretical level, there are reasons why the nominal interest rate may not conform exactly to changes in inflation. Arguments exist to justify the relationship being less than one-to-one, as well as more. Robert Mundell, followed by James Tobin, present a theory where changes in the expected rate of inflation raise or lower the nominal rate of interest by less than the expected inflation rate change.[8] In the case of an increase in expected inflation, this change is said to be reflected in both an increase in the nominal rate of interest and a decrease in the real rate. (The change in the differential between the two rates equals the increase in the expected rate of inflation.)

The crux of Mundell's contention that the real rate of interest declines under such circumstances is that inflation reduces real money balances. In other words, money assets depreciate in real terms. As a result, real wealth declines, and this stimulates increased savings. In turn, this brings downward pressure on the real rate of interest. Finally, the decline in the real rate of interest stimulates investment and an acceleration in growth, according to this theory.

In the case of a decrease in expected inflation or increased deflation, the opposite occurs. Here the real rate rises and, as a result, the nominal rate falls by less than the change in inflation. Accompanying this is a deceleration of growth. Mundell concludes that fluctuations in the rate of inflation affect real economic activity and not just nominal rates of interest. Thus, the Mundell-Tobin hypothesis is that real rates of interest fluctuate over time in part because of the portfolio adjustments that accompany a change in expected inflation.[9] Because the change in real rate is opposite to that of the change in expected inflation, the response of the nominal rate of interest to the expected inflation change is less than one-to-one.

The principal argument for the response being more than one-to-one has to do with taxes. This argument has been advanced by Michael R. Darby and by Martin Feldstein.[10] With taxes, it is shown that a rise in expected inflation results in nominal rates rising by a greater percent. The after-tax real return to a lender whose loan is specified in nominal

[8]Robert Mundell, "Inflation and Real Interest," *Journal of Political Economy*, 71 (June 1963): 280–83; and James Tobin, "Money and Economic Growth," *Econometrica*, 33 (October 1965): 671–84.

[9]Frank G. Steindl, "Price Expectations and Interest Rates," *Journal of Money, Credit and Banking* 5 (November 1973): 939–49, suggests that the hypothesis is appropriate only if the reduced real demand for money balances that accompanies an increase in expected inflation is reflected in an increased real demand for bonds. As it is not clear a priori that the decreased real demand for money will not be felt primarily in the commodity markets as opposed to the bond market, Steindl concludes that it is not possible to predict the exact impact of changes in inflation on nominal rates of interest.

[10]Michael R. Darby, "The Financial and Tax Effects of Monetary Policy on Interest Rates," *Economic Inquiry*, 13 (June 1975): 266–76; and Martin Feldstein, "Inflation, Income Taxes and the Rate of Inflation: A Theoretical Analysis," *American Economic Review*, 66 (December 1976): 809–20.

dollars is

$$R^* = i - it - \alpha \qquad (4\text{-}5)$$

where i is the nominal rate of interest
$\quad\quad t$ is the marginal tax rate
$\quad\quad \alpha$ is the expected rate of inflation

all of which are expressed in terms of the length of the loan.
Rearranging Eq. (4-5), the nominal rate of interest is

$$i = \frac{(R^* + \alpha)}{(1 - t)} \qquad (4\text{-}6)$$

Suppose now that expected inflation increases from α to α', but that the marginal tax rate remains unchanged, as does the after-tax real return that is required. From Eq. (4-6) it is seen that the nominal rate must rise by

$$\Delta i = \frac{\alpha' - \alpha}{(1 - t)} \qquad (4\text{-}7)$$

If the tax rate were positive, the nominal rate would increase by more than the increase in anticipated inflation.[11] This is needed simply to pay the additional taxes. The higher the tax rate, the greater the nominal rate increase that is required.

To illustrate, suppose the expected rate of inflation is presently 10 percent and that it rises to 12 percent. If the lenders' effective tax rate is 40 percent, the nominal interest rate must rise by

$$r = \frac{12\% - 10\%}{(1 - .4)} = 3\tfrac{1}{3}\%$$

in order for lenders to be as well off in real terms on new loans as they were before the change in expected inflation. The implication is that lenders require compensation not only for inflation, but for the additional tax burden as well. Before examining empirical evidence on the relationship

---

[11]Arthur E. Gandolfi, "Inflation, Taxation, and Interest Rates," *Journal of Finance*, 37 (June 1982): 797–807, argues a relationship close to one-to-one could occur even with taxes. Such a situation would happen if the capital gains tax equals that on ordinary income and if the elasticity of investment with respect to after-tax real rates significantly exceeds that of savings. As the capital gains tax exceeds that on ordinary income, he concludes that the empirical relationship should lie between the Darby effect (more than one-to-one) and the Fisher effect (one-to-one). Maurice D. Levi and John H. Makin, "Anticipated Inflation and Interest Rates: Further Interpretation of Findings on the Fisher Equation," *American Economic Review*, 68 (December 1978): 801–12, also contend that the Fisher effect and the Darby effect are simplistic and do not capture the interactions in a general equilibrium approach to the real rate of interest. The authors include a labor sector in their model.

between nominal interest rates and inflation, it is important to distinguish between anticipated and unanticipated inflation.

Anticipated and Unanticipated Inflation

Anticipated (or expected) inflation is that inflation presently recognized by financial market participants and embodied in expected security returns. In this regard, we assume a single index exists which effectively portrays the general price level at various moments in time. The anticipated rate of inflation is defined in terms of the expected annual rate of change in this index. If the inflation that actually occurs over the life of a security is exactly that which was anticipated when its terms were set, neither borrowers nor lenders gain (or lose) with respect to inflation. Lenders receive the real return they expected when the loan was made, and borrowers pay the real return they expected to pay. An *unanticipated* (or unexpected) change in inflation represents a change in the rate of expected inflation that was unanticipated in advance. If the present rate of inflation is 8 percent and it shifts upward to 11 percent in a way unanticipated by market participants, we would say that there was a 3 percent unanticipated increase in inflation.

EMPIRICAL EVIDENCE ON NOMINAL INTEREST RATES

Theoretically, we see—depending on the strength of the argument—that inflation may affect nominal interest rates in different ways. The Fisher effect postulates a one-to-one change in the nominal rate of interest to a change in expected inflation. Other arguments suggest that it is less than one-to-one (Mundell-Tobin) or more than one-to-one (Darby-Feldstein). The actual effect is an empirical question, and one to which a great deal of inquiry has been directed. As we will see, the results are mixed, ranging from little relationship between nominal interest rates and inflation to a highly significant one.

Problems in Empirical Testing

A problem in empirical testing is that both the real rate of interest and expected inflation are not directly observable. Both must be estimated. Fisher himself regressed the nominal rate on a geometrically declining weighted average of past rates of price change. (Despite the effect bearing his name, he discovered only a weak relationship between nominal interest rates and expected inflation for the earlier part of this century.)

There have been several approaches to deriving proxies for the real rate of interest. In the capital market equilibrium approach, one attempts to infer rates of expected inflation from differences in the expected returns on two different types of assets; the asset whose return tends to be expressed in real terms and the asset whose return tends to be expressed in nominal terms. Fisher studied the difference in yield on bonds payable in gold and bonds payable in money.[12] Milton Friedman and Anna J. Schwartz, as well as a number of others, have used the difference in return on stocks and bonds.[13] The idea is that stocks and bonds are close substitutes and that equilibrium in the capital markets is based on expected real returns and not nominal returns.

A second approach to estimating the real rate of return is a loanable funds model.[14] In this approach, the real rate is broken down into two components: (1) the *equilibrium real rate*, which equates *ex ante* savings and investment; and (2) the *deviation of the current real rate from the equilibrium rate*. The equilibrium real bond rate is said to be a function of such variables as the change in real output, the Federal deficit, real income, tax rates, and real wealth. The deviation of the current real bond rate from the equilibrium real rate is said to depend on the variables that shift the demand for bonds, such as changes in the monetary aggregates. In yet another approach to estimating the real bond rate, a Keynesian liquidity-preference model may be employed. Here, the principal determinants of the real bond rate are the real stock of liquidity and the level of real income.

All these approaches represent attempts to estimate the real expected rate of return on bonds. As the latter is not directly observable, these indirect estimates vary widely from study to study depending on the model used and the sample period studied. The concern, of course, is with the expected future real rate of interest, not the present or past real rates. Consequently, past levels of, and changes in, various series of data may not be a good proxy for the expected future real rate of interest.

Similarly, estimates of the inflation premium often are based on past levels of, and changes in, some price index. Here too the past may not be a good proxy for the future, particularly when inflation is rapidly changing as it was in the 1970s and 1980s. It is not surprising then that when past inflation rates are used the distributed lag estimates of future inflation vary

---

[12]Irving Fisher, *The Theory of Interest* (New York: The Macmillan Co., 1930), pp. 401–7.

[13]Milton Friedman and Anna J. Schwartz, *A Monetary History of the United States, 1867–1960* (New York: National Bureau of Economic Research, 1963), pp. 583–4. For an excellent analysis of these studies and their shortcomings, see Richard Roll, "Interest Rates on Monetary Assets and Commodity Price Index Changes," *Journal of Finance*, 28 (May 1972): 251–78.

[14]See, for example, Thomas J. Sargent, "Commodity Price Expectations and the Interest Rate," *Quarterly Journal of Economics*, LXXXIII (February 1969): 127–40.

widely. A possible solution is to use direct inflation estimates by various people. However, these estimates are not without their problems. The sample of people surveyed is usually small and specialized, so generalization to all market participants is difficult. Also, the survey technique often biases the results, and the method by which a "consensus" inflation estimate is derived is inconsistently applied over time. The most famous of the direct estimates is Joseph A. Livingston's semiannual consensus estimates of about sixty business economists, which is published in the *Philadelphia Bulletin*.

Another problem common to most studies involves the period over which inflation is estimated. Conceptually, we are interested in expected inflation over the life of the debt instrument. For a 15-year bond, it would be a weighted average of expected inflation rates for each of the next 15 years; for a 5-year bond, the next 5 years. The anticipated rate of price change may vary with the length of the loan contract. For example, if the current rate of inflation were 8 percent and this rate were expected to decline gradually to 3 percent over the next 5 years and level off thereafter, the anticipated rate of price change for a 1-year loan would be much higher than that for a 10-year loan. As a result, the nominal rate of interest on the 1-year loan would be higher than that on a 10-year loan, all other things being the same.

Most of the studies of the impact of inflation on nominal yields use the same estimated future rate of inflation for all maturities being examined. Implied is that expected future inflation in all future periods is the same as that which is expected to occur in the next period. Thus, a change in short-term inflation estimates changes inflation estimates for all future periods as well. While this may be a reasonable approximation of reality theoretically it certainly need not occur. In concept expected inflation in the next period can change without inflation estimates for subsequent periods changing at all. As a result, the inflation premium embodied in a long-term bond would change very little with a change in expected inflation for the next period. In practice, we might expect inflation estimates for all future periods to change roughly together. However, they need not change by the same magnitude. Unfortunately, there has been little testing involving differing inflation expectations for different future periods.

Testing for the Fisher Effect

Despite these problems, there have been numerous direct and indirect tests of the Fisher effect. While there are too many to discuss all of them, it is useful to describe some of the more important, as well as representative, tests.

If the Fisher effect holds and the relationship between changes in nominal interest rates and changes in inflation is one-to-one, we have

$$r = R + \alpha \qquad (4\text{-}8)$$

where, as before, r is the nominal rate of interest, R is the real rate, and α is the expected inflation rate. Rearranging, we obtain

$$\alpha = r - R \qquad (4\text{-}9)$$

If, on the average, inflation estimates by market participants are realized, the actual rate of inflation could be used as an estimate of the expected inflation rate, α. This is not to say that the expected inflation rate always equals the realized rate, only that the average forecasting error is zero. Eugene F. Fama tested the following equation on 1-month Treasury bills over the period 1953–1971:[15]

$$P = a + b(r) + e \qquad (4\text{-}10)$$

where P is the actual inflation rate, a is the constant term, b is the regression coefficient, r is the nominal rate, and e is the error term. For the Fisher effect to hold, b should approximate 1.0 and a should be negative and approximate the real interest rate in magnitude. In the regressions, Fama found $b = .98$, consistent with the Fisher effect. Moreover, the results were found to support the idea of a constant real rate of interest throughout the period studied, as well as the notion of an efficient market for Treasury bills.

Using more sophisticated econometric techniques, Fama and Michael R. Gibbons tested Eq. (4-10) and again found that b was close to 1.0.[16] However, they also discovered that the expected real rate of interest varied negatively with expected inflation. Rather than attribute the results to the Mundell-Tobin hypothesis of a less than one-to-one Fisher effect, they conclude that real returns—the capital expenditures process, in particular— vary with real activity in the economy. The negative relationship between real returns and inflation is said to be the consequence of proxy effects. Employing a different tack, G. J. Santoni and Courtenay C. Stone used various real, as well as financial, variables as substitutes for the real rate

---

[15]Eugene F. Fama, "Short-Term Interest Rates as Predictions of Inflation," *American Economic Review*, 65 (June 1975): 269–82.

[16]Eugene F. Fama and Michael R. Gibbons, "Inflation, Real Returns and Capital Investment," *Journal of Monetary Economics*, 9 (May 1982): 297–323. See also James A. Wilcox, "Why Real Rates were so Low in the 1970s," *American Economic Review*, 73 (March 1983), 44–53 for evidence of a stable real rate over time.

of interest.[17] On the basis of evidence for the 1954–80 period, they support the notion of a constant real rate of interest over time.

Other studies, using different inflation expectation variables and/or different maturity securities and sample periods, have challenged the notion of a constant real interest rate. R. W. Hafer and Scott E. Hein rejected the hypothesis that the expected real rate of interest on short-term investments has been constant when they test various subperiods over 1955–79.[18] In addition, others have found the real rate of interest to vary over time.[19] These results, like those of Fama and Gibbons, imply that the real interest rate is primarily a function of economic activity.

With respect to the response of the nominal rate of interest to changes in expected, or anticipated, inflation, empirical testing also is mixed. No studies have found the relationship to be significantly more than one-to-one, which would need to occur to support a tax effect. For the behavior of interest rates prior to World War II, investigators found the relationship to be weak, or, in some cases, negligible. However, in the post–World War II period, a number of scholars found that inflation expectations played the dominant role in the determination of nominal interest rates. In many cases, the relationship was less than one-to-one.[20] In others, it was essentially one-to-one.[21] Even the hypothesis of a dominant relationship between nominal rates of interest and expected inflation is open to question, as some studies show only small effect even in the post–World War II period.[22] Other than the period of the mid-1960s to early 1970s and the late 1970s, there is a lack of a strong relationship.

[17]G. J. Santoni and Courtenay C. Stone, "What Really Happened to Interest Rates?": pp. 3–14.

[18]R. W. Hafer and Scott E. Hein, "Monetary Policy and Short-Term Real Rates of Interest," *Economic Review of the Federal Reserve Bank of St. Louis*, 64 (March 1982): 13–19.

[19]See, for example, John A. Carlson, "Short-term Interest Rates as Predictors of Inflation: Comment," *American Economic Review*, 67 (June 1977): 469–75; Charles R. Nelson and G. William Schwert, "Short-Term Interest Rates as Predictors of Inflation: On Testing the Hypothesis that the Real Rate of Interest is Constant," *American Economic Review*, 67 (June 1977): 478–86; and Kenneth J. Singleton, "Real and Nominal Factors in the Cyclical Behavior of Interest Rates, Output and Money," Working Paper, National Bureau of Economic Research, 1981.

[20]Vito Tanzi, "Inflation Expectations, Economic Activity, Taxes, and Interest Rates," *American Economic Review*, 70 (March 1980): 12–21; Benjamin M. Friedman, "Who Puts the Inflation Premium into Nominal Interest Rates?" pp. 833–45; and Friedman, "Price Inflation, Portfolio Choice and Nominal Interest Rates," *American Economic Review*, 70 (March 1980), 32–48.

[21]See, for example, T. F. Cargill, "Direct Evidence of the Darby Hypothesis for the United States," *Economic Inquiry*, 15 (January 1977): 132–5. Also see, J. A. Carlson, "Expected Inflation and Interest Rates," *Economic Inquiry*, 17 (October 1979): 597–608.

[22]See Lawrence H. Summers, "The Non-Adjustment of Nominal Interest Rates."

Summing Up the Evidence

As is clear from the foregoing discussion, empirical results are mixed. Most studies point to a positive relationship between unanticipated changes in inflation and changes in nominal rates of interest in the post–World War II period. However, the relationship is less than one-to-one and often is rather weak. Thus, when there is an unanticipated increase in inflation, interest rates are found not to rise sufficiently to cover the erosion in purchasing power and the additional taxes occasioned by the increased interest income. Overall, the evidence of the 1960s and 1970s implies that leaders' after-tax real rates of return decline with unanticipated increases in inflation.

However, the relationship between the nominal rate of interest and expected inflation is far from simple, as implied by the Fisher effect. It is clear that there is an interaction with real economic activity. But even when such variables are introduced, we cannot explain nominal interest rates in any consistent manner over time. In the 1980s, inflation abated, but nominal rates of interest remained high until the fall of 1982. As a result, high real rates of interest were available to lenders in 1981 and 1982. This experience puzzled virtually all followers of financial markets trying to explain things with the traditional, less than one-to-one Fisher effect. The relationship between inflation and interest rates does not lend itself to simple explanations, nor does it appear to be consistent over time. Toward the end of the 1970s, many thought a sensible explanation of nominal interest rates was possible if expected inflation were known. The experience of the early 1980s dashed such hopes. Only time will tell whether this experience was an aberration from the experience of the mid-1960s to late 1970s or whether there was more fundamental instability requiring new explanations. Our ability to explain, let alone predict, nominal rates of interest in terms of inflation leaves much to be desired.

DEBTOR-CREDITOR CLAIMS

With unanticipated changes in inflation, an existing loan is not repaid in keeping with the real return expected at the time the loan was made. If there is an unanticipated increase in inflation, the borrower tends to gain. This gain occurs in an opportunity sense in that the loan is repaid with "cheaper" money than originally anticipated. To illustrate, suppose the nominal rate of interest on a 10-year loan is 12 percent, of which 4 percent is the expected real rate and 8 percent represents a premium for expected inflation. However, suppose that over the 10 years, inflation of 10 percent per annum actually occurs. As a result, the borrower's real interest cost is 2 percent instead of 4 percent. The lender loses, of course, because the real return is less than anticipated at the time the loan contract was made. With an unanticipated decrease in inflation, the borrower loses, in that the loan has to be repaid in more "expensive" dollars than originally anticipated, whereas the lender gains.

Unanticipated increases in inflation result in a transfer of real wealth from net creditors to net debtors, whereas the opposite occurs with unanticipated decreases. A *net creditor* is defined as an economic unit whose financial assets exceed its financial liabilities, whereas the opposite holds for the *net debtor*. Whether a given economic unit gains or loses with respect to inflation depends upon whether there is an unanticipated increase or decrease in inflation and whether the economic unit is a net debtor or a net creditor. In the aggregate, nonfinancial corporations have been consistent net debtors. However, individual companies can be net debtors or net creditors, and this can vary over time.

In the 1946–1979 period, a sizable portion of the inflation that occurred was unanticipated. Twenty-five years ago, no one would have thought double-digit levels of inflation were possible, yet they occurred in the late 1970s. Exactly how much of the inflation was unanticipated is difficult to say, because we do not know what was expected.[23] However, estimates of one-third to one-half of the inflation that actually occurred being unanticipated several years in advance are not uncommon. These estimates mean that nonfinancial corporations as net debtors, in the aggregate, gained in the 1946–1979 period. Put another way, there was a drop in the value of existing debt instruments, accruing to the benefit of firms in the aggregate and their stockholders. On the other hand, households as net creditors, suffered a loss in wealth, owing to unanticipated inflation. In contrast, the decline in inflation in the early 1980s was largely unanticipated in advance. Here net creditors gained and net debtors lost.

Money Illusion by Corporate Stockholders?

With increasing inflation and rising interest rates, Franco Modigliani and Richard A. Cohn argued that stockholders of a corporation suffer a money illusion, which results in a valuation of the stock lower than its true value.[24] Because corporations are able to deduct all of the higher interest expense, even though part of it is a return of capital, accounting profits are said to seriously underestimate the "true" profits of the cor-

---

[23]G. L. Bach and James B. Stephenson, "Inflation and the Redistribution of Wealth," *Review of Economics and Statistics*, 56 (February 1974): 1–13 estimate that the total dollar of creditors' claims wiped out by inflation in the period 1946–1971 was $1.2 trillion. However, part of this inflation was anticipated, and creditors were compensated with higher interest rates.

[24]Franco Modigliani and Richard A. Cohn, "Inflation, Rational Valuation and the Market," *Financial Analysts Journal*, 35 (March–April 1979): 24–44.

poration. By increasing its nominal debt to offset an increase in inflation, a company is able to hold constant its debt in real terms. Modigliani and Cohn suggest that the increase in nominal debt generates sufficient funds not only to pay interest, but to maintain real dividends and reinvestment. To the extent stockholders are fooled by accounting earnings, as opposed to real dividends, stock prices will suffer. The Modigliani-Cohn proposition has stirred considerable controversy, both theoretically and empirically. One troubling aspect of their proposition, however, is that the money illusion applies only to one set of security holders—namely, stockholders— and not to the other set, lenders. Often economic units are both lenders and investors in stock. If both suffer money illusion or if neither lenders nor investors in stock suffer it, the proposition does not hold.

Empirical Testing

There have been a number of studies of possible debtor-creditor wealth transfers with inflation. Early studies by Kessel, Alchian and Kessel, and Bach and Ando suggested that there is a wealth transfer from net creditors to net debtors in times of inflation.[25] Many of these studies were based on examination of companies with high and low debt ratios in periods of high and low inflation. One problem with this work is that it does not distinguish between anticipated and unanticipated inflation. Using more sophisticated empirical tests involving unanticipated inflation and stock returns, holding constant systematic risk, Gershon N. Mandelker and S. Ghon Rhee found no evidence to support the notion of a wealth transfer between net debtors and net creditors due to unexpected inflation.[26]

Kenneth R. French, Richard S. Ruback, and G. William Schwert also tested stock returns for corporate wealth effects caused by unanticipated inflation.[27] Based on a careful study involving a number of variables, they too concluded that large corporate net debtors did not benefit from un-

---

[25]Reuben A. Kessel, "Inflation-Caused Wealth Redistribution: A Test of a Hypothesis," *American Economic Review*, 46 (March 1956): 43–66; Armen A. Alchian and R. A. Kessel, "Redistribution of Wealth through Inflation," *Science*, 130 (September 1959): 635–9; R. A. Kessel and A. A. Alchian, "Effects of Inflation," *Journal of Political Economy*, 70 (December 1962), 521–37; and George L. Bach and A. Ando, "The Redistribution Effects of Inflation," *Review of Economics and Statistics*, 39 (February 1957): 1–13. In contrast, Hai Hong, "Inflation and the Market Value of the Firm: Theory and Tests," *Journal of Finance*, 32 (September 1977): 1031–55, using a cross-sectional multiple regression equation, does not find support for the debtor-creditor hypothesis.

[26]Gershon N. Mandelker and S. Ghon Rhee, "Redistribution of Wealth through Inflation: A Reexamination of the Fisher-Keynes-Kessel Hypothesis," Research Paper, University of Pittsburgh, 1981.

[27]Kenneth R. French, Richard S. Ruback, and G. William Schwert, "Effects on Nominal Contracting on Stock Returns," Working Paper, University of Rochester, 1981.

expected inflation relative to net creditor firms in the period 1947–1979. In contrast, Lawrence H. Summers employed the revision of expectations about the entire future path of inflation instead of current-period unexpected inflation as the inflation variable.[28] His results are partially consistent with the debtor-creditor hypothesis. Thus, like earlier evidence on the Fisher effect, empirical tests of the debtor-creditor hypothesis are mixed. Most of the tests have involved only corporations, and increasingly we are seeing a focus on stock returns as a proxy for wealth. Often, it is difficult to sort out the effect of corporate debt on stock returns from the many other factors that affect these returns.

INFLATION-PROMPTED CHANGES IN FINANCIAL MARKETS

The high and unstable inflation that occurred in the decade of the 1970s and the early 1980s was unsettling to financial markets. During 1980, there was almost a 10 percent decline in short-term interest rates from March to June and over a 10 percent rise from July to December. Those financial institutions that make fixed-rate, long-term loans are unable to live with such volatility. On the one hand, their return on assets is locked in, while their cost of funds usually is more directly related to current interest rates in the market. This relationship is due to the fact that the maturity structure of liabilities typically is shorter in maturity than that of assets. With unanticipated increases in inflation, nominal rates of interest for all maturities rise; and those who "lend long and borrow short" are hurt.

Response of Financial Institutions

This phenomenon, coupled with considerable uncertainty, was untenable for many financial institutions. No longer could they afford to make fixed-rate, long-term loans where they had little control over their costs of funds during the life of the loan. Many came to the conclusion that they had to adapt and learn to live with variability. One means for doing so was to shorten the maturity of loans to conform more nearly with the maturity structure of their liabilities.

Another means was to use floating-rate, as opposed to fixed-rate, loans. In a floating-rate loan, the interest rate is adjusted periodically, in

---

[28]Lawrence H. Summers, "Inflation and the Valuation of Corporate Equities," Working Paper, National Bureau of Economic Research, 1981.

keeping with changes in the short-term cost of funds to the lending institution. For a bank, the lending rate frequently is geared to the prime rate, with changes occurring whenever there is a change in the prime rate. Other banks gear interest-rate changes on loans to changes in such money-market rates as Treasury bills or commercial paper. Here the loan rate is adjusted more frequently—often daily—than in the case of a floating-rate loan geared to the prime rate. On the liability side, financial institutions increasingly have issued floating-rate notes. These notes have a specific term, such as 5 years; but the rate of interest to the investor floats in keeping with the Treasury bill or the commercial paper rate. For example, the rate might be set at $\frac{1}{2}$ percent above the Treasury bill rate and be adjusted daily. The notes usually are redeemable at their face value. Originated by Citicorp in 1974, the floating-rate note was not used extensively by financial institutions until the late 1970s and the 1980s. In recent years, floating-rate notes have been sold not only to institutional investors, but also to individuals.[29]

By using floating-rate loans and issuing floating-rate notes, the financial institution neutralizes itself with respect to the vagaries of inflation and fluctuating interest rates. Its profit comes in the margin between the floating-loan rate and the floating-note rate. In addition to floating-rate loans, the use of variable-rate mortgages has become more pronounced. With a variable-rate mortgage, the rate is adjusted up or down either annually or semiannually. Usually there is a ceiling on the amount of each adjustment, which is imposed by state law. As a result, the variable-rate mortgage is not nearly so effective in shielding the lender from interest-rate volatility as is the floating-rate loan. For this reason, we have seen increasing use of short-term mortgages, in which, at maturity, the loan is rolled over at prevailing interest rates. Again, the idea is to neutralize the effects of inflation and volatile interest rates. Another means for offsetting the effect of changing interest rates is the interest rate futures market.[30] Here, a futures position is established so that movements in its value will offset either those of financial securities held outright or of financial liabilities issued by the financial institution. By establishing an overall hedged position, the institution protects itself against changing interest rates.

While we do not yet have a complete indexing of financial claims to inflation in the United States, as exists in some countries, the moves described above are in that direction. The underlying objective is to nullify the risk associated with volatile interest rates, which, in turn, are caused by turbulent inflation.

---

[29]See Kenneth R. Marks and Warren A Law, "Hedging Against Inflation with Floating-Rate Notes," *Harvard Business Review,* 58 (March-April 1980): 106–12.

[30]Chapter 7 is devoted to the interest rate futures markets and should be referred to by the interested reader.

Implications for Financing

The changes discussed have a number of implications for economic units in their financing. For one thing, these units sometimes experience difficulty obtaining long-term, fixed-rate loans, particularly mortgage loans. Increasingly, they must settle for shorter-term loans. While corporations and municipalities are able to place long-term, fixed-rate bonds in the public market, they often find a more receptive market for inter-mediate-term bonds. In trying to tailor their financing to the market, some corporations have issued floating-rate notes or bonds. As was the case with financial institutions, the return to the lender fluctuates in keeping with changes in overall market interest rates.

When interest rates are high and expected to fall, the economic unit has a considerable incentive to borrow either on a short-term basis or through a floating-rate loan. By avoiding long-term financing, the unit hopes to refinance at lower interest rates in the future. Increasingly, in times of high interest rates, corporate borrowers insist on special call and/or conversion features, subjects discussed later. The purpose of these features is to provide the firm flexibility or to make the instrument more attractive to investors, thereby realizing an interest-cost savings.

While often an economic unit will try to forecast interest rates and plan their financing accordingly, increasingly many of them are coming to the realization that it is difficult to do such forecasting. High and volatile inflation is the root of the uncertainty. Rather than rely completely on one's ability to forecast interest rates, it may be better to provide flexibility so one is not badly hurt, no matter which way interest rates go. This is done not only in the maturity and terms of the financial liabilities issued, but sometimes also by hedging in the financial futures market. For the same reasons that financial institutions have become so wary of volatile interest rates, borrowers increasingly are looking for ways to neutralize the effects of interest-rate variability.

SUMMARY

Changing inflation has an important and pervasive influence on interest rates. With inflation, the real return on a security is less than its nominal return, and the difference is known as an inflation premium. The Fisher effect suggests that the nominal return on a bond is the sum of the real rate of interest plus the rate of inflation expected over the life of the instrument. When changes in monetary policy are integrated into the study of inflation and interest rates, nominal rates have been theorized to adjust only over time to changes in monetary policy. In the case of money expansion, nominal rates are said to decline first as a result of a liquidity effect and then to rise with the inflation that accompanies increased spending.

The Fisher effect implies that the nominal rate of interest changes exactly, or on a one-to-one basis, with changes in expected inflation. In theory, a real money effect argues for a less than one-to-one relationship, whereas a tax effect argues for a more than one-to-one relationship. It is important to distinguish between anticipated inflation, which is embodied in existing interest rates, and unanticipated inflation, which is not. Certain empirical evidence was reviewed in regard to the Fisher effect, after first exploring problems that plague such testing. While the evidence is mixed, many studies find a positive relationship between changes in nominal interest rates and changes in expected inflation, and none find the relationship to be more than one-to-one. However, the relationship is not consistent over time, and it appears to be influenced by economic activity variables.

With an unanticipated increase in inflation, debtors gain and creditors lose in real terms, while the opposite occurs with a decrease in unanticipated inflation. Empirical testing of the debtor-creditor hypothesis is mixed, particularly for corporations where stock returns are used as a proxy for wealth. Finally, high and volatile inflation affects financial markets, financial institutions, and the economic unit in its financing. A number of new instruments have developed, and these affect the economic unit in its financing.

SELECTED REFERENCES

Bach, G.L., and James B. Stephenson, "Inflation and the Redistribution of Wealth," *Review of Economics and Statistics,* 56 (February 1974): 1–13.

Cagan, Phillip, and Robert E. Lipsey, *The Financial Effects of Inflation.* Chicago: University of Chicago Press and National Bureau of Economic Research, 1980.

Carlson, John A., "Expected Inflation and Interest Rates," *Economic Inquiry.* 17 (October 1979): 597–608.

Darby, Michael R., "The Financial Effects of Monetary Policy on Interest Rates," *Economic Inquiry,* 13 (June 1975): 266–76.

Fama, Eugene F., "Short-Term Interest Rates as Predictors of Inflation," *American Economic Review,* 65 (June 1975): 269–82.

——— , and Michael R. Gibbons, "Inflation, Real Returns and Capital Investment," *Journal of Monetary Economics,* 9 (May 1982): 297–323.

——— , and G. William Schwert, "Asset Returns and Inflation," *Journal of Financial Economics,* 5 (November 1977): 115–46.

Feldstein, Martin, "Inflation, Income Taxes and the Rate of Inflation: A Theoretical Analysis," *American Economic Review,* 66 (December 1976): 809–20.

Fisher, Irving, *Appreciation and Interest.* New York: The Macmillan Co., 1896.

———— , *The Theory of Interest.* New York: The Macmillan Co., 1930.

Friedman, Benjamin M., "Price Inflation, Portfolio Choice and Nominal Interest Rates," *American Economic Review,* 70 (March 1980): 32–48.

———— , "Who Puts the Inflation Premium into Nominal Interest Rates?" *Journal of Finance,* 33 (June 1978): 833–45.

Gandolfi, Arthur E., "Inflation, Taxation, and Interest Rates," *Journal of Finance,* 37 (June 1982): 797–807.

Gibson, William E., "Interest Rates and Inflationary Expectations: New Evidence," *American Economic Review,* LXII (December 1972): 854–65.

———— , "Price Expectations Effects on Interest Rates," *Journal of Finance,* 25 (March 1970): 19–34.

Hendershott, Patric H., and James C. Van Horne, "Expected Inflation Implied by Capital Market Rates," *Journal of Finance,* 28 (May 1973): 301–14.

Kessel, Reuben A., "Inflation-Caused Wealth Redistribution: A Test of a Hypothesis," *American Economic Review,* 46 (March 1956): 43–66.

Modigliani, Franco, and Richard A. Cohn, "Inflation, Rational Valuation and the Market," *Financial Analysts Journal,* 35 (March-April 1979): 24–44.

Mundell, Robert, "Inflation and Real Interest," *Journal of Political Economy,* 71 (June 1963): 280–83.

Roll, Richard, "Interest Rates on Monetary Assets and Commodity Price Index Changes," *Journal of Finance,* 28 (May 1972): 251–78.

Santoni, G.J., and Cortenay C. Stone, "What Really Happened to Interest Rates?: A Longer Run Analysis," *Review of the Federal Reserve Bank of St. Louis,* 63 (November 1981): 3–14.

Summers, Lawrence H., "The Non-Adjustment of Nominal Interest Rates: A Study of the Fisher Effect," Working Paper, National Bureau of Economic Research, 1982.

Tanzi, Vito, "Inflation Expectations, Economic Activity, Taxes, and Interest Rates," *American Economic Review,* 70 (March 1980): 12–21.

Tobin, James, "Money and Economic Growth," *Econometrica,* 33 (October 1965): 671–84.

Wilcox, James A., "Why Real Rates were so Low in the 1970's," *American Economic Review,* 73 (March 1983): 44–53.

5

THE TERM STRUCTURE
OF INTEREST RATES

In the previous two chapters, our focus was on the determination of equilibrium rates of interest in the economy with and without
the consideration of inflation. We assumed implicitly, either a single rate
of interest or interest rates in general. In this and the next five chapters,
we are concerned with why rates of interest differ for different financial
instruments. We study the relationship among yields on fixed-income securities by examining the term structure of interest rates in this chapter;
the effect of coupon rates in the next; default risk in Chapter 8; callability
and sinking funds in Chapter 9; and the effect of taxes in Chapter 10. In
each of these chapters, we attempt to hold constant the other factors.
Together, these factors should allow us to explain most of the observed
differences in yield and expected return for nonequity securities.

The relationship between yield and maturity on securities differing
only in length of time to maturity is known as the *term structure of interest
rates*. All factors other than maturity must be held constant if the relationship studied is to be meaningful. Term structure may be approximated
graphically by plotting yield and maturity for equivalent-grade securities
at a moment in time. Maturity is plotted on the horizontal axis and yield
is plotted on the vertical axis, and their relationship is described by a yield

curve fitted to the observations. An example of a yield curve for default-free Treasury securities is shown in Fig 5-1.[1]

Typically, yield curves are upward-sloping during a period of low inflation and economic activity and moderately downward-sloping in periods of high inflation and/or vigorous economic expansion. For the period 1975–1982, the range of yields observed for U. S. Treasury securities of various maturities is shown in Fig. 5-2. As can be seen, the range is wide, going from about 4 percent to 17 percent for short-term securities and from 7 percent to 15 percent for long-term securities. Thus, short-term yields fluctuate within a wider band than do long-term yields.

In this chapter, we investigate why the term structure of interest rates has different shapes and different overall levels over time. It generally is agreed that expectations of the future course of interest rates are an important influence; controversy arises, however, as to whether there are other important influences. We begin by considering the pure expectations theory, where the term structure is explained entirely by interest-rate expectations. Using this theory as a building block, we then consider rival theories for explaining the yield-maturity relationship on securities differing only in the length of time to maturity.

THE PURE EXPECTATIONS THEORY

In broad terms, the expectations theory states that the *expected* one-period rate of return on investment is the same, regardless of the maturity of security in which one invests. That is, if an individual's investment horizon were 1 year, it would make no difference whether he or she initially invested in a 1-year security, invested in a 2-year security and sold it at the end of 1 year, or invested in a 5-year security and sold it at the end of 1 year. The expected holding period return at the time of initial investment would be the same for all possible maturity strategies. This theory was first expressed by Irving Fisher and was developed further by Friedrich Lutz.[2]

---

[1]The Treasury yield curve shown in Fig. 5-1 is fitted by eye to the data, using high coupon issues. For various methods of mathematically fitting yield curves to data, see Michael E. Echols and Jan Walter Elliott, "A Quantitative Yield Curve Model for Estimating the Term Structure of Interest Rates," *Journal of Financial and Quantitative Analysis,* 11 (March 1976): 87–114; J. Huston McCulloch, "Measuring the Term Structure of Interest Rates," *Journal of Business,* 44 (January 1971): 19–31; and Willard T. Carleton and Ian A. Cooper, "Estimation and Uses of the Term Structure of Interest Rates," *Journal of Finance,* 31 (September 1976): 1067–84.

[2]Irving Fisher, "Appreciation and Interest," *Publications of the American Economic Association,* XI (August 1896): 23–29, 91–92; and F. A. Lutz, "The Structure of Interest Rates," *Quarterly Journal of Economics,* LV (November 1940): 36–63.

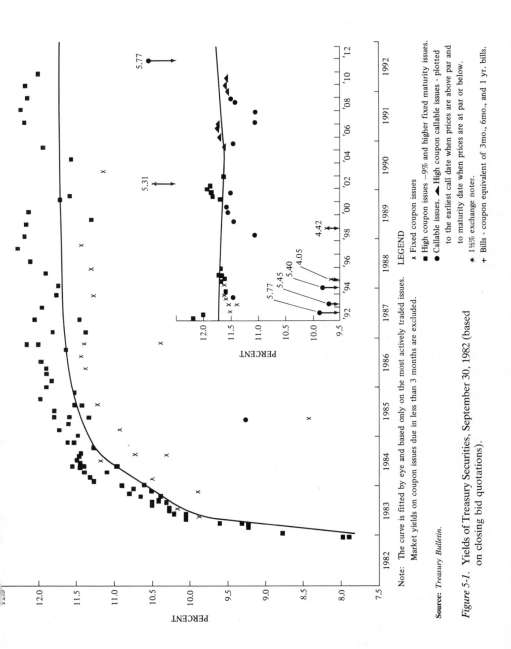

Note: The curve is fitted by eye and based only on the most actively traded issues. Market yields on coupon issues due in less than 3 months are excluded.

Source: *Treasury Bulletin.*

LEGEND

x Fixed coupon issues
■ High coupon issues –9% and higher fixed maturity issues.
● Callable issues. ▲ High coupon callable issues - plotted to the earliest call date when prices are above par and to maturity date when prices are at par or below.
★ 1½% exchange notes.
+ Bills - coupon equivalent of 3mo., 6mo., and 1 yr. bills.

Figure 5-1. Yields of Treasury Securities, September 30, 1982 (based on closing bid quotations).

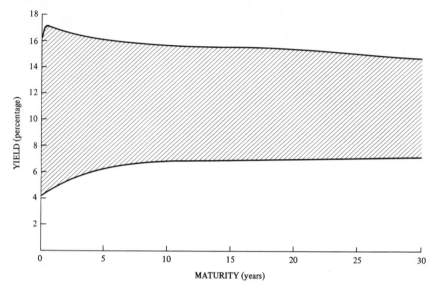

Figure 5-2. Range of yields on U. S. Treasury securities by maturity, 1975–1982.

In the theoretical presentation to follow, we assume the presence of pure discount securities as opposed to securities having coupon payments. (In the next chapter, we analyze securities with coupon payments and the effect of the coupon rate.) A pure discount bond is simply an instrument that promises to pay a stated amount of money at a single future date, with no other payments to be received. For example, the amount paid 1 year hence might be $1,000 and the security sells in the market for $900. The rate of interest is embraced in the discount from future value—in our example, $100. The interest rate in our illustration is $100/$900 = 11.11 percent. To go to a 2-year example, suppose the security sells for $800 with the promise to pay $1,000 two years from now. The interest rate is that rate r such that

$$\$800 = \frac{\$1,000}{(1+r)^2}$$

When we solve for r, we find it to be 11.80 percent. These two rates, 11.11 percent and 11.80 percent, are known as *spot rates of interest* for 1- and 2-year loans.

When considering the expectations theory, it is useful to transform actual spot rates of interest into *forward rates*. Implied in the term structure at any moment is a set of forward rates:[3]

$$(1 + {}_tR_n)^n = (1 + {}_tR_1)(1 + {}_{t+1}r_{1t})(1 + {}_{t+2}r_{1t}) \cdots (1 + {}_{t+n-1}r_{1t}) \quad (5\text{-}1)$$

where ${}_tR_n$ represents the actual spot rate of interest at time t on an N-period loan, ${}_tR_1$ is the actual rate on a one-period loan at time t, and ${}_{t+1}r_{1t}$, ${}_{t+2}r_{1t}$, and ${}_{t+n-1}r_{1t}$ are forward rates for one-period loans beginning at times $t+1$, $t+2$, and $t+n-1$, implied in the term structure at time t. Thus, a loan for 4 years is equivalent to a 1-year loan plus a series of forward contracts, each renewing the loan for a successive year. The formula for deriving the one-period forward rate beginning at time $t+n$, implied in the term structure at time t, is

$$
\begin{aligned}
1 + {}_{t+n}r_{1t} &= \frac{(1 + {}_tR_{1t})(1 + {}_{t+1}r_{1t}) \cdots (1 + {}_{t+n-1}r_{1t})(1 + {}_{t+n}r_{1t})}{(1 + {}_tR_{1t})(1 + {}_{t+1}r_{1t}) \cdots (1 + {}_{t+n-1}r_{1t})} \\[2mm]
&= \frac{(1 + {}_tR_{n+1})^{n+1}}{(1 + {}_tR_n)^n} \quad (5\text{-}2) \\[2mm]
{}_{t+n}r_{1t} &= \frac{(1 + {}_tR_{n+1})^{n+1}}{(1 + {}_tR_n)^n} - 1
\end{aligned}
$$

This formula permits calculation of the implied one-period forward rate for any future period based upon actual rates of interest prevailing in the market at a specific time. The forward rate computed need not be a one-period rate, but may span any useful length of time. The calculation of the J-period forward rate beginning at time $t+n$ implied in the term structure at time t is

$$
{}_{t+n}r_{jt} = \sqrt[j]{\frac{(1 + {}_tR_{n+jt})^{n+j}}{(1 + {}_tR_{nt})^n}} - 1 \quad (5\text{-}3)
$$

The forward rate defined in this way is merely a mathematical calculation which has no behavioral meaning. A version of the pure expectations theory, however, adds behavioral content to the concept of the forward rate by implying that expected future interest rates are equivalent

---

[3]For such a derivation, see, for example, J. R. Hicks, *Value and Capital*, 2nd ed. (London: Oxford University Press, 1946), pp. 141–5. If coupon bonds were involved, the formula implicitly assumes that the coupon payments are reinvested, the lender receiving the principal and reinvested interest at maturity. The formula contrasts with one in which interest and principal payments are discounted back to present value in accordance with the times when they are to be received.

to the computed forward rates. According to this version, $_{t+n}p_{1t} = {}_{t+n}r_{1t}$, where p_1 is the future one-period rate expected at time t to prevail at time $t+n$. To illustrate, suppose that the actual rates of interest prevailing in the market were 10 percent for a 2-year loan and 11 percent for a 3-year loan. The implied forward rate on a 1-year loan 2 years hence would be

$$_{t+2}r_{1t} = \frac{(1 + {}_tR_3)^3}{(1 + {}_tR_2)^2} - 1 = \frac{(1.11)^3}{(1.10)^2} - 1 = 13\% \qquad (5\text{-}4)$$

Because forward rates are equivalent to expected future rates, the version of the pure expectations theory discussed implies that the expected 1-year rate 2 years hence is 13 percent.

Substitutability of Maturities

If we ignore transaction costs and assume for the moment that the pure expectations theory is valid, securities of different maturity would be expected substitutes for one another.[4] Prospective investors at any time have three choices: they may invest in an obligation having a maturity corresponding exactly to their anticipated holding period; they may invest in short-term securities, reinvesting in short terms at each maturity over the holding period (known as a *rollover*); or they may invest in a security having a maturity longer than the anticipated holding period. In the last case, they would sell the security at the end of the given period, realizing either a capital gain or a loss. According to another version of the pure expectations theory, the investors' expected return for any holding period would be the same, regardless of the alternative or combination of alternatives they chose. This return would be a weighted average of the current short-term interest rate plus future short rates expected to prevail over the holding period; this average is the same for each alternative.

To illustrate, suppose that the following yields prevailed in the market for default-free treasury securities, all of which are pure discount bonds:

Maturity	Yield
1 year	10%
2 year	11
3 year	12
4 year	$12\frac{1}{2}$

---

[4]For certain technical reasons, they may not be perfect expected substitutes. This concern will be explored later in the chapter.

The 1-year forward rates, implied in this term structure, may be derived with Eq. (5-2) and are found to be:

Forward Rate	Percent
$_{t+1}r_{1t}$	12.01
$_{t+2}r_{1t}$	14.03
$_{t+3}r_{1t}$	14.01

If investors have an anticipated holding period of 3 years, they may invest in the 3-year security, from which a yield to maturity of 12 percent will be obtained. However, the investor also may invest in a 1-year security and reinvest in 1-year securities at maturity over the intended holding period. In this case, the expected return is

$$\sqrt[3]{(1.10)(1.1201)(1.1403)} - 1 = 12\% \qquad (5\text{-}5)$$

or the same as that for investment in the 3-year security. Finally, the investor can invest in a 4-year security and sell it at the end of 3 years. Assuming again a pure discount bond, its price would have to be $62.43 (per $100 face value) for it to yield 12½ percent over 4 years. At the end of the third year, its expected market price would need to be $87.71 in order for it to provide a return of 14.01 percent in the last year. (The latter is the 1-year forward rate beginning 3 years hence.) Over the 3-year holding period, the expected return to the investor can be found by solving the following equation for r:

$$\$62.43 = \frac{\$87.71}{(1+r)^3} \qquad (5\text{-}6)$$

Solving for r, we find it also to be 12 percent. Thus, the investor could expect to do no better by investing in securities with maturities other than 3 years. Regardless of the maturity in which an investment is made, the expected return at the time of initial investment is the same. In other words, securities of different maturities are perfect substitutes for one another; one maturity strategy is as good as the next.

Technical Problems

In our discussion, we have expressed the pure expectations theory in two ways. First, forward rates of interest embodied in the term structure are unbiased estimates of expected future spot rates of interest. Second, for a specific holding period the expected returns arising from different maturity strategies are the same. With respect to the first expression, forward rates will not be unbiased estimates of expected future spot rates if there is autocorrelation of spot rates and/or if the distributions of possible future spot rates are wide. Rather, they will be biased estimates, and usually upwardly biased if the autocorrelation is positive. With respect to the second expression, expected returns for a holding period are technically the same only for a specific future holding period, not all possible holding periods. (In a strict sense, this holding period should be the next instantaneous interval of time.)

It also follows from this discussion that the second expression of the pure expectations theory is inconsistent with the first.[5] As these arguments are complex, involving stochastic calculus to resolve, we do not delve into them in this book. The interested reader should refer to the references cited below. For most situations, the biases are not large and, in many cases, can be safely ignored. We assume in this chapter that both expressions of the pure expectations theory hold, and move on to consider the more general implications of the theory. However, one should be mindful of the technical problems involved with different expressions of the pure expectations theory.

Arbitrage Support

Behaviorally, support for the pure expectations theory comes from the presence of market participants who are willing and able to exploit profit opportunities. Should forward rates differ from expected future rates, a large enough speculative element is said to exist in the market to drive the two sets of rates together.[6] With different rates, various market participants, sensing opportunity for expected gain, would exploit the opportunity until it was eliminated. As a result, forward rates would be unbiased estimates of expected future rates—i.e., the two would be the same. Market participants are said to seek to maximize their return based upon their expectations. By buying and selling securities of different maturities, the individual can, in effect, engage in forward transactions. Such a transaction may consist only of shifting from a 6-year bond to a 7-year one, a shift

---

[5]The classic paper in this regard is John Cox, Jonathan E. Ingersoll, Jr., and Stephen A. Ross, "A Reexamination of Traditional Hypotheses about the Term Structure of Interest Rates," 36 (September 1981): 769–99. See also Robert A. Jarrow, "Liquidity Premiums and the Expectations Hypothesis," *Journal of Banking and Finance,* 5 (December 1981): 539–46; and David Pyle, "Term Structure, Spot Rates and Forward Rates, the Relationship between Forward Rates and Realized Spot Rates, Yield Curves," Berkeley Program in Finance, September 12, 1982.

[6]David Meiselman, *The Term Structure of Interest Rates* (Englewood Cliffs, N.J.: Prentice-Hall, Inc., 1962), p. 10.

that is marginally the same as making a forward contract for a 1-year loan 6 years in the future.

The action of these market participants seeking profit results in the term structure's being determined solely by expectations about future interest rates. According to the pure expectations theory, a horizontal yield curve implies that market participants expect future short rates to be the same as the current short rate. A downward-sloping yield curve signifies that future short rates are expected to fall. Investors are willing to buy long-term securities yielding less than short-term ones because they can expect to do no better by the continual reinvestment in short-term securities. On the other hand a positively sloped yield curve implies that future short rates are expected to rise. Investors are then unwilling to invest in long-term securities unless the yield is in excess of that on short terms. They would be better off investing in short terms and reinvesting at maturity. With forward rates as unbiased estimates of expected future rates, different maturity securities must be perfect expected substitutes.

Market Efficiency

The pure expectations theory implies that the bond markets are highly efficient. Efficient financial markets are said to exist when security prices reflect all available information which bears on the valuation of the instrument. Implied is that market prices of individual securities adjust very rapidly to new information. If excess profits were possible, a sufficient number of market participants with sufficient resources would recognize the opportunity and exploit it. In exploiting it, they would cause security prices to be valued in keeping with all available information. Thus, efficient markets imply an absence of market imperfections that impede the rapid diffusion of information and the rapid reaction to this information by market participants.

In the context of the expectations theory, it is suggested that all relevant information is incorporated in expectations about the future course of interest rates. To be sure, new information can develop, but when it does it is rapidly reflected in revised expectations. Consequently, there does *not* exist the opportunity for arbitrage profits to be earned on the basis of expectations about future interest rates. Once expectations adjust to new infomation, security prices for various maturities are said to fluctuate randomly about their intrinsic values. As a result, forward rates, which are calculated from these prices, would also fluctuate randomly. Only new information will cause prices to change in one direction or the other, and then the change is extremely rapid.[7] While a necessary condition

[7]For the development of the application of the efficient markets theory to the term structure of market rates, see Richard Roll, *The Behavior of Interest Rates: An Application of the*

for the pure expectations theory is the efficient markets notion, a combined theory of expectations and liquidity premiums is also consistent with this notion. We now turn to this topic.

UNCERTAINTY AND LIQUIDITY PREMIUMS

If complete certainty existed in the market, it is clear that forward rates would be exact forecasts of future short-term interest rates. Arbitrage would make all maturities consistent with expectations, so that the investor would receive the same return regardless of the maturity in which an investment in a pure discount bond is made. The forward rate would contain no compensation for risk. When we go to an uncertain world, however, the question of risk is raised.

Here, J. R. Hicks and others argue, the pure expectations theory must be modified. The longer the maturity of the security, the greater is said to be the risk of fluctuation in value of principal to the investor. Because of this greater risk, investors are said to prefer to lend short. Borrowers, however, are said to prefer to borrow long in order to reduce the risk of inability to meet principal payments. Because of this "constitutional weakness" on the long side, a risk, or liquidity, premium must be offered to induce investors to purchase long-term securities. This premium is over and above the average of the current short rate and expected future short rates. The premium structure itself is said to correspond to "normal backwardation" in the commodities futures market.[8]

The theory of normal backwardation supposes that the securities market is dominated by risk averters, who prefer to lend short unless offered a premium sufficient to offset the risk of lending long. Forward rates, therefore, would be biased estimates of future interest rates, exceeding them by the amount of the risk, or liquidity, premium. Thus,

$$_{t+n}r_{1t} = {}_{t+n}\rho_{1t} + {}_{t+n}L_{1t} \tag{5-7}$$

where $_{t+n}r_{1t}$, as before, is the forward one-period rate beginning at $t + n$ implied in the term structure at time t, $_{t+n}\rho_{1t}$ is the expected future rate for that period, and $_{t+n}L_{1t}$ is the Hicksian liquidity premium embodied in the forward rate. If risk increases with the remoteness of the future, li-

---

Efficient Market Model to U.S. Treasury Bills (New York: Basic Books, Inc. 1970); and Thomas J. Sargent, "Rational Expectations and the Term Structure of Interest Rates," *Journal of Money, Credit and Banking,* 4 (February 1972): 74–97.

[8]J. R. Hicks, *Value and Capital,* pp. 146–47.

quidity premiums would be an increasing function of this distance.[9]

$$0 <_{t+1}L_{1t} <_{t+2}L_{1t} < \cdots <_{t+n}L_{1t} \tag{5-8}$$

The presence of liquidity premiums implies a bias toward upward-sloping yield curves. Indeed, the yield curve could decrease monotonically only when expected future short rates were lower than the current short rate by amounts exceeding their respective liquidity premiums.[10] To illustrate, suppose that market participants expected future short-term interest rates to be the same as the current short rate. On the basis of these expectations alone, the yield curve would be horizontal. However, with liquidity premiums embodied in forward rates, it would be upward-sloping, as illustrated in Fig. 5-3. If a positive bias does exist in forward rates, securities of different maturities would not be perfect expected substitutes for one another. Investment in a long-term security would provide a higher expected return than would investment in a short-term security and reinvestment in short terms at each maturity.

Proponents of the pure expectations theory contend that speculators need not be offered a liquidity premium because they are risk seekers and will search for advantages in the term structure where forward rates exceed corresponding expected future rates. Speculators, together with investors

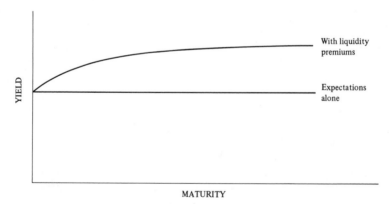

MATURITY

Figure 5-3. Combined expectations and liquidity premiums.

[9]For the derivation of term structure liquidity premiums based on the utility of consumption, see Joseph E. Stiglitz, "A Consumption-Oriented Theory of the Demand for Financial Assets and the Term Structure of Interest Rates," *Review of Economic Studies,* 37 (July 1970): 321–50; and Gordon S. Roberts, "Term Premiums in the Term Structure of Interest Rates," *Journal of Money, Credit, and Banking,* 12 (May 1980): 184–97.

[10]For determination of the liquidity premium when interest rates are assumed to follow a stochastic process, see Terrence C. Langetieg, "A Multivariate Model of the Term Structure," *Journal of Finance,* 35 (March 1980): 71–97.

who are indifferent as to maturity, are said to squeeze out any premium that might exist in the forward rate. All maturities then would have expected equal liquidity, according to the pure expectations theory.

Level of Interest Rates

If forward rates do contain liquidity premiums, these premiums are not necessarily constant over time. A widely held rationale for investor behavior suggests that risk in the market for loans varies with the overall level of interest rates.[11] If, on one hand, interest rates in general were believed to be high by "recent historical standards" and were not expected to go much higher, risk would seem to be relatively moderate. Risk averters would not be overly fearful about loss of principal. Additionally, those long-term investors interested primarily in certainty of income probably would be actively seeking investments, thereby exerting pressure analogous to a negative liquidity premium. If overall interest rates are believed to be low and susceptible to a rise, however, the balance is said to shift in the direction of a greater positive liquidity premium. Risk averters demand a higher liquidity premium in forward rates, anticipating a probable rise in interest rates and a corresponding drop in security prices. It also follows that those long-term investors interested in income certainty are less active in seeking investments at these lower prevailing rates of interest.

Borrowers, on the other hand, would have an incentive to issue securities if interest rates were low and expected to rise because of the lower interest cost. By the same token, they would want to refrain from borrowing when interest rates were believed to be high and were expected to fall. The foregoing discussion implies that the level of interest rates has an influence apart from that of expectations in determining the term structure of interest rates. More specifically, liquidity premiums are said to vary inversely with the level of interest rates relative to a level which is considered normal. In other words, interest rates have a tendency toward mean reversion. This behavior would tend to accentuate the positive slope of the yield curve in cyclical troughs and to accentuate the downward-sloping portion of the yield curve at cyclical peaks.

The idea of an inverse relationship between liquidity premiums and the level of interest rates contrasts with the view of Reuben A. Kessel, who claimed that the relationship is direct.[12] His position stems from the belief that securities serve as money substitutes. Kessel reasoned that be-

---

[11]See John Maynard Keynes, *The General Theory of Employment Interest and Money* (New York: Harcourt, Brace & World, Inc., 1936), pp. 201–2.

[12]Reuben A. Kessel, *The Cyclical Behavior of the Term Structure of Interest Rates* (New York: National Bureau of Economic Research, 1965), pp. 25–26.

cause a rise in interest rates increases the cost of holding money, this rise also increases the cost of holding money substitutes. Because short-term securities are better money substitutes than longer-term securities, an increase in interest rates implies that the opportunity cost of holding short-term securities rises relative to the opportunity cost for holding longer-term, less liquid securities. With the greater relative opportunity cost for holding short-term securities, Kessel contended that yields on longer-term securities increase relative to those on short-term securities. As a result, liquidity premiums embodied in forward rates must rise. On the other hand, when interest rates fall, opportunity costs decline, and as a result liquidity premiums embodied in forward rates fall. Thus, Kessel maintained that liquidity premiums vary directly with the level of interest rates. More will be said about the effect of the level of interest rates on the term structure when we take up empirical testing later in this chapter.

MARKET SEGMENTATION

A third theory of the term structure suggests that the segmented market behavior of lenders and borrowers basically determines the shape of the yield curve.[13] Because of legal and behavioral restrictions, institutional lenders are said to have preferred maturity ranges in which they operate. For example, commercial banks typically prefer short- to medium-term maturities because of the nature of their deposit liability and a traditional emphasis upon liquidity. Insurance companies and other lenders with long-term liabilities prefer longer maturities. On the other hand, borrowers are described as relating the maturity of their debt to their need for funds. Thus, a corporation constructing a plant often takes steps to assure that the maturity of the debt it undertakes in financing the plant corresponds to the expected cash flow to be generated from the plant.

In the extreme, a market segmentation theory implies that the rate of interest for a particular maturity is determined solely by demand and supply conditions for that maturity, with no reference to conditions for other maturities. In other words, borrowers and lenders have rigid maturity preferences and do not deviate from these preferences no matter how attractive the yields for other maturities. Thus, the markets for loans would be entirely segmented, or compartmentalized, according to maturity. In turn, the segments would be determined by the rigid maturity preferences of borrowers and lenders.

A more moderate version of the segmentation theory is that of Franco

---

[13]One of the first proponents of this theory was J. M. Culbertson, "The Term Structure of Interest Rates," *Quarterly Journal of Economics,* LXXI (November 1957): 489–504.

Modigliani and Richard Sutch.[14] They suggested that different categories of lenders have *preferred maturity habitats*. While lenders prefer their own habitats, they will leave them if significant yield inducements are offered on one side or the other. In the absence of sizable yield inducements, however, lenders will stay in their preferred maturity areas, thereby causing the market for loans to be partially segmented. Therefore, arbitrage across maturities would not entirely eliminate inconsistencies in yield for various maturity areas.

The question with which we later will be concerned empirically is whether market segmentation affects the term structure of interest rates over and above the combined influences of expectations and possible systematic risk aversion by lenders. A market segmentation theory on the demand side implies that changes in the relative supplies of various maturities will affect the shape of the term structure of interest rates. For example, if a large relative quantity of long-term debt is offered, long-term rates presumably would rise relative to short-term rates. The opposite presumably would occur if a large relative amount of short-term offerings occurred. Thus, the debt management policies of the Treasury, of municipalities, and of corporations would influence the term structure of interest rates if a partial market segmentation theory held.

TRANSACTION COSTS

In addition to the factors already considered, transaction costs also may have an influence upon the shape of the yield curve.[15] On the basis of number of transactions alone, the long-term investor would find holding long-term securities more attractive than holding short-term securities and reinvesting in short terms at maturity. If the investor had a five-year holding period, investment in a five-year bond would involve only one transaction. If that investor were to invest in one-year securities, there would be five transactions. In contrast, if the investor had a holding period of only one year, the purchase of a one-year security would involve only one transaction, whereas the purchase of a five-year security would involve two—the *purchase* and the *sale*.

All other things being the same, each investor would have an incentive to invest in a security with a maturity corresponding to the intended holding period. If the distribution of holding periods for all investors were shorter

---

[14]Franco Modigliani and Richard Sutch, "Innovations in Interest Rate Policy," *American Economic Review*, LVI (May 1966): 178–97.

[15]This section draws on Burton G. Malkiel, *The Term Structure of Interest Rates* (Princeton, N.J.: Princeton University Press, 1966), Chapter 5.

in maturity than that of securities outstanding, and if transaction costs per transaction for all maturities were equal, a bias toward a positively sloped yield curve would exist. All other things the same, longer-term securities would have to yield more than securities which corresponded in maturity to investors' holding periods, to offset the higher total transaction costs for investment in them. The opposite is implied if the distribution of holding periods is longer in maturity than the distribution of securities outstanding. However, transaction costs in the secondary market tend to increase with maturity. This phenomenon reduces the previously described disadvantage to the long-term investor of investing in short-term securities and reinvesting in short terms upon maturity. On the other hand, the short-term investor must pay substantially higher transaction costs to purchase a long-term security and to sell it at the end of a holding period than if a security were purchased which corresponded to the holding period.

Malkiel contended that low transaction costs for very short-term securities make it possible for a long-term investor to buy short terms, as total transaction costs would be very similar to the cost of a single long-term purchase. If this were true, there would be a bias toward an upward-sloping yield curve, all other things being the same. Long-term investors would be roughly indifferent to transaction costs, while short-term investors would prefer short-term securities. Accordingly, there would be buying pressure in favor of short-term securities relative to long-term ones, resulting in a tendency toward a positively sloped yield curve.

From the standpoint of the borrower, transaction costs (comprised of underwriting and selling costs, legal fees, and inconvenience) make the relative cost per unit of time higher for short-term securities than for long-term securities. Available evidence on corporate and municipal offerings suggests that the percentage cost of flotation varies inversely with the absolute amount of the issue being offered.[16] As a result of these factors, debt financing tends to be "lumpy." Thus, issuers are not inclined to sell bonds with maturities shorter than the time for which they will need the funds.

To the extent that the maturity distribution of debt outstanding is longer than the distribution of desired holding periods of investors, there is a bias toward a positively sloped yield curve. However, if the distribution of debt outstanding is shorter than the distribution of desired holding periods, the effect of transaction costs on the term structure will be neutral, according to Malkiel's analysis. The longer the holding periods of investors, the less the effect of transaction costs on the term structure, all other things the same.

---

[16]See James C. Van Horne, "Implied Fixed Costs of Long-Term Debt Issues," *Journal of Financial and Quantitative Analysis,* 8 (December 1973): 821–34.

CYCLICAL BEHAVIOR OF THE TERM STRUCTURE

In the preceding sections several factors were considered that may influence the term structure of interest rates: expectations, liquidity preference, the level of interest rates, market segmentation, and, finally, transaction costs. The support of these various theories must be based upon empirical testing, a subject we consider shortly. However, a certain amount of insight can be gained by examining the shape of the yield curve over various interest-rate cycles.

Since World War II, term structures of interest rates for Treasury and corporate securities have shown the greatest positive slope at cyclical troughs and usually have evidenced a hump and downward slope at the peaks. Despite certain leads and lags, there has been a strong correspondence between interest-rate cycles and business cycles in most of the post–World War II period. However, in recent years this correspondence has been dampened by inflation. In the 1981–1982 recession and to a lesser extent in the 1974–1975 recession, inflation expectations remained high for some time. As a result, interest rates remained high for some time after the recessions began, and yield curves were humped and downward sloping. The troughs in these interest-rate cycles lagged significantly behind the troughs in business cycles. This was not the case in earlier years, when inflation tended to correspond more closely with the level of economic activity.

If the term structure were determined solely by interest-rate expectations, we might expect the negative yield differential between long- and short-term securities at cyclical peaks to approximate the positive differential at cyclical troughs in interest rates. Since World War II, however, the positive yield differential between long- and short-term Treasury securities has been quite pronounced at interest-rate troughs, the negative differential at cyclical peaks being relatively small in comparison.

This evidence is consistent with an expectations theory modified for liquidity preference. Hicksian liquidity premiums would tend to cushion any downward slope in the yield curve at cyclical peaks and to accentuate the upward slope at the troughs in interest rates. Thus, the bias would be toward a positively sloped yield curve, holding expectations constant. To illustrate this notion, consider the yield curves in Fig. 5-4. In the upper panel of the figure, a yield curve based upon expectations alone is assumed to be downward-sloping. However, when liquidity premiums are added, the yield curve becomes humped in the early maturities and downward-sloping thereafter. Thus, liquidity premiums cushion the downward slope. The lower panel of the figure depicts a positively sloped yield curve based upon expectations alone. Here, liquidity premiums result in the slope becoming more accentuated. A theory of expectations, modified for liquidity

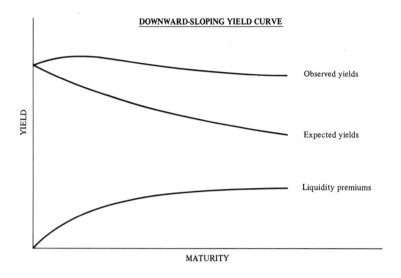

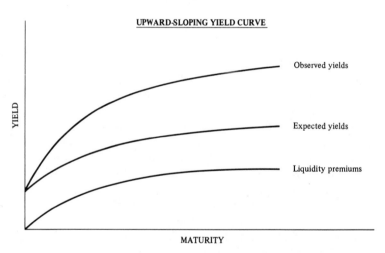

Figure 5-4. Expectations and liquidity premiums.

premiums, then is consistent with the observed predominance of yield differentials in favor of long-term over short-term yields.

EMPIRICAL EVIDENCE

In recent years there have been numerous empirical tests of the term structure of interest rates. We cannot hope to cover them all, but can give a representative sample for each of the various theories. At the outset, we should understand that virtually all the tests to date have involved coupon bonds, as opposed to pure discount bonds. Consequently, there is not an exact correspondence between the theories presented, where we assumed pure discount bonds, and the empirical evidence to follow. Still, such evidence casts a good deal of light on the matter. As we shall see, many of the studies have been concerned either directly or indirectly with whether forward rates are accurate forecasts of future rates of interest. If it can be shown that forward rates correspond exactly to expected future rates, the pure expectations theory is supported. However, if the forward rates are found to be systematically biased in a particular direction, the evidence casts light on other theories of the term structure. The difficulty in testing is that expectations by market participants are not directly observable. Consequently, only indirect estimates can be made.

Tests of Expectations and Liquidity Premiums

One way in which various investigators have attempted to test the pure expectations theory is through the use of a perfect-foresight model. Such a model assumes that not only are expectations held by market participants but also, on the average, they are realized. As expectations cannot be determined directly, the *actual* short rate for a given period of time is substituted for the rate predicted at some earlier time to prevail during the given period. If the long rate at the earlier point in time agrees closely with the average of actual short rates, substituted for expected short rates, the pure expectations theory supposedly is supported. Although this model provides meaningful information, it is not a truly valid test of the pure expectations theory. Actual short rates (*ex post*) cannot be substituted for expected short rates (*ex ante*) and then be used to determine long rates.

Another variation of a perfect-foresight model is to compare forward rates, as implied in the term structure at one point in time, with the actual short rates that they attempt to forecast. Regardless of which variation is used, it is not possible to refute the pure expectations theory simply by showing that implied forward rates at one point in time were poor forecasts of actual short rates. In essence, a perfect-foresight model tests whether predictions in the market, as evidenced by various forward rates, are accurate. Culbertson employed a variation of the perfect-foresight model in his analysis of holding-period yields in order to determine whether holding-period yields for securities of different maturity were equal for all holding periods. For his analysis, he used Treasury bills and long-term Treasury bonds for 1-week and 3-month holding periods. He concluded that the wide differences in holding-period yields that he found rendered the pure expectations theory inadequate as a means of explaining the term structure of interest rates.[17]

While it is reasonable to have errors in prediction, we would not expect these errors to take on any pattern or bias. Over a very long period of time, errors should be distributed randomly about the actual rate, with forward-rate forecasts being above actual rates about as often as below them. However, if a bias in one direction were evident, it would suggest that factors other than pure expectations were at work in the determination of the term structure. In computing the average forecasting error, one should try to eliminate any secular trend. Otherwise, the bias in forecasting error may be attributable to this trend.

David Meiselman was the first to apply an error-learning model to the term structure of interest rates.[18] He asserted that interest-rate expectations are revised whenever previously held expectations prove to be in error. An error-learning model was introduced, which implied that expectations are a function of past and present learning experiences. As new information is received, expectations are adjusted in keeping with the learning process. In his model, changes in 1-year forward rates are related to errors in forecasting the actual 1-year rate of interest:

$$_{t+n}r_{1t} - {}_{t+n}r_{1t-1} = a + b(Et_1) + u \qquad (5\text{-}9)$$

where u is the error term, and Et_1 is the 1-year forecasting error, defined as

$$Et_1 = {}_t R_{1t} - {}_t r_{1t-1} \qquad (5\text{-}10)$$

Thus, the forecasting error is the actual 1-year rate in period t minus the forward-rate forecast of a 1-year loan beginning at time t embodied in the term structure one year earlier.

Market participants are assumed to adjust their expectations in keeping with unanticipated changes in the actual one-year rate of interest. Using the Durand basic corporate bond yield data, Meiselman computed the degree of correlation between forecasting errors and changes in various forward rates for the period 1900–1954.[19] He assumed a linear function and found that correlation coefficients ranged from .95 for changes in

[17]John M. Culbertson, "The Term Structure of Interest Rates," *Quarterly Journal of Economics* LXXI (November 1957): 499–502, 507–9.

[18]See Meiselman, *Term Structure.*

[19]In the Durand annual basic yield data, estimates are made of the yield on the highest-grade corporate bonds. David Durand, *Basic Yields on Corporate Bonds, 1900–1942* (New York: National Bureau of Economic Research, 1942); and David Durand and Willis J. Winn, *Basic Yields of Bonds, 1926–1947: Their Measurement and Pattern* (New York: National Bureau of Economic Research, 1947).

forward rates one year from t to .59 for changes eight years from t. In addition to high positive association, Meiselman found that the regression coefficients reflecting the responsiveness of dependent-variable changes to forecasting errors decreased with the remoteness in the future of the dependent variable.

Moreover, the constant terms were not found to differ significantly from zero. Meiselman argued that constant-term values were measures of liquidity premiums; and since these values did not differ significantly from zero, liquidity premiums were not present in the term structure. From this evidence, it was inferred that a significant portion of the variation in expectations could be explained by the 1-year forecasting error. Meiselman contended that the evidence was consistent with the pure expectations theory, in which forward rates are equivalent to expected future short rates.[20]

Using U.S. Treasury yield-curve data, I tested certain variations of the error-learning model.[21] A high degree of positive correlation was discovered between changes in forward rates and errors in forecasting the one-year actual rate. For all the forward rates tested, the Treasury data resulted in a higher degree of correlation than that which Meiselman had found using the Durand basic corporate yield data. The results supported the notion that interest-rate expectations are important in explaining the term structure of interest rates and that they are revised systematically when actual rates of interest differ from those that had been anticipated. Furthermore, all of the constant-term values were significantly different from zero, a finding that supports the hypothesis that forward rates of interest contain both expectations and a liquidity premium. Moreover, the pattern of intercepts on the horizontal axis for the various regression studies

---

[20] John H. Wood, "Expectations, Errors, and the Term Structure of Interest Rates," *The Journal of Political Economy*, LXXI (April 1963): 165–6, points out a logical weakness in this argument. If liquidity premiums are embodied in the forward rate, Meiselman's error-learning model, Eq. (5-9), becomes

$$\left(_{t+n}\rho_{1t} + _{t+n}L_{1t}\right) - \left(_{t+n}\rho_{1t-1} + _{t+n}L_{1t-1}\right) = a + b\left[_t R_{1t} - \left(_t\rho_{1t-1} + _t L_{1t-1}\right)\right]$$

Rearranging them gives

$$\left(_{t+n}\rho_{1t} - _{t+n}\rho_{1t-1}\right) + \left(_{t+n}L_{1t} - _{t+n}L_{1t-1}\right) = a + b\left[_t R_{1t} - \left(_t\rho_{1t-1} + _t L_{1t-1}\right)\right]$$

where, as before, ρ is the expected future rate, and L is the liquidity premium. We can see readily that when the expectations are realized and the constant term is zero, the first term above equals $b\left[_t R_{1t} - _t\rho_{1t-1}\right]$, and we are left with

$$\left(_{t+n}L_{1t} - _{t+n}L_{1t-1}\right) = b\left(_t L_{1t-1}\right)$$

Thus, a constant term of zero can be consistent with the presence of liquidity premiums embodied in forward rates.

[21] James Van Horne, "Interest-Rate Risk and the Term Structure of Interest Rates," *Journal of Political Economy*, 73 (August 1965): 344–51.

was consistent with liquidity premiums increasing at a diminishing rate with the remoteness of the future period.[22]

Kessel, in his investigation of the term structure, also tested for the presence of liquidity premiums in forward rates of interest. Using error-learning models similar to those discussed, he analyzed the residuals in the regression results when the models were applied to the Durand yield-curve data and to certain Treasury bill data. In both cases, he found systematic positive bias in forward rates as estimates of expected future interest rates—i.e., they were high estimates.[23] In addition to this evidence and his theoretical argument for liquidity preference, Kessel pointed out that on the average, long-term yields on government securities exceeded short-term yields. This finding also might be considered to be consistent with liquidity preference, if one isolated the effect of trend.

Benjamin M. Friedman analyzed forward rates of interest on Treasury bills in relation to estimates of future Treasury bill spot rates of interest.[24] The interest-rate estimates were by professional investors, traders, and underwriters, as reported in the biweekly *Goldsmith-Nagan Bond and Money Market Letter*. The liquidity premium was defined as the forward rate embraced in the actual Treasury bill yield minus the estimated yield. The difference was found to be positive and significant, which was consistent with Hicksian liquidity premiums being embodied in Treasury bill yields.

In an extensive study of liquidity premiums in the post-accord period (after 1952), J. Huston McCulloch also found evidence of positive pre-

---

[22]If liquidity premiums are embodied in forward rates and no other factors exist that would cause the regression line not to pass through the origin, we have from footnote 20 in this chapter:

$$(_{t+n}\rho_{1t} - _{t+n}\rho_{1t-1}) + (_{t+n}L_{1t} - _{t+n}L_{1t-1}) = b[_tR_{1t} - (_t\rho_{1t-1} + _tL_{1t-1})]$$

We assume that $(_{t+n}\rho_{1t} - _{t+n}\rho_{1t-1})$ is revised relative to $_tR_{1t} - _t\rho_{1t-1}$. If $_{t+n}L_{1t}$ equaled $_{t+n}L_{1t-1}$, then the constant term would be $b(_tL_{1t-1})$. The intercept on the horizontal axis would be $-_tL_{1t-1}$ and would be the same for all regression studies.

Now, if $_{t+n}L_{1t-1}$ exceeds $_{t+n}L_{1t}$, the regression line and the constant term would be lower than if the two liquidity premiums were equal. If liquidity premiums increase with the remoteness of the future period, $_{t+n}L_{1t-1}$ would exceed $_{t+n}L_{1t}$. Thus, the intercept on the X, or horizontal, axis would be

$$X\text{-intercept} = -_tL_{1t} - \frac{_{t+n}L_{1t} - _{t+n}L_{1t-1}}{b}$$

If the negative X-intercepts increased in magnitude with successive regression studies, this occurrence would be consistent with liquidity premiums increasing at a diminishing rate with the remoteness of the future period. The X-intercepts in the results for the Treasury securities followed this pattern through $n = 8$ for the dependent variable, after which point ($n = 9$ through 11) they leveled off and fluctuated. Thus, the evidence was consistent with liquidity premiums increasing at a diminishing rate.

[23]See Kessel, *Cyclical Behavior of Term Structure*, pp. 12–25; Chapter 3.

[24]Benjamin M. Friedman, "Interest Rate Expectations versus Forward Rates: Evidence from an Expectations Survey," *Journal of Finance*, 34 (September 1979): 965–73.

mums.[25] However, liquidity premium estimates for long-term forward loans were very inaccurate. For very short forward loans, however, the estimates increased at a decreasing rate and eventually leveled off. Also, McCulloch found no evidence of liquidity premiums varying over the sample period.

Tests Concerning the Level of Rates

If liquidity premiums are embodied in forward rates and affect the term structure it is important to know whether they vary with the level of interest rates over time. Recall from our earlier discussion that one rationale for investor behavior suggests that risk premiums vary inversely with the level of interest rates, relative to an accustomed (normal) interest-rate range. If interest rates were low and were expected to rise, investors would be expected to demand a relatively high risk premium; the opposite would hold if interest rates were high and were expected to fall.

Malkiel tested the hypothesis that the spread between long-term and short-term interest rates varied inversely with the deviation of the long rate from the midpoint of a "normal" range.[26] After transforming the variables to eliminate certain statistical problems, he tested this hypothesis on the Durand basic corporate yield data for the periods 1900–1942 and 1951–1965. The results were found to support the hypothesis of an inverse relationship, thereby supporting indirectly the idea of an inverse relation between liquidity premiums and the level of interest rates relative to a normal level.

Charles R. Nelson also found an inverse relationship between estimated liquidity premiums and the level of interest rates.[27] Using the 1901–1958 Durand yield data, Nelson computed liquidity premiums as the difference between forward rates and corresponding conditional expectations implied by a linear process model. Regressing these liquidity premium estimates against the level of interest rates and also against an index of business confidence, he found the regression coefficients for both to be negative and significant. He holds that this is consistent with the level of interest rates being a measure of risk since downward movements are bounded at zero.

Finally, certain empirical studies I undertook supported in some measure the notion that liquidity premiums vary inversely with the level of interest rates. In these studies, changes in forward rates were made a function of the one-year forecasting error and of the deviation of the level

[25]J. Huston McCulloch, "An Estimate of the Liquidity Premium," *Journal of Political Economy,* 83 (January–February 1975): 95–119.

[26]Malkiel, *Term Structure,* Chapter 3.

[27]Charles R. Nelson, *The Term Structure of Interest Rates* (New York: Basic Books, Inc., 1972), Chapter 6.

of forward rates from an accustomed level.[28] The results of regression studies using Treasury yield-curve data indicated alteration of forward rates depending upon whether interest rates were believed to be high or low with respect to an accustomed interest-rate range. These results, like the other two, were consistent with the idea of an inverse relationship between liquidity premiums and the relative level of interest rates.

Others, however, have found evidence of a positive relationship between estimated liquidity premiums and the level of interest rates. These results are consistent with Kessel's theory that short-term securities are close substitutes for money. On the basis of tests of Treasury bills, Kessel discovered a positive relationship between estimated liquidity premiums and the level of interest rates.[29] Benjamin M. Friedman, in testing liquidity premiums for Treasury bills, also discovered a positive relationship between liquidity premiums and current interest-rate levels.[30] In somewhat the same vein, Phillip Cagan tested for the effect of the level of interest rates using Treasury bills.[31] These results also were consistent with a positive relationship between estimated liquidity premiums and the level of interest rates.

Tests Concerning the Market Segmentation Theory

If the term structure is compartmentalized into separate markets according to maturity, a change in the relative supply or demand in one of these markets should change the shape of the yield curve. For example, an increase in the relative supply of long-term securities should result in an increase in long rates relative to short rates, if all other things remain the same. The reason is that because of institutional specialization investors in other markets can be induced into long-term bonds only with the offer of higher interest rates.

One interesting study regarding market segmentation is that by Franco Modigliani and Richard Sutch, who employed a variant of an expectations model.[32] They labeled their theory "preferred habitat"; supposedly it blended

---

[28]James C. Van Horne, "Interest-Rate Risk and Term Structure of Interest Rates" *Journal of Political Economy,* 73 (August 1965): 344–51; Richard Roll, "Comment," *Journal of Political Economy,* 74 (December 1966): 629–32; and Van Horne, "Reply," *Journal of Political Economy,* 74 (December 1966): 633–35.

[29]Kessel, *Cyclical Behavior of Term Structure,* pp. 22–26.

[30]Benjamin M. Friedman, "Interest Rate Expectations versus Forward Rates," p. 969.

[31]"Liquidity Premiums on Government Securities," in Jack M. Guttentag and Phillip Cagan, *Essays on Interest Rates,* Vol. 1 (New York: National Bureau of Economic Research, 1969), pp. 223–42.

[32]Modigliani and Sutch, *op. cit.,* 178–197; and Modigliani and Sutch, "Debt Management and the Term Structure of Interest Rates: An Empirical Analysis of Recent Experience," *Journal of Political Economy,* 75 (Supplement: August 1967): 569–89.

the theories of expectations, liquidity preference, and market segmentation. The authors suggested that expectations of future interest rates are formed on the basis of past interest rates. However, there are two distinct influences in this history: the recent trend in interest rates and the "normal" level of interest rates based upon long-run experience. The first influence suggests that over the short run market participants expect current trends in interest rates to continue. The second influence is that interest rates are expected to regress toward a normal level.

Modigliani and Sutch combine both of these expectational influences into a single expectations variable, using an Almon lag structure, which resembles an inverted U. The yield differential between long and short rates is made a function of a moving average of past short rates, weighted according to the lag structure. Their model is

$$R_{Lt} - R_{st} = a - b_0 R_{st} + \sum_{i=1}^{16} B_i R_{st-i} + u \qquad (5\text{-}11)$$

where R_{Lt} is the long rate at time t, R_{st} is the short rate, the third term on the right represents the lag structure, and u is the error term. Through various tests, the most suitable lag was found to be 16 quarters. It should be noted that there is no explicit use of future rates; Modigliani and Sutch relate current spot rates to current and past spot rates. The data used to test the model was based on 3-month Treasury bills and the average yield on long-term government securities, both on a quarterly basis. Overall, the model was successful in explaining the *ex post* differential between the long and short rates; the regression coefficients had the right sign and size. Because the lag structure had the predicted shape, the authors concluded that interest-rate expectations are based upon both of the influences discussed above.

In a second paper (*Journal of Political Economy*, 1967), they tested the influence of maturity composition of Treasury debt upon the spread between the long and short rates. Their approach consisted of adding various maturity-composition variables to their expectations model and seeing if the effect of these additions was significant. Using their original data, they failed to uncover any significant relationships between the yield spread and the various measures of maturity composition. However, when the authors used average yield-to-maturity data prepared by Morgan Guaranty Trust Company, they discovered significant and positive relationships between the yield spread of intermediate and very short rates and variations in the supply of debt in the intermediate range. However, these relationships were not evident for yield spreads involving longer-term securities. Even from the evidence for intermediate-term securities, the term structure could not be considered very responsive to changes in the maturity composition of the debt.

In a related study, Steven W. Dobson, Richard C. Sutch, and David E. Vanderford undertook an extensive analysis of those predictive models of the term structure based on past interest-rate observations.[33] In all, eight distinct models were analyzed: (1) inertial, where the best estimate of the next period's rate is the present period's rate; (2) a linear regressive model, where interest rates are expected to return to some "normal" rate over time; (3) a weighted regressive model, where the "normal" rate is taken to be a weighted average of past rates with the most recent past rates being weighted more heavily; (4) a simple extrapolative model, where the change in next period's rate is a constant fraction of recent changes in rates; (5) a weighted extrapolative model, where the extrapolation is based on a weighted average of recent past rates; (6) an extrapolative-regressive model that combines both elements, as in the Modigliani-Sutch version described above; (7) an adaptive model, such as the error-learning models examined earlier, based on an exponential weighting of past rate observations; and (8) a convex model, where expectations are taken to be a weighted average of multiple adaptive expectation processes.

All of the models examined endeavor to predict future interest rates based on a linear combination of past yield observations. The general form of the models was

$$R\ (m)_t = \sum_{t=0}^{\infty} \beta\ (m)_i r_{t-i} + Y\ (m)_t \qquad (5\text{-}12)$$

where $R(m)_t$ = the yield on an m-period loan at time t
$\beta(m)_i$ = a distributed lag function for past rates
r_{t-i} = the one-period rate at time $t-i$
$Y(m)_t$ = the liquidity premium for an m-period loan

The summation of the $\beta(m)_i$ should equal 1. Thus, Eq. (5-12) is a general expression which states that the term structure is determined primarily by expectations of future short-term interest rates; these, in turn, are determined by a distributed lag on past short rates, plus a liquidity premium, which is assumed to be constant. Dobson, Sutch, and Vanderford went on to test the various models using monthly U.S. Treasury security data. Of the eight models, only the linear, the simple extrapolative, and the extrapolative-regressive models were found to be internally consistent, with the latter having the most explanatory power. When unconstrained, the estimated distributed lag exhibits a humped shape. The authors contend

[33]Steven W. Dobson, Richard C. Sutch, and David E. Vanderford, "An Evaluation of Alternative Empirical Models of the Term Structure of Interest Rates," *Journal of Finance*, 31 (September 1976): 1035–65.

that this shape is consistent with the pattern predicted by the Modigliani and Sutch version of the extrapolative-regressive model. As this model performs better than the various other models of expectations formation for the data examined, the authors contend that there is little advantage to using a more restrictive model.

However, a number of other scholars have questioned Modigliani and Sutch's model of term structure behavior. Llad Phillips and John Pippenger, for example, tested the model using the same sample period, but with both corporate and Treasury yield data.[34] They found that the linkage between the current long-term rate of interest and the distributed lag on short-term rates did not persist across time and space. The authors concluded that the results do not support Modigliani and Sutch's model as a description of term structure behavior. Similarly, other authors have found that long-term interest rates do not depend in any important way on past short-term rates. According to these studies, past short-term rates are not very useful in predicting future interest rates.[35]

John S. McCallum tested the pure expectations theory, the combined expectations and liquidity premium theory, and the preferred habitat model using Canadian government securities.[36] He analyzed the risk-return pattern for a 3-month holding period for various maturity securities ranging from 3 to 240 months. While risk, as measured by the standard deviation and the beta, increased with maturity of the instrument held, the expected return did not. (The latter was "corrected" for unanticipated interest rate movements.) Expected returns were found to rise with maturity up to 3 years, but to level off thereafter. McCallum interprets this evidence as consistent with the preferred habitat theory. He reasons that investors were not able to acquire premiums commensurate with risk across the spectrum of maturities available. Only in the early maturities were they able to obtain such premiums. While this interpretation may follow from the evidence, there is some problem in adjusting for unanticipated changes in interest rates. As a result, the return data employed may not reflect true expected returns.

[34]Llad Phillips and John Pippenger, "The Term Structure of Interest Rates in the MIT-PENN-SSRC Model," *Journal of Money, Credit, and Banking,* 11 (May 1979): 151–64.

[35]See Michael J. Hamberger and Cynthia A. Latta, "The Term Structure of Interest Rates: Some Additional Evidence," *Journal of Money, Credit, and Banking,* 1 (February 1969): 71–83; Llad Phillips and John Pippenger, "Preferred Habitat vs. Efficient Market: A Test of Alternative Hypotheses," *Review of the Federal Reserve Bank of St. Louis* (May 1976): 11–19; Thomas F. Cargill and Robert A. Meyer, "A Spectral Approach to Estimating the Distributed Lag Relationship between Long and Short Term Interest Rates," *International Economic Review,* 13 (June 1972): 223–38; John R. Brick and Howard E. Thompson, "Time Series Analysis of Interest Rates: Some Additional Evidence," *Journal of Finance,* 33 (March 1978): 93–104; and James E. Pesando, "On the Efficiency of the Bond Market: Some Canadian Evidence," *Journal of Political Economy,* 86 (December 1978): 1057–76.

[36]John S. McCallum, "The Expected Holding Period Return, Uncertainty and the Term Structure of Interest Rates," *Journal of Finance,* 30 (May 1975): 307–23.

Benjamin M. Friedman, in a study described previously, tested for a supply effect with respect to Treasury bill liquidity premiums. He found only a faint relationship between liquidity premiums and the relative supplies of short-term Treasury securities and no relationship for the average maturity of the entire government debt.[37]

Richard W. Lang and Robert H. Rasche analyzed the price elasticity of Treasury securities with respect to debt-management policy.[38] Using a Modigliani-Sutch equation of the term structure, they found little evidence of market segmentation. The authors concluded that debt management activities by the Treasury have little effect on the term structure of interest rates. In another test of market segmentation, I analyzed changes in authority of the Treasury to issue long-term bonds.[39] The 4¼ percent interest-rate ceiling on long-term bonds imposed by Congress effectively precludes their issuance when prevailing interest rates are higher. The restrictiveness of this ceiling was greatly altered in 1971 and 1976 (and later as well), when Congress allowed the Teasury to sell long-term securities apart from the ceiling. As a result, the supply of long-term securities would be expected to increase. To test whether long-term interest rates rose relative to short-term rates around the time of the change in authority, several widely used term structure models were employed. There was no evidence that long-term rates rose relative to short-term rates after the change in authority. Thus, the market segmentation theory was not supported.

In contrast, J. W. Elliott and M. E. Echols analyze Treasury yield data for direct signs of discontinuities, which might support the notion of market segmentation.[40] Using piecewise linear regression, the method detected the presence of statistically significant discontinuities in the yield curve. In turn, this was said to be evidence of market segmentation. In another study of corporate and Treasury securities, Wayne Y. Lee, Terry S. Maness, and Donald L. Tuttle also claimed to find evidence of market segmentation.[41] Analyzing the pattern of liquidity premiums, the authors discovered peaking and troughing, which they interpreted to be consistent with market segments. In both of these studies, there are data and maturity categorization problems, which temper the strength of the conclusions.

Michael E. Echols and Jan Walter Elliott tested the premise that

[37]Benjamin M. Friedman, "Interest Rate Expectations versus Forward Rates," pp. 969–70.

[38]Richard W. Lang and Robert H. Rasche, "Debt-Management Policy and the Own Price Elasticity of Demand for U. S. Government Notes and Bonds," *Review of the Federal Reserve Bank of St. Louis,* 59 (September 1977): 8–22.

[39]James C. Van Horne, "The Term Structure of Interest Rates: A Test of the Segmented Markets Hypothesis," *Southern Economic Journal,* 47 (April 1980): 1129–40.

[40]J. W. Elliott and M. E. Echols, "Market Segmentation, Speculative Behavior, and the Term Structure of Interest Rates,"*Review of Economics and Statistics,* LVIII (February 1976): 40–49.

[41]Wayne Y. Lee, Terry S. Maness, and Donald L. Tuttle, "Nonspeculative Behavior and the Term Structure," *Journal of Financial and Quantitative Analysis,* 15 (March 1980): 53–83.

interest-rate expectations are based largely on economic variables.[42] Using yield curve data for U. S. Treasury securities up to 20 years in maturity, their model had considerable explanatory power with respect to forward rates. Most of the variables behaved as expected. However, forward rates were positively related to the level of interest rates, a finding consistent with the Kessel thesis. The institutional demand variable was significant for maturities up to ten years, whereas a bond supply variable was not significant. The former finding is consistent with a degree of market segmentation existing in the market for government securities. Finally, V. Vance Roley studied the demand for U. S. Treasury securities using a structural model of portfolio adjustment.[43] When Treasury security supplies were introduced into the model, security yields were found to be responsive to them. The short-run impact of absolute and relative security supplies on the yield curve is consistent, of course, with market segmentation.

Empirical Studies: Summary

In summary, the evidence cited, plus additional empirical studies, attests to the importance of interest-rate expectations in the term structure of interest rates. The market appears to forecast the future course of interest rates, and these forecasts are important in determining the yield on securities. In addition, empirical studies dealing with post–World War II data suggest that forward rates are biased and high estimates of expected future rates. Market participants during this period appear to have gauged their activities on expected future interest rates, plus a liquidity premium.

However, the evidence is mixed as to the shape of the liquidity premium profile. Most of the studies examined suggest that premiums increase at a decreasing rate with maturity, for the early maturities. However, the evidence for later maturities differs as to whether liquidity premiums increase monitonically with maturity. Moreover, the evidence is mixed as to whether liquidity premiums vary inversely or directly with the level of interest rates. Some studies show an inverse relationship; others show a direct relationship, whereas still other studies show no relationship at all.

The market-segmentation theory has been tested by studying the effect of shifts in the relative supply of various maturity securities and shifts in maturity demand by institutional investors. While certain studies suggest that market segmentation has some influence on the term structure, other studies point out no effect at all. On balance, the empirical evidence on

[42]Michael E. Echols and Jan Walter Elliott, "Rational Expectations in a Disequilibrium Model of the Term Structure," *American Economic Review,* 66 (March 1976): 28–44.

[43]V. Vance Roley, "The Determinants of the Treasury Yield Curve," *Journal of Finance,* 36 (December 1981): 1103–26.

market segmentation would have to be regarded as largely inconclusive. If there is an effect, the effect is of only moderate importance. That is, the term structure is largely determined by factors other than market segmentation. However, the impact of market segmentation could vary over time, being more important at some times than at others. We simply need to learn more about market imperfections.

It must be pointed out that the empirical evidence examined in this section is by no means all inclusive. Constraints of space have kept us from reviewing many other studies that have been undertaken. It should also be mentioned that the generalizations presented in this summary are not universally accepted. The question of what theory best explains the term structure of interest rates remains a subject of heated controversy.

SUMMARY

The term structure of interest rates portrays the yield-maturity relationship on securities that differ only in length of time to maturity and that are pure discount bonds. A number of theories attempt to explain the term structure. The pure expectations theory states that expectations of the future course of interest rates are the sole determinant. When the yield curve is upward-sloping, this theory implies that market participants expect interest rates to rise in the future; a downward-sloping curve implies that interest rates are expected to fall; while a horizontal yield curve suggests that interest rates are not expected to change. One version of the theory implies that securities of different maturity are perfect substitutes in the sense that the expected return is the same, while another version implies that forward rates are unbiased estimates of expected future spot rates of interest. Although the chapter was written as if both versions hold, we pointed out certain technical problems that may not make this so.

A combined theory of expectations and liquidity preference suggests that market participants generally prefer to lend short unless offered a premium sufficient to offset the risk of lending long. Thus, the term structure would be affected not only by expectations but also by Hicksian liquidity premiums. If risk increases with the remoteness of the future, these premiums would increase at a decreasing rate with remoteness, or maturity. The presence of liquidity premiums in the term structure implies a bias toward upward-sloping yield curves. These premiums may vary with the level of interest rates; the theory that interest rates return to some normal level suggests an inverse relationship between liquidity premiums and the level of interest rates whereas a money-substitute theory implies a direct relationship.

A market segmentation theory implies that maturity preferences of lenders and borrowers are so strong that they usually will not leave their preferred maturity range to take advantage of yield differentials. As a result, there are a number of different markets, and interest rates are said to be determined by the interaction of supply and demand in each. With partial market segmentation, lenders and borrowers have preferred habitats, but they will leave their preferred maturity areas if there are significant yield inducements on either side. In addition to the theories considered, transaction costs may also influence the yield curve. We examined the role of these costs and their effect on the term structure. We also analyzed cyclical changes in the term structure over time.

The empirical studies examined give considerable insight into the factors that best explain the term structure. Most of the studies show the important role of expectations of the future course of interest rates. Also, there is indication of an upward bias in forward rates of interest. This evidence is consistent with an expectations theory modified for liquidity preference. Whether or not liquidity premiums vary with the level of interest rates is an inconclusive topic, as some evidence is consistent with an inverse relationship whereas other evidence is consistent with a direct relationship. In addition, tests of the market segmentation theory have been mixed. If there is an effect here, it would appear to be modest.

SELECTED REFERENCES

Brink, John R., and Howard E. Thompson, "Time Series Analysis of Interest Rates: Some Additional Evidence," *Journal of Finance,* 33 (March 1978): 93–104.

Cox, John, Jonathan E. Ingersoll, Jr., and Stephen A. Ross, "A Reexamination of Traditional Hypotheses about the Term Structure of Interest Rates," 36 (September 1981): 769–99.

Culbertson, John M., "The Term Structure of Interest Rates," *Quarterly Journal of Economics,* LXXI (November 1957): 485–517.

Dobson, Steven W., Richard C. Sutch, and David E. Vanderford, "An Evaluation of Alternative Empirical Models of the Term Structure of Interest Rates," *Journal of Finance,* 31 (September 1976): 1035–65.

Elliott, J. W., and M. E. Echols, "Market Segmentation, Speculative Behavior, and the Term Structure of Interest Rates," *Review of Economics and Statistics,* LVIII (February 1976): 40–49.

———— , "Rational Expectations in a Disequilibrium Model of the Term Structure," *American Economic Review,* LXVI (March 1976): 28–44.

Friedman, Benjamin M., "Interest Rate Expectations versus Forward Rates: Evidence from an Expectations Survey," *Journal of Finance,* 34 (September 1979): 965–73.

Hicks, J. R., *Value and Capital,* 2nd ed. London: Oxford University Press, 1946.

Jarrow, Robert A., "Liquidity Premiums and the Expectations Hypothesis," *Journal of Banking and Finance,* 5 (December 1981): 539–46.

Kessel, Reuben H., *The Cyclical Behavior of the Term Structure of Interest Rates.* New York: National Bureau of Economic Research, 1965.

Langetieg, Terrence C., "A Multivariate Model of the Term Structure," *Journal of Finance,* 35 (March 1980): 71–97.

Lutz, Friedrich A., "The Structure of Interest Rates," *Quarterly Journal of Economics,* LV (November 1940): 36–63.

Malkiel, Burton G., "Expectations, Bond Prices, and the Term Structure of Interest Rates," *Quarterly Journal of Economics,* LXXVI (May 1962): 197–218.

———— , *The Term Structure of Interest Rates.* Princeton, N.J.: Princeton University Press, 1966.

McCulloch, J. Huston, "An Estimate of the Liquidity Premium," *Journal of Political Economy,* 83 (January-February 1975): 95–119.

Meiselman, David, *The Term Structure of Interest Rates.* Englewood Cliffs, N.J.: Prentice-Hall, Inc., 1962.

Modigliani, Franco, and Richard Sutch, "Innovations in Interest Rate Policy," *American Economic Review,* LVI (May 1966): 178–97.

———— , "Debt Management and the Term Structure of Interest Rates: An Empirical Anaylsis of Recent Experience," *Journal of Political Economy,* 75 (Supplement August 1967): 569–89.

Nelson, Charles R., *The Term Structure of Interest Rates.* New York: Basic Books, Inc., 1972.

Phillips, Llad, and John Pippenger, "The Term Structure of Interest Rates in the MIT-PENN-SSRC Model," *Journal of Money, Credit and Banking,* 11 (May 1979): 151–64.

Roll, Richard, *The Behavior of Interest Rates: An Application of the Efficient Market Model to U.S. Treasury Bills.* New York: Basic Books, Inc., 1970.

Roley, V. Vance, "The Determinants of the Treasury Yield Curve," *Journal of Finance,* 36 (December 1981): 11–3–26.

Stiglitz, Joseph E., "A Consumption-Oriented Theory of the Demand for Financial Assets and the Term Structure of Interest Rates," *Review of Economic Studies,* 37 (July 1970): 321–50.

Van Horne, James, "Interest-Rate Expectations, the Shape of the Yield Curve, and Monetary Policy," *Review of Economics and Statistics,* XLVIII (May 1966): 211–15.

———— , "Interest-Rate Risk and the Term Structure of Interest Rates," *Journal of Political Economy,* 73 (August 1965): 344–51.

———— , "The Term Structure of Interest Rates: A Test of the Segmented Markets Hypothesis," *Southern Economic Journal,* 47 (April 1980): 1129–40.

———— , and David A. Bowers, "The Liquidity Impact of Debt Management," *The Southern Economic Journal,* XXXIV (April 1968): 526–37.

Wood, John H., "Expectations, Error, and the Term Structure of Interest Rates," *Journal of Political Economy,* 71 (April 1963): 160–71.

6

COUPON RATE EFFECT
AND IMMUNIZATION

In the last chapter we explored various theories of the term structure of interest rates, as well as empirical evidence related to these theories. The latter was examined without regard to differences in coupon rates. However, such differences usually result in different valuations and yields of otherwise identical securities. In this chapter, we investigate the coupon rate phenomenon as it relates to the bond-value equation. We then examine the use of the duration measure, which takes account of both interest and principal payments and is used as a substitute for maturity. This is followed by a discussion of how we might immunize the payments stream of a bond investment relative to some desired payments stream. Finally, we explore the increasing presence of pure discount bonds in the marketplace and their implication for the valuation of bonds.

THE COUPON EFFECT

We know in general that the longer the maturity of a debt instrument, the greater the change in price that accompanies a shift in interest rates.[1] However, price changes also are dependent on the level of

---

[1]For a thorough examination of the mathematics of bond price movements, see Sidney Homer and Martin L. Leibowitz, *Inside the Yield Book* (Englewood Cliffs, N. J.: Prentice-Hall, Inc., 1972).

coupon. This phenomenon is known as the *coupon effect*. It is important to distinguish the coupon effect that arises from the mathematics of interest rates, to be studied here, from that which arises from the call feature and/or the taxation of interest income and capital gains at different rates. Our concern in this chapter is solely with the former. The latter effects are explored in Chapters 9 and 10, when we deal with callability and taxability.

Sensitivity of Price Changes to Coupons

For a given bond, the lower the coupon the greater the price change for a given shift in interest rates. This is illustrated in Table 6-1 for 10- and 20-year bonds. In the upper part of the table, a yield increase is assumed, while in the lower part a yield decline is assumed to occur. We see that the lower the coupon, the more sensitive market prices are to changes in yields. The reason for this is that with lower coupons more of the total return to the investor is reflected in the principal payment at maturity as opposed to interest payments, which are discounted from nearer coupon dates. In effect, then, the "true" maturity is longer for a low coupon bond than it is for a high coupon one. Put another way, investors realize their returns sooner with a high coupon bond than with a low coupon one.

In general, the further in the future an income stream, the more volatile its present value when changes in the discount rate occur.[2] This phenomenon is evident in Table 6-1, when we compare the column for 20-year bonds with that for 10-year bonds. To illustrate it for a single future receipt, suppose a contract is to pay $100, 15 years hence, and another contract is to pay $100, 30 years hence. If the present discount rate were 13 percent and we wished to know the effect of changes in it to 16 percent and to 10 percent, the following present values would be relevant with annual compounding:

Discount Rate	Present Value 15-Year Contract	Present Value 30-Year Contract
16%	$10.79	$1.16
13	15.99	2.56
10	23.94	5.73

[2]For very long maturities, volatility can decrease with further increases in maturity. We will investigate this situation shortly.

Percentagewise, the changes in the two contracts are as follows:

Change in Discount Rate	15-Year Contract	30-Year Contract
From 13% to 16%	− 32.52%	− 54.69%
From 13% to 10%	49.72	123.83

The point of these examples is to emphasize that one gets very different market price movements, depending on the coupon rate. With high coupons, the total income stream (interest and principal payments) is closer to realization than it is with low coupons. The nearer the income stream, the less the present value effect, given a change in yields. Thus, even if high and low coupon bonds have the same maturity, the low coupon bonds tend to be more volatile.

Table 6-1. Changes in Price Accompanying a Shift in Yield for Various Coupons

	YIELD INCREASE FROM 12% TO 15%	
Coupon	Price Decline 10-Year Bond	Price Decline 20-Year Bond
15%	− 14.68%	− 18.41%
12	− 15.29	− 18.89
9	− 16.16	− 19.65
6	− 17.48	− 21.03
3	− 19.74	− 24.34
0	− 24.50	− 43.00

	YIELD DECREASE FROM 12% TO 9%	
Coupon	Price Increase 10-Year Bond	Price Increase 20-Year Bond
15%	18.62%	26.63%
12	19.51	27.60
9	20.78	29.15
6	22.71	31.97
3	26.02	38.72
0	32.98	76.84

THE DURATION MEASURE

The problems associated with different market price move-ments for different coupon rates has led many to question the usefulness of maturity as a measure of the length of a financial instrument. Instead they suggest the use of another measure—the duration of a security, which is simply a weighted average of the times in the future when interest and principal payments are to be received. This measure was first proposed in 1938 by Frederick R. Macaulay in his monumental study of yields.[3] Macaulay made it clear that the number of years to maturity is an inadequate measure of the time element of a loan because it tells only the date of final payment and omits essential information about the size and date of payments that occur before the final payment.

To remedy this problem, he proposed the following measure, which he called *duration*.

$$D = \frac{\displaystyle\sum_{t=1}^{n} \frac{C_t(t)}{(1+r)^t}}{\displaystyle\sum_{t=1}^{n} \frac{C_t}{(1+r)^t}} \tag{6-1}$$

where C_t = interest and/or principal payment at time t
 (t) = length of time to the interest and/or principal pay-ments
 n = length of time to final maturity
 r = yield to maturity

The denominator of the equation is simply the present value of the stream of interest and principal payments. The numerator is the present value, but the interest and principal payments are weighted by the length of the interval between the present time and the time that the payment is to be received. Rather than estimate interest rates for each future period and use them to discount the payments to present value, for computational convenience Macaulay used yield-to-maturity as the discount rate throughout. He then employed duration as a measure of the life of a coupon-paying bond.

---

[3]Frederick R. Macaulay, *Some Theoretical Problems Suggested by the Movements of Interest Rates, Bond Yields, and Stock Prices in the United States since 1856* (New York: National Bureau of Economic Research, 1938). For a historical review of the duration measure and its use, as well as alternative specifications, see Roman L. Weil, "Macaulay's Duration: An Appreciation," *Journal of Business*, 46 (October 1973): 589–92; Jonathan E. Ingersoll, Jr., Jeffrey Skelton, and Roman L. Weil, "Duration Forty Years Later," *Journal of Financial and Quantitative Analysis*, 13 (November 1978): 627–50 ; and G. O. Bierwag, George G. Kaufman, and Alden L. Toevs, "Single Factor Duration Models in a Discrete General Equilibrium Framework," *Journal of Finance*, 37 (May 1982): 325–38.

To illustrate the duration measure shown in Eq. (6-1), suppose that we hold a bond with 4 years to maturity which had an 8 percent coupon rate and yielded 10 percent to maturity. Assume also that interest payments are received at the end of each of the 4 years and that the principal payment is received at the end of the fourth year. The duration of the bond would be:

$$D = \frac{\dfrac{\$80(1)}{(1.10)} + \dfrac{\$80(2)}{(1.10)^2} + \dfrac{\$80(3)}{(1.10)^3} + \dfrac{\$1,080(4)}{(1.10)^4}}{\dfrac{\$80}{(1.10)} + \dfrac{\$80}{(1.10)^2} + \dfrac{\$80}{(1.10)^3} + \dfrac{\$1,080}{(1.10)^4}} = 3.56 \text{ years}$$

If the coupon rate were 4 percent, its duration would be:

$$D = \frac{\dfrac{\$40(1)}{(1.10)} + \dfrac{\$40(2)}{(1.10)^2} + \dfrac{\$40(3)}{(1.10)^3} + \dfrac{\$1,040(4)}{(1.10)^4}}{\dfrac{\$40}{(1.10)} + \dfrac{\$40}{(1.10)^2} + \dfrac{\$40}{(1.10)^3} + \dfrac{\$1,040}{(1.10)^4}} = 3.75 \text{ years}$$

If the coupon rate were zero, however, duration would be:

$$D = \frac{\dfrac{\$1,000(4)}{(1.10)^4}}{\dfrac{\$1,000}{(1.10)^4}} = 4 \text{ years}$$

Thus, if there is but a single payment, duration equals maturity. For bonds with interim coupon payments, however, duration is always less than maturity.

In examining Eq. (6-1), we can visualize also that the higher the interest rate, as denoted by r, the shorter the duration. For the bond with an 8 percent coupon, 4 years to maturity, and a 10 percent yield, we determined earlier that its duration was 3.56 years. Suppose now that its yield to maturity were 14 percent instead of 10 percent. The duration of the bond then would be:

$$D = \frac{\dfrac{\$80(1)}{(1.14)} + \dfrac{\$80(2)}{(1.14)^2} + \dfrac{\$80(3)}{(1.14)^3} + \dfrac{\$1,080(4)}{(1.14)^4}}{\dfrac{\$80}{(1.14)} + \dfrac{\$80}{(1.14)^2} + \dfrac{\$80}{(1.14)^3} + \dfrac{\$1,080}{(1.14)^4}} = 3.53 \text{ years}$$

Thus, the higher the interest rate, the shorter the duration of the instrument, all other things the same.

In summary, duration can be considered a measure of the average life of a debt instrument on a present-value basis.[4] That is, it is a weighted average of the present values of coupon and principal payments. The weights represent proportions of the total present value of the bond, which are associated with specific future payments. As we will see later in the chapter, it is assumed in the duration measure that the term structure of interest rates shift in a parallel manner.

The Relationship Between Duration and Maturity

For bonds selling at their par value or above, duration increases at a decreasing rate with maturity. For bonds selling at a discount, duration increases at a decreasing rate up to some fairly long maturity and then declines. Lawrence Fisher and Roman L. Weil calculate duration measures for various discount bonds and their results for bonds yielding 8 percent to maturity are shown in Table 6-2.[5] We see that for 2, 4, and 6 percent coupon rates, duration declines with maturity after 50 years. For the 8 percent coupon bond selling at par, duration increases with maturity

Table 6-2. *Duration for Bonds Yielding 8 Percent (Semiannual Coupons)*

Years to Maturity	COUPON RATE			
	2%	*4%*	*6%*	*8%*
1	0.995 year	0.990 year	0.985 year	0.981 year
5	4.742	5.533	4.361	4.218
10	8.762	7.986	7.454	7.067
20	14.026	11.966	10.922	10.292
50	14.832	13.466	12.987	12.743
100	13.097	13.029	13.006	12.995
Perpetual	13.000	13.000	13.000	13.000

Source of data: Lawrence Fisher and Roman L. Weil, "Coping with the Risk of Interest-Rate Fluctuations: Returns to Bondholders from Naive and Optimal Strategies," *Journal of Business,* 44 (October, 1971), 418.

[4]See Michael H. Hopewell and George G. Kaufman, "Bond Price Volatility and Term to Maturity: A Generalized Respecification," *American Economic Review,* LXIII (September 1973):749–53.

[5]Lawrence Fisher and Roman L. Weil, "Coping with the Risk of Interest-Rate Fluctuations: Returns to Bondholders from Naive and Optimal Strategies," *Journal of Business,* 44 (October 1971): 418.

at a decreasing rate throughout. Thus, for bonds selling at a discount, duration eventually declines with maturity. However, this occurs many years out. As most bond issues have original maturities of 30 years or less, duration increases with maturity for most of the bonds we observe. However, it is important to recognize that for discount bonds this need not be the case.

IMMUNIZATION OF BOND PORTFOLIOS

When investors have desired patterns of cash flows to be received at various future times, it is appropriate for them to arrange their bond portfolios in such a way that the desired patterns can be approximated. In other words, they *dedicate* their portfolios to a specific stream of cash payouts and hope to come as close as possible to this stream. To illustrate with a simple example, suppose we were concerned with realizing a single payment of dollars 5 years from today. For ease of exposition, assume the use of default-free securities. If a pure discount bond (zero coupon) existed with 5 years to maturity, it would be an easy matter. We would simply invest in that security. By buying enough of these bonds, we can assure ourselves of the receipt of X dollars 5 years from now. Because the future value of the position is known with certainty, it is said to be perfectly *immunized,* in that it is insensitive to subsequent fluctuations in interest rates. Put another way, the payoff will equal precisely the amount desired at the end of the holding period.

Immunization with Coupon Issues

Whenever possible, one should look first to pure discount bonds. As these bonds have increased dramatically in number in recent years, as we discuss later, it often is possible to immunize only with them. However, it also is possible to immunize with coupon bonds, though usually less than perfectly. With coupon bonds, two types of risk are germane: *price risk* and *coupon reinvestment risk*. Price risk is the risk that—with changing interest rates—the bond will need to be sold at a different price from what was expected. Of course, price risk could be reduced to zero if bonds whose maturity equaled the intended holding period were selected. However, there would still be coupon reinvestment risk, which is the risk associated with reinvesting the coupons received at yields that are different from the yield of the bond when it was purchased.

Together, these two risks represent the total risk associated with a bond investment for an investor with an intended holding period. Moreover, these risks vary in opposite directions. An increase in interest rates reduces the price of a bond, but increases the yield possible from reinvestment of coupons. In contrast, a decline in interest rates results in a price increase, but lowers the yield possible from coupon reinvestment. Thus, the two types of risk are offsetting. To "immunize" a bond investment from subsequent interest-rate changes, these two risks must be balanced so that they are completely offsetting.

To illustrate this notion, suppose that $1,210 must be realized in 2 years.[6] At present, the term structure is flat with a 10 percent yield-to-maturity throughout. However, at the end of the first year, there is a possibility of a single, parallel shift in interest rates, either to 12 percent or to 8 percent, as well as the possibility that interest rates will remain unchanged. Available for investment is a 2-year bond with a 10 percent annual coupon. For an investment in this bond, the amounts realized at the end of 2 years under the three possible states of the world would be as follows:

	TERM STRUCTURE LEVEL		
	8%	10%	12%
Principal Payment	$1,000	$1,000	$1,000
Reinvested First-Year Coupon	108	110	112
Second-Year Coupon	100	100	100
	$1,208	$1,210	$1,212

Only if interest rates remain at 10 percent will the $1,210 desired at the end of the holding period be able to be realized. If there is a shift in interest rates, the bond will not provide perfect immunization. The reason is that the reinvestment rate on the first-year coupon payment changes.

Suppose, however, that there also exists a 10 percent coupon bond with 2.1 years to maturity. Assume that this bond pays a $10 coupon at maturity (one-tenth of a full year coupon), together with $100 at the end of the first and second years. In this case, the bond will need to be sold before maturity. If interest rates turn out to be 8 percent, the market value of the bond at the end of 2 years, with one-tenth of a year to go, will be approximately $1,002. That is, the $1,000 principal amount and $10 coupon at the end of one-tenth of a year will be worth approximately $1,002 at the beginning of the period with an 8 percent discount rate. Contrarily, the market value of the bond at the end of 2 years will be approximately

---

[6]This example comes from Jeffrey Skelton, "Recent Results in Term Structure Theory," Berkeley Program in Finance Seminar, September 13, 1982.

$998 if the term structure shifts from 10 percent to 12 percent. Therefore, the amounts realized at the end of 2 years for a 2.1 year bond will be:

	TERM STRUCTURE LEVEL		
	8%	*10%*	*12%*
Market Value on Sale	$1,002	$1,000	$ 998
Reinvested First-Year Coupon	108	110	112
Second-Year Coupon	100	100	100
	$1,210	$1,210	$1,210

In this case, the bond is perfectly immunized in the sense that the amounts received are exactly the same under all possible states. The changes in principal value at the end of 2 years exactly offset the changes in reinvestment rate on the first-year coupon.

Using Eq. (6-1), the duration of the 2.1-year bond is:

$$D = \frac{\dfrac{\$100(1)}{(1.10)} + \dfrac{\$100(2)}{(1.10)^2} + \dfrac{\$1,010(2.1)}{(1.10)^{2.1}}}{\dfrac{\$100}{(1.10)} + \dfrac{\$100}{(1.10)^2} + \dfrac{\$1,010}{(1.10)^{2.1}}} = 2.0 \text{ years}$$

Thus, the duration is equal to the intended holding period. Whenever the term structure is flat and only parallel shifts in interest rates occur, it can be shown that a bond investment is always immunized when its duration equals the intended holding period.[7] If the duration of the bond exceeds the intended holding period, reinvestment risk would be zero, but price risk would be positive. If the duration is less than the intended holding period, there will be reinvestment risk and often price risk as well.[8] Only when the duration of the coupon bond equals the intended holding period is the investment perfectly immunized under the stated assumptions. Moreover, one would want to immunize with noncallable bonds. For callable bonds, the actual horizon often is less than maturity due to the bond being called. (See Chapter 9.)

[7]For proof of this statement, see G. O. Bierwag and George G. Kaufman, "Coping with the Risk of Interest-Rate Fluctuations: A Note," *Journal of Business,* 50 (July 1977): 364–70; and Paul A. Samuelson, "The Effect of Interest-Rate Increases on the Banking System," *American Economic Review,* 35 (March 1945), Appendix B.

[8]The exception to the latter risk is when the maturity of the bond equals the holding period.

Qualifications to Immunizing with Coupon Bonds

In our illustration, we assumed a flat term structure of interest rates and parallel shifts. It is clear that these assumptions do not hold in practice. As a result, it usually is not possible to achieve perfect immunization simply by finding a coupon bond with a duration equal to the intended holding period. However, the relevant question is how effective the use of Macaulay's duration measure is in approximating perfect immunization. If we could model precisely the stochastic processes governing interest-rate behavior, we could devise an investment strategy that would achieve perfect immunization. In order to determine if this is feasible, let us turn to some of the literature. Fisher and Weil were the first to test various immunization strategies with bond data.[9] In this regard, they tested both Macaulay's duration measure, Eq. (6-1), as well as a duration measure in which the weights were based on one-period discount rates, as opposed to yield-to-maturity. The latter duration measure avoids the assumption of a flat term structure. However, parallel interest-rate shifts are still implied, because unexpected changes in interest rates are assumed to follow an additive stochastic process. The authors found that the duration strategies consistently outperformed a buy-and-hold maturity strategy, as well as a naive strategy of annually rolling over a 20-year bond. They concluded that very effective immunization was possible with duration measures.

Others have developed single-factor duration measures, which attempt to map the stochastic processes governing interest-rate fluctuations.[10] However, these studies are mainly theoretical and based on the investor's predicting the correct stochastic process. In simulating alternative strategies for the period 1925–1978 using corporate bond data, G. O. Bierwag, George G. Kaufman, Robert Schweitzer, and Alden Toevs tested five alternative assumptions about the nature of the stochastic process for interest-rate changes.[11] They conclude that the simple Macaulay duration measure does about as well as more complex measures. In all cases, immunization was less than perfect.

Rather than a single-factor model, a number of authors argue for multiple-factor models to give a more complex mapping to the stochastic

[9]Fisher and Weil, "Coping with the Risk."

[10]See G. O. Bierwag, "Immunization, Duration and the Term Structure of Interest Rates," *Journal of Financial and Quantitative Analysis*, 12 (December 1977): 725–43; Chulsoon Khang, "Bond Immunization when Short-Term Rates Fluctuate More than Long-Term Rates," *Journal of Financial and Quantitative Analysis*, 14 (December 1979): 1085–89; and G. O. Bierwag and George G. Kaufman, "Coping with the Risk of Interest-Rate Fluctuations: A Note," *Journal of Business*, 50 (July 1977): 364–70.

[11]G. O. Bierwag, et al., "The Art of Risk Management in Bond Portfolios," *Journal of Portfolio Management*, 7 (Spring 1981): 27–36.

processes governing interest-rate movements.[12] For example, a two-factor model might consist of a duration measure and the spread between long- and short-term rates. Another two-factor model might consist only of the long-term rate and the short-term rate. In the case of a model with more than two factors, many different points on the term structure could be used.

The problem with all these models is that the stochastic process is not stable over time. If it were and the process were known, it could be mapped and appropriate immunization strategies could be devised. The results of limited empirical testing suggest that multiple factor models are relatively unpromising when it comes to immunization.[13] Again, the simple, single-factor Macaulay duration measure does about as well as more complex and rigorous models. Thus, it can be used with about as much confidence as any other immunization model when coupon bonds are involved.

In addition to the immunization procedures described, interest-rate futures markets can be used to obtain similar results. Instead of adjusting the duration of a portfolio by buying and selling bonds, one can buy and sell future contracts to achieve approximate immunization. One advantage of using the futures market is that costs of transactions are much less.[14] Financial futures are the subject of the next chapter, and they represent a logical extension of our discussion of immunization.

PRESENCE OF PURE DISCOUNT BONDS

At the outset of the previous section, we stated that immunization should be undertaken with pure discount (zero-coupon) bonds whenever feasible. One can achieve perfect immunization by locking in a single future payment, which is known with certainty.[15] Until recently, the problem has been that, with the exception of certain fairly short-term securities, the instruments available were coupon securities.[16] This no longer is the case. In 1981, many corporations began to offer zero-coupon bonds,

---

[12]See John C. Cox, Jonathan E. Ingersoll, Jr., and Stephen A. Ross, "Duration and the Measurement of Basis Risk," *Journal of Business,* 52 (January 1979): 51–61.

[13]For an overall discussion of the issues, see G. O. Bierwag, George G. Kaufman, and Alden L. Toevs, "Single Factor Duration Models in a Discrete General Equilibrium Framework," *Journal of Finance,* 37 (May 1982): 325–38. Also, Stephen Schaefer, "Managing Interest Rate Risk," Berkeley Program in Finance Seminar, September 13, 1982.

[14]See Robert W. Kolb and Gerald D. Gay, "Immunizing Bond Portfolios with Interest Rate Futures," *Financial Management,* 11 (Summer 1982): 81–90.

[15]The zero-coupon bond also provides call protection, and certain tax issues are involved. These facets are explored in Chapters 9 and 10.

[16]For a method for deriving zero-coupon interest rates from the market prices of nonzero-coupon bonds, see John Caks, "The Coupon Effect on Yield to Maturity," *Journal of Finance,* 32 (March 1977): 103–15.

as well as bonds with low coupons relative to prevailing rates of interest. If the coupon rate is zero, the bond's return is expressed entirely in terms of the price appreciation to maturity. For a zero-coupon, $1,000 face value, 10-year bond to yield 14 percent to maturity, its initial price must be approximately $258. The return is captured in the present-value difference between the $258 investment and the $1,000 paid at maturity.

Coupon Stripping

In addition to original issue pure discount bonds, a process known as *coupon stripping*—the separation of the coupons from the principal amount of a bond—began in 1982. Once separated, each coupon and each principal payment become separate zero-coupon bonds. For example, if a 13 percent, 5-year bond issue totaling $10 million were sold, there would be $650,000 in semiannual, zero-coupon bonds and a $10 million 5-year, zero-coupon bond. For the most part, the stripping is indirect. An investment banking firm will buy a Treasury security and hold it in trust. Participations are sold in the coupons and principal payments. A participation represents ownership of either a future coupon or principal payment on a Treasury bond held in trust for the participants. Thus, each is a zero-coupon bond and will trade in the market at the appropriate spot rate of interest. To the extent the market was incomplete before, issuers of debt instruments tailor security offerings to the unfilled desires of investors.[17] Institutional investors, such as pension funds, are said to have an appetite for pure discount bonds for immunization purposes. This demand, as well as that of other investors, was a principal impetus to this financial innovation. Why zero-coupon bonds were so long in coming is difficult to understand. Now that they are here, investors should look first to pure discount bonds when contemplating immunization.

Term Structure of Pure Discount Bonds

The increasing presence of pure discount instruments and the developing secondary market for such instruments allow a yield curve based on them to be constructed. This yield curve is known as the *spot rate yield curve,* as described in the previous chapter. While its construction may be crude, owing to a lack of certain observations, as more pure discount bonds become available in the secondary market precision will be added. The

---

[17]Complete markets exist when every contingency in the world corresponds to a distinct marketable security. Incomplete markets exist when the number and types of securities available do not span these contingencies.

spot rate yield curve will almost always differ from a yield curve based on coupon paying bonds. The former is represented by yield observations for a single payment at the end of year n. For coupon paying bonds, the yield observations pertain to a principal payment at the end of year n, together with coupon payments through year n. In this case, yield-to-maturity is a weighted average of the spot discount rates applicable to each of the coupon and principal payments. Obviously the durations of the two bonds are different, and this difference increases with the maturity of the observation, as well as with the coupon rate of the coupon bond. In short, apples and oranges are involved in the construction of the two yield curves.

For each future payment of a bond, there exists in theory a spot rate that discounts that payment to its present value. Earlier, these spot rates were mainly theoretical, as we did not have markets for pure discount bonds. Such observations now are possible in increasing number. To determine if coupon stripping results in a higher valuation for the sum of the parts than for the whole, each coupon and principal payment should be discounted by the appropriate rate on the spot rate yield curve. If the present-value sum of these discounted payments exceeds the bond's price in the market, stripping a bond's coupons and selling the separate parts is worthwhile. Of course, this opportunity will persist only as long as the market remains incomplete in the sense that there is an unsatisfied demand for pure discount bonds. We would expect the forces of competition among coupon strippers, as well as original issuers selling zero-coupon bonds, to eventually satisfy the demand. At that point, the markets for pure discount bonds and coupon bonds would be in equilibrium and financial markets would be complete with respect to this dimension. It is only if the supply of pure discount bonds is not responsive to the demand function that an incomplete market exists.

With a complete market, there would be sufficient pure discount bonds spanning all maturity areas, and they would be efficiently priced in relation to coupon bonds. More specifically, all future coupon and principal payments would be discounted by the appropriate market spot rates for pure discount bonds, and the valuation of all bonds would be so determined. The distinction between maturity and coupon effects would disappear with such asset pricing. As a result, the investor would be provided with considerable flexibility in matching the cash flows arising from bond investments with a desired cash flow pattern. Moreover, investors would be able to manage their risk-return tradeoffs more effectively. Indeed, the increasing presence of pure discount bonds is changing dramatically the management of bond portfolios.

SUMMARY

Price changes in bonds that accompany a shift in interest depend in part on the coupon rate. The lower the coupon, the greater the price change for a given shift in interest rates. The reason for this is that more of the total return is realized at maturity when the principal is paid, as opposed to interim coupon payments. The problems associated with the coupon effect led to the development of the duration measure, which is a time-weighted average of interest and principal payments. Duration represents the average life of an investment on a present-value basis. For a coupon bond, duration is always less than maturity. While duration increases with maturity for bonds trading at par or above, for discount bonds it eventually declines with maturity.

Immunization consists of arranging a bond portfolio so that its payouts approximate a desired stream of payouts as nearly as possible. A single payout is perfectly immunized if it is insensitive to subsequent fluctuations in interest rates. Whenever feasible, one should immunize with pure discount bonds. With coupon bonds, immunization is more difficult. Both price risk and coupon reinvestment risk are involved, and these risks work in opposite directions. If the term structure were flat and only parallel interest rate shifts occurred, perfect immunization could be achieved by finding a bond whose duration equaled the intended holding period. As these assumptions do not hold in practice, a number of authors have devised more complicated models to map the stochastic processes governing interest-rate fluctuations. However, these models appear to do little better in immunizing a coupon-bond portfolio than a simple duration measure. In all cases, immunization is less than perfect with coupon bonds.

In recent years, there have been a number of zero-coupon, original-issue bonds, as well as indirect zero-coupon bonds that result from coupon stripping. The existence of an incomplete market made such instruments valuable in satisfying the needs of certain investors. As equilibrium is established between pure discount bonds and coupon bonds, we will be able to construct a spot rate yield curve. This yield curve will differ from one based on coupon bonds, owing to differences in duration, but it will serve as the foundation for discounting future payments to present value and, accordingly, for bond valuation.

SELECTED REFERENCES

Bierwag, G. O., and George G. Kaufman, "Coping with the Risk of Interest Rate Fluctuations: A Note," *Journal of Business,* 50 (July 1977): 364–70.

Bierwag, G. O., George G. Kaufman, and Alden Toevs, eds., *Innovations in Bond*

Portfolio Management: Duration Analysis and Immunization. Greenwich, Conn.: JAI Press, 1982.

Bierwag, G.O., George G. Kaufman, and Alden L. Toevs, "Single Factor Duration Models in a Discrete General Equilibrium Framework," *Journal of Finance,* 37 (May 1982): 325–38.

Caks, John, "The Coupon Effect on Yield to Maturity," *Journal of Finance,* 32 (March 1977): 103–16.

Cox, John C., Jonathan E. Ingersoll, Jr., and Stephen A. Ross, "Duration and the Measurement of Basis Risk," *Journal of Business,* 52 (January 1979): 51–61.

Fisher, Lawrence, and Roman L. Weil, "Coping with the Risk of Interest-Rate Fluctuations: Returns to Bondholders from Naive and Optimal Strategies," *Journal of Business,* 44 (October 1971): 408–31.

Homer, Sidney, and Martin L. Leibowitz, *Inside the Yield Book,* Englewood Cliffs, N.J.: Prentice-Hall, Inc., 1972.

Hopewell, Michael H., and George G. Kaufman, "Bond Price Volatility and Term to Maturity: A Generalized Respecification," *American Economic Review,* LXIII (September 1973): 749–53.

Ingersoll, Jonathan E., Jr., Jeffrey Skelton and Roman L. Weil, "Duration Forty Years Later," *Journal of Financial and Quantitative Analysis,* 13 (November 1978): 627–50.

Leibowitz, Martin L., and Alfred Weinberger, "The Uses of Contingent Immunization," *Journal of Portfolio Management,* 8 (Fall 1981): 51–55.

Macaulay, Frederick R., *Some Theoretical Problems Suggested by the Movements of Interest Rates, Bond Yields, and Stock Prices in the United States since 1856.* New York: National Bureau of Economic Research, 1938.

Weil, Roman L., "Macaulay's Duration: An Appreciation," *Journal of Business,* 46 (October 1973): 589–92.

7

INTEREST RATE FUTURES

In the 1970s and 1980s, there developed a number of financial futures markets, and interest in them has boomed. Transactions have multiplied rapidly, and a wide variety of parties participate. By way of definition, a *futures contract* is a standardized agreement traded on an exchange that calls for delivery of a commodity at some specified future date. In the case of financial futures, the commodity is a security. Once a contract is traded, the clearinghouse of the exchange interposes itself between the buyer and seller. Its creditworthiness is substituted for that of the other party, and each exchange has a number of rules governing transactions. As in commodities, very few financial futures contracts involve actual delivery at maturity. Rather, buyers and sellers of a contract independently take offsetting positions to close out the contract. The seller cancels a contract by buying another contract; the buyer, by selling another contract. As a result of offsetting positions before maturity, only a small percentage of contracts come to actual delivery. The *open interest* is the number of futures contracts outstanding, which have not been closed.

While futures markets for commodities have been around for some time, the first financial futures market began in late 1975. The number of markets has grown and their development and use represents an important financial innovation. Table 7-1 lists the markets for interest rate futures. The rapid spread of these markets has been nothing short of sensational, and other futures markets are on the drawing board. One impetus to this

Table 7-1. *Financial Futures Markets for Fixed Rate Instruments at the End of 1982*

Market	Treasury Bills	Treasury Notes	Treasury Bonds	Commercial Paper	Bank C.D.'s	GNMA	Euro-dollars
Contract Size:	$1 million	$100,000	$100,000	$3 million, 30-Day. $1 million, 90-day.	$1 million	$100,000	$1 million
Security Delivered:	Treasury bill specified (91-day, 182-day or 1 year)	4-6 year maturity Treasury note, based on 8% coupon	15 year or more maturity Treasury bond, based on 8% coupon	Prime commercial paper approved by Exchange of 30 or 90 days	3 month C.D. of prime grade banks approved by Exchange	Modified pass-through mortgage backed certificates GNMA guaranteed, based on 8% coupon, 12 yrs.	Cash settlement contract at LIBOR rate for 3-month deposit
Exchanges*:	ACE COMEX IMM	CBOT IMM	ACE CBOT	CBOT	ACE CBOT COMEX	IMM CBOT NYFE	IMM
Date Started:	Jan. 1976	June 1979	Aug. 1977	Sept. 1977	July 1981	Oct. 1975	Dec. 1981

*Exchanges: ACE = Amex Commodities Exchange
CBOT = Chicago Board of Trade
COMEX = Commodity Exchange, New York
IMM = International Monetary Market of the Chicago Mercantile Exchange
NYFE = New York Futures Exchange of the New York Stock Exchange

boom was the high and volatile interest rates that occurred in the late 1970s and early 1980s. The desire to transfer risk is a prominent factor in the growth of transactions. Of the futures markets shown in Table 7-1, the strongest are Treasury bills, Treasury bonds, and GNMA (Government National Mortgage Association) pass-through mortgages.

TRANSACTIONS IN FUTURES MARKETS

To illustrate a transaction, first consider the market for 91-day Treasury bills on the Chicago Mercantile Exchange. Each contract is for $1 million face value of 90- to 92-day bills, with delivery months of March, June, September, and December (third week of the month). At present, eight delivery months are traded, going out to nearly two years. Suppose the price of 91-day bills for delivery in March of next year is $90. The discount from the face value of $100 is $10, and the yield on a bank discount basis is $10/$100 = 10 percent. Suppose a contract representing $1 million of Treasury bills to be delivered in the third week of March next year is purchased. In order to assure payment, *margin* of $2,000 per contract must be put up. This is effectively a security deposit.

Each day, the futures contract is *marked-to-market* in the sense that it is valued at the closing price. If the price declines and the account goes below the prescribed minimum, additional margin is required in order to maintain the position. If the price rises, excess margin occurs and may be drawn out. The seller of the contract also must maintain margin, again as a security deposit. If the price of the futures contract declines, excess margin occurs for the seller; if the price increases, the seller must put up additional margin. Thus, price movements of futures contracts affect the margin positions of the buyer and seller in opposite ways. Settlement occurs not at the end of the contract, but daily. In other words, the winners and losers make daily adjustments in cash.

To illustrate the nature of a longer-term market, consider interest-rate futures for Treasury bonds. Futures markets for these instruments are provided on the Chicago Board of Trade and the Amex Commodities Exchange. The trading unit for a single contract is $100,000, in contrast to $1 million for Treasury bills. Price quotations are given as a percentage of the face value ($100) of an 8 percent coupon with 20 years to maturity. A quotation of $81\frac{4}{32}$ would mean $81\frac{1}{8}$ percent of $100, or $81.125. The initial margin requirement on Treasury bond futures is around $1,500 per contract. As with Treasury bills, the contract is marked-to-market daily and appropriate settlements are made.

Delivery months are March, June, September, and December, and contracts go out about 2¾ years. For delivery, any Treasury bond with at least 15 years to the earliest call date or to maturity may be used. This contrasts with Treasury bills, where a specific maturity bill is specified in the contract. Because most bonds have a coupon rate other than 8 percent, the invoice is the settlement price multiplied by a conversion factor. Recall that the futures contract settlement price is based on a coupon rate of 8 percent. Therefore, the conversion factor is greater than 1.00 for coupon rates greater than 8 percent, 1.00 for an 8 percent coupon bond, and less than 1.00 for coupon rates less than 8 percent. The greater the deviation in coupon rate from 8 percent, the greater the deviation in conversion factor from 1.00. Conversion factors are established for each delivery date and are used in all transactions. Naturally, the sellers of a contract will attempt to deliver the "cheapest" bond of those that qualify. This is the bond that has the highest conversion value (futures contract settlement price times the conversion factor) relative to the spot price for the bond in the market.

In both Treasury bills and bonds, exchanges impose limits on daily price movements. For example, the price limit on Treasury bonds is $2 per $100 of face value, or $2,000 per contract. The reasons for these limits are controversial, but their presence in futures markets is well established and likely to continue.

HEDGING A POSITION

Hedging represents taking a future contract position opposite to a position taken in the spot market. The purpose is to reduce risk exposure by protecting oneself from unexpected price changes. In contrast, a *speculator* takes positions in futures markets in the pursuit of profits and assumes price risk in this endeavor. The speculator buys or sells futures contracts based on an interest-rate forecast. For a futures market to operate effectively, there must be both hedgers and speculators. Otherwise the shifting of risk would depend on hetereogeneous expectations. In what follows, we describe in general two types of hedges. This is followed by a more detailed inquiry into the amount of remaining risk after a hedged position is undertaken.

Long Hedges

A *long hedge* involves buying (going long in) a futures contract. It is generally employed to lock in an interest rate that is believed to be high. Suppose an investor will have $1 million to invest in Treasury bonds 2 months hence—on November 1, for example. The investor believes interest rates have peaked at present and wishes to lock in the current high rates (on September 1), even though the funds will not be available for investment for 2 months.

Suppose the conditions shown in Table 7-2 held for September 1 and December 1, respectively. In the example, we ignore transaction costs and margin deposits. We also assume the use of 8 percent coupon bonds in the spot market, so we do not need a conversion factor. The investor buys ten futures contracts on September 1, and prices rise and yields fall as expected. By selling the contracts on November 1, the investor realizes a gain of $62,500. On the same day, the investor purchases $1 million in Treasury bonds at a higher price and lower yield than prevailed on September 1. The opportunity loss is $67,187.50. Thus, the opportunity loss is offset, but not entirely so, by the gain on the futures contracts. The hedge was less than perfect, but it was largely successful in insulating the investor from price changes.

Short Hedges

A *short hedge* involves the opposite sort of transactions. Here the idea is to sell a futures contract now because of a belief that interest rates will rise. The sale of the futures contract is used as substitute for the sale of an actual security held. Another example of a short hedge is a corporation that needs to borrow in the future and sells a futures contract now to protect itself against an expected rise in interest rates. Suppose on February 1, a corporation knows it will need to borrow $1 million in the long-term bond market 3 months hence. The company feels interest rates will rise and wishes to hedge against this possibility.

Unfortunately, there is no futures market for long-term corporate bonds. Therefore, the company must look to a related market and settles on the Treasury bond futures market. While interest rates in these two markets do not move entirely in concert, there is a close relationship, so

Table 7-2. Illustration of a Long Hedge

Cash Market	Futures Market
September 1: 8% Treasury bond sells at $71\frac{15}{32}$. Investor wants to lock in high yield.	September 1: Buys ten December Treasury bond futures contracts at $72\frac{9}{32}$.
November 1: Buys $1 million of 8% Treasury bond at $78\frac{6}{32}$.	November 1: Sells ten December bond futures contracts at $78\frac{17}{32}$.
Loss: $67,187.50	Gain: $62,500

Table 7-3. Illustration of a Short Cross Hedge

Cash Market	Futures Market

February 1:
  $13\frac{1}{2}\%$ high grade, 20-year corporate bond sells at $99\frac{3}{8}$. Issuer wants to protect against rise in rates.
	February 1:
	  Sells fourteen June 8% Treasury bond futures contracts at $72\frac{2}{32}$.

May 1:
  Issues $13\frac{1}{2}\%$ corporate bond at $91\frac{7}{8}$.
	May 1:
	  Buys fourteen June 8% Treasury bond futures contracts at $66\frac{8}{32}$.

Loss: $75,000.	Gain: $81,375

a *cross hedge* across markets makes sense. This type of hedge is shown in Table 7-3. Again we ignore transaction costs and margin deposits. Instead of selling ten Treasury bond futures contracts, the company sells fourteen, to bring its total commitment to a little over $1 million in the futures market. Thus, the *hedge ratio* is 1.4. The reason that the hedge ratio is greater than 1.0 is that the price is lower on the 8 percent coupon Treasury bond used in the futures market than it is on the 13½ percent coupon corporate bond. Because the cross markets do not have exactly the same price movements, a perfect hedge is not achieved. In this case the gain in the futures market more than offsets the opportunity loss in the spot market. These examples are sufficient to illustrate the principles of hedging and some of the terms. We turn now to a more in-depth analysis.

Basis in Hedging

The examples show that hedging is not perfect in eliminating all the risk of a position. In hedging, market participants are concerned with fluctuations in the *basis,* which portrays the risk to the hedger.[1] The basis is simply the price of a security in the spot market minus its futures price (adjusted by the appropriate conversion factor). Hedgers, of course, are concerned about their net positions at the closeout of a futures contract. If the hedger holds 8 percent Treasury bonds long and sells futures contracts in equivalent amount, both the spot price and the futures price are uncertain at the closeout. At this close, the hedger will receive $\tilde{S}_c$ in the spot market for each bond held long. The futures price at that time is depicted by $\tilde{F}_c$,

---

[1]This example is based on Douglas T. Breeden, "Some Common Misconceptions about Futures Trading," Stanford Business School Teaching Note, June, 1981.

whereas the futures price at the time the contract is sold is F_0. The latter is known with certainty.

At the closeout the net funds received are the funds realized from the sale of the bonds held long, together with the gain or loss on the futures position. This can be expressed as

$$\text{net funds received} = Q\tilde{S}_c - Q(\tilde{F}_c - F_o) \qquad (7\text{-}1)$$

where Q is the number of bonds involved in both the long position and the short position in the futures market. Rearranging the equation, we have

$$\text{net funds received} = QF_0 + Q(\tilde{S}_c - \tilde{F}_c) \qquad (7\text{-}2)$$

Thus, the net funds received depend on the futures price at the time of the hedge, which is known, and the difference between the price received on the sale of bonds in the spot market and the futures price at the close, both of which are uncertain. As both terms of the basis are uncertain at the closeout, the overall hedge is not free of risk. To be sure, risk has been reduced considerably from what would occur with only a long position or only a futures position, because spot and futures markets tend to move in similar ways. However, risk is not totally eliminated and the residual risk is represented by the fluctuations in the basis, or in *basis risk,* as it is known.

Fluctuations in basis for the 14 percent Treasury bonds of 2006–11 are shown in Fig. 7-1. At the top of the figure, the prices over time of the bond and of the futures contract are shown. Because the bond has a higher coupon rate than the 8 percent coupon used for Treasury bond futures contracts, it is necessary to adjust it by a conversion factor. (The need for this adjustment was previously discussed.) In this case, the conversion factor is 1.6359, and the price of the futures contract is multiplied by that factor. When the adjusted futures price is subtracted from the bond's spot price, the basis is obtained; it is shown in the lower panel of the figure. While the basis fluctuates much less than either of the two price series in the top panel, it nonetheless does vary over time. As the delivery month approaches, the two sets of prices tend to converge and the basis approaches zero. However, prior to this time there is basis risk for the hedged position.

MARKET EFFICIENCY

If a future price is significantly out of line with prices in the spot market, there is opportunity for arbitrage. For financial futures, such an opportunity can be judged by comparing the rate of return on a futures

Source: Chicago Board of Trade, *An Introduction to Financial Futures,* p. 39. Chart courtesy of Data Lab Corp., Chicago, Ill.

Figure 7-1. Spot, futures and basis prices 14% Treasury Bonds of 2006–2011.

contract with the corresponding forward rate embodied in the term structure of interest rates. A futures contract on Treasury bills, for example, specifies a given return on 91-day bills so many days in the future, numbering m. If there existed an m-day Treasury bill and an $(m+91)$-day Treasury bill in the spot market, a forward rate may be derived using the formula given in Chapter 5. If rates of interest on future contracts differ significantly from forward rates, the markets are said to be inefficient. On the other hand, if arbitrage brings the returns into parity, no further opportunities for arbitrage would exist and the markets would be said to be efficient.

Should the futures rate exceed the forward rate, an arbitrager could buy a futures contract for 91-day Treasury bills delivered m days hence and essentially short a forward contract in the spot market for the same period, namely m to $m + 91$ days in the future. The latter might be accomplished by establishing a short position in Treasury bills maturing in $m + 91$ days and using the exact proceeds of the short sale to buy Treasury bills maturing in m days. Ignoring transaction costs and margin requirements, the cash inflows from the proceeds of the bills maturing on the mth day will exceed the cash outflow needed to take delivery on the futures contract on the mth day. On the $(m+91)$st day, the proceeds realized on the maturing bills will equal the outflow associated with maturation of the originally shorted $(m+91)$-day bills.

If the forward rate exceeds the futures rate, the arbitrager will wish to sell a futures contract for 91-day bills to be delivered m days hence and buy a forward contract for the same time frame. In this case, the latter might be accomplished by establishing a short position in m-day Treasury bills and using the exact proceeds to buy $(m + 91)$-day bills. On the mth day, the Treasury bills held long are used to make delivery on the futures contract. The cash inflows realized from delivery of the bills on this contract will exceed the cash outflow associated with maturation of the originally shorted m-day bills if we again ignore transaction costs and margin requirements. In both of these situations, there is no risk to the arbitrager. In efficient markets then, arbitrage could be expected to bring forward rates and future rates into parity.

Possible Reasons for Deviation of Forward and Futures Rates

However, there are reasons that the futures rate may not equal the forward rate. For one thing there are transaction costs to arbitrage. These consist of: (1) costs involved in opening and closing a futures position, including margin requirements; (2) costs of buying and selling securities long in the spot market; and (3) cost of establishing a short position in the spot market. With respect to a short position, the arbitrager must post collateral equal in value to the securities borrowed, as well as pay a percentage premium for such securities. This premium, around $\frac{1}{2}$ percent on an annualized basis for Treasury bills, means that the dollar cost of the premium increases with the time to maturity. The effect here would be a tendency for forward rates to exceed futures rates for more distant maturities, all other things the same.[2] For both margin deposits on futures contracts and collateral deposits on short positions, securities can be deposited. As a result, the arbitrager does not suffer an opportunity loss on the funds. The costs of opening and closing a futures position and of buying and selling securities long in the spot market are relatively small in magnitude. Moreover, they are nondirectional; they simply establish a band within which arbitrage is not profitable. Only the cost of short selling for longer maturities is directional, and it argues for forward rates exceeding futures rates.

Futures and forward contracts are different in that there are daily settlements of the futures position, while settlement of the forward contract comes only at maturity. As discussed previously, the futures position is marked-to-market with daily settlements throughout the life of the contract. Each day the losing party, either the buyer or the seller of the futures contract, must pay the full amount of the futures price change that day. If the daily interest rate at which such funds can be invested is stochastic, the arbitrage hedge described above would not be entirely free of risk. Technically, the day-to-day debits and credits must be taken into account. John C. Cox, Jonathan E. Ingersoll, Jr., and Stephen A. Ross developed a model for valuing futures and forward contracts that incorporates differences in settling-up procedures.[3] The instantaneous interest rate is assumed to follow a mean reverting diffusion process. Under this assumption, they find that if futures and spot prices are positively correlated, the futures contract price will be less than the forward contract price, because more risk is involved with the former. If they are negatively correlated, the futures contract price will exceed the forward contract price. However, differences in settling-up procedures on futures and forward contracts generally result in relatively small differences in prices of the two contracts using the Cox, Ingersoll, and Ross model.[4]

A third factor perhaps responsible for differences in futures and forward rates is differences in default risk on the two types of contracts. In the case of a purchase of a Treasury security, there is no default risk. In a futures contract for a Treasury security, however, there is a slight risk of nondelivery. The futures contract is backed by the clearinghouse in-

---

[2]See Dennis R. Capozza and Bradford Cornell, "Treasury Bill Pricing in the Spot and Futures Markets," *Review of Economics and Statistics,* 61 (November 1979): 517–19, for a detailed analysis of these costs.

[3]John C. Cox, Jonathan E. Ingersoll, Jr. and Stephen A. Ross, "The Relation between Forward Prices and Futures Prices," *Journal of Financial Economics,* 9 (December 1981): 321–46. See also Robert A. Jarrow and George S. Oldfield, "Forward and Futures Contracts," *Journal of Financial Economics,* 9 (December 1981): 373–82.

[4]See Richard J. Rendelman, Jr. and Christopher E. Carabini, "The Efficiency of the Treasury Bill Futures Market," *Journal of Finance,* 34 (September 1979): 897. However, if interest rates get very volatile, the effect will be more important.

volved in the transaction, but still it is not entirely free of risk. In the case of a short position needed to produce a forward contract, the risk is perhaps that of nonperformance by the other party. However, if this party is a major financial institution, there is little such risk. For both futures and the forward contracts, there is little in the way of default risk and any net directional effect is unclear.[5]

Empirical Evidence on Market Efficiency

There have been a number of tests comparing returns on futures contracts and derived forward contracts. Most have involved Treasury bills, a fact not surprising in view of the vitality of this futures market and the fact that it was one of the first to open (early 1976). Overall, the evidence is mixed as to whether the Treasury bill futures and forward markets are efficient in the sense of future rates equaling forward rates. For the most part, the focus has been on the presence or absence of arbitrage opportunities.

Earlier tests of Treasury bills by Donald J. Puglisi and also Richard W. Lang and Robert H. Rasche proclaimed to find market inefficiency.[6] The former found that investors could earn higher returns with combinations of different maturity Treasury bills and bill futures contracts than Treasury bills alone. Lang and Rasche tested for systematic arbitrage opportunities and found that with the exception of short distant contracts, future rates were significantly above forward rates. Arbitrage opportunities were more frequent in the more distant contracts, and here the authors found no tendency for this inefficiency to diminish over the sample period. The authors performed essentially the same tests as William Poole in an earlier study and sample period,[7] but with different results. In Poole's study, some future rates were found to be significantly below forward rates.

---

[5]Prior to the 1981 Tax Act for individuals but not dealers, there was a differential taxation of futures contracts held over 6 months and forward contracts. It was possible to realize capital gains on the futures contract if the contract had a profit. If not, the individual could take delivery of the security and sell it in the spot market for an ordinary income loss. For Treasury bill forward contract transactions in the spot market, all gains and losses were reported as ordinary income regardless of maturity. This asymmetric tax treatment may have resulted in greater demand for and lower interest rates on futures contracts of over 6 months than forward contracts. See Bradford Cornell, "A Note on Taxes and the Pricing of Treasury Bills Futures Contracts," *Journal of Finance,* 36 (June 1981): 1169–76. The 1981 Tax Act eliminated this differential tax effect, making uniform the tax treatment.

[6]Donald J. Puglisi, "Is the Futures Market for Treasury Bills Efficient?" *Journal of Portfolio Management,* 4 (Winter 1978): 64–7; and Richard W. Lang and Robert H. Rasche, "A Comparison of Yields on Futures Contracts and Implied Forward Rates," *Review of the Federal Reserve Bank of St. Louis,* 60 (December 1978): 21–30.

[7]William Poole, "Using T. Bill Futures to Gauge Interest Rate Expectations," *Review of the Federal Reserve Bank of San Francisco,* (Spring 1978): 7–19.

However, the deviations were not sufficient to make arbitrage profitable. He concluded that futures prices were efficient.

Rodney L. Jacobs and Robert A. Jones also tested Treasury bill futures during the late 1970s and found evidence of significant arbitrage opportunities.[8] This was particularly true for more distant contracts, where the futures rate exceeded the forward rate on many occasions. However, contracts introduced near the end of the sample period, 1978, did not offer nearly the arbitrage opportunities as earlier contracts. In another study, Dennis R. Capozza and Bradford Cornell tested for profitable arbitrage opportunities in Treasury bills.[9] The authors found that while near-term contracts were efficiently priced, more-distant contract forward rates exceeded future rates, and the differential increased with maturity. The authors attributed this phenomenon to the premium cost of short selling, described earlier, and to a possible reluctance of institutions to enter the futures market. The former would limit arbitrage profitability, so the finding of a significant difference between forward and futures rates does not necessarily support the presence of arbitrage opportunities.

Richard J. Rendelman and Christopher E. Carabine tested whether arbitrage opportunities were possible with Treasury bills.[10] They found that futures contracts in the nearest contract month tended to be overpriced relative to forward contracts, while long-term futures contracts were underpriced. However, when transactions costs were taken into account, there was little in the way of arbitrage opportunity. Therefore, futures markets were concluded to be largely efficient. Brian G. Chow and David J. Brophy extensively analyzed the Treasury bill futures market and concluded that habitat premiums are needed to explain futures rates relative to forward rates in the spot market.[11] This premium, which is either demanded or sacrificed, is said to be necessary to attract certain investors into the futures market, as opposed to the spot market. The authors analyzed arbitrage opportunities available to owners not only of spot Treasury bills, but also combinations of spot and futures bills. They claimed that the yield differentials between futures and forward markets can be explained only in terms of differential habitat premiums.

For futures markets other than Treasury bills, there have been very few studies. In an exception to this statement, Bruce G. Resnick and Elizabeth Hennigar studied the futures and spot markets for U. S. Treasury

---

[8]Rodney L. Jacobs and Robert A. Jones, "The Treasury Bill Futures Market," *Journal of Political Economy*, 88 (August 1980): 699–721.

[9]Cappoza and Cornell, "Treasury Bill Pricing," pp. 513–20.

[10]Richard J. Rendelman and Christopher E. Carabini, "The Efficiency of the Treasury Bill Futures Market," *Journal of Finance*, 34 (September 1979): 895–914.

[11]Brian G. Chow and David J. Brophy, "Treasury Bills Futures Market: A Formulation and Interpretation," *Journal of Futures Markets*, 2 (Spring 1982): 25–47. See Chapter 5 of this book for a discussion of the habitat notion.

bonds.[12] The authors analyzed whether arbitrage profits are possible. Their analysis focuses on the Treasury bond which is "cheapest to deliver" in the sense of buying it in the spot market to satisfy a futures contract. A number of different hedges were tested, using this issue and a futures contract to establish the hedge. After adjusting for transaction costs and some abnormal observations, the authors found that the average net return on hedges was very small. As these hedges were not perfectly riskless and large investments were necessary, they interpreted their results to be consistent with *ex post* market efficiency.

In summary, most tests of market efficiency involve the possibility of arbitrage profits due to differences between forward rates in the spot market and futures rates. Almost all studies have focused on Treasury bills, a preoccupation that we hope will change as experience is gained with other, newer futures markets. The majority suggest that near-term futures contracts are efficiently priced, particularly in recent years. For longer-term contracts, a significant differential between forward and future rates appears on occasion. This differential may offer an arbitrage opportunity after transaction costs. However, the direction of the bias differs depending on the study and the time frame investigated. Therefore, it is difficult to generalize as to market efficiency for longer-term Treasury bill contracts. In the only study of Treasury bond futures reviewed, the results were consistent with market efficiency.

SUMMARY

Interest rate futures markets have grown tremendously in importance in recent years and now span a number of financial instruments. The contract itself is standardized and traded on an exchange; it calls for the delivery of either a specific financial instrument or one of a basket of approved instruments at a specified future date. Both the buyer and the seller must maintain a small amount of margin as a security deposit. Each day the value of the contract is marked-to-market, with the losing party required to put up additional margin in a daily settlement procedure.

Hedging involves taking a futures position opposite to that taken in the spot market in order to substantially reduce exposure to risk. There are long hedges, short hedges, and cross hedges (across different financial instruments). A speculator takes positions in the futures market in anticipation of profiting from interest-rate movements. Hedging usually does not eliminate all risk; basis risk remains. The basis is the spot price minus the futures price, and fluctuations in this basis represent risk to the hedger.

---

[12]Bruce G. Resnick and Elizabeth Hennigar, "The Relationship between Futures and Cash Prices for U.S. Treasury Bonds," paper presented at the Financial Management Association meetings, October 14, 1982.

Market efficiency concerns whether or not there are arbitrage opportunities between the futures and the spot markets. Such opportunities usually are judged by comparing the futures rate with the forward rate embodied in the spot market for the same future period. Several possible reasons exist for deviations. These are transactions costs, particularly those associated with short selling in the spot market, different settlement procedures for the two types of contracts, and possible differences in default risk. The empirical evidence on market efficiency (mostly Treasury bills) was reviewed, and it was sufficiently mixed to make generalizations difficult.

SELECTED REFERENCES

An Introduction to Financial Futures. Chicago: Chicago Board of Trade, 1983.

Arak, Marcelle, and Christopher J. McCurdy, "Interest Rates Futures," *Federal Reserve Bank of New York Quarterly Review*, 4 (Winter 1979–80): 33–46.

Capozza, Dennis R., and Bradford Cornell, "Treasury Bill Pricing in the Spot and Futures Markets," *Review of Economics and Statistics*, 61 (November 1979): 513–20.

Chow, Brian G., and David J. Brophy, "Treasury Bills Futures Market: A Formulation and Interpretation," *Journal of Futures Markets*, 2 (Spring 1982): 25–47.

Cornell, Bradford, "A Note on Taxes and the Pricing of Treasury Bills Futures Contracts," *Journal of Finance*, 36 (June 1981): 1169–76.

Cox, John C., Jonathan E. Ingersoll, Jr., and Stephen A. Ross, "The Relation between Forward Prices and Futures Prices," *Journal of Financial Economics*, 9 (December 1981): 321–46.

Jacobs, Rodney L., and Robert A. Jones, "The Treasury Bill Futures Market," *Journal of Political Economy*, 88 (August 1980): 699–721.

Jarrow, Robert A., and George S. Oldfield, "Forward and Futures Contracts," *Journal of Financial Economics*, 9 (December 1981): 373–82.

Jones, Frank J., "The Integration of the Cash and Futures Markets for Treasury Securities," *Journal of Futures Markets*, 1 (Spring 1981): 33–58.

———, "Spreads: Tails, Turtles and All That," *Journal of Futures Markets*, 1 (Winter 1981): 565–96.

Lang, Richard W., and Robert H. Rasche, "A Comparison of Yields on Futures Contracts and Implied Forward Rates," *Review of the Federal Reserve Bank of St. Louis*, 60 (December 1978): 21–30.

Rendelman, Richard J., Jr., and Christopher E. Carabini, "The Efficiency of the Treasury Bill Futures Market," *Journal of Finance*, 34 (September 1979): 895–914.

Resnick, Bruce G., and Elizabeth Hennigar, "The Relationship between Futures and Cash Prices for U.S. Treasury Bonds," paper presented at the Financial Management Association meetings, October 14, 1982.

8

THE DEFAULT-RISK STRUCTURE
OF INTEREST RATES

In Chapters 5 and 6 we examined two reasons for relative differences in market rates of interest—the term to maturity and the coupon rate.

In this chapter, an additional reason is examined—the default risk of the security involved. This is simply the risk that the borrower will default in the contractual payment of principal or interest. The default-risk structure of interest rates depicts the relationship between the yield on securities and their risk of default, holding all other factors constant. In particular, maturity is held constant by studying different financial instruments of the same maturity. The relationship between yield and default risk may be similar to that shown in Fig. 8-1. In the figure, yield is plotted along the vertical axis and risk along the horizontal. The intercept on the vertical axis represents the yield on a default-free security; for all practical purposes, it represents the yield on Treasury securities. The figure shows that investors demand a higher yield, the greater the perceived risk of default.

PROMISED, REALIZED, AND EXPECTED RATES

In this chapter a *risk premium* is defined as the differential in yield between a security being studied and a default-free one, with all factors other than default risk being held constant. It is represented in Fig. 8-1 by the distance on the vertical axis between the intercept and the yield on the security being studied.

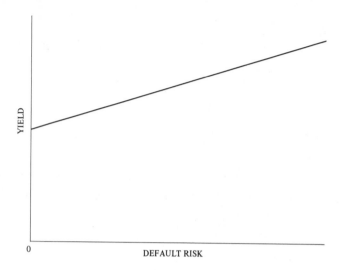

Figure 8-1. Yield-default risk relationship.

The *promised rate* on a security is the *ex ante* yield at a moment in time. If a corporation issues a bond with a 14 percent coupon rate at a price of $1,000 to the public, the rate promised by the issuer is 14 percent. However, if the bond rises in price so that 1 month later it yields $13\frac{1}{2}$ percent to maturity, the promised rate at that time would be $13\frac{1}{2}$ percent. It is important to recognize that the promised rate is not necessarily the rate actually realized if the bond is held to maturity.

The *realized rate* is the rate of discount that equates all payments actually received by investors, including the final principal payment, with the market price of the security at the time the security was purchased. Any difference between the promised rate at the time the security was bought and the realized rate is known as the *loss rate* attributable to default.[1] It is clear that if the issuer does not default in the payment of principal and interest, the promised and the realized rates are the same.

At any moment in time, the risk structure of interest rates is determined by differences between promised rates and *expected* rates—the latter being the rate investors at the margin actually expect to receive. If there is a possibility of default, the expected yield on a security will be less than the promised one. To carry this reasoning one step further, if financial markets were perfect and investors' risk neutral, the rate expected by investors at the margin would equal the rate on a default-free security. In other words, the difference between the promised rate and the expected rate on a security would correspond to the risk premium defined earlier.

[1]This assumes that we have held constant all other factors, in particular callability. See W. Braddock Hickman, *Corporate Bond Quality and Investor Experience* (New York: National Bureau of Economic Research, 1958), introductory chapter and pp. 64–66.

The implication of this notion is that the differential between the promised and default-free rates is equal to the expected default loss for investors at the margin.

Distribution of Possible Returns

To better understand this notion, consider the behavior of a perspective investor. At some moment in time, the investor foresees a number of possible returns associated with owning a risky fixed-income security. We might picture the investor forming a subjective probability distribution of these returns. This distribution is not symmetrical, but highly skewed to the left. For the typical fixed-income security, there is a high probability that the issuer will meet all principal and interest payments. However, no probability exists for the realized yield to exceed the promised yield, assuming the security is held to maturity.[2] The promised rate, then, represents the highest return possible from holding the security to maturity. However, if the issuer defaults in any of the principal or interest payments, the realized rate will be less than this promised rate.

Legally, an issuer defaults anytime it is unable to meet the terms of the contract. However, degrees of default vary from a simple extension all the way to liquidation involving legal procedures. An extension is nothing more than creditors extending the maturity of the obligation voluntarily or allowing the postponement of interest payments. Because of the time value of money, however, the realized yield will be less than the promised yield even in the case of an extension. To illustrate, suppose that the promised yield on a 20-year security at the time of issuance were 15 percent, the market price $1,000, and the coupon rate 15 percent. Suppose, however, that the issuer was unable to meet the annual interest payment at the end of the third year and that this payment were postponed until the end of the fourth year, at which time it was paid. Suppose further that the regular interest payment at the end of the fourth year as well as all other payments were met by the borrower. With annual interest payments,[3] the realized yield on the security would be found by solving the following equation for r:

$$\$1,000 = \frac{\$150}{(1+r)} + \frac{\$150}{(1+r)^2} + \frac{\$300}{(1+r)^4} + \frac{\$150}{(1+r)^5}$$

$$+ \cdots + \frac{\$150}{(1+r)^{20}} + \frac{\$1,000}{(1+r)^{20}} \quad (8\text{-}1)$$

[2] Again, maturity is held constant. Any selling of the security prior to maturity would be based upon considerations taken up in Chapters 5 and 6.

[3] For simplicity, we assume annual interest payments. The problem can be worked out for semiannual or quarterly payments with Eq. (3-2) in Chapter 3. All of the problems associated with the yield-to-maturity measure raised in Chapters 5 and 6 hold here. Because it is almost always employed, however, we use it to illustrate the general concepts about to be discussed.

The yield realized in this case would be 14.80 percent—only slightly less than the promised rate.

With the liquidation of a corporate borrower, investors are likely to receive much less. To illustrate, suppose that the issuer of the security described above paid interest for the first 3 years, but defaulted at the end of the fourth year because of inadequate liquidity. Suppose further that investors felt the borrower had no hope of turning the situation around and that liquidation was the only feasible alternative. Through bankruptcy proceedings, its assets are liquidated and investors receive an eventual settlement of 50¢ on the dollar at the end of the fifth year. In this case, the investors' cash outflow of $1,000 exceeds the total cash inflows they receive. As a result, the realized yield on the security will be negative. For negative yields, Eq. (8-1) is not appropriate; it computes smaller and smaller negative yields the further in the future that final settlement occurs. The implication is that it is more desirable to receive the $500 final settlement at the end of year 5 than it is at the end of year 4, when default actually occurs. Obviously, investors would like to receive final settlement as early as possible, all other things the same. To take account of the investor's opportunity cost, it is necessary to modify Eq. (8-1) when total cash inflows to the investor are less than the cash outflow.

To *approximate* the realized yield in an economic sense, we discount the final settlement amount back to the time of the actual default—the end of year 4. The discount rate used is the initial promised yield on the security. If this yield is significantly out of line with prevailing yields in the market for the time span considered, however, an opportunity rate more closely in line with market rates of interest should be used. Using the promised rate, the realized yield for our example can be found by solving the following equation for r:

$$\$1,000 = \frac{\$150}{(1+r)} + \frac{\$150}{(1+r)^2} + \frac{\$150}{(1+r)^3} + \frac{\dfrac{\$500}{(1.15)}}{(1+r)^4} \qquad (8\text{-}2)$$

When we solve for r, we find it to be -3.99 percent. In a manner similar to that in Eqs. (8-1) and (8-2), the realized yields for other possible default situations can be determined.

For each possibility, a probability should be attached and the possibilities ordered according to the magnitude of realized yield to form a probability distribution. An example of such a distribution is shown in Fig. 8-2. The figure illustrates that a relatively high probability exists for all interest and principal payments to be met by the borrower, resulting in the realized yield's equaling the promised one. However, the distribution is skewed to the left, indicating that a definite possibility exists for default. The further to the left in the figure, the higher the degree of default.

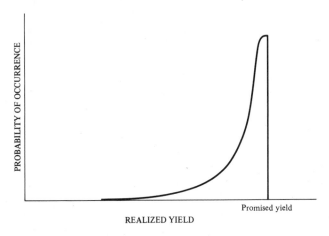

Figure 8-2. Distribution of possible returns.

The *expected rate* for a security can be approximated by

$$ER = \sum_{x=1}^{n} Y_x P_x \tag{8-3}$$

where Y_x is the xth possible yield, P_x is the probability of occurrence of that yield, and n is the total number of possibilities. Suppose that an individual formulated the probability distribution of possible yields for a corporate security shown in Table 8-1. The approximate expected yield for the security would be

$$\begin{aligned}
ER = &(15\%)0.80 + (14\%)0.04 + (13\%)0.03 + (12\%)0.02 + (10\%)0.015 \\
&+ (8\%)0.015 + (6\%)0.015 + (3\%)0.01 + (0\%)0.01 \\
&- (5\%)0.01 - (10\%)0.01 - (15\%)0.01 - (20\%)0.005 \\
&- (30\%)0.005 - (40\%)0.005 \\
= &12.83\%
\end{aligned} \tag{8-4}$$

Thus at time t the prospective investor expects an approximate return of 12.83 percent on the security.

The *expected default loss* on the security is the difference between its promised and expected yields, or

$$15.00\% - 12.83\% = 2.17\% \tag{8-5}$$

This percentage may or may not correspond to the *market risk premium,* defined as the differential between the promised yield and the yield on a

Table 8-1. Probability Distribution of
Possible Yields

Possible Yield (%)	Probability
15 (promised yield)	0.80
14	0.04
13	0.03
12	0.02
10	0.015
8	0.015
6	0.015
3	0.01
0	0.01
−5	0.01
−10	0.01
−15	0.01
−20	0.005
−30	0.005
−40	0.005

comparable risk-free security. If the risk premium in the market is more than the prospective investor's expected default loss, one rationale would suggest that he or she should invest in the security. The investor stands to benefit from an expected yield, adjusted for expected default loss, which is higher than that available on a risk-free security. By the same reasoning, if the investor's subjectively formulated expected default loss exceeds the risk premium on the security, he or she should not invest. Here, the expected yield realized from the security would be less than that from a default-free one. If the expected default loss equaled the risk premium in the market, the investor should be willing simply to hold the security.

The action of all investors behaving in this manner would tend to raise or lower the differential between the promised and the default-free rates until it equals the default loss expected by investors at the margin.[4] Thus, the market risk premium would equal the expected default loss, and the expected rate would equal the default-free one, according to this school of thought. If the actual default-free rate in the example above were 12.83

---

[4]In efficient markets, investors would be able to diversify in order to average out some default risk. However, a certain amount of risk of net default losses would remain. For example, in a depression, there are likely to be default losses. See Hickman, *Corporate Bond Quality*, pp. 15–16. With diversification, the probability distributions in the above example would be formulated on the basis of nondiversifiable default losses. This is the systematic risk that remains after efficient diversification has been undertaken. See Chapter 3 for an additional discussion of this point.

percent, the risk premium would be 2.17 percent, and this premium would equal the default loss expected by investors at the margin.

The equilibrating process described above implies that market participants are neutral with respect to risk; only the expected value of the distribution of possible realized returns is important. However, the distribution not only displays dispersion, but it is highly skewed to the left. Such a distribution means that there is a possibility for very unfavorable returns. To the extent that investors at the margin demand a higher return for dispersion and skewness, the risk premium in the marketplace would exceed the default loss expected by these investors.[5] The more risky the security, of course, the greater the expected default loss. Thus, over a long period of time we would expect that the average promised rate for a large sample of bonds would exceed the average realized rate and that this differential would vary inversely with the quality of the security.

In summary, investors are assumed to form subjective probability distributions of possible realized returns for each security. Differences in these probability distributions will determine differences in risk premiums for the securities and, accordingly, will determine yield differentials between the securities. Figure 8-3 illustrates several of these distributions. The first probability distribution *a* represents the least risky security, while the last *c* is the most risky. On the basis of probability distributions of this sort, risk premiums are assumed to be determined in the market. However, these premiums may or may not conform to the expected default loss. We turn now to the empirical evidence.

EMPIRICAL EVIDENCE ON DEFAULT LOSSES

The most logical way to test the ideas discussed thus far is to compare actual realized yields on a large sample of securities with previous promised yields. The opportunity to test for default, however, depends upon a severe economic downturn. Only then are a significant number of issues likely to default. In other words, the probability of default on most securities is very small; it takes a sharp downturn to shake out those issuers possessing significant default risk. In this century, the depression of the 1930s provides the most valid test.

If risk premiums consistently equaled expected default losses by investors at the margin, we would expect that the average difference between the promised yield at time t and the realized yield at maturity would equal the average risk premium at time t for a large sample of bonds over a long

---

[5]Theoretically the required return would vary with the amount of undiversifiable dispersion and skewness—that is, the incremental variance and skewness of a security as part of an efficiently diversified portfolio. In theory, this portfolio would be the market portfolio which is comprised of all financial assets (see Chapter 3).

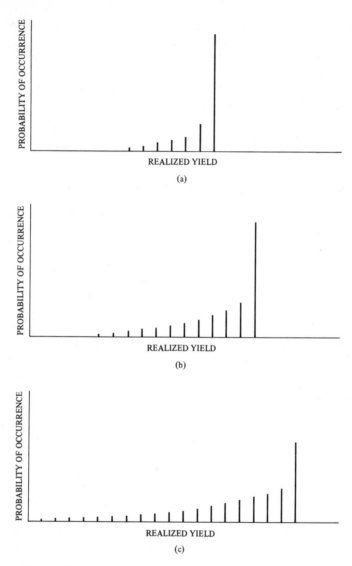

Figure 8-3. Illustration of different distributions of possible returns.

period of time. The most comprehensive testing of this sort has been by Hickman, who investigated the default experience of fixed-income, single-maturity corporate bonds over the period 1900–1943.[6] The sample consisted of all bonds over $5 million and a 10 percent sample of smaller issues. For the sample, "life-span" default rates were computed, depicting the proportion of bonds offered that defaulted between the offering date and

[6]*Ibid.*

extinguishment. In addition, loss rates representing the difference between promised and realized rates were computed.

Hickman's loss rate differed somewhat from the rate used earlier to measure default loss. For one thing, the call feature was not held constant. If a bond were called, there was usually a capital gain because the call price was in excess of the par value of the bond. As a result, realized rates tended to be higher than they would have been otherwise. Additionally, there were a number of bonds outstanding at the end of the sample period, January 1, 1944. The realized rates computed for these bonds were based upon the market prices of the bonds at that date. Because of wartime controls on interest rates, however, yields were low and bond prices were relatively high at that time. This occurrence caused the realized rates on bonds outstanding at the end of the sample period to be artificially high. Both of these factors tended to bias the results in the direction of high realized rates in relation to promised ones. For all bonds, Hickman found that the weighted averages of both promised and realized rates were 5.6 percent. Thus, the loss rate, as defined, was zero—an unusual phenomenon, explained primarily by the biases described. Capital gains from calls and favorable conditions at the end of the sample period simply offset the capital losses attributable to default.[7]

Harold G. Fraine and Robert H. Mills attempted to correct for these biases by removing the effect of market influences on final liquidating values from the estimates of realized yields and loss rates.[8] The authors derived modified averages for large corporate bonds, using Hickman's data for the period 1900–1943. For bonds that did not default and whose realized yield was in excess of the promised one, they substituted the contractual yield for the realized yield. (The implication of this modification is that bonds called at premiums are assumed to run until maturity, when they are redeemed at par. The same implication applies to undefaulted bonds outstanding at the end of the sample period.) After these substitutions were made, modified realized yields were computed; these yields are shown in Table 8-2. The results show that when realized yields are modified for gains attributable to changes in interest rates, the realized yield is less than the promised one. Still, the difference between the two yields was somewhat smaller than the typical yield spread between corporate and government securities (the risk premium as defined) from 1920 to 1943.[9] Therefore, the results still would appear to be biased.

[7]Over the sample period, different loss rates were experienced for the various subperiods. For bonds offered during 1900–1931 and extinguished during 1932–1943, the average promised yield was 5.4 percent and the average realized yield 4.6 percent, the average loss rate being 0.8 percent. For securities both offered and extinguished during the period 1932–1943, the loss rate was more than offset by capital gains. The average promised yield in this case was 4.9 percent and the average realized yield 6.0 percent.

[8]Harold G. Fraine and Robert H. Mills, "Effects of Defaults and Credit Deterioration on Yields of Corporate Bonds," *Journal of Finance,* 16 (September 1961): 423–34.

[9]Prior to World War I, there were few U. S. Treasury securities outstanding. Because the market for government bonds was so thin, comparisons are not possible.

*Table 8-2. Promised vs. Modified Realized Yields,
1900–1943*

	WEIGHTED MEAN ANNUAL RATE	
Agency Rating	*Promised Yield (%)*	*Modified Realized Yield (%)*
I	4.5	4.3
II	4.5	4.3
III	4.9	4.3
IV	5.4	4.5
I–III	4.7	4.3
I–IV	4.8	4.3

Source of data: Harold G. Fraine and Robert H. Mills, "Effects of Defaults and Credit Deterioration on Yields of Corporate Bonds," *Journal of Finance,* 16 (September, 1961), 428.

In a follow-up study, Thomas R. Atkinson extends the analysis of corporate bond quality through 1965.[10] Average annual default rates for the period 1900–1965 are shown in Table 8-3. These rates represent the ratio of the amount of bonds that went into default during a year to the amount of bonds *not* in default at the beginning of the year. Both the numerator and the denominator are based on par values, as opposed to market values. (If market values were used, default rates undoubtedly

*Table 8-3. Corporate Bond
Average Annual
Default Rates,
1900–1965*

Period	*Default Rate (%)*
1900–1943	1.70
1944–1965	0.10
1900–1909	0.90
1910–1919	2.00
1920–1929	1.00
1930–1939	3.20
1940–1949	0.40
1950–1959	0.04
1960–1965	0.03

Source of data: Thomas R. Atkinson, *Trends in Corporate Bond Quality* (New York: National Bureau of Economic Research, 1967), p. 43.

[10]Thomas R. Atkinson, *Trends in Corporate Bond Quality* (New York: National Bureau of Economic Research, 1967).

would have been less.) As seen in the table, the incidence of default in the post–World War II era was very small. The defaults that did occur were concentrated in the railroad industry. From this, as well as from previous evidence, we can conclude that default experience is highly correlated with the economic cycle. Put another way, it takes a severe economic downturn before the *ex ante* possibility of default becomes a significant reality and realized yields differ from those originally promised.

If the evidence were extended into the 1970s and 1980s, I am sure the incidence of corporate bankruptcy would have increased, to accompany the bankruptcies of Penn Central, W. T. Grant & Co., Wickes Corporation, Braniff Airways, and a host of lesser-known companies. Moreover, the number of bankruptcies increased during the three recessions—1970, 1974–1975 and 1981–1982. Particularly in the last recession, the combination of hard economic times and high interest rates caused many a company to succumb. The bankruptcy courts sagged under an unprecedented case load.

Similar in many ways to the Atkinson study, George H. Hempel studied the default experience for municipal securities over the period 1839–1965.[11] The results are reported in terms of number of defaults, as opposed to ratio of default or the relative amount of defaults in dollar terms. As the total number of state and local governments has increased dramatically over the period studied, there is a bias toward exaggerating the default experience in the later years relative to the earlier ones. These problems notwithstanding, the numbers are still revealing. They suggest that defaults increase significantly in periods of major depressions. Studying these depressions in more detail, Hempel found:

Depression	Percent of Debt Outstanding Defaulting
1837–1843	51.0
1873–1879	24.5
1893–1899	10.0
1929–1937	15.4

Furthermore, he found that most payment problems occurred in the latter stages of a depression. For milder economic reversals, significant debt payment problems did not seem to occur although some municipalities failed even in good times. As with corporate bonds, then, only a severe economic downturn will cause significant default losses and differences between promised and realized returns for municipal bonds (see Table 8-4).

[11]George H. Hempel, *The Postwar Quality of State and Local Debt* (New York: National Bureau of Economic Research, 1971).

Table 8-4. Number of Defaults of State and Local Government Bonds, 1839–1965

Period	Number of Defaults	Period	Number of Defaults
1839–1849	13	1910–1919	36
1850–1859	17	1920–1929	186
1860–1869	38	1930–1939	4,770
1870–1879	168	1940–1949	79
1880–1889	97	1950–1959	112
1890–1899	258	1960–1965	192
1900–1909	149		

Source of data: George H. Hempel, *The Postwar Quality of State and Local Debt* (New York: National Bureau of Economic Research, 1971), p. 30

Default Prediction with Financial Ratios

In recent years there has been considerable empirical testing of the use of financial ratios and other accounting information as predictors of various future events. One of the events of principal concern is that of *corporate bankruptcy.* By studying the past behavior of significant financial ratios, one hopes to determine the relative probability of future default. This suggests that the causes for failure evolve gradually and that these causes emit certain signals which can be detected in advance of actual failure. If this is true, the lender may be able to take corrective action before actual failure occurs.

In an extensive research study, William H. Beaver used financial ratios to predict failure.[12] The study encompassed a sample of seventy-nine relatively large firms that failed.[13] Another firm was compared to each of these companies—a firm that did not fail, was in the same industry, and was of approximately the same size as the firm that failed. The data collected for the nonfailed companies were for the same years as those for the failed firms. These samples were used to test the predictive ability of thirty financial ratios. The mean values of the ratios for the two samples were compared over the 5-year period prior to failure. An example of such a comparison, using the ratio of cash flow to total debt, is shown in Fig. 8-4. We see that the mean ratio for the failed firms differs significantly from that for the nonfailed firms. Not only is it lower, but it deteriorates markedly as failure approaches. In addition to a comparison of mean values, Beaver tested the samples by using a form of discriminant analysis

[12]William H. Beaver, "Financial Ratios as Predictors of Failure," *Empirical Research in Accounting: Selected Studies,* supplement to *Journal of Accounting Research* (1966): 71–111.
[13]*Failure* was defined as the inability of a firm to meet its financial obligations.

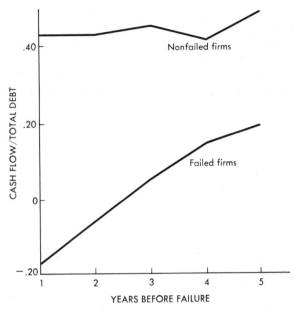

Figure 8-4. Comparison of mean values for failed and non-failed firms.

and then went on to analyze the evidence using likelihood ratios. Although not all of the financial ratios examined predicted failure equally well, many showed excellent predictive power.

In a similar type of study, Edward I. Altman employed multiple discriminant analysis to predict bankruptcy, using various financial ratios.[14] Altman worked with a sample of thirty-three corporations that filed for bankruptcy. Like Beaver, he collected a paired sample of thirty-three non-bankrupt firms on a stratified random basis. Starting with twenty-two financial ratios, he selected the five that did the best combined job of predicting bankruptcy. These ratios were used to discriminate between bankrupt and nonbankrupt firms, using data from 1 to 5 years prior to bankruptcy. As expected, the predictive accuracy of the multiple discriminant model declined with the increase in years prior to bankruptcy; however, the model was able to forecast failure quite well up to 2 years before bankruptcy.

Altman also tested the model with secondary samples of bankrupt and nonbankrupt firms. Using the parameter estimates obtained in the original

[14]Edward I. Altman, "Financial Ratios, Discriminant Analysis and the Prediction of Corporate Bankruptcy," *Journal of Finance,* 23 (September 1968): 589–609. For a discussion of discriminant analysis as it applies to finance problems as well as an analysis of Altman's approach, see O. Maurice Joy and John O. Tollefson, "On the Financial Application of Discriminant Analysis," *Journal of Financial and Quantitative Analysis*, 10 (December 1975): 723–39; and Robert A. Eisenbeis, "Pitfalls in the Application of Discriminant Analysis in Business Finance and Economics," *Journal of Finance*, 32 (June 1977): 875–900.

sample, he found the model to have considerable predictive accuracy when used in conjunction with the secondary samples. In his investigation, Altman, like Beaver, found that the financial ratios of bankrupt firms deteriorated as bankruptcy approached, the greatest deterioration occurring between the third and the second year. Altman concluded that through discriminant analysis, a creditor can successfully predict potential bankruptcy.

In another study, Edward I. Altman, Robert G. Haldeman, and P. Narayanan extended the original Altman discriminant function model to include, among other things, the capitalization of leases, and they updated its application.[15] A sample of fifty-three bankrupt firms and a matched sample of fifty-eight nonbankrupt firms were employed. Manufacturing and, for the first time in any study, retailing companies were included. On the basis of discriminatory ability, twenty-seven original variables were reduced to seven: the return-on-assets ratio, the stability of earnings, the interest coverage ratio, the retained earnings to total assets ratio, the current ratio, the common equity to total capital ratio, and the size of total assets. Using a linear discriminant model, the authors were successful in predicting bankruptcy up to 5 years prior to failure. Successful classification ranged from 96 percent 1 year before failure to 70 percent 5 years before failure. In comparing their model with alternative models, including the original Altman model, the authors found it more accurate.

Robert O. Edmister tested the usefulness of financial ratio analysis for predicting the failure of small businesses.[16] Similar to the others, his work employed multiple discriminant analysis and found it to be an accurate predictor of failure if ratios were averaged over a 3-year span. Unlike the results of Beaver and Altman, however, an analysis based upon one year's financial statements was not sufficient to discriminate failing from non-failing firms. Consecutive financial statements were necessary for the successful analysis of small-business failures.

On the basis of the empirical studies described above, it would appear that signs of potential failure are evident before actual failure occurs. For the creditor, the lag may allow time to take corrective actions. However, it is important to recognize that the parameters of a model change over time. Indeed, most investigators have found them to be unstable. In order

[15]Edward I. Altman, Robert G. Haldeman, and P. Narayanan, "Zeta Analysis: A New Model to Identify Bankruptcy Risk of Corporations," *Journal of Banking and Finance,* 1 (June 1977). Both quadratic and linear models were tested, with the linear function winning out. For an analysis of the failure of credit unions using the Altman type model and one where financial data from more than one period is used, see Robert A. Collins, "An Empirical Comparison of Bankruptcy Prediction Models," *Financial Management,* 9 (Summer 1980): 52–57.

[16]Robert O. Edmister, "An Empirical Test of Financial Ratio Analysis for Small Business Failure Prediction," *Journal of Financial and Quantitative Analysis,* 7 (March 1972): 1477–93.

for the models to have predictive power, then, they must be constantly updated with new empirical testing.

CREDIT RATINGS AND RISK PREMIUMS

For the typical investor, risk is judged not by a subjectively formulated probability distribution of possible returns, but in terms of the credit rating assigned to the bond by investment agencies. The principal rating agencies are Moody's Investors Service and Standard & Poor's. The issuer of a new corporate or municipal bond contracts with the agency to evaluate and rate the bond, as well as to update the rating throughout the bond's life. For this service, the issuer pays a fee. In addition, the rating agency charges subscribers to its rating publications. While the assignment of a rating for a new issue is current, changes in ratings of existing bond issues tend to lag behind the events that prompt the change. More will be said about this shortly.

Based on their evaluations of a bond issue, the agencies give their opinion in the form of letter grades, which are published for use by investors. In their ratings, the agencies attempt to rank issues according to the probability of default. The highest grade bonds, whose risk of default is felt to be negligible, are rated triple A. The ratings used by the two agencies, as well as brief descriptions, are shown in Table 8-5. The first four grades in either case are considered to represent investment quality issues, whereas other rated bonds are considered speculative. For each rating category, a modifier of 1, 2, or 3 is applied. For example, Aa-1 means that a security is in the higher end of the Aa rating category. Baa-3 indicates that a security is in the lower end of the Baa category. The ratings by the two agencies are widely respected and are recognized by various government regulatory agencies as measures of default risk. In fact, many investors accept them without further investigation of the risk of default.

Hickman investigated the reliability of these ratings for corporate bonds over the period 1900–1943 and found a close correspondence between the rating category and the subsequent default experience.[17] The results of his investigation and the correspondence described are shown in Table 8-6. Hickman concluded that the record of the rating agencies over the sample period was remarkably good. Issues that were rated as high grade at the time of the offering generally had a much lower default rate than issues rated in lower categories.[18] On the basis of this study, confidence in the ability of the rating agencies to discriminate among issues of bonds as to the probability of default would seem to be justified. However, it is im-

[17]Hickman, *Corporate Bond Quality*, p. 176.
[18]*Ibid.*, p. 141.

Table 8-5. Credit Ratings by Investment Agencies

Moody's	Explanation
Aaa	Best quality
Aa	High quality
A	Upper medium grade
Baa	Medium grade
Ba	Possess speculative elements
B	Generally lack characteristics of desirable investment
Caa	Poor standing; may be in default
Ca	Speculative in a high degree; often in default
C	Lowest grade; very poor prospects

Standard & Poor's	Explanation
AAA	Highest grade
AA	High grade
A	Upper medium grade
BBB	Medium grade
BB	Lower medium grade
B	Speculative
CCC-CC	Outright speculation
C	Reserved for income bonds
DDD-D	In default, with rating indicating relative salvage value

Table 8-6. Default Experience, 1900–1943 (Percent)

Size of Issues	RATING					
	I	II	III	IV	V–IX	No Rating
Large issues (over $5 million)	5.9	6.0	13.4	19.1	42.4	28.6
Small issues (under $5 million)	10.2	15.5	9.9	25.2	32.6	27.0

Source of data: W. Braddock Hickman, *Corporate Bond Quality and Investor Experience* (New York: National Bureau of Economic Research, 1958), p. 176.

portant to understand that the rating categories portray *relative risk* among issuers of securities, not *absolute risk*. As evident in the depression of the 1930s, the possibility of default for all classes of risky bonds can increase. As a result, the yield differential between bonds subject to default and Treasury securities can increase. More will be said about this when we examine the cyclical behavior of risk premiums.

A number of scholars have investigated the reasons for the assignment of a rating by a rating agency. Using the rating as the dependent variable, they have searched for statistically significant relationships between this variable and measures of past performance.[19] For corporate debt, higher ratings generally are associated with: (1) lower debt ratios; (2) higher return-on-asset ratios; (3) lower relative variation in earnings over time; (4) larger companies; (5) higher interest-coverage ratios; and (6) the lack of subordination. The studies varied somewhat in explanatory variables employed and in the sample periods tested. Over all, these studies were able to predict correctly anywhere from 60 percent to 90 percent of the ratings assigned by the rating agencies.

Other tests have involved the reaction of bond prices to rating changes. If agencies change an existing bond's rating only after the events that eventually trigger the change, the market price may already have adjusted. Therefore, the rating change itself would have no informational content for investors. In an extensive test of corporate bond price movements surrounding the announcement of a rating change, Mark I. Weinstein found no reaction of bond prices during the 6 months prior to the rating change when overall market movements were held constant.[20] However, there was some evidence of price change $\frac{1}{2}$ to $1\frac{1}{2}$ years prior to the rating change, indicating a lag in adjusting a rating by agencies as a result of information to which the market had previously reacted.

The Fisher Study and Other Studies

In an extensive and classic study of risk premiums, Lawrence Fisher undertook a multiple regression analysis of five cross-sectional samples of corporate bonds for 1927, 1932, 1937, 1949, and 1953.[21] Using the risk premium (market yield less the corresponding default-free rate) as the dependent variable, he regressed this variable against four explanatory

---

[19]See Thomas F. Pogue and Robert M. Soldofsky, "What Is in a Bond Rating?" *Journal of Financial and Quantitative Analysis,* 4 (June 1969): 201–28; George E. Pinches and Kent A. Mingo, "A Multivariate Analysis of Industrial Bond Ratings," *Journal of Finance,* 28 (March 1973): 1–18; and Richard R. West, "An Alternative Approach for Predicting Corporate Bond Ratings," *Journal of Accounting Research,* 8 (Spring 1970): 118–27; James S. Ang and Kiritkumar A. Patel, "Bond Rating Methods: Comparison and Validation," *Journal of Finance,* 30 (May 1975): 631–40; Shyam B. Bhandari, Robert M. Soldofsky, and Warren J. Boe, "Bond Quality Rating Changes for Electric Utilities: A Multivariate Analysis," *Financial Management,* 8 (Spring 1979): 74–81; and Ahmed Belkaoui, "Industrial Bond Ratings: A New Look," *Financial Management,* 9 (Autumn 1980): 44–52.

[20]Mark I. Weinstein, "The Effect of a Rating Change Announcement on Bond Price," *Journal of Financial Economics,* 5 (1977): 329–50. See also Steven Katz, "The Price Adjustment Process of Bonds to Rating Reclassifications: A Test of Bond Market Efficiency," *Journal of Finance,* 29 (May 1974): 551–9.

[21]Lawrence Fisher, "Determinants of Risk Premiums on Corporate Bonds," *Journal of Political Economy,* 67 (June 1959): 217–37.

variables: the earnings variability of the company, the length of time the company has been solvent and creditors have not taken a loss, the equity/ debt ratio, and the market value of all publicly traded bonds of the company. The first three variables relate to the risk of default, while the last attempts to depict the marketability of the bond. The last measure was justified on the basis of the market value of publicly traded bonds being a proxy for transaction frequency. Supposedly, the fewer bonds that change hands, the thinner the market and the more uncertain the market price.

Fisher found that the four variables explained approximately 75 percent of the variance in the logarithm of the risk premium. Moreover, the elasticity of the dependent variable with respect to these four variables was relatively stable over time. The regression coefficients for the explanatory variables all had the proper sign, and practically all were significant over the five dates. The sign for the first variable was positive, indicating that the greater the variability of earnings of the firm, the greater the default risk and the greater the risk premium embodied in the bond yield. The signs of the remaining three variables were negative. The second and third suggest that the greater the period of solvency and the greater the equity/ debt ratio, the less the default risk and the lower the risk premium required. The sign for the last variable suggests that the greater the market value of total bonds outstanding, the greater the marketability of the issue to investors and the lower the risk premium. Overall, Fisher's study represents the first thorough and direct study of factors responsible for risk premiums.

Richard R. West reexamines the Fisher model in relation to bond ratings.[22] In addition, he gives a historical perspective on the origination and development of ratings and on the use of ratings as tools for the regulation of investments by financial institutions. This use began in the late 1930s and was in the form of a constraint on investment behavior of financial institutions to "investment grade" issues (Baa or better.) Using Fisher's data, West analyzed the residuals according to their Moody's rating. For the 1927, 1932, and 1937 results, the residuals were mixed as to sign and showed no significant relationship to the bond ratings. For 1949 and 1953, however, the residuals for the speculative grade ratings (Ba or lower) were mostly positive and significant, while those for the investment grades (Baa or higher) showed a lesser tendency toward negative residuals. West interprets this finding to be consistent with the argument that ratings have an independent impact on yields because of their use as tools for financial regulation. In other words, speculative grade issues show higher yields than predicted by the Fisher model, whereas investment grade issues show lower yields. Put yet another way, this finding is consistent with institutional restrictions on investment leading to a segmented market for

---

[22] Richard R. West, "Bond Ratings, Bond Yields and Financial Regulation: Some Findings," *Journal of Law and Economics,* 16 (April 1973): 159–68.

bonds. The implication of a segmentation effect will be examined later in this chapter.

In another study, which is similar in many respects to that of Fisher's, Avery B. Cohan investigated the behavior of yields on a sample of direct placements.[23] A direct placement is a corporate debt or equity instrument which is sold directly to one or more institutional investors, such as to a life insurance company. Cohan regressed the logarithm of yield against certain variables said to depict the quality of the promise to pay. They were the size of issue, the total capitalization of the company, the debt ratio, the amount of earnings before interest and taxes (EBIT), the maturity of the instrument, the average length of time the principal was expected to be outstanding, the length of time to the first call date, the type of security (senior or junior debentures, or mortgage bonds), the classification of the borrower as to line of business, the total interest paid by the borrower on all debt outstanding. As hypothesized, all but the last variable had a negative sign and all were significant. Like Fisher's study, Cohan's study assesses the relationship between various risk variables and promised yields. For both public debt issues and direct placements, then, there is a significant and positive relationship between the yield required by investors and the degree of risk as depicted by various risk measures.

It should be noted that the causal relationship between interest rates paid by a borrower and its default risk works both ways. The higher the interest rate, the larger is the amount of debt charge and the lower is the cash flow ability of the borrower to service these charges, all other things the same. Hence, higher interest rates raise the probability of default and hence the default risk of the security. Thus, the causal relationship between interests rates and default risk runs both ways, and a case can be made for their simultaneous determination.

CYCLICAL BEHAVIOR OF RISK PREMIUMS

Another aspect of risk premiums is their cyclical behavior over time. A priori, we might expect risk premiums in the market for bonds to fluctuate in a systematic manner with the business cycle. During periods of economic downturn the risk premium might be expected to widen, while during periods of economic prosperity it might be expected to narrow. This pattern of behavior may be attributable to investors' utility preferences for bonds changing with different states of nature. In a recession, their prime concern may be with safety. To invest in more risky bonds, the investor would have to be offered a substantial risk premium. On the other hand, during a period of prosperity, investors may be less concerned with safety

[23]Avery B. Cohan, *Yields on Corporate Debt Directly Placed* (New York: National Bureau of Economic Research, 1967).

and may be willing to bear more risk of default. During such a time, there may be a tendency for them to seek out the highest yielding investments. A sufficient number of investors behaving in this manner would narrow risk premiums in periods of prosperity and widen them in times of recession.

A related reason for this behavior has to do with liquidity and marketability. If liquidity is more valued in a recession than it is in a period of economic expansion, investors may seek out Treasury and other high-grade, marketable securities. In this way they achieve a high degree of liquidity. This changing preference for liquidity would tend to widen risk premiums in periods of economic contraction and narrow them in periods of economic expansion.

It is important to differentiate these effects from the effect of underlying changes in the default risk of borrowers over the business cycle. In a recession, the default risk for some borrowers increases as their cash flow ability to service debt charges deteriorates. The opposite tends to occur in an economic expansion. While the rating services tend to downgrade issues in the contraction phase of a business cycle and upgrade them in the expansion phase, the number of changes is relatively small. Therefore, it is likely that some changes in underlying default risk occur without commensurate adjustments in ratings. In other words, the ratings are "sticky" and do not altogether capture cyclical variations in default risk. The import of all of this is that changes in yield differentials between various-grade securities may reflect more than changes in the way that investors view risk. They may also reflect underlying changes in default risk.

Yield Differentials over Time

Recognizing this limitation, let us examine the cyclical behavior of yield differentials. In Fig. 8-5, yield differentials between long-term Treasury bonds and Aaa corporates and between Treasury bonds and Baa corporates are shown for the period 1946–1982. Economic recessions are denoted by the shaded areas. In the figure, we see that the yield differential between Treasury bonds and Baa corporates widened during the recessionary periods. This widening was particularly evident in 1957–1958, 1970, 1974–1975 and 1981–1982. Moreover, during periods of economic expansion, the differential narrowed from the previous peak. The fact that the troughs in 1973 and 1978 were higher than earlier troughs is not surprising in view of the high levels of interest rates that prevailed during those times relative to the low and stable levels of 1961–1965.

The pattern for the yield differential between Treasuries and Aaa corporates is not as distinct as that for the differential between Treasuries and Baa corporates. The former differential is seen to widen somewhat in the 1953–1954, 1957–1958, and 1960 recessions and to widen more distinctly

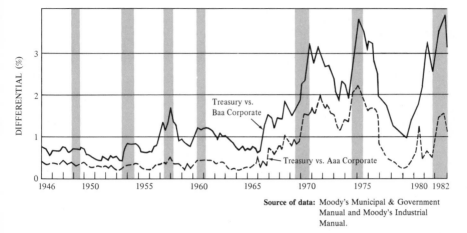

Source of data: Moody's Municipal & Government
Manual and Moody's Industrial
Manual.

Figure 8-5. Yield differentials between Treasury bonds, Aaa corporate bonds, and Baa corporate bonds, 1946–1982.

in the 1974–1975, 1980, and 1981–1982 recessions. For the 1970 recession,
the differential widened but remained wide well into the subsequent recovery. The patterns during periods of economic expansion were much the
same as that for the Baa corporate–Treasury yield differential described
previously, but less pronounced. Because of the relatively low default risk
of Aaa corporates, the less pronounced fluctuation of this differential is
to be expected. In Fig. 8-6, the yield differential between Aaa corporate
bonds and Baa corporate bonds is shown. While this can be deduced from
Fig. 8-5, it is useful to show it separately. As seen in the figure, the widening
of yield differentials during the 1949, 1957–1958, 1970, 1974–1975, 1980,
and 1981–1982 recessions is more pronounced than that shown in Fig. 8-5,
as is the subsequent narrowing of the differential in periods of economic
expansion. Again, this is attributable to the lesser variation of Aaa corporate yields over the business cycle.

When we examine the yield differential for different grades of municipal bonds, the pattern is less clear. Figure 8-7 shows the differential
between Aaa municipal bonds and Baa municipals during the period 1946–
1982. As seen in the figure, there is a tendency for the differential to widen
during the 1949, 1953–1954, 1957–1958, 1960, 1980, and 1981–1982 recessions. There also is a pronounced narrowing of the differential during the
1950–1952 period of economic expansion and again during the 1961–1965
and the 1977–1979 periods of prosperity. However, there is no widening
of the differential during the 1970 recession, in sharp contrast to the evidence on corporate bonds. As is also seen in the figure, the most pronounced widening in yield differential occurred from mid-1974 to mid-
1976. This spans the 1974–1975 recession, and such a widening during a
recession is consistent with the evidence for corporates. However, in con-

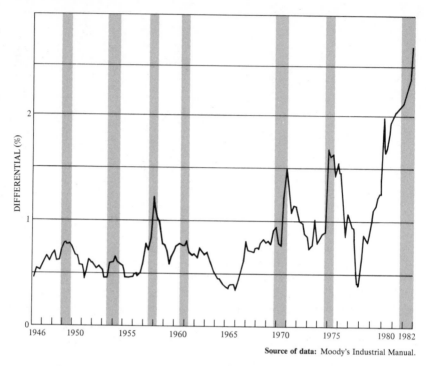

Source of data: Moody's Industrial Manual.

Figure 8-6. Yield differential between Aaa corporate bonds and Baa corporate bonds, 1946–1982.

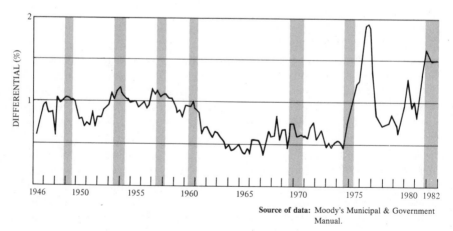

Source of data: Moody's Municipal & Government Manual.

Figure 8-7. Yield differential between Aaa municipal bonds and Baa municipal bonds, 1946–1982.

trast to corporates, the differential continued to widen well after the recession was over.

The main explanation of this occurrence is that during this time the financial condition of New York City triggered great concern over default risk for municipal securities in general. In 1975, the city was on the verge of default and such default was prevented only by the Federal government eventually providing a $2.3 billion, 3-year revolving credit. During 1975, there were also potential default problems for the state of Massachusetts, for the New York Port Authority, and for various housing agencies of the state of New York. These problems caused great uncertainty in the market for municipal securities and a general reassessment of the default risk of municipal securities in general—and the securities of large urban cities in particular. The "flight to quality" at this time is said to be the reason for the widening of the yield differential between Aaa municipals and Baa municipals.

Over all, however, the evidence on municipals gives only moderate support to the notion that risk premiums widen during recessions and narrow during periods of economic expansion. This contrasts with the evidence on corporates, which was much stronger.

Other Studies of Cyclical Behavior

For the earlier period 1900–1943, Hickman found that when low-grade corporate bonds were purchased near the troughs of an investment cycle and sold during the peaks, investors fared better than they did with similar purchases and sales of high-grade corporates. On the other hand, investors fared better with high-grade corporates bought near peaks and sold near troughs. He concluded that the market usually overpriced low-grade issues (and underestimated default risks) near the peaks of major investment cycles.[24] This behavior is consistent with risk premiums narrowing during periods of prosperity and widening during recessions.

In another study, Michael D. Joehnk and James F. Nielsen examined promised yields and the volatility of such yields for speculative-grade corporate bonds in relation to investment-grade bonds.[25] The speculative-grade bonds consisted of samples of industrial and railroad issues rated Ba and B by Moody's. The investment-grade bonds consisted of a sample of Aa rated industrial and public utility bonds. Two 4-year time periods were studied: 1961–1964, which was characterized as a period of interest-rate

---

[24]Hickman, *Corporate Bond Quality*, p. 15.

[25]Michael D. Joehnk and James F. Nielsen, "Return and Risk Characteristics of Speculative Grade Bonds," *Quarterly Review of Economics and Business,* 15 (Spring 1975): 27–46. The authors also examine realized returns and their volatility, but we do not review this part of their article.

stability, and 1968–1971, which was more volatile in comparison. For the period 1970–1971, in which there was a recession, yield differentials tended to be wider and variability larger relative to the other two periods. This evidence is roughly consistent with evidence on corporate bonds rated Baa or better which we examined earlier. Yield differentials tend to widen during recessions and narrow during periods of economic expansion.

In an extensive study of the causes of the cyclical behavior of risk premiums, Dwight M. Jaffee regressed corporate yield differentials against certain business cycle variables.[26] These variables included a measure of consumer sentiment, the unemployment rate, the growth of corporate retained earnings, the growth of capital expenditures, and an inflation variable. The dependent variable involved yield differentials for Baa grade bonds and high-grade issues (Aaa, Aa, and A).These differentials were for overall corporates and for the various components—industrial, utilities, and railroads. Tests for the period 1954–1969 showed that yield differentials were negatively related to consumer sentiment, to growth in retained earnings, and to growth in investment, while they were positively related for the most part to unemployment and inflation. The first three variables were said to portray the degree of optimism with respect to economic activity. Yield differentials would be expected to narrow as optimism increased. In contrast, unemployment and the growth in prices are associated with uncertainty and economic contraction. Therefore, yield differentials would be expected to widen as these variables increased.[27]

Of the explanatory variables examined, consumer sentiment was by far the most significant. Other variables tended to be significant for the overall corporate and industrial categories. For the utility category, however, the results were mixed both with respect to sign and significance. For railroads, they were mixed with respect to significance. Over all, however, the Jaffee study supports the notion that people's utility toward investing varies with the phase of the economic cycle. In turn, this variation causes changes in yield differentials between various grades of corporate bonds.

In another study of this sort, Timothy Q. Cook and Patric H. Hendershott tested for the effect of economic activity variables on yield spreads.[28]

[26]Dwight M. Jaffee, "Cyclical Variations in the Risk Structure of Interest Rates," *Journal of Monetary Economics,* 1 (July 1975): 309–25.

[27]The results were the most pronounced for the Baa–Aaa yield spread with respect to such things as the goodness of fit and the size and significance of the coefficients; the results lessened as one moved to the Baa–A yield spread.

[28]Timothy Q. Cook and Patric H. Hendershott, "The Impact of Taxes, Risk and Relative Security Supplies on Interest Rate Differentials," *Journal of Finance,* 33 (September 1978): 1173–86. Jess B. Yawitz and William J. Marshall, "Measuring the Effect of Callability on Bond Yields," *Journal of Money, Credit and Banking,* 13 (February 1981): 60–71, develop an improved callability variable for the Cook-Hendershott model. Using it, they obtain a higher degree of explanatory power. The measure of consumer sentiment remained highly important and significant, while the employment pressure index did not.

Regressing the yield differential between corporate and Treasury bond yields against a measure of consumer sentiment and an employment pressure index, among other variables, they found both to be negative and significant. These results support the idea that yield spreads vary inversely with the level of economic activity. (This study is described in more detail in the next section, when we take up market segmentation.)

David S. Kidwell and Charles A. Trzcinka also analyzed yield spreads for various grades of corporate bonds in the 1960s and 1970s.[29] These authors also found the relative yield spread to vary countercyclically with the business cycle, as represented by several economic activity variables.

Earl D. Benson, David S. Kidwell, Timothy W. Koch, and Robert J. Rogowski tested yield differentials for various grades of general-obligation, new-issue municipal bonds.[30] In their study, the yield of the new issue relative to Aaa new issue municipal yields was regressed against the size of the issue, the number of bids received, the Moody's credit rating, the change in real gross national product, a measure of consumer sentiment, and the relative net purchases of commercial banks in the overall municipal market. The first three variables were statistically significant. As a measure of marketability, size had the expected U-shaped relationship with respect to relative yield. The greater the number of bids, the lower the relative yield; and the higher the credit rating, the lower the relative yield. All these results were in keeping with earlier studies and were not surprising. Primary interest was in the variables of economic activity and bank segmentation, which we discuss later in the chapter. The change in real GNP was negative and highly significant, indicating that the yield differential between various quality municipal bonds widens in economic contractions and narrows in economic expansions. The inclusion of the consumer sentiment measure was not statistically significant, and the authors concluded that real GNP change alone is adequate for explaining the relationship between economic activity and default risk.

Finally, David S. Kidwell and Timothy W. Koch tested the cyclical behavior of the differential between two types of municipal securities.[31] As revenue bonds generally are believed to be more risky than general obligation bonds, the authors tested the hypothesis that the yield differential varies inversely with the level of economic activity. Using a very large sample of individual bond issues during the 1960s and 1970s, a multiple regression analysis with macroeconomic data suggested that the yield

[29]David S. Kidwell and Charles A. Trzcinka, "The Risk Structure of Interest Rates and the Penn Central Crisis," *Journal of Finance,* 34 (June 1979): 751–60.

[30]Earl D. Benson et al., "Systematic Variation in Yield Spreads for Tax-Exempt General Obligation Bonds," *Journal of Financial and Quantitative Analysis*, 16 (December 1981): 685–702.

[31]David S. Kidwell and Timothy W. Koch, "The Behavior of the Interest Rate Differential Between Tax-Exempt Revenue and General Obligation Bonds," *Journal of Finance,* 37 (March 1982): 73–85.

differential varies countercyclically with the level of economic activity. In addition, the authors analyzed individual bond issues using microeconomic data and three cyclical variables. Here, too, the results were consistent with the countercyclical behavior described above.

In summary, for yield differentials between corporate bonds and Treasuries, for yield differentials between different grades of corporate bonds, and, to a lesser extent, for yield differentials between different grades of municipals, there appears to be a tendency for risk premiums to vary with the level of economic activity. Certain evidence gives support to the notion that risk premiums narrow during periods of economic expansion and widen during periods of economic downturn. One explanation for this phenomenon is that the utility of investors changes with the changes in the state of the economy. Put another way, investors are said to be more safety conscious in a recession than they are in a period of economic prosperity.

THE MARKET SEGMENTATION EFFECT

Other investigators say that the cause of the cyclical behavior of yield differentials is more complex. Some argue that the pattern of behavior is affected by institutional restrictions on investing in and on issuing securities. In turn, these restrictions are said to lead to segmented financial markets in the same sense as we discussed for the term structure of interest rates. In this case, segmentation refers to the type and grade of security in which one can invest or which one can issue. We have already discussed one type of institutional restriction, the 4¼ percent coupon-rate ceiling on Treasury bond offerings. This restriction effectively precluded long-term Treasury borrowings from 1966 to 1971 and may explain in part the widening in yield differentials between corporates and Treasuries observed during this time.

Other institutional restrictions on the supply side include voter constraints on borrowing by municipalities. In many state and local governments, voter approval is required before a bond issue can be floated. Moreover, some municipalities have a legal ceiling on what they can pay in interest. If interest rates in general move up, these municipalities may be precluded from borrowing unless voter approval to remove the ceiling can be obtained. When inflation occurs, it typically brings with it not only higher interest rates, but increased costs to the municipality and higher property taxes. Since few people like higher taxes, there tends to be a correspondence between the percentage of bond issues turned down by the electorate and inflation. As lower-grade municipalities pay higher interest rates and typically have more funded indebtedness outstanding, it is not unreasonable to expect them to feel restrictions on borrowing to a greater extent than do prime-grade municipalities.

On occasion, corporations also face restrictions on the issuing of bonds. If a company has existing debt outstanding that is covered by a loan agreement or bond indenture, there frequently exists a restriction on the company with respect to future debt. This constraint is likely to be more binding for the lower-grade company than it is for the prime-grade company. For both municipalities and corporations, then, it is not unreasonable to expect lower-grade borrowers to feel institutional restrictions to a greater extent than do higher-grade borrowers in times of inflation and economic contraction or stagnation. As a result, the supply of various-grade securities may be affected differently by institutional restrictions over the business cycle.

On the demand side there are institutional restrictions as well. For example, a common restriction is the limiting of the types and grades of securities in which certain institutions can invest. In turn, these restrictions on institutions may cause them to select different securities than they would if they were free to invest in any security. In other words, institutional restrictions may cause greater relative demand for restricted securities vis-à-vis unrestricted securities, if all other conditions are the same. This notion is illustrated in Fig. 8-8, where it is seen that restricted investors can invest only in restricted securities, while unrestricted investors can invest in all securities.

The restrictions placed on investment take many forms. For all practical purposes, commercial banks cannot invest in corporate bonds, being restricted to Treasury securities and municipals. Public deposits in commercial banks must be secured by collateral, principally U.S. Treasury or government agency securities. This restriction affects their investment behavior. For commercial banks not members of the Federal Reserve System, part of their reserve requirement can be satisfied by holding Treasury securities. Obviously this may influence their investment behavior. Life insurance companies and certain other institutions are restricted in their

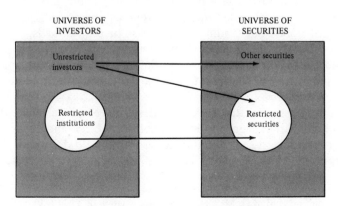

Figure 8-8. Effect of institutional restrictions on demand.

investment by the states in which they operate. They are allowed to invest only in securities on the "legal list." With respect to bonds, this restriction frequently takes the form of investment-grade bonds—those rated Baa or better. Bonds rated Ba and below would not qualify, and the institution involved would be precluded from buying them. Similarly, commercial banks tend to be restricted to investment-grade bonds. These are only examples of some of the more important restrictions on the type and grade of security in which an institution may invest.

The combination of restrictions on the supply of and the demand for different types and grades of securities may lead to a market segmentation effect. If significant, this effect would have an influence on the cyclical behavior of yield differentials and risk premiums apart from the influences already discussed.

Empirical Evidence on Segmentation Effect

Certain empirical studies bear on the question of whether there is a market segmentation effect on the risk structure of interest rates. We already have described the West study, in which he concluded that whether or not a corporate bond was rated investment grade had an effect on yield differentials apart from underlying factors accounting for risk. An investment-grade rating (Baa or above) was said to give a bond additional demand owing to restrictions on the investment behavior of financial institutions.

Ray C. Fair and Burton G. Malkiel tested the hypothesis that government bonds, high-grade utility bonds, and high-grade industrial bonds are not perfect substitutes.[32] Because of legal requirements and other market imperfections affecting the demand for bonds, these markets may be segmented to a degree. As a result, changes in relative supply would affect yield differentials between the various types of bonds mentioned above. Fair and Malkiel regressed yield differentials against differences in the amounts of bonds outstanding. In the case of utility bonds, the "visible supply" of bonds during the next six months was added as an explanatory variable. Testing for the period 1961–1969, the supply and anticipated new financial variables were found to have a significant effect on yield differentials.

Let us now review four previously described empirical studies for their insights into market segmentation. Timothy Q. Cook and Patric H. Hendershott tested for a segmentation effect in the yield differential between Aa corporate bonds and U.S. Treasury bonds. Rather than use existing

---

[32]Ray C. Fair and Burton G. Malkiel, "The Determination of Yield Differentials between Debt Instruments of the Same Maturity," *Journal of Money, Credit and Banking,* 3 (November 1971): 733–49.

yield series, however, they constructed a new Treasury bond series to isolate the influence of taxes and, as nearly as possible, to hold constant maturity.[33] Cook and Hendershott then regressed the adjusted yield differential against a measure of consumer sentiment, an employment pressure index, an interest-rate expectations proxy, and a measure of the relative supplies of the two types of securities. The first two variables attempted to capture the cyclical effect on yield spreads while the third dealt with call risk. Although the first three variables were significant, the relative security supply variable was not. Thus, when the yield series was adjusted for tax and other effects, Cook and Hendershott did not find relative security supplies to be a significant explainer of the observed yield spread between corporate and Treasury securities. This finding is contrary to the results of Fair and Malkiel, who use unadjusted yield series.

In addition to the aspect discussed previously, Jaffee's study tested for market segmentation. He contended that if perfect market segmentation exists, yields would depend only on those exogeneous forces which influence the supply and demand for bonds. On the other hand, if a perfect substitutes hypothesis holds, the risk structure would be fixed over time and the yield on a bond would be a function only of the risk-free rate. Jaffee suggested that a mix of these two results would be consistent with the preferred habitat theory, where partial segmentation exists. Using the corporate data previously described, Jaffee could find no evidence of market segmentation. For municipal bonds, however, certain variables pertaining to the ability of commercial banks to invest were found to be significant, supporting the notion of a segmentation effect. However, the tests were not well suited to pick up this effect; the primary contribution of the study was the analysis of other factors which explain the cyclical behavior of yield differentials.

In the study of municipal bond yield differentials by Earl D. Benson, David S. Kidwell, Timothy W. Koch, and Robert J. Rogowski, also described earlier, the market segmentation variable was the ratio of net purchases by banks to total net purchases of municipal securities. This variable had a negative and significant impact on yield differentials for Aa and A rated bonds and a positive and significant effect on yield differentials for Baa and lower rated bonds.[34] The authors contended that these findings are consistent with a market segmentation effect, as commercial banks exhibit a definite preference for A or higher rated bonds.[35] Even though

---

[33]To isolate the effect of the Consolidated Edison failure to pay a dividend in 1974, a utility yield series was used up to that time and the industrial yield series after.

[34]The yield differentials are Aa–Aaa, A–Aaa, Baa–Aaa and so forth.

[35]In another study of municipal securities, Timothy S. Campbell, "On the Extent of Segmentation in the Municipal Securities Market," *Journal of Money, Credit and Banking*, 12 (February 1980): 71–83, also tested for segmentation in the municipal securities market. His findings did not indicate a market segmentation effect when he tested prime and good grade municipal securities. However, the lack of inclusion of lower grade securities does not permit a true test of investment restriction by commercial banks.

Baa bonds are investment grade, banks apparently shy away from them, as they do altogether from lower-grade bonds in which they cannot invest.

In the other study of municipal bonds, David S. Kidwell and Timothy W. Koch tested for a market segmentation effect in their study of the yield differential between revenue and general obligation municipal bonds. Because of both supply restrictions on general obligation bonds in times of high interest rates and the preference of commercial banks for general obligation as opposed to revenue bonds, a case is made for market segmentation. The results of empirical tests with a very large sample showed the yield differential to narrow as banks increase their relative demand for municipal securities and to widen as the supply of revenue bonds increases relative to the supply of general obligation bonds.

Overall, the empirical results are mixed on whether there is a market segmentation effect on the behavior of yield differentials over time. While there is some evidence of it for bank investment in municipal bonds, there is less evidence for corporate bonds. Until further studies are undertaken, it is not possible to make strong generalizations on the importance of this effect on the default risk structure of interest rates.

RISK STRUCTURE AND THE TERM STRUCTURE

With differences in both default risk and the length of time to maturity, yield curves may differ for different grades of securities. In other words, the default risk premium is not necessarily a constant function of the length of time to maturity. If the default risk premium were 2 percent on a long-term bond, it does not follow that the premium on a short-term security of the same grade also would be 2 percent. A priori, it might seem that the risk of default as perceived by investors for a particular grade of bond would vary directly with maturity. As the length of time to maturity grows shorter and the issuer does not default, a degree of uncertainty is resolved. With this resolution, investors may require a risk premium different from before, all other things the same.[36]

However, the direction of the bias may differ for different rating categories. For those where the financial condition of the typical company is sufficient to service debt, the probability of default perceived by investors would seem to lessen as maturity approaches. However, for rating categories where the financial condition of the typical company is insufficient

---

[36]Roland I. Robinson, in comparing the yield spread between Aaa and Baa municipal securities with the length of time to maturity, found that in most cases yield differentials were greater for long-term securities than they were for short-term ones. He concluded that default risk was an increasing function of maturity. *Postwar Market for State and Local Government Securities* (New York: National Bureau of Economic Research, 1960), pp. 184–88.

or marginal with respect to servicing debt and meeting the final redemption, the perceived probability of default may increase as maturity decreases.[37] Consequently, for lower-grade categories of bonds, the risk of default may not be an increasing function of maturity. For these grades, the probability of default may increase as the final redemption date grows nearer and the company is unable to improve its financial condition. Implied is a bias toward a downward-sloping yield curve.

Ramon E. Johnson defines the latter problem as "crisis-at-maturity."[38] This viewpoint, which arose during the depression, suggests that because of the difficulty of refinancing and meeting the final redemption payment during crisis periods, short maturities are more risky than long maturities. During periods of economic prosperity, crisis-at-maturity would be a factor only for lower quality bonds. The two types of bias are illustrated in Fig. 8-9. In both cases, the yield curve for default-free securities is assumed to be horizontal. The upper panel shows the pattern for high-grade securities, and the lower one the pattern for low-grade securities.

Empirical Evidence

The most interesting part of Johnson's study was the construction of yield curves based upon empirical data for five grades of corporate securities and the comparison of these yield curves with Durand's basic corporate yield curves. Recall from the previous chapter that Durand's yield curves depict the yield-maturity relationship for corporate bonds of the lowest default risk. Johnson plotted yield curves for 1910 through 1944, although only fourteen of them were shown in the article. Of particular interest were the yield curves which occurred during the depression. From 1933 on, the highest-grade issues tended to be upward-sloping, as was Durand's basic yield curve, while lower-grade issues were downward-sloping. Examples of yield curves for 1934 and 1938 are shown in Fig. 8-10. The line with the *B*'s refers to the basic yield curve, while the numbers 1 to 5 refer to different grading categories, from high to low.

Johnson postulated that the downward-sloping yield curves for lower quality issues, seen particularly during the depression, were primarily the result of crisis-at-maturity considerations. Upward-sloping yield curves for low-grade bonds occurred only when the prospect for crisis-at-maturity was slight. Moreover, Johnson contended that upward-sloping yield curves for

---

[37] In many cases, the redemption of a bond issue comes through refinancing with a new bond issue. As the ability to go to market with a new bond issue depends upon the financial condition of the company, the above argument holds regardless of the intended means for redemption.

[38] Ramon E. Johnson, "Term Structures of Corporate Bond Yields as a Function of Risk of Default," *Journal of Finance,* 22 (May 1967): 318–21.

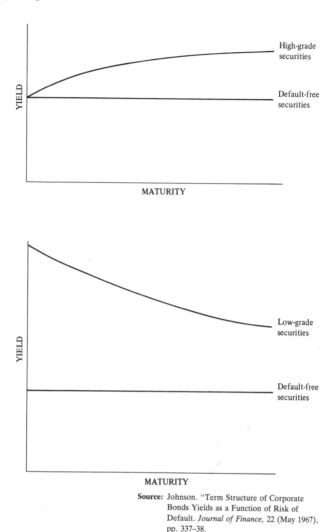

Source: Johnson. "Term Structure of Corporate
Bonds Yields as a Function of Risk of
Default. *Journal of Finance,* 22 (May 1967),
pp. 337–38.

Figure 8-9. Default risk premiums and maturity.

high-grade securities were the result of risk premiums increasing with maturity. On the other hand, U-shaped curves were said to result from a combination of crisis-at-maturity considerations and expectations that default risk premiums would increase in the future. Similarly, yield curves of other shapes were explained in terms of risk premiums increasing with maturity, crisis-at-maturity, and expectations of changing risk premiums.

Rather than compare yield differentials with maturity, J. B. Silvers investigates the behavior of derived certainty equivalent coefficients.[39] This approach can be expressed as

[39]J. B. Silvers, "An Alternative to the Yield Spread as a Measure of Risk," *Journal of Finance,* 28 (September 1973): 933–55.

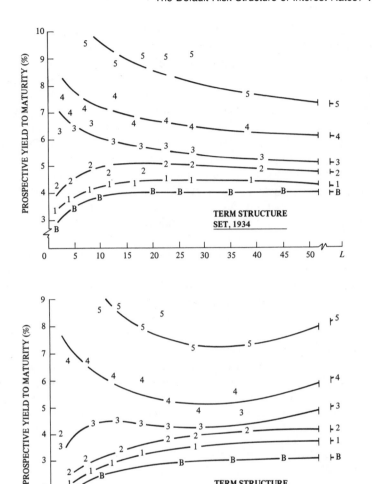

Figure 8-10. Term structure for various grade bonds.

$$P_0 = \frac{\alpha_1 C_1}{(1+i_1)} + \frac{\alpha_2 C_2}{(1+i_2)^2} + \cdots + \frac{\alpha_n C_n}{(1+i_n)^n} \qquad (8\text{-}6)$$

where P_0 is the market price of the bond at time 0

α_t is the certainty equivalent coefficient for period t

C_t is the payment of interest and/or principal in period t

n is the number of years until the final payment

i_t is the risk-free rate in period t

The coefficient α_t is a value between 0 and 1.00 and it varies inversely with the degree of risk. It supposedly represents the ratio of what market participants would regard as a certain cash flow in period t to the promised amount of cash flow.

Silvers studies the pattern of the α_t with respect to maturity, i.e., when t is varied. Recall from our discussion of Fig. 8-9 that "normal" risk adjustment for high-grade securities implies that risk premiums increase with maturity as uncertainty increases. For lower-grade securities, however, the crisis-at-maturity argument implies that risk premiums decrease with maturity. These two situations are illustrated in Fig. 8-11 for certainty equivalent coefficients. On the left-hand side, the relationship between yield and maturity is illustrated, similar to the relationship shown in Fig. 8-9. On the right-hand side, these relationships are transformed into patterns of relationship between certainty equivalent coefficients and maturity. In the case of crisis-at-maturity, certainty equivalent coefficients drop very rapidly at first and then decrease at a decreasing rate. For the risk adjustment of high-grade securities, certainty equivalent coefficients decline much more gradually at first. Thus, the shape of the certainty equivalent curve gives evidence of the pattern of risk premium variation with maturity.

Silvers estimated certainty equivalent coefficients for 5-, 15-, and 30-year maturities, attempting to hold constant the effects of marketability, callability, and capital gains. The sample period was 1952 to 1964, and Aaa through Baa grade corporate bonds were studied. On the basis of the three observations, certainty equivalent curves were drawn. The results for Aaa and A ratings are shown in Fig. 8-12. Among other things, Silvers found that the certainty equivalent coefficients tended to be lower, the lower the grade of the bond. Also, the coefficients tended to be lower in a period of economic contraction than they were in a period of expansion. (In the figure, recessions are denoted by the shaded areas.) Together these findings

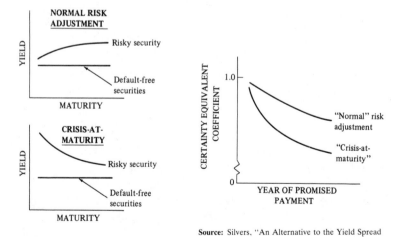

Source: Silvers, "An Alternative to the Yield Spread as a Measure of Risk." *Journal of Finance,* 28 (September, 1973), 938.

Figure 8-11. Patterns of certainty equivalent coefficients.

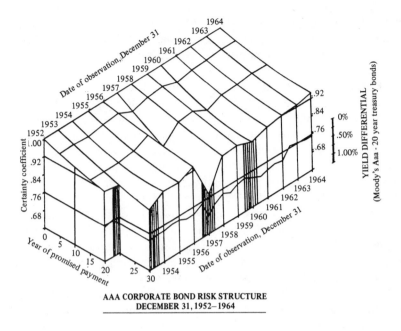

**AAA CORPORATE BOND RISK STRUCTURE
DECEMBER 31, 1952–1964**

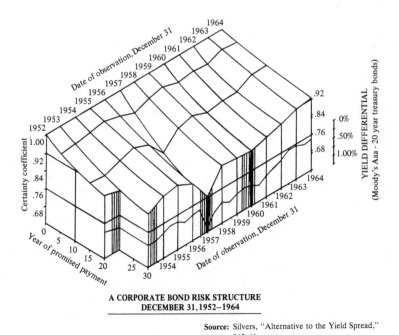

**A CORPORATE BOND RISK STRUCTURE
DECEMBER 31, 1952–1964**

Source: Silvers, "Alternative to the Yield Spread,"
945–46.

Figure 8-12. Certainty equivalent coefficients and maturity over time.

are consistent with previous evidence on the cyclical behavior of risk premiums. Additionally, the findings give indication that the "crisis-at-maturity" argument is more important during recessions and for lower-grade securities.

Through the use of certainty equivalent coefficients, Calvin M. Boardman and Richard W. McNally also attempted to decompose the payments stream of a bond into a time component and a default-risk component.[40] Unlike Silvers, however, the coefficients are not constrained in the estimating process. Also, the authors added explanatory variables dealing with callability, sinking fund status, security status, marketability, listing, industrial classification, and the beta measure of the bond's systematic volatility. Using Aaa through Baa corporate bonds for each of the years 1972–1975, the authors plotted the certainty equivalent coefficients. These coefficients result from regressions for each of the four credit rating classes, holding statistically constant the other variables. In general, the coefficient weights are less than one and decline at a decreasing rate with futurity. Also, there is a tendency for the higher-rated bonds to have higher certainty equivalents. One of the most interesting aspects of the study has to do with the spread between plots for the four credit rating categories. For 1972, a good economic year, the spreads are small and do not increase much with futurity. For 1974, a recession, the certainty equivalent coefficients decline much more markedly with futurity and the spreads widen. This behavior is consistent with the crisis-at-maturity hypothesis for lower-grade securities. The authors concluded that economic conditions directly influence the shape and spread of the term structures for various grades of corporate bonds.

In another study of default risk premiums for different maturities, I analyzed commercial paper and long-term bond rates for a sample of individual companies over the period 1972–1974.[41] Risk premiums for short- and long-term debt instruments were found to behave differently over time. In the latter part of the sample period, the average commercial paper risk premium was above the average long-term bond risk premium, whereas it was below in the earlier part. In the 1974 recession, there was an alleged "flight to quality" in the capital markets, where investors were said to seek high-grade securities, in particular Treasury securities. The late 1973–1974 evidence for commercial paper risk premiums, relative to long-term bond risk premiums, was consistent with crisis-at-maturity. However, when default risk premiums were analyzed company by company, the notion that short-term default risk premiums should be higher in relation to long-term risk premiums for lower-grade companies than they are for higher-grade

---

[40]Calvin M. Boardman and Richard W. McNally, "Factors Affecting Seasoned Corporate Bond Prices," *Journal of Financial and Quantitative Analysis,* 16 (June 1981): 207–26.

[41]James C. Van Horne, "Behavior of Default-Risk Premiums for Corporate Bonds and Commercial Paper," *Journal of Business Research,* 7 (December 1979): 301–13.

companies was not supported. In this regard, a number of risk measures were used to depict the grade of company. Moreover, factor analysis was employed and it did not reveal any underlying pattern of relationship for the company-by-company behavior of short- and long-term default risk premiums over time.

In a similar test for municipal bonds, Thomas H. McInish also found that the default risk premiums were not invariant with respect to maturity.[42] Testing risk premiums for 1-, 5-, 10-, 15- and 20-year maturities, the author found significant differences in them, but no clear-cut pattern between the risk premiums and maturity.

In summary, the various studies reviewed give us insight into the relationship between risk premiums and maturity, as well as insight into changes in this relationship depending on the phase of the economy. In the first three studies, there is indication that the lower the grade of the bond, the greater the risk premium tends to be. Also, the crisis-at-maturity argument appears to be important in depressions and recessions, but not important in periods of economic expansion. It seems clear that risk premiums are not invariant with respect to maturity, though there is little consistent pattern over time. In studying the risk structure of interest rates, we have been concerned with differences in yield for different types and grades of securities, holding maturity constant. However, one must be mindful that the risk structure is different for different maturities and that the relationship between the risk structure and maturity can change over time.

SUMMARY

The relationship between yield and the risk of default, with other factors constant, is known as the risk structure of interest rates. This relationship usually is studied through the analysis of risk premiums, the difference between the yield on a security and the yield on a corresponding security which is free of default risk. The promised yield on a security is its *ex ante* yield at a moment in time. The expected yield, on the other hand, is the expected value of the probability distribution of possible realized yields. The distribution itself is highly skewed to the left. In perfect markets and with risk neutrality, the expected yield for investors at the margin should equal the risk-free rate. If this relationship held, the expected default loss on a security would equal the market-determined risk premium. However, to the extent that the market as a whole is adverse to dispersion and skewness to the left of the probability distribution, the

---

[42]Thomas H. McInish, "Behavior of Municipal Default-Risk Premiums by Maturity," *Journal of Business Research,* 8 (December 1980): 418–28.

risk premium will exceed the default loss expected by investors at the margin.

Empirical studies of default losses show that default experience is highly correlated with the economic cycle. It is only with a severe economic downturn, such as a depression, that widespread default occurs and there are differences between promised and realized returns for a significant number of securities. Various investment agencies rate securities as to their probability of default. Available evidence suggests that these ratings are reasonably consistent with respect to default risk. They also suggest consistency with respect to certain financial ratios involving earnings, earnings stability, and debt coverage. Another method for analyzing yield differentials is through regression analysis, and various studies concerning its use were examined. For both public debt issues and private placements, there is a significant and positive relationship between promised yields and various variables which depict the risk of a corporation. In recent years, considerable attention has been directed toward predicting corporate bankruptcy on the basis of the pattern of past financial ratios. The empirical studies examined suggest that signs of potential failure are evident before actual failure occurs.

An important facet of the default risk structure of interest rates is the cyclical behavior of risk premiums. Various evidence indicates a tendency for risk premiums to widen during a period of economic contraction and to narrow during a period of expansion. This is consistent with investors' utility preferences changing with the state of the economy—investors being more concerned with safety in an economic downturn than they are in a period of prosperity. Whether this is the cause or not, it is clear that risk premiums are affected by the level of economic activity.

In addition to the cyclical behavior of risk premiums over time, there may be a market segmentation effect. Various institutional restrictions on the demand for and the supply of bonds of various types and grades were discussed. Empirical testing is largely inconclusive regarding whether these restrictions have a meaningful impact on the behavior of risk premiums over time. The possible exception is indication of a segmentation effect for commercial bank investment in the municipal bond market.

Finally, the default-risk structure and the term structure of interest rates were examined jointly in an effort to explain differing shapes of yield curves for different risk categories of securities. The idea that uncertainty is resolved as maturity grows shorter implies a bias toward an upward-sloping yield curve for high-grade securities and a downward-sloping yield curve for low-grade securities. Empirical studies have shown this tendency to be evident during periods of economic contraction. Also, risk premiums are found not to be constant with respect to maturity.

SELECTED REFERENCES

Atkinson, Thomas R., *Trends in Corporate Bond Quality*. New York: National Bureau of Economic Research, 1967.

Benson, Earl D., David S. Kidwell, Timothy W. Koch, and Robert J. Rogowski, "Systematic Variation in Yield Spreads for Tax-Exempt General Obligation Bonds," *Journal of Financial and Quantitative Analysis*, 16 (December 1981): 685–702.

Boardman, Calvin M., and Richard W. McNally, "Factors Affecting Seasoned Corporate Bond Prices," *Journal of Financial and Quantitative Analysis*, 16 (June 1981): 207–26.

Campbell, Timothy S., "On the Extent of Segmentation in the Municipal Securities Market," *Journal of Money, Credit and Banking*, 12 (February 1980): 71–83.

Cohan, Avery B., *Yields on Corporate Debt Directly Placed*. New York: National Bureau of Economic Research, 1967.

Cook, Timothy Q., and Patric H. Hendershott, "The Impact of Taxes, Risk and Relative Security Supplies on Interest Rate Differentials," *Journal of Finance*, 33 (September 1978): 1173–86.

Fair, Ray C., and Burton G. Malkiel, "The Determination of Yield Differentials between Debt Instruments of the Same Maturity," *Journal of Money, Credit and Banking*, 3 (November 1971): 733–49.

Ferri, Michael G., and James P. Gaines, "A Study of Yield Spreads in the Money Market," *Financial Management*, 9 (Autumn 1980): 52–59.

Fisher, Lawrence, "Determinants of Risk Premiums on Corporate Bonds," *Journal of Political Economy*, 67 (June 1959): 217–37.

Fraine, Harold G., and Robert H. Mills, "Effects of Defaults and Credit Deterioration on Yields of Corporate Bonds," *Journal of Finance*, 16 (September 1961): 423–34.

Hempel, George H., *The Postwar Quality of State and Local Debt*. New York: National Bureau of Economic Research, 1971.

Hickman, W. Braddock, *Corporate Bond Quality and Investor Experience*. New York: National Bureau of Economic Research, 1958.

Jaffee, Dwight M., "Cyclical Variations in the Risk Structure of Interest Rates," *Journal of Monetary Economics*, 1 (July 1975): 309–25.

Joehnk, Michael D., and James F. Nielsen, "Return and Risk Characteristics of Speculative Grade Bonds," *Quarterly Review of Economics and Business*, 15 (Spring 1975): 27–46.

Johnson, Ramon E., "Term Structures of Corporate Bond Yields as a Function of Risk of Default," *Journal of Finance*, 22 (May 1967): 313–45.

Kidwell, David S., and Timothy W. Koch, "The Behavior of the Interest Rate Differential Between Tax-Exempt Revenue and General Obligation Bonds," *Journal of Finance*, 37 (March 1982): 73–85.

Robinson, Roland I., *Postwar Market for State and Local Government Securities*. New York: National Bureau of Economic Research, 1960.

Silvers, J. B., "An Alternative to the Yield Spread as a Measure of Risk," *Journal of Finance,* 28 (September 1973): 933–55.

Soldofsky, Robert M., and Dale F. Max, *Holding Period Yields and Risk-Premium Curves for Long-Term Marketable Securities: 1910–1976.* New York: New York University Salomon Brothers Center for the Study of Financial Institutions, 1978.

Van Horne, James C., "Optimal Initiation of Bankruptcy Proceedings by Debt Holders," *Journal of Finance,* 31 (June 1976): 897–910.

———, "Behavior of Default-Risk Premiums for Corporate Bonds and Commercial Paper," *Journal of Business Research,* 7 (December 1979): 301–13.

———, and Samuel S. Stewart, "A Simultaneous Equations Analysis of the Bond Markets," *The Southern Economic Journal,* XXXVIII (April 1972): 538–46.

West, Richard R., "Bond Ratings, Bond Yields and Financial Regulations: Some Findings," *Journal of Law and Economics,* 16 (April 1973): 159–68.

9

THE CALL FEATURE AND
SINKING FUND PROVISION

In the preceding four chapters, the influences of maturity and default risk on fixed-income security returns were analyzed. Also investigated, from a mathematical standpoint, was the coupon rate effect. We saw that the higher the coupon rate, the shorter the duration of the instrument; in turn, it was shown that this can have an effect on the yield to maturity. In this chapter we consider the impact that a call feature can have on returns, as well as the effect of the *type* of call feature employed. As we shall see, discount bonds and callability are intertwined in the sense that the discount in some measure protects the investor from a call. Consequently, callability has an influence on the valuation of discount bonds. (Another factor affecting their value is *taxability,* a topic considered in the next chapter.)

In this chapter we also explore the workings of the sinking fund provision and its effect on a bond's value. Depending on callability and sinking fund influences, two bonds, which are alike in all other respects, may be valued differently in the market and have different yields. Thus, this chapter is an extension of our on-going effort to explain interest rate differentials.

THE NATURE OF THE CALL FEATURE

A call provision gives the issuer the option to buy back the instrument at a specified price before maturity. The price at which this occurs is known as the *call price* and it usually is above the *face value* or *par value* of the security. In most cases, it declines over time. For example, a 25-year corporate bond might be callable at $112 ($1,120 per $1,000 face value bond) the first 2 years, at $111 the second 2 years, $110 the next 2, and so on. Frequently, the call price in the first year is established at 1 year's interest above the face value of the bond. If the coupon rate were 14 percent, the initial price might be $114 ($1,140 per $1,000 face value).

Forms of the Provision

The call feature itself may take several forms. The security may be *immediately callable,* which simply means that the instrument may be bought back by the issuer at the call price at any time. Even here, the investor is partially protected from a call because the initial call price is above the face value of the bond. Moreover, there are a number of expenses and inconveniences associated with refunding a bond issue which must be factored in by the borrower before a decision to call a bond issue is made. However, should interest rates decline significantly, the issuer may wish to call the bond. Rather than being immediately callable, the call provision may be *deferred* for a period of time. This means that the instrument cannot be called during the deferment period; thus, the investor is protected from a call.

Virtually all corporate bond and preferred stock issues have a call feature. Between the end of World War II and the late 1950s, most issues to the public were immediately callable. Because of increasing interest rates and the accompanying fear of investors that in a cyclical interest-rate decline many issues would be called, the *deferment period* became an attractive feature in selling an issue. Corporations responded accordingly. From this time until the late 1960s, both immediately callable and deferred callable bonds were issued in the corporate market. In the late 1960s, however, interest rates increased to such levels that immediately callable bonds found little favor in the market. Since then, the vast majority of corporate bond issues have had a call feature with a deferment period. Most utility issues carry a deferment period of 5 years, while industrial issues have a 10-year deferment period. While 5 and 10 years are the most typical deferment periods, some corporate issues have deferment periods between 5 and 10 years.

Behavior of Noncorporate Borrowers

In contrast to corporate bonds, where virtually all bond issues are callable, only some municipal bonds are callable. It is important to distinguish between the two principal types of municipal securities: general credit obligations and revenue bonds. *General credit obligation bonds* are backed by the "full faith and credit" of the municipality—e.g., its full taxing power. *Revenue bonds,* however, are backed only by the revenue of the specific project and not by the taxing power of the municipality. An example of a revenue bond issue is a bond issue to build a toll road. Most revenue bond issues contain a call feature; this makes sense since it is logical to retire some of the bonds outstanding if there is any excess cash as a result of revenues exceeding projections. For general obligation issues, the percentage with a call feature is much less. In this case, callable bonds are the exception rather than the rule.[1] One reason for this may be the nature of political life. If a municipal security were made callable, in most cases the immediate interest cost to the municipality would rise. Gordon Pye suggests that the issuance of callable bonds would result in higher current taxes, with the possibility of tax savings some time in the future.[2] Because public officials may not be in office in the future, Pye reasons that they place a higher utility on lower taxes now than on possible savings in the future.

Another reason for state and local governments to issue noncallable bonds is the difference between their borrowing and lending rates. Because interest on municipal securities is exempt from federal income taxes, the borrowing rate is lower than the lending rate; the latter rate might be the return on a Treasury or corporate bond. Richard R. West theorizes that public officials may discount possible future interest savings by the lending, rather than the borrowing, rate. If that is true, the present value of expected cash savings from the exercise of the call privilege would usually be less than the cost of the privilege, and thereby its attractiveness would be reduced considerably.[3]

While most Treasury securities are noncallable, the call provision for those that are is geared to final maturity. For example, the 11¾ percent bonds of February 2005–2010 have a call feature which enables the Treasury to call the bonds anytime between February 2005 and the final maturity five years later, February 2010. The primary purpose of the call privilege is to give flexibility in refinancing to the Treasury. Unlike that of some corporations, the debt of the federal government is rolled over at maturity. The Treasury is primarily concerned with the tone of the market when it

---

[1]David S. Kidwell, in "The Inclusion and Exercise of Call Provisions by State and Local Governments," *Journal of Money, Credit and Banking,* 8 (August 1976): 391–8, analyzed almost all municipal bond issues between 1959 and 1967. He found that 31 percent of the general-obligation issues contained call provisions, whereas 94 percent of the revenue issues contained call provisions. The annual percentages ranged from 24 to 40 percent and from 88 to 97 percent for general-obligation and revenue issues, respectively.

[2]Gordon Pye, "The Value of the Call Option on a Bond," *Journal of Political Economy,* 74 (April 1966): 200–1.

[3]Richard R. West, "On the Noncallability of State and Local Bonds: A Comment," *Journal of Political Economy,* 75 (February 1967): 98–9.

has to refinance its maturing obligations. By having 5 years in which to roll over the debt, the Treasury can be flexible in the timing of its refinancing. Thus, the principal purpose of the call privilege is not to achieve a savings in interest, but rather to obtain flexibility in financing near the final maturity of the existing obligation. The call feature is basically restricted to long-term Treasury bonds; only about one-sixth of the bonds outstanding carry this feature. Because the maturity of the Treasury bond can be shortened by only 5 years, the call feature does not pose the same disadvantage to investors as does the call privilege for a corporate bond.[4]

A form of call privilege exists for mortgages. Unless otherwise specified in the contract, the borrower may pay off the loan at any time. In other words, the loan is callable immediately. Frequently, however, lenders demand a prepayment penalty if the loan is paid off before a certain date. For example, insurance companies usually require a prepayment penalty on mortgages, graduated downward through 5 years. After 5 years, the loan can be paid without penalty. In times of high interest rates, banks and savings and loan associations also impose prepayment penalties on their mortgage loans.

Putable Bonds

In recent years, there have been a limited number of fixed-income security issues having a put feature. With this feature, after a specified period of time the investor has the option to "put" the securities back to the borrower at a specified price. The first example occurred in June 1976, when Beneficial Corporation issued $150 million of 8 percent, 25-year debentures, which gave the holder the option to have the company redeem the bonds at their face value anytime from the seventh to the twenty-fourth year. A second example of a reverse call feature is the Federal Home Loan Mortgage Corporation's guaranteed mortgage certificates. Here the investor has the option of requiring the corporation to repurchase the certificate at its face value at a specified date (usually 15 to 20 years from the date of issue). Since being first offered in 1976, a limited number of putable bonds have appeared. Interestingly, foreign borrowers in the U.S. market (Yankee bonds) have made significant use of this feature.

The advantage of the put feature to investors is obvious; in times of rising interest rates they may put the bonds to the issuer and invest in bonds providing higher yields. Instead of the option to exercise lying with

[4]For callable Treasury bonds, yield to maturity is computed on the basis of final maturity when the market price of the bond is *below* its face value and on the basis of the earliest call date when its market price is *above* face value. When it is below face value, the implication is that the Treasury is unlikely to call the security.

the borrower, as it does with a call feature, the option rests with the investor. As the principles of valuation of a putable bond are nearly the mirror image of those for the regular call feature, we confine our attention to call features where the option rests with the borrower.

THE VALUE OF THE CALL FEATURE

The call provision gives the borrower flexibility. Should interest rates decline significantly, the borrower can call the debt instrument and refinance at a lower interest cost. However, the decline in interest rates must be sufficient to offset the fact that the call price is above the face value of the instrument and the fact that there are flotation, legal, and inconvenience costs.[5] With a call provision, the borrower does not have to wait until final maturity to refinance. The optimal time for an issuer to call bonds is when the present value of the difference between the price at which the new, or refunding, bonds can be issued and the call price is greatest (holding constant the coupon rate and the final maturity).[6] In addition to flexibility, the call provision may be advantageous to a corporation with unduly restrictive protective covenants in its existing bond indenture. (The indenture is a legal document spelling out the conditions of the loan and the covenants under which default occurs.) By calling the bonds before maturity, the company can eliminate these restrictions.

The call privilege works to the benefit of the borrower but to the detriment of investors. If interest rates fall and the bond issue is called, they can invest in other bonds only at a sacrifice in yield to maturity. From the standpoint of an investor, bonds with the call feature have a different probability distribution of possible returns from bonds that have no call feature. To illustrate, suppose that an investor had the probabilistic beliefs about a callable bond and a noncallable bond shown in Fig. 9-1. We assume that the two bonds are alike in all other respects and both have 20 years to maturity. The distributions are skewed to the left because of the possibility of default, an influence examined in the previous chapter. The most favorable outcome is that all principal and interest payments will be met on time, so that the realized rate of return equals the promised yield at the time of purchase. Should interest or principal payments not occur as

---

[5]For an analysis of the profitability of refunding by the borrower, see Oswald D. Bowlin, "The Refunding Decision: Another Special Case in Capital Budgeting," *Journal of Finance,* 21 (March 1966): 55–68; and Aharon R. Ofer and Robert A. Taggart, Jr., "Bond Refunding: A Clarifying Analysis," *Journal of Finance,* 32 (March 1977): 21–30; Jess B. Yawitz and James A. Anderson, "The Effect of Bond Refunding on Shareholder Wealth," *Journal of Finance,* 32 (December 1977): 1738–46; and W.M. Boyce and A.J. Kalotay, "Optimum Bond Calling and Refunding," *Interfaces, The Institute of Management Science,* 9 (November 1979): 36–49.
[6]See Pye, "Value of the Call Option," pp. 200–1.

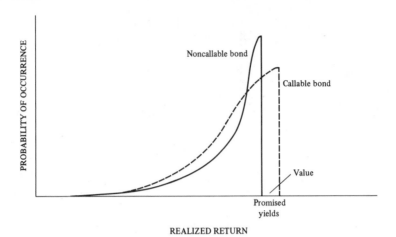

Figure 9-1. Probability distributions for noncallable and callable corporate bonds.

scheduled, the realized yield will be less. (The deviation from promised yield for the noncallable bond depends entirely on the degree of default.)

On the right-hand side of the figure, the likely consequence of the bond having a call feature is shown. We see that there is still the strong possibility that the actual yield will equal the promised yield, although the probability is less. However, there is now a reasonable probability that the bond will be called and that the investor's actual return over the 20 years, including reinvestment, will be less than the promised yield. This negative factor is *in addition* to the possibility of default. As a result, for the callable bond there is a greater probability that the realized return, including reinvestment in a lower-yielding bond, will be less than that of the noncallable bond. This is noticeable in the midrange of realized returns. The extreme tail of the distribution for the callable bond is not altered materially, because it depends on a severe default occurring and not on the bond being called. It is the intermediate part of the distribution which is altered by the addition of the call feature.

Because of the disadvantage to the investor, the call privilege usually does not come free to the borrower. Its cost, or value, is measured by the difference in yield on the callable bond and the yield that would be necessary if the security were noncallable. In Fig. 9-1, it is represented on the horizontal axis by the distance between the two promised yields. In other words, the promised yield of the callable bond should be such that the marginal investor is indifferent between it and a noncallable bond. More fundamentally, this yield is determined by supply and demand forces in the market for callable securities. In equilibrium, the value of the call feature will be just sufficient to bring the demand for callable securities by investors into balance with the supply of callable securities by borrowers.

Interest-Rate Expectations

In the equilibrating process, both borrowers and investors are influenced by expectations regarding the future course of interest rates. When interest rates are high and are expected to fall, the call feature is likely to have significant value. Investors are unwilling to invest in callable bonds unless such bonds yield more than bonds that are noncallable, all other things being the same. In other words, they must be compensated for the risk that the bonds might be called. On the other hand, borrowers are willing to pay a premium in yield for the call privilege in the belief that yields will fall and that it will be advantageous to refund the bonds. In equilibrium, both the marginal borrower and the marginal investor will be indifferent as to whether the bond is callable or noncallable.[7]

When interest rates are low and expected to rise, the call privilege may have negligible value, in that the borrower might pay the same yield if there were no call privilege. For the privilege to have value, interest-rate expectations must be such that there is a possibility that the issue will be called. If interest rates are very low and are not expected to fall further, there is little probability that the bonds will be called. The key factor is that the borrower has to be able to refund the issue at a profit. For it to do so, interest rates have to drop significantly, since the issuer must pay the call price, which usually is at a premium above par value, as well as flotation costs involved in the refunding. If there is no probability that the borrower can refund the issue profitably, the call feature is unlikely to have a value.

Asymmetrical Tax Effects

In the equilibrating process, which determines the value of the call feature, taxes may play a role. When a bond is called, the *call premium* is treated as a capital gain from the standpoint of the investor. (The call premium is simply the difference between the call price and the face value of the bond.) On the other hand, the premium is treated as an expense by the corporation calling the bond. It is able to deduct this expense against income that otherwise would be taxed at the full corporate tax rate. On the average, the capital gains tax to the investor tends to be less than the corporate tax rate. Jess B. Yawitz and William J. Marshall contended that the total taxes paid by investors and the corporation will be less for a called bond than for a noncallable bond.[8] As a result, there is an incentive

---

[7]Pye, "Value of the Call Option," p. 203.

[8]Jess B. Yawitz and William J. Marshall, "Why Firms Issue Callable Debt: A Bias in the Tax Laws," Working Paper, Washington University, 1978. See also William Marshall and Jess B. Yawitz, "Optimal Terms of the Call Provision on a Corporate Bond," *Journal of Financial Research,* 3 (Fall 1980): 203–11.

to issue callable bonds. The authors suggested that the present value of the expected tax reduction represents a net gain, which is shared between the investor and the borrowing corporation in the yield equilibrating process.

In a different vein, W.M. Boyce and A.J. Kalotay argued that there is a net tax advantage anytime the marginal tax rate of the borrower exceeds that of the typical investor.[9] Their argument was that parties having high marginal tax rates will have lower after-tax discount rates than low-tax parties. Investors with lower tax rates and higher discount rates prefer a decreasing interest stream because of the present value implications. On the other hand, borrowers with higher tax rates and lower discount rates prefer to pay a decreasing stream of interest payments. Since the interest payments schedule on a callable bond and its possible refunding bond can never increase, but may well decrease, it is said to be favored by both parties over a noncallable bond. Precisely the opposite would occur if the borrower had a lower marginal tax rate than the typical investor. However this is unlikely for corporate bonds because a large portion is held by tax-exempt institutional investors. Thus, differences in tax rates between the borrower and lender may explain in part the absence of noncallable corporate bonds in recent years.

EMPIRICAL EVIDENCE ON VALUATION

Because virtually all corporate bonds have call features, empirical studies of the differential in yield on a noncallable bond and a callable bond are not possible. However, it is possible to examine the yield differential between newly issued corporate bonds having an immediate call privilege and those of the same grade having a 5-year or 10-year deferred call. For the immediate call privilege to have a value over the deferred call privilege, interest-rate expectations must be such that the immediately callable bond might be called during the deferment period. If there is no probability of its being called during this period, the value of the immediate over the deferred call privilege will be zero.

An examination of the yield differential between newly issued bonds of the same grade but with different call privileges reveals that the differential tends to increase in times of high interest rates and tight money, and to decline in periods of easy money and low interest rates. The differential for immediately callable and five-year deferred callable Aa public utility bonds over the period 1958–1970 is shown in Fig. 9-2. Unfortunately for empirical testing purposes, after the early 1970s utilities ceased to issue immediately callable bonds and issued only deferred callable bonds. In the

[9]W.M. Boyce and A.J. Kalotay, "Tax Differentials and Callable Bonds," *Journal of Finance,* 34 (September 1979): 825–38.

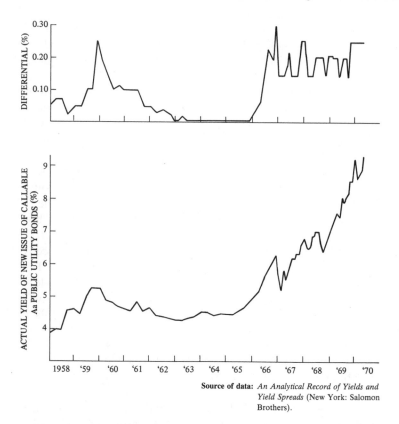

Source of data: *An Analytical Record of Yields and Yield Spreads* (New York: Salomon Brothers).

Figure 9-2. Yield differentials: new issues of callable and deferred callable Aa public utility bonds, 1958–1970.

figure, we see that for the periods of relatively high interest rates, 1959, 1966, and 1968–1970, the differential was fifteen to thirty basis points, whereas during the period 1963–1965, an immediately callable bond offered no premium over a deferred callable bond.

Frank C. Jen and James E. Wert tested the offering yields of newly issued utility bonds over the period 1960–1964 and found the yield differential to be around zero when coupon rates were low and positive when coupon rates were high.[10] In another test, Jen and Wert computed and compared average callable yields and average call-free yields on 434 utility issues issued between 1956 and 1964.[11] The authors found that in periods

---

[10]Frank C. Jen and James E. Wert, "The Value of the Deferred Call Privilege," *National Banking Review,* 3 (March 1966): 369–78. For an extension of this study, see Jen and Wert, "The Deferred Call Provision and Corporate Bond Yields," *Journal of Financial and Quantitative Analysis,* 3 (June 1968): 157–69.

[11]Jen and Wert, "The Effect of Call Risk on Corporate Bond Yields," *Journal of Finance,* 22 (December 1967): 637–51.

of relatively high interest rates, a number of issues were called. As a result, the average yield actually realized by investors on bonds issued in periods of high interest rates was only slightly higher than the average yield realized on bonds issued in moderate interest-rate periods.

In another study of callable corporate bonds, Mark W. Frankena analyzed yield spreads between low coupon and higher coupon public utility bonds during 1957–1967.[12] His findings were consistent with low coupon bonds having much less possibility of being called than high coupon bonds; hence they provide a lower yield to maturity. Frankena also found that because high coupon bonds were in danger of a call in an interest rate trough, their market prices did not rise significantly above their call prices. Finally, the presence of a deferment period was found to make such bonds more attractive than immediately callable bonds and, hence, to result in a lower relative yield.

One problem in testing returns on called bonds is that corporate bond refundings, by which an issue is called and refinanced with a new issue having a lower interest cost, occur in waves. Only when interest rates decline significantly below previous cyclical peaks are refundings profitable from the standpoint of the issuer. In the 1970s, peak yields occurred in 1970, 1974, and 1979. While interest rates declined from their 1970 peak and remained lower from 1971 through 1973, bonds issued in 1970 were protected by their deferment periods. Bonds issued in peak periods during the 1960s had coupon rates below the yields of 1971–1973, so it was not profitable to refund them. Only in late 1976 and 1977 did interest rates dip below those that prevailed in late 1969 and 1970. Both before and after (to 1980), interest rates were higher. Therefore, the only time refundings were meaningful in the decade of the 1970's was during 1976–1977.

For corporate bonds called during this time, I compared the initial yield to maturity of the called bond with the combined yield of this bond together with the refunding bond.[13] In all cases, the investor suffered an opportunity loss, ranging from a few basis points up 0.90 percent. A second test involved the comparison of the realized return from the time of issuance to the time of call of the called bond with the realized return over the same holding period for a lower coupon bond of the same company. The return to call was found to be significantly higher than the return available on the lower coupon bond, which was not called, the average differential being 1.61 percent. Two things explained this occurrence: the call price premium and the fact that the lower coupon bonds have capital gains tax advantages

[12]Mark W. Frankena, "The Influence of Call Provisions and Coupon Rate on Yields of Corporate Bonds," in Jack M. Guttentag, ed., *Essays on Interest Rates,* Vol. 2 (New York: National Bureau of Economic Research, 1971), pp. 134–86.

[13]James C. Van Horne, "Called Bonds: How did the Investor Fare?," *Journal of Portfolio Management,* 6 (Summer 1980): 58–61.

associated with them, resulting in a somewhat lower before-tax yield. Until the time of call then, called bonds tended to provide a higher return than noncalled bonds of the same company; however, the investor suffered an opportunity loss on reinvestment, which more than offset this gain.[14]

In a study of municipal securities, Kidwell analyzed 9,420 issues between 1959 and 1967 regarding the incidence and nature of a call feature.[15] Both general obligations and revenue issues were analyzed. Surprisingly, no statistically significant relationship was found between the percentage of issues which had a call provision and the level of interest rates. Of the bonds that were callable, Kidwell could find no relationship between the number of years to first call (12.2- to 13.2-year range for general obligation and 8.9- to 9.9-year range for revenue bonds) and the level of interest rates. One might expect the deferment period to lengthen as interest rates rose. In testing another hypothesis, Kidwell found that the observed exercise of the call provision by municipalities decreased with the level of interest rates. This makes sense, of course, because only when interest rates decline would we expect a significant number of bonds outstanding to be refunded at a lower interest cost. However, while the relationship was statistically significant, the explanatory power was relatively low, particularly for revenue issues. Kidwell suggests that refunding may not be the dominant motive for the exercise of the call feature by a municipality.

In general, the evidence on corporate bonds is consistent with the notion that the call privilege has the most value, and the most cost to the issuer, when interest rates are high and are expected to fall. By the same token, the call privilege has the greatest potential benefit to the corporation at this time. However, for this privilege the corporation must pay a cost at the time the bonds are sold, for the investor suffers an opportunity loss on reinvestment should the bonds be called. The higher the coupon rate, the greater the danger to the investor of a call, if interest rates should decline. In contrast, a low coupon rate protects the investor because it lessens the probability of a call. However, the market for callable bonds of different coupon rates should equilibrate so that at a moment in time, the marginal investor is indifferent among the various issues. While some of these notions are apparent when municipal bond evidence is examined, there has been a lack of empirical work here. Virtually no work has been done on the call feature for Treasury bonds or on the value of the prepayment penalty for mortgages.

---

[14]Michael G. Ferri, "Systematic Return Risk and the Call Risk of Corporate Debt Instruments," *Journal of Financial Research,* 1 (Winter 1978): 1–13, relates call risk to systematic fluctuations in a bond's price with the market. He finds that bonds with high systematic risk and, hence, call risk have higher yields than bonds with low systematic risk.

[15]Kidwell, "Inclusion and Exercise of Call Provisions."

THE CALL FEATURE AS AN OPTION

The call feature, of course, is an option given by investors to the borrower. Like any option, its value depends on the associated asset. With an option on common stock, for example, it is easy to demonstrate that the greater the variability of the stock, the greater the possibility of upside movements in the associated asset and the greater the value of the option. If the stock performs poorly, the option is not exercised and it has no value. However, its market price is bounded at zero on the downside. This feature, together with its upside potential, results in the distribution of possible returns on the option being skewed to the right. As a result, the greater the variability of the stock's price, the greater the possibility that the option may be exercised in the future at a profit, and the more valuable it becomes. Thus, the volatility of the associated asset's price is what is important in the valuation of options. (These concepts are explored in detail in Chapter 11 when we take up convertible securities.)

In the case of a call option, the associated asset is the bond that may be used to refund the one called. Consequently, it is the variance or likely volatility of interest rates which is important in determining the value of the call option to the borrower. The greater the volatility of future interest rates, the greater the possibility that the issuer of a callable bond may refund it with a bond having a lower interest cost, and the more valuable the option becomes.

This concept is illustrated in Fig. 9-3, where we assume that the call option pertains only to a given future date. In other words, the option can be exercised at only one time, this being the option date. The value of the bond is shown on the vertical axis and the interest rate in the market on

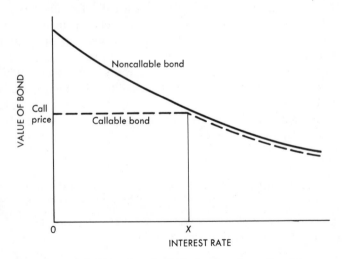

Figure 9-3. Valuation of callable bond on the option date.

the horizontal axis. For a noncallable bond, value decreases at a decreasing rate as the interest rate increases. For a callable bond, value is constrained on the upside by the call price. This occurs for lower levels of interest rates—to the left of X on the horizontal axis. In this range, the difference between the value of a noncallable bond and the value of a callable bond represents the value of the option on the option date. If interest rates are such that the bond's value as a noncallable bond is less than the call price, the company obviously will not call the issue. As a result, the value of the callable bond is the same as that of a noncallable bond for interest rates higher than X on the horizontal axis. The key to valuation of the option is the likelihood that interest rates will be less than X on the horizontal axis on the option date. This, in turn, depends on the variance of the distribution of possible interest rates. The greater the variance, the greater the expected value of the call option to the company.

In summary, the principles of option pricing theory, which we explore in detail in Chapter 11, apply in general to the valuation of the call feature. The greater the variance or uncertainty of future interest rates, the greater the value of the option to the borrower. In efficient financial markets, this means that the cost is greater as well, represented by the difference in promised yield on the callable bond and what would prevail if a noncallable bond were issued.

THE SINKING FUND PROVISION AND ITS CHARACTERISTICS

The majority of industrial bond issues and about one-quarter of public utility and other corporate bond issues carry a provision for a *sinking fund*. With this provision, the borrower is required to retire a specified face value portion of the issue each year. The idea is to "sink" most of the issue before maturity. Some sinking funds begin not at the time of issuance, but after a period of 5 or 10 years. Sinking fund payments need not retire the entire bond issue; there can be a balloon payment at final maturity. All bonds in an issue have the same maturity, although specific bonds are retired before that date. These bonds differ from *serial* bonds. For example, in a $20 million issue of serial bonds, $1 million of the bonds might mature each year for 20 years. While serial bonds are employed extensively in the municipal bond market, they are not in the corporate bond market, where the sinking fund provision is prevalent.

The sinking fund retirement of a bond issue can take two forms.

1. The corporation can make a cash payment to the trustee, who in turn calls the bonds for redemption at the sinking fund call price.[16] Usually

---

[16]This price can and usually does differ from the call price of the overall issue, discussed earlier in the chapter.

the bonds are called on a lottery basis by their serial numbers, which are published in the *Wall Street Journal* and other papers.

2. The corporation can purchase bonds in the open market and pay the trustee by delivering to it a given number of bonds. If the market price of the bonds is less than the sinking fund call price, the company will buy bonds in the open market and deliver them to the trustee. If the market price exceeds the call price, it will make a cash payment to the trustee.

A problem some corporations face in purchasing bonds in the market is the presence of *accumulators*. An accumulator is an institutional or other investor who buys bonds in advance of the corporation going into the market to acquire them for sinking-fund purposes. If supply is sufficiently restricted, the corporation will be able to purchase bonds only by bidding up the price. In this way, the accumulator hopes to sell the bonds at an inflated price, knowing the corporation must purchase them in order to satisfy the sinking-fund requirement. For example, an accumulator might buy bonds at a price of $740 per bond to yield 16½ percent and sell them to the corporation for $820, which corresponds to a yield of 14.8 percent. Although the price is significantly above the previous going market price, imperfections allow the accumulator to partially corner the market, thereby forcing the corporation to pay the inflated price.

While perfectly legal, accumulators are not looked upon with favor by corporate borrowers. Only when the bonds sell at a discount from the sinking fund call price, of course, does accumulation occur. Otherwise, the corporation will make a cash payment to the trustee, who will purchase bonds at the call price. Consequently, the sinking fund call price sets an upper limit on the price the accumulator can receive. In an era of high interest rates and discount bonds, the presence of accumulators is common, much to the dismay of corporate borrowers with sinking fund provisions.[17]

In the situations described above, the sinking fund was assumed to pertain to an individual bond issue. A less-known and much less-used provision is a blanket sinking fund, which pertains to multiple bond issues of a corporation. Known as a *funnel sinking fund,* the provision specifies the amount of periodic payment to the sinking fund that is required to retire outstanding bonds. However, the corporate borrower can funnel its sinking fund payment to a single issue or to several issues. Put another way, it has the choice of which issue or issues to retire. In order to reduce its overall interest costs, the corporation will usually focus on high coupon issues. Public utilities are the principal users of "funnel sinkers," though not of the sinking fund provision in general.

---

[17] For an analysis of the accumulation problem, see Andrew J. Kalotay, "On the Management of Sinking Funds," *Financial Management,* 10 (Summer 1981), 34–40.

VALUE OF SINKING FUND PROVISION

Because of the orderly retirement of sinking fund debt, some feel that it has less default risk than nonsinking fund debt.[18] This argument supposes that the ability of the corporation to make sinking fund payments is evidence of solvency and that these payments reduce the possibility of a crisis-at-maturity, discussed in the previous chapter. In addition, steady repurchase activity adds liquidity to the market, which may be beneficial to investors. Also, a sinking fund bond has a shorter duration than a nonsinking fund bond of the same maturity.[19] This factor also may be attractive to investors, but it will depend on the term structure of interest rates. The reasons cited above may result in bonds with a sinking fund provision being more valuable in the market than nonsinking fund bonds, thereby providing lower yields.

Working in the opposite direction is the fact that the sinking fund provision represents an option to the corporation. It can satisfy the provision either by paying cash to the trustee or by repurchasing bonds in the market. In other words, the corporation has the option to retire its debt at the sinking fund call price—usually the face value—or at the market price, whichever is lower.[20] This option works to the advantage of the corporation and its stockholders and to the disadvantage of bondholders. As a result, the yield on a sinking fund bond issue should be reduced relative to a comparable serial bond.[21] The net effect of the various factors discussed above is not clear. Let us turn now to the empirical evidence.

Empirical Evidence

Unfortunately there has been little testing of the value of the sinking fund provision. However, a few studies shed light on the issue. In an early study, F. C. Thompson and R. L. Norgaard found that the typical yield on a sinking fund bond was significantly less than that on a nonsinking fund bond of the same maturity.[22] The authors suggested that this differ-

---

[18]Edward A. Dyl and Michael D. Joehnk, "Sinking Funds and the Cost of Corporate Debt," *Journal of Finance,* 36 (September 1979): 887–93.

[19]For an analysis of sinking fund bond yields in relation to the slope of the yield curve, see Frank C. Jen and James E. Wert, "Inputed Yields of a Sinking Fund Bond and the Term Structure of Interest Rates," *Journal of Finance,* 21 (December 1966): 697–713.

[20]For an analysis of the sinking fund in an option pricing model framework, see Thomas Ho and Ronald F. Singer, "The Value of Sinking Fund Provisions on Corporate Debt," Working Paper, New York University, 1981.

[21]The presence of successful accumulators would tend to reduce the value of the option to the corporation.

[22]F. C. Thompson and R. L. Norgaard, *Sinking Funds: Their Use and Value* (New York: Financial Executives Research Foundation, 1967).

ential can be explained in part by the shorter duration of the sinking fund bond.

In an extensive study of both industrial and public utilities bonds in the 1960s and 1970s, Edward A. Dyl and Michael D. Joehnk found that sinking fund bonds in aggregate provided a yield 16 basis points lower than matched pairs of nonsinking fund bonds.[23] Whether the result was due to a lower perceived default risk, better liquidity, or shorter duration is unclear. The data were further analyzed according to bond quality, level of interest rates, and industry category. The yield differential was significantly greater for medium-grade bonds than for high-grade bonds, for high levels of interest rates than for low levels, and for industrial bonds than for public utility bonds. The authors attribute the first result to the sinking fund provision being more valuable as the perceived risk of default becomes greater. Other than a possible correlation between default risk overall and interest rates, the authors have little explanation for the second result. The last result was the most substantial—a differential of 48 basis points for industrials versus 9 for utilities. Here, the authors suggest that utilities as a group may be perceived to be safer than industrials. However, this conjecture is contrary to the lower yields we observe for industrials for all rating categories. Though the segmented sample results are interesting, the possible reasons are ambiguous.

A. J. Kalotay argues that different maturity structures of sinking fund and nonsinking fund bonds make comparisons misleading.[24] To make the two securities comparable, the author assumed that a sinking fund must be rolled over for the remainder of the bond's horizon. When roll-over costs were considered, he found that sinking fund bonds did not necessarily have a lower cost to the borrower. That depended on subsequent movements of interest rates. If rates rise, Kalotay maintained that sinking fund purchases of the discount bonds must be funded at higher prevailing rates of interest, which is said to be a disadvantage to the borrower. On the other hand, when rates fall, Kalotay affirmed that the issue will be called whether or not it has a sinking fund provision. As a result, the lower cost advantage of the sinking fund provision is good only up to the time of call. On the whole, the author suggested that the provision may well cost the issuer more.

Thus, the empirical evidence on sinking fund bonds is limited. It seems clear that these bonds provide a lower yield than nonsinking fund bonds of the same maturity and grade. However, the reasons for this occurrence are hazy, as there are several possibilities.

---

[23]Edward A. Dyl and Michael D. Joehnk, "Sinking Funds and the Cost of Corporate Debt," *Journal of Finance*, 36 (September 1979): 887–93.
[24]A. J. Kalotay, "Sinking Funds and the Realized Cost of Debt," *Financial Management*, 11 (Spring 1982): 43–54.

SUMMARY

An additional factor that influences relative yields in the marketplace is callability. A call provision gives the issuer the ability to buy back the debt instrument prior to maturity. Almost all corporate bond issues have a call feature, while only some municipal and Treasury bonds have such a feature. Securities can be immediately callable or callable after a deferment period, usually 5 or 10 years. While the call feature gives the borrower flexibility in refinancing, it works to the disadvantage of the investor. If a security is called, investors usually suffer an opportunity loss because they can invest in other bonds only at a sacrifice in yield.

For this reason, the call feature has significant value when interest rates are high and expected to fall. By value, we mean that there is a differential between what the callable bond yields and what it would yield if it were noncallable. The call feature usually has value only as long as there is some probability that the issue might be called. In turn, this probability depends on interest-rate expectations. Different tax treatments for corporate borrowers and investors may create an incentive for callable, as opposed to noncallable, bonds to be issued. Empirical evidence on corporate bonds is consistent with the call feature having the most value when interest rates are relatively high and little or no value when they are low. There has been little testing of the value of the call feature for other issuers. As with any option, the value of it depends on variability; for the call option, the volatility of future interest rates is what is important.

The call feature influences the valuation of bonds selling for less than their face value. The greater the discount, the less the probability that the bond will be called. To the extent that investors value this protection, it will influence upward the demand for discount bonds relative to that for other bonds. Another and more important factor influencing the valuation of discount bonds is taxability, which we will take up in the next chapter.

A sinking fund provision requires the borrower to retire a specified portion of a bond issue periodically. To do so, the corporation can either make a cash payment to the trustee, who calls certain bonds, or it can purchase bonds in the open market. It will choose the former if the market value is at or above the sinking fund call price and the latter on other occasions. A funnel sinking fund pertains to multiple bond issues of a corporation and the borrower has the choice of issue or issues to which it directs its payments.

The valuation of the sinking fund provision depends on several factors. The possibility of lower default risk, greater liquidity and shorter duration suggest a lower yield for a sinking fund bond than for a nonsinking fund bond of the same maturity. However, the fact that the provision is an option to the corporation as to the method of payment works to the disadvantage of investors. Empirical evidence is limited. While sinking fund bonds have a lower yield on average than nonsinking fund bonds, the reasons are hard to delineate.

SELECTED REFERENCES

Bodie, Zvi, and Benjamin M. Friedman, "Interest Rate Uncertainty and the Value of Bond Call Protection," *Journal of Political Economy,* 86 (February 1978): 19–43.

Boyce, W.M., and A.J. Kalotay, "Optimum Bond Calling and Refunding," *Interfaces, The Institute of Management Science,* 9 (November 1979): 36–49.

_____ , "Tax Differentials and Callable Bonds," *Journal of Finance,* 34 (September 1979): 825–38.

Brennan, Michael J., and Eduardo S. Schwartz, "Savings Bonds, Retractable Bonds and Callable Bonds," *Journal of Financial Economics,* 5 (1977): 67–88.

Dyl, Edward A., and Michael D. Joehnk, "Sinking Funds and the Cost of Corporate Debt," *Journal of Finance,* 36 (September 1979): 887–93.

Frankena, Mark W., "The Influence of Call Provisions and Coupon Rate on Yields of Corporate Bonds," in Jack M. Guttentag, ed., *Essays on Interest Rates,* Vol. 2, pp. 134–86. New York: National Bureau of Economic Research, 1971.

Ho, Thomas, and Ronald F. Singer, "The Value of Sinking Fund Provisions on Corporate Debt," Working Paper, New York University, 1981.

Jen, Frank C., and James E. Wert, "The Deferred Call Provision and Corporate Bond Yields," *Journal of Financial and Quantitative Analysis,* 3 (June 1968): 157–69.

_____ , "The Effect of Call Risk on Corporate Bond Yields," *Journal of Finance,* 22 (December 1967): 637–51.

_____ , "The Value of the Deferred Call Privilege," *National Banking Review,* 3 (March, 1966): 369–78.

Kalotay, Andrew J., "On the Management of Sinking Funds," *Financial Management,* 10 (Summer 1981): 34–40.

_____ , "Sinking Funds and the Realized Cost of Debt," *Financial Management,* 11 (Spring 1982): 43–54.

Kidwell, David S., "The Inclusion and Exercise of Call Provisions by State and Local Governments," *Journal of Money, Credit and Banking,* 8 (August 1976): 391–98.

Pye, Gordon, "The Value of the Call Option on a Bond," *Journal of Political Economy,* 74 (April 1966): 200–5.

_____ , "The Value of Call Deferment of a Bond: Some Empirical Results," *Journal of Finance,* 22 (December 1967): 623–36.

Van Horne, James C., "Called Bonds: How did the Investor Fare?" *Journal of Portfolio Management,* 6 (Summer 1980): 58–61.

Yawitz, Jess B., and James A. Anderson, "The Effect of Bond Refunding on Shareholder Wealth," *Journal of Finance,* 32 (December 1977): 1738–46.

_____ , and William J. Marshall, "Optimal Terms of the Call Provision on a Corporate Bond," *Journal of Financial Research,* 3 (Summer 1980): 203–11.

10

THE INFLUENCE
OF TAXES

Another influence that we observe on the market yields is that of taxes. Up until now this effect has been ignored as we tried to explain the influences of maturity, default risk, and callability on yields. In this chapter we remedy this deficiency by extending our analysis to consider the consequences of a taxable world on yields and on yield differentials.

In the absence of taxes, the yield of a fixed-income security with a $1,000 face value and annual interest payments is found by solving the following equation for r:

$$P_0 = \sum_{t=1}^{n} \frac{C_t}{(1+r)^t} + \frac{\$1,000}{(1+r)^n} \qquad (10\text{-}1)$$

where P_0 is the current market price
  C_t is the coupon payment at time t
  n is the number of years to final maturity

The yield, r, represents the promised rate of return applicable to all investors.

With taxes, r no longer represents the relevant return for all investors. The reason is that Eq. (10-1) does not take into account whether or not interest income is taxed and whether or not part of the yield to maturity is comprised of capital gains which are taxed at a different rate from that for interest income. Therefore, the equation does not allow one to determine the effective after-tax rate of return which, for the rational investor, is the relevant consideration. We would expect financial markets to equilibrate in terms of after-tax rates of return. Because of different tax situations, a financial instrument will imply different after-tax yields for different investors despite the fact that the before-tax yield [r in Eq. (10-1)] is the same for all of them.

The after-tax yield for a financial instrument held to maturity can be expressed as the discount rate $\bar{r}$, which equates its current market price with the present value of after-tax cash returns. Thus,

$$P_0 = \sum_{t=1}^{n} \frac{C_t(1-T)}{(1+\bar{r})^t} + \frac{(\$1,000-P_0)(1-G)}{(1+\bar{r})^n} + \frac{P_0}{(1+\bar{r})^n} \qquad (10\text{-}2)$$

where T is the marginal tax rate on ordinary income for the investor and G is the marginal tax rate on capital gains. We see that interest payments are taxed as ordinary income while any capital gain which occurs at final maturity, denoted by ($\$1,000-P_0$), is taxed at the capital gains rate.

In cases where a security is bought at a premium over its face value— i.e., where $P_0>\$1,000$—a capital loss is involved. Investors have two options. They may amortize the premium over the remaining life of the instrument and deduct the prorated amount each year from ordinary income. For example, if a bond were purchased for $1,080 and it had a remaining life of 20 years, the investor would be entitled to deduct $4 each year.[1] The other option is to wait until maturity or until the instrument is sold and then declare a capital loss. As the former tax treatment usually is more favorable to the investor, it is typically employed.[2]

For premium bonds that are amortized, Eq. (10-2) needs to be modified so that

$$P_0 = \sum_{t=1}^{n} \frac{C_t(1-T) + T(P_0-\$1,000)/n}{(1+\bar{r})^t} + \frac{\$1,000}{(1+\bar{r})^n} \qquad (10\text{-}3)$$

The first term on the right takes account of the annual after-tax receipt of interest payments, as well as the tax shield afforded by the yearly amortization of the premium. The last term is the face value of the bond at maturity. Note in the equation that the capital gains tax, G, does not come into play, as it does in Eq. (10-2) for discount bonds and for unamortized premium bonds. Our principal focus in this chapter is on discount bonds, as opposed to premium bonds.

Therefore, Eq. (10-2) will serve as a focal point for the discussion of a number of tax issues. We assume that rational investors attempt to maximize their after-tax rates of return, as denoted by $\bar{r}$ in Eq. (10-2), relative

[1] If a bond is callable, the premium over the call price may be amortized to the first call date if this results in a smaller deduction than occurs if the full premium is amortized to maturity.
[2] For an analysis of the valuation of premium bonds in the presence of taxes, see Miles Livingston, "The Pricing of Premium Bonds," *Journal of Financial and Quantitative Analysis*, 14 (September 1979): 517–27.

to the perceived risk involved. As marginal tax rates for interest income and capital gains vary across investors, equilibration in financial markets is considerably complicated. In concept, prices should adjust so that in equilibrium the risk-adjusted after-tax yield to marginal investors is the same for all financial instruments considered. This proposition may need to be modified for market imperfections. However, to the extent that it serves as an appropriate generalization of static equilibrium in financial markets, we shall use it. In the remainder of the chapter, we wish to analyze the effect of taxes on yields and on yield differentials. Our concern is with whether interest income is taxed, with the differential tax on interest income and capital gains, and with the effect of certain special tax considerations on yields.

TAXATION OF INTEREST INCOME

The tax treatment of interest income is different for different financial instruments. As a result, the after-tax rate of return computed with Eq. (10-2) is affected. Interest on state and local government securities is exempt from federal income taxes, while that for other financial instruments is taxed at the ordinary income tax rate.[3] Consequently, observed before-tax yields are lower for municipal securities than they are for other securities of equivalent risk. The usual comparison is with corporate bonds. In Fig. 10-1, the yield differential between Aaa public utility bonds and Aaa municipal bonds is shown for the 1955–1982 period. It is seen that the yield differential is always positive, ranging between 1 and 6 percent.

We see also that the yield differential varies to some extent with the level of interest rates. This is because the tax benefit is proportional to the level of interest rates. To illustrate, suppose the marginal tax rate for an investor were 40 percent and the yield on taxable bonds were 13 percent. The yield on the tax exempt security would then need to be $13\%\,(1.0-0.4)$ = 7.8 percent in order for investors to be indifferent between the two securities on an after-tax basis. Under these circumstances, the yield differential would be 5.2 percent. Suppose now that interest rates rose and that the taxable bond yielded 16 percent. The tax-exempt security then would need to yield 9.6 percent for the investor to be indifferent between the two, and the yield differential would be 6.4 percent. Thus, the yield differential would be expected to vary with the overall level of interest rates.[4]

---

[3]In addition, the interest income for municipal securities is usually not subject to state income taxes if the security is an obligation of the state involved or an obligation of a local government within the state. However, if the security is of another state, the interest is taxable. In contrast, the interest on Treasury securities is subject to federal income taxes, but is exempt from any state or local income tax.

[4]This argument supposes that the marginal tax rate of the investor at the margin is invariant to the level of interest rates.

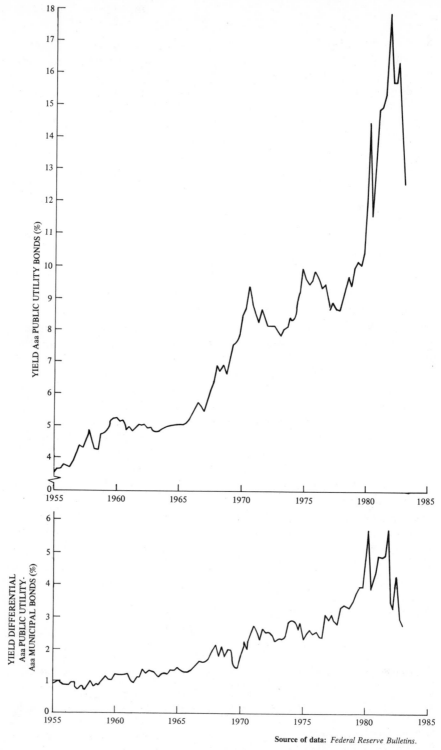

Source of data: *Federal Reserve Bulletins.*

Figure 10-1. Aaa public utility bond yields and yield differentials with Aaa municipal bond yields, 1955–1982.

As seen in Fig. 10-1, the spread between the two yields tends to rise and fall to some degree in keeping with rises and falls in the corporate rate. While the tax effect certainly is not the only explanation for the movement in the yield differential over time, it is an important one. If tax laws and other relevant factors were constant over time, we might expect proportional changes in yields for corporate and municipal bonds. Even though these factors are not constant, we still see a reasonable correspondence between movements in the two series of yields. However, this correspondence is less in the volatile (and high) interest-rate period of the 1980s.

The Segmented Nature of the Municipal Market

Because of the tax-exempt feature, municipal securities are of interest mainly to individuals in high tax brackets and to financial intermediaries paying taxes at or nearly at the full corporate tax rate. A nonprofit organization which pays no taxes would have little reason to invest in municipal securities, considering that yields on default-free Treasury securities are higher. Similarly, life insurance companies, which pay only a limited tax, are able to take only partial advantage of the tax-exempt feature. As a result, the demand for municipals is relatively segmented. The market consists mainly of commercial banks, high income individuals, either directly or through municipal bond mutual funds, and fire and casualty companies. This segmentation is further characterized by the volatile participation of commercial banks and fire and casualty companies.

When banks experience a period of high loan demand and monetary restriction by the Federal Reserve, their relative commitment to municipal securities declines. In contrast, in periods of low loan demand and "easy" monetary policy, banks bid aggressively for municipal securities. The participation by fire and casualty companies is a function of the flow of funds into them and their casualty losses. Here, too, investment behavior fluctuates rather sharply over time. The household sector represents the residual. When the amount of municipal securities issued is in excess of that desired by banks and fire and casualty companies, individuals must be drawn into the market. As the shortfall increases, these investors can be attracted only by higher and higher yields. In periods of high demand by institutions, the role of households in the municipal market is considerably lessened. This usually corresponds to a period of lower interest rates.

The ebb and flow between these three sectors with respect to net investment in municipal securities is seen in Table 10-1. As shown, the investment behavior of commercial banks fluctuated widely over the period 1965–1982. In the monetary restrictive and/or high loan demand eras of 1966, 1969, 1975–1976, and 1981, net purchases by commercial banks con-

Table 10-1. Net Changes in Holdings of Municipal Securities, 1965–1981 (In billions)

Year	Commercial Banks	Households	Fire and Casualty Companies	Other	Total Change
1965	$ 5.2	$ 1.7	$ 0.4	$ 0.0	$ 7.3
1966	2.3	3.6	1.3	−1.6	5.6
1967	9.1	−2.2	1.4	−1.5	7.8
1968	8.6	−0.8	1.0	0.7	9.5
1969	0.2	9.6	1.2	−1.1	9.9
1970	10.7	−0.8	1.5	−0.1	11.3
1971	12.6	−0.2	3.9	1.3	17.6
1972	7.2	2.3	4.3	0.9	14.7
1973	5.7	5.3	3.6	0.1	14.7
1974	5.4	8.3	2.2	0.6	16.5
1975	1.8	6.2	2.6	5.5	16.1
1976	3.0	2.0	5.4	5.3	15.7
1977	9.2	−1.5	10.7	3.5	21.9
1978	9.6	1.8	13.5	1.2	26.1
1979	9.5	2.4	9.9	0.0	21.8
1980	13.6	3.0	8.2	2.1	26.9
1981	5.0	14.9	1.9	4.0	25.8

Source of data: *Flow of Funds Accounts*, Federal Reserve System.

tracted considerably. In contrast, in periods like 1965, 1967–1968, 1970–1971, and 1977–1980, banks dramatically increased their net purchases of municipal securities. Increasingly in the 1970s, commercial banks found other tax-avoidance investment vehicles in the form of direct leasing, foreign operations, and certain types of special depreciation investments. These competing demands may have lessened their overall appetite for municipal securities.

Throughout this time frame, the investment behavior of fire and casualty companies also varied. Owing to favorable cash flows and low loss experiences in the late 1970s, they were large purchasers of municipal securities on both an absolute and relative basis. However, as competition set in and profit margins eroded, these companies substantially reduced their net purchases in 1981. The "other" sector was large in 1975 and 1976 primarily because of the substantial purchase of city of New York obligations by the state of New York and by city retirement funds and general funds. These purchases were made in conjunction with the near default of the city of New York described earlier. Because state or local governments do not pay taxes, they usually invest in taxable bonds where yields are more attractive. Also included in the other category are municipal bond mutual funds; these funds were important investors in 1981.

As the balancing factor between the desired supply of municipal securities and the desired demand by institutions, participation by the household sector fluctuated the most over time. This sector substantially increased its holdings in 1966, 1969, 1973–1975 and in 1981. In the earlier years, its investment behavior seesawed with that of commercial banks; when banks expanded, households contracted their rate of accumulation, and vice versa. In the period 1976–1980, fire and casualty companies were heavy net purchasers of municipal securities, as were banks. As a result, households accounted for little of the net change. In 1981 and into 1982 (not shown in table), banks and fire and casualty companies sharply reduced their net purchases. As a result, individuals had to be drawn into the market and they accounted for the bulk of the net purchases. The inducement, of course, was higher rates of interest.

The segmented market for municipal securities, the fluctuating investment behavior of commercial banks and fire and casualty companies and the heavy and growing demand for funds by municipalities have caused yields in the municipal market to fluctuate somewhat more than yields in other markets.[5] The importance of commercial banks in the municipal bond market on the demand side affects not only the variability of yields, but also the term structure. Because of the nature of their deposit liabilities, banks are interested primarily in shorter maturities. Very seldom will a bank purchase a long-term municipal. As a result, there may be a greater relative demand for short-term securities than for long-term securities. In fact, the yield curve for municipals is almost always upward-sloping.

Value of the Tax-Exemption Feature

One of the interesting aspects of the municipal market is the value placed on tax exemption. For an investor to be indifferent between a municipal security and, say, a corporate security of equal risk, the following would need to hold for par value bonds:

$$r_{\text{muni.}} = r_{\text{corp.}}(1 - T) \tag{10-4}$$

where $r_{\text{muni.}}$ = the yield on the municipal security
$r_{\text{corp.}}$ = the yield on the corporate
T = the marginal tax rate of the investor

We assume that the return on both securities is comprised solely of interest income, with no capital gains or losses.[6] If $r_{\text{muni.}}$ were greater than $r_{\text{corp.}}(1 - T)$,

---

[5]For an empirical study indicating the greater variability of municipal bonds versus taxable bonds, see Jeffrey L. Skelton, "The Relative Pricing of Tax-Exempt and Taxable Debt," Research Paper, University of California, Berkeley, 1979.

[6]For bonds selling at a discount or a premium, the formula above is but an approximation. Under such circumstances capital gains tax considerations are involved. For an analysis of their effect on market equilibrium relationships, see Miles Livingston, "The Pricing of Municipal Bonds," *Journal of Financial and Quantitative Analysis*, 17 (June 1982): 179–93.

rational investors would invest in municipal securities; if it were less, they would invest in corporates. The implied marginal tax rate in the market can be determined by

$$T_{\text{mkt.}} = 1 - \frac{r_{\text{muni.}}}{r_{\text{corp.}}} \tag{10-5}$$

If rational investors had a marginal tax rate (comprised of both federal and state and local income taxes) greater than $T_{\text{mkt.}}$, they would invest in municipals; if the marginal tax rate were less, the investors would invest in corporates.

If we regard Aaa municipal long-term bonds and Aaa public utility bonds as comparable from the standpoint of risk, the implied marginal tax rate for long-term bonds would be that shown in Fig. 10-2 for the period 1955–1982. [The calculations involved use Eq. (10-5).] As seen in the figure, the implied tax rate fluctuated between 18 and 43 percent over the period studied.

Particularly noticeable is the pattern since 1975. In early 1975, the implied tax rate was around 26 percent. It rose sharply in 1976, stayed at a plateau for several years in the high thirties, and then peaked at 43 percent in 1979. As interest rates in general rose rather dramatically in 1980–1981, the tax rate then declined to the lower thirties. In late 1981 and 1982, the implied tax rate dropped to a low of 22 percent and fluctuated. A partial reason for the sharp drop in 1981 may be the *Economic Recovery Tax Act of 1981,* which lowered tax rates in general and the maximum effective tax rate on interest income in particular. Relative to taxable securities, tax-exempt securities were less attractive than they were before.

In addition to changes in taxation, the fluctuations observed are due to the segmented nature of the municipal securities market. When interest

Figure 10-2. Implied marginal tax rate using Aaa public utility and Aaa municipal bonds, 1955–1982.

rates are high and monetary restriction prevails, state and local govern-ments generally have to offer sizable yield inducements to attract marginal investors. The opposite tends to occur in an interest rate trough. This pattern occurs because only a limited number of investors are able to take advantage of the tax-exempt feature. This was illustrated in our analysis of net purchases of municipal securities in Table 10-1.

Apart from fluctuations in the implied tax rate over time, this rate varies by maturity. It is lowest in the long-term end of the market. For short- and intermediate-term securities, yields on municipal securities typically are less, relative to taxable yields, than they are for long-term securities. Therefore, the implied tax rate is higher. This phenomenon may be attributable primarily to commercial banks restricting their investment activities to short- and intermediate-term securities. In fact, they dominate the market in the short-term end. In an extensive study of implicit tax rates for the period 1952–1976, Michael L. Mussa and Roger C. Kormendi found that the implied tax rate went from about 45 percent for very short-term securities, to 40 percent for intermediate-term securities, to about 30 percent for long-term securities.[7] The average implied tax rate, weighted according to the maturity distribution of new issues, was approximately 36 percent. However, Jeffrey L. Skelton took issue with the notion of different implied tax rates for different maturities.[8] Based on simulated term structures for taxable and tax-exempt bonds adjusted for relative risk, Skelton suggested that a single marginal tax rate may govern relative pricing for all maturities. The key to Skelton's argument rests with the adjustment of yields for future marginal tax brackets and for risk. Application of a more standard type of formula, such as Eq. (10-5), results in implied tax rates varying inversely with maturity.

Regardless of the fluctuation in implied marginal tax rate and the question of maturity, it seems clear that the average implied tax rate is somewhere in the 30 to 40 percent range, and probably about in the middle. As we know, investors in municipal securities are comprised of high-income individuals and financial institutions whose marginal tax rate, when state and local income taxes and federal income taxes are taken into account, must approach 50 percent. This suggests that the tax-exemption feature is not fully priced in the marketplace.[9] Put another way, municipalities are not obtaining the full benefit of the tax exemption feature. A sizable portion of it goes to investors.

---

[7]Michael L. Mussa and Roger C. Kormendi, *The Taxation of Municipal Bonds* (Washington, D.C.: American Enterprise Institute, 1979), Chapter 4.

[8]Skelton, "Relative Pricing."

[9]This point was first made by Roland T. Robinson, *Postwar Market for State and Local Government Securities* (New York: National Bureau of Economic Research, 1960), Chapter 6.

Broadening the Municipal Market

The tax-exemption feature has been criticized because a sizable and fluctuating portion of the total tax revenues forgone by the Treasury goes to investors and not to the state and local governments for which the feature was intended. Rough estimates suggest that between 25 and 30 percent of the tax revenues forgone go to investors.[10] In order to broaden the market for municipal securities and lower the interest portion of the tax exemption subsidy going to investors, a taxable bond option has been proposed for the municipality. This option would give the state or local government the ability to issue bonds in the taxable market and then receive a federal subsidy. In other words, the municipality would receive a subsidy from the federal government and would sell bonds without the tax-exemption feature. To be sure, the interest cost would be higher, but the municipality would be appealing to a broader market. The *ex ante* higher interest cost would be more than offset by the subsidy; otherwise the municipality would elect to issue bonds in the tax-exempt market. In short, the option would be that of the municipality in determining in which market—the taxable market or the tax-exempt market—it wished to borrow.[11]

The critical factor is the percent of the municipality's interest cost the federal government would subsidize. Most proposals call for a subsidy of between 30 and 40 percent of the interest cost. The higher the subsidy, of course, the greater the use that would be made of the taxable, as opposed to the tax-exempt, market. At a very high subsidy, of course, only taxable bonds would be employed. Also, proposals call for a fixed percentage subsidy across maturities and over time. As the portion of the present tax-exempt subsidy going to investors is greatest for long-term maturities, the taxable bond option would have the greatest benefit to the municipality for that end of the maturity structure. In fact, municipalities might issue bonds in the early maturities on a tax-exempt basis and bonds in the later maturities on a taxable basis. In addition, the fixed rate subsidy would be more valuable at the peaks of an interest-rate cycle than at the troughs. Therefore, municipalities would be expected to make greater use of the option to issue bonds in the taxable market at interest-rate peaks than they would at the troughs.

[10]See John Peterson, *Changing Conditions in the Market for State and Local Government Debt,* Joint Economic Committee, 94th Congress, 2nd Session (Washington, D.C.: U. S. Government Printing Office, April 16, 1976), pp. 56–58.

[11]Mechanically, the best way to make the federal payment subsidy is to the interest-paying agent. Only upon receipt of funds from the municipality for the balance of the interest payment would the subsidy funds be disbursed to investors. If the federal government paid investors directly, it would be underwriting a portion of the default risk of the municipality. If it paid the funds to the municipality, it would be a form of revenue sharing. Only if the payment of the subsidy is linked to the ability of the municipality to service its debt does the federal government avoid these problems. By restricting the interest paying agent in the manner described above, the federal government interferes least in the market process.

These are but some of the issues associated with the taxable bond option. The purpose is to allow municipalities to avoid some of the problems that arise from the segmented nature of the present municipal market by tapping a broader market. Proponents contend it would lower the portion of the tax-exempt feature that goes to investors. A contrary position is that of Michael L. Mussa and Roger C. Kormendi, who argued that when inflation is factored into consideration, municipalities realize over 90 percent of the benefit of the subsidy.[12] They concluded that the taxable bond option is not needed, is inefficient, and would have some bad effects if it were to be adopted. Therefore, the case for positive effects is not universal. The proposal itself has surfaced several times, but Congress has not enacted the option.

DIFFERENTIAL TAXES ON INTEREST AND CAPITAL GAINS

As discussed in the introduction, interest income and capital gains are taxed at different rates. Recall that for discount bonds, bonds trading at par, and for premium bonds where the premium is not amortized,[13] the after-tax rate of return for a bond held to maturity is determined by solving the following equation for $\bar{r}$:

$$P_0 = \sum_{t=1}^{n} \frac{C_t(1-T)}{(1+\bar{r})^t} + \frac{(\$1,000-P_0)(1-G)}{(1+\bar{r})^n} + \frac{P_0}{(1+\bar{r})^n} \quad (10\text{-}6)$$

where C_t is the interest payment at the end of year t
             P_0 is the present market price
             n is the number of years to final maturity
     T and G are the marginal tax rates on interest income
             and capital gains respectively for the investor

If T exceeds G, it is clear that a dollar of capital gains on a discounted present-value basis is more valuable than a dollar of interest income, again on a discounted present-value basis. This applies to all fixed-income securities other than municipals, which we will discuss shortly.

The favorable tax treatment of capital gains makes taxable fixed-income securities selling at a discount from their face values attractive to some taxable investors.[14] As a result, their pretax yield to maturity tends

---

[12]Mussa and Kormendi, *Taxation of Municipal Bonds.*

[13]For premium bonds where the premium is amortized over the remaining life of the bond, Eq. (10-3) is applicable.

[14]Treasury bills and certain other money-market instruments are sold in the market without coupons. The yield is determined by the amount of discount. In these cases, the discount is taxed at the ordinary income tax rate despite the fact that the instrument might be held for a period longer than that required for capital gains purposes. The tax itself is payable in the year the instrument is sold by the investor or at maturity if held to that time.

to be lower than the yield of comparable bonds with higher coupon rates. The greater the discount, the greater the capital gains attraction of the bond and the lower its yield relative to what it would be if the coupon rate were such that the bond sold at par. However, Eq. (10-6) shows that the effect depends on maturity. The longer the maturity of a bond, the less important the capital gains feature in going from one year to the next. To be sure, the discount will be eliminated at maturity. Mathematically, however, a bond appreciates at an increasing rate as maturity is approached, all other things the same. At first, a long-term bond appreciates very slowly to reduce the discount. As a result, the tax effect also is small in the early years. As maturity is approached, it appreciates much more rapidly and the tax effect is significant.

Tax Treatment of Original-Issue Deep Discount Bonds

In our discussion, we assumed that a bond was originally sold near par and that it went to a discount because of a subsequent rise in interest rates. If a person buys the discount bond in the secondary market and holds it to maturity, the increase in value is subject to the capital gains tax rate. However, we know from Chapter 6 that in recent years there has been a number of original-issue, zero-coupon bonds (pure discount bonds), as well as low coupon bonds, which are sold initially at a substantial discount. Here the tax treatment is different. For the taxable investor, the discount must be amortized over the life of the bond and reported as interest income. Moreover, all subsequent purchasers of the bond in the secondary market are subject to the original amortization schedule in the reporting of interest income. For the issuer, the annual amortization of the discount is treated as an interest expense.

The amoritzation schedule is not straight line, in the sense of dividing the discount by the number of years to maturity to determine annual interest. Rather, annual interest increases at an incrasing rate, to take account of the funds actually "borrowed" by the issuer. More specifically, the amount of amortized discount in a particular year is: (1) the bond's adjusted issue price multiplied by (2) the yield-to-maturity minus (3) the interest, if any, paid during the year. The *adjusted issue price* is the original issue price plus the amount of the original issue discount amortized in all prior years. To illustrate, suppose a zero-coupon bond of 10 years were sold for $226.68, to give a yield-to-maturity of 16 percent. In the first year, the amount of imputed interest is $226.68 × .16 = $36.27. In the second year, it is ($226.68 + $36.27) × .16 = $42.07. For all 10 years the annual amortization is:

Year	Discount Amortization
1	$36.27
2	42.07
3	48.80
4	56.61
5	65.67
6	76.18
7	88.36
8	102.50
9	118.90
10	137.96
	$773.32

The total of $773.32 is, of course, equal to the original discount of $1,000 − $226.68 = $773.32.

Both the issuer and the taxable investor are required to use the above interest amounts for tax purposes. Therefore, there are no implications of capital gains versus interest income. In what follows, we are concerned with discount bonds that evolve from increasing interest rates subsequent to original issue, and not with original-issue discount bonds.

The Attraction of Discount Bonds

The attractiveness of discount bonds can be visualized by comparing the yields for low coupon bonds already outstanding with yields for newly issued bonds, where the coupon rate reflects the current level of interest rates. More specifically, we compare yields on Aa public utility bonds having approximately an $8\frac{3}{4}$ percent coupon with newly issued Aa public utility bonds having a 5-year deferred call feature. The yield differential between the two sets of yields, as well as the yield on the newly issued bonds, are shown in Fig. 10-3 for the period 1973–1982. As seen in the figure, the yield differential tends to widen as interest rates rise and narrow as interest rates decline. In the beginning year, 1973, yields on new issues were below $8\frac{3}{4}$ percent, and the differential (new issue yield minus $8\frac{3}{4}\%$ seasoned bond yield) was negative. From mid-1974 through 1975, new issue yields exceeded $8\frac{3}{4}$ percent, and the differential was positive. In 1976–1978, the new issue yield hovered around $8\frac{3}{4}$ percent and the differential

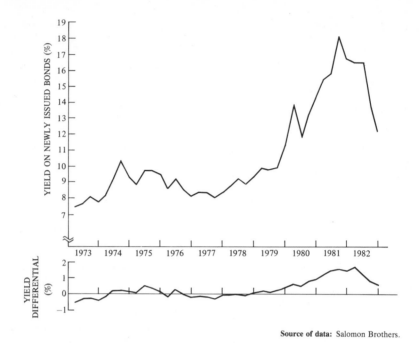

Source of data: Salomon Brothers.

Figure 10-3. Yields on newly issued Aa public utility bonds and differential with $8\frac{3}{4}$ percent coupon seasoned Aa public utility bonds, 1973–1982.

was both above and below zero, but mostly below. As interest rates rose in 1979 and beyond, the differential was always positive and mostly increasing up to the spring of 1982, after which it fell. Thus, the figure gives indication of the different yield behavior of bonds with different coupon rates.

   To probe further into discount bonds, suppose an investor were in a 50 percent tax bracket with respect to interest income and 20 percent with respect to capital gains. Suppose further that the coupon rate on a seasoned bond were $8\frac{3}{4}$ percent with a maturity of 25 years. If the investor were interested in the before-tax yield necessary for a newly issued bond of 25 years to provide an after-tax yield equal to that of the seasoned bond, the relationships in Fig. 10-4 would hold.[15] The horizontal axis shows after-tax yield and the vertical axis shows before-tax yield. The diagonal lines represent the relationships between before- and after-tax yields for the new issue, for the $8\frac{3}{4}$ percent coupon bond, and for the yield differential between the two. The after-tax yield for the new issue is simply $(1.0 - .5)$ times

[15]The idea of this example came from Timothy Q. Cook, "Some Factors Affecting Long-Term Yield Spreads in Recent Years," *Monthly Review of the Federal Reserve Bank of Richmond,* 59 (September 1973): 7.

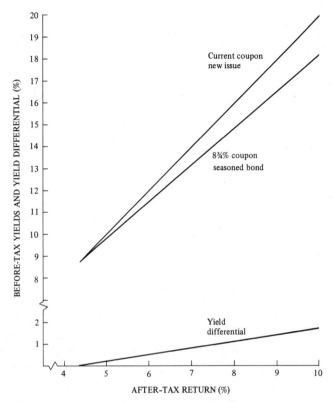

Figure 10-4. Yields on newly issued current coupon bonds, 8¾ percent coupon seasoned bonds, and yield differential for various after-tax rates of return. Assumptions: 25-year maturity, 50% ordinary income tax applicable to interest income and 20% capital gains tax applicable to capital gains at maturity.

the before-tax yield. Because capital gains are involved for the seasoned bond, a variation of Eq. (10-6) is used to compute the after-tax yield. At 8¾ percent of course, the after-tax yield for both securities is the same, 4.375 percent, because there is no capital gain for the seasoned bond. For before-tax yields in excess of 8¾ percent, however, the after-tax yields differ.

Changing Tax Laws

Changes in the tax code make capital gains less or more important relative to interest income. As a result, the before-tax yields for various coupon bonds change (Fig. 10-3), which causes changes in the relationships shown in Figure 10-4 for the market as a whole. In the Tax Reform Act of 1969, the maximum capital gains tax was increased from

25 percent to 32.5 percent for individuals and to 30 percent for corporations. In the Tax Reform Act of 1976, the length of the holding period was increased in steps from 6 months to 1 year, and changes in the minimum and maximum taxes effectively raised the capital gains tax rate for certain individuals. Following the change, the maximum tax rate on capital gains was over 49 percent. These two changes lessened the attraction of discount bonds, all other things the same.

Reversing this trend, the Revenue Act of 1978 lowered the capital gains tax rate. Instead of 50 percent of long-term gains being excluded from taxable income, 60 percent was excluded. The maximum capital gains tax rate for individuals was reduced to 28 percent. This act made capital gains more attractive relative to interest income. The Economic Recovery Tax Act of 1981 lowered tax rates overall and reduced the maximum tax on interest and dividend income to 50 percent. Therefore, the maximum capital gains tax rate for individuals was reduced to 20 percent $(1.0 - .6).5$. However, interest income also was more attractive to high income individuals, since the top rate was reduced from 70 percent to 50 percent. Whether interest income or capital gains are more attractive to investors overall as a result of this tax change is unclear.

To summarize, an unexpected increase (decrease) in the effective capital gains tax rate relative to that for interest income would be expected to be associated with an increase (decrease) in yield on discount bonds relative to those trading near par.

Discount Bonds—Demand and Supply

Further affecting the type of relationship shown in Fig. 10-4 for the market as a whole are underlying changes in the demand for and the supply of discount bonds. On the demand side, the market for discount bonds may be partially segmented. The basic appeal of a discount bond is to taxable investors. Investors who pay no taxes, such as a pension fund, would be indifferent between a dollar of interest on a discounted present-value basis and a dollar of capital gains on the same basis, if all other things were the same. However, if taxable investors bid up the price of discount bonds, the tax-exempt investor is better off investing in high coupon bonds. In this way, yield need not be sacrificed for a feature, namely, the prospect of a capital gain, which has no tax value to the investor. The same applies to a lesser extent to other institutional investors that pay limited taxes, such as life insurance companies.

While commercial banks typically are in high tax brackets, they are unable to avail themselves of the favorable tax rate on capital gains. Unfortunately for them, capital gains are treated as ordinary income when it comes to paying taxes. Therefore, commercial banks do not seek discount bonds, but rather bonds selling more nearly at par or above.[16] As before, the reason is simply that yields on these bonds are more attractive. By the process of elimination, discount bonds are attractive primarily to higher-income individuals and to fire and casualty companies. Thus, the capital gains tax feature associated with discount bonds result in a segmented market for these bonds. Demand is largely determined by the flow of funds to fire and casualty companies and the ability of high-income individuals to invest.

On the other hand, the supply of (nonoriginal issue) discount bonds changes with changes in the level of interest rates. At cyclical peaks in interest rates, there are far more discount bonds than there are at cyclical troughs. By definition, at these times there are bonds issued in the past at coupon rates lower than prevailing interest rates in the market. In other words, the supply of discount bonds varies directly with the interest-rate level. The combination of a segmented market on the demand side and rather sharp shifts in supply, caused by changes in the level of interest rates, results in a shifting relationship between yields on discount and par bonds. Further affecting the relationship, of course, are changes in tax laws, which we previously discussed.

Some Empirical Tests

While there have been only a limited number of empirical tests of the valuation of discount bonds, it is useful to review them. Robert J. Shiller and Franco Modigliani developed a regression model for testing the yield differential between new issues of corporate bonds and seasoned bonds, which often sell at a discount.[17] Under the assumption of a single representative tax bracket and unchanging tax laws, the differential is related to the spread between the new issue yield and the coupon rate on the seasoned bond. Therefore, the regression coefficient is a measure of differential implied tax rates on interest income and capital gains. Testing with data for the period 1960–1978, the authors found that the differential taxation of interest and capital gains income is of major importance in explaining the behavior of the yield differential. The results were consistent with the equalization of after-tax returns for seasoned and new issue bonds for persons in high tax brackets (above 60 percent).

[16]For an analysis of the investment behavior of institutional investors with respect to taxes and likely future reinvestment rates on coupon payments, see Robert H. Cramer and Stephen L. Hawk, "The Consideration of Coupon Levels, Taxes, Reinvestment Rates, and Maturity in the Investment Management of Financial Institutions," *Journal of Financial and Quantitative Analysis,* 10 (March 1975): 67–84.

[17]Robert J. Shiller and Franco Modigliani, "Coupon and Tax Effects on New and Seasoned Bond Yields and the Measurement of the Cost of Debt Capital," *Journal of Financial Economics,* 7 (1979): 297–318.

In another approach, I derived implied tax rates for individual and corporate investors who are indifferent between discount and par bonds under the condition that these implied tax rates can change over time.[18] Using a modification of Eq. (10-6), the yield on a bond trading near par multiplied by one minus the tax rate is used as the after-tax return required by investors at the margin. It then is possible to solve for the implied tax rate at a moment in time, given the price and terms of a discount bond and the yield of a bond of approximately the same duration that sells near par. The implied tax rate computed is not a weighted average of the tax rates of all investors in the market.[19] Rather, it represents an approximation of the tax rate for investors who are indifferent between yields on a discount and par bond.

The test involved Treasury bonds over the period 1975–1979. The discount bond employed was the 6⅜s of February 15, 1993, which in all but one month had a market price less than par. Various bonds were used for the par bond. The evidence showed that the valuation of the tax benefits associated with discount bonds is not constant over time. The implied tax rate varied inversely with the level of Treasury bond yields. These results are seen in Fig. 10-5. While the implied tax rate at the interest-rate peaks seems too high, its variation over time is consistent with a segmented market for discount bonds on the demand side. As interest rates rise, the supply of discount bonds increases, and investors in increasingly lower tax brackets must be attracted to them. In addition, the evidence was consistent with the 1976 and 1978 changes in tax laws, the first making capital gains less attractive vis-à-vis interest income and the second making them more attractive.

John S. McCallum studied the effect of changes in the capital gains tax on bond yields.[20] He hypothesized that as the capital gains tax increases, the yield on discount bonds will increase which, of course, is as we discussed before. The author analyzed the Canadian capital market at the time the capital gains tax was introduced; it was introduced January 1, 1972, after being recommended in 1969. Prior to this time, there was no such tax. His empirical results for the period immediately subsequent to the announcement supported the hypothesis mentioned above. Earlier or later yields on discount bonds did not reflect this behavior, a finding which is consistent with an efficient market.

[18]James C. Van Horne, "Implied Tax Rates and the Valuation of Discount Bonds," *Journal of Banking and Finance,* 6 (June 1982): 145–60.

[19]Stephen M. Schaefer, "Taxes and Security Market Equilibrium," in William F. Sharpe and Cathryn M. Cootner, *Financial Economics: Essays in Honor of Paul Cootner* (Englewood Cliffs, N.J.: Prentice-Hall, 1982), pp.159–78, shows that with perfect and complete financial markets, one cannot have different taxes for different investors and market equilibrium. With imperfections, however, the market can be comprised of individuals in many tax brackets and price equilibrium can still be achieved.

[20]John S. McCallum, "The Impact of the Capital Gains Tax on Bond Yields," *National Tax Journal,* 26 (December 1973): 575–84.

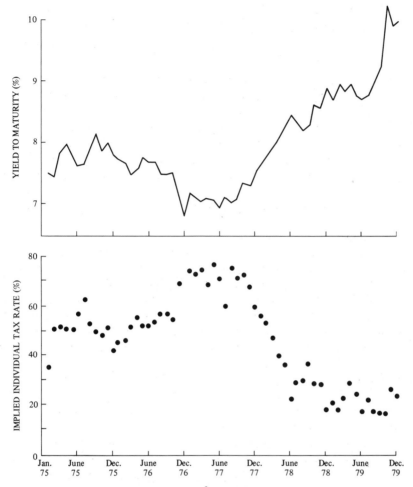

Figure 10-5. Yield-to-maturity of 6¾s of February 15, 1993, and implied individual tax rate, 1975–1979.

Stephen M. Schaefer tested British government securities for evidence of tax clienteles.[21] The sample period was 1955 to 1978, and the question addressed was whether a particular security is held by investors of a particular tax bracket depending on whether its expected return has a capital gains component. Using a dominance criterion, the author was able to demonstrate the existence of tax clienteles.

In summary, empirical evidence gives strong indication that the differential taxation of interest income and capital gains affects the valuation of discount bonds. There is some indication that the market is partially

---

[21]Stephen M. Schaefer, "Tax Induced Clientele Effects in the Market for British Government Securities," *Journal of Financial Economics,* 10 (July 1982): 121–60.

segmented and that yields on such bonds, relative to those on par bonds, vary with changes in tax laws and with the level of interest rates. Efforts to derive an implied tax rate are hampered by several theoretical short-comings, but insight from such calculations is still possible.

Capital Gains Valuation for Municipal Bonds

While capital gains are attractive to taxable investors for most fixed-income securities, they are not for investors in municipal bonds. Any capital gain realized upon the sale of a municipal security or upon its final redemption is subject to a capital gains tax. This contrasts with interest income, which is tax exempt. As a result, the yield behavior of discount bonds is opposite to that which occurs for bonds in the taxable market. Municipal bonds selling at a discount typically provide a yield higher than comparable bonds selling at par. In other words, bonds selling at par are more attractive than discount bonds because their return is comprised entirely of interest and the final principal payment, neither of which are subject to taxation. Referring to our basic valuation formula for deter-mining the after-tax rate of return, Eq. (10-6), it is clear that if $T=0$ and G is positive, the discount bond will provide a lower after-tax rate of return for the investor who is taxed than will a bond whose market price equals $1,000, all other things being the same. If market equilibration occurs in terms of after-tax rates of return, the discount bond must provide a higher yield than the municipal bond selling at par.[22]

ESTATE TAX BONDS

For certain Treasury bonds, there is yet another phenomenon associated with discount bonds. Certain bonds issued prior to 1963 can be used in the payment of federal estate taxes, if they are owned by the deceased at the time of death. Known as *flower bonds,* these bonds count at their full face value in the settlement of estate taxes. For example, if a flower bond had a coupon rate below current prevailing interest rates such that its market price was $850, it could be purchased and at the time of death would be worth $1,000 in the payment of federal estate taxes.

This advantage was reduced, but not eliminated, by the Tax Reform Act of 1976. Beginning in 1977, the estate paid capital gains taxes based on the original cost of the security or upon its market value at December 31, 1976, whichever was higher. Moreover, the holding period necessary

---

[22]For an analysis of the effect of discounts and premiums on market valuation when there are capital gains tax considerations, see Livingston, "Pricing of Municipal Bonds."

to qualify for a capital gains tax treatment was extended from 6 months to 1 year. Thus, the difference in price between what is paid for a flower bond and its face value when used in the settlement of estate taxes is subject to taxation, whereas before it was not. Moreover, the security must be purchased at least 1 year before death to qualify for the more favorable capital gains tax treatment.

The Value of Flower Bonds

Because of these benefits and the resulting demand for them, flower bonds tend to sell at much lower yields than do other Treasury bonds of roughly the same maturity. This is illustrated in Table 10-2, where ask quotations and yields are shown for all longer-term flower bonds, as well as for surrounding issues with respect to maturity. We see that the longest-term flower bonds provide the lowest yields. The 3s of 1995 yield 4.41 percent and the $3\frac{1}{2}$s of 1998 yield 4.69 percent. Note that these yields are some 6 percent below yields on surrounding issues. For example, the 7s of 1993–1998, which also have a capital gains tax attraction because their coupon rate is much below prevailing yields in the market, sell at $62\frac{20}{32}$, to yield 12.47 percent. In contrast, the $3\frac{1}{2}$s of 1998 have a lower

Table 10-2. Ask Quotations and Yields on Selected Long-Term Treasury Bonds

	AUGUST 12, 1982	
Issue	*Ask Price*	*Yield*
$10\frac{3}{4}$s, 1989 November	89\frac{1}{32}$	13.13%
*$3\frac{1}{2}$s, 1990 February	$86\frac{22}{32}$	5.70
$8\frac{1}{4}$s, 1990 May	$79\frac{15}{32}$	12.46
$13\frac{3}{4}$s, 1992 May	$101\frac{8}{32}$	13.51
*$4\frac{1}{4}$s, 1987–1992 August	$86\frac{24}{32}$	6.03
$7\frac{1}{4}$s, 1992 August	$69\frac{2}{32}$	12.84
*4s, 1988–1993 February	86	5.80
$6\frac{3}{4}$s, 1993 February	$66\frac{18}{32}$	12.58
9s, 1994 February	$76\frac{5}{32}$	13.05
*$4\frac{1}{8}$s, 1989–1994 May	$86\frac{15}{32}$	5.73
$10\frac{1}{8}$s, 1994 November	$81\frac{20}{32}$	13.19
*3s, 1995 February	$86\frac{16}{32}$	4.41
$10\frac{1}{2}$s, 1995 February	$83\frac{12}{32}$	13.26
7s, 1993–1998 May	$62\frac{20}{32}$	12.47
*$3\frac{1}{2}$s, 1998 November	$86\frac{18}{32}$	4.69
$8\frac{1}{2}$s, 1994–1999 May	$69\frac{31}{32}$	12.92

*Flower Bonds

Table 10-3. Estate Tax Bonds Outstanding (in millions)

Bond	1965	1970	1975	1980	1982
$3\frac{1}{2}$s, 1990 February	$4,902	$4,780	$3,656	$2,333	$1,812
$4\frac{1}{4}$s, 1987–1992 August	3,818	3,812	3,553	2,537	2,180
4s, 1988–1993 February	250	248	222	150	121
$4\frac{1}{8}$s, 1989–1994 May	1,560	1,555	1,353	921	817
3s, 1995 February	2,290	1,318	720	446	360
$3\frac{1}{2}$s, 1998 November	4,421	4,115	2,790	1,654	1,383

Source: *Treasury Bulletins.*

coupon, but a price of $86\frac{18}{32}$, to yield 4.69 percent. The difference in price and yield can be attributed primarily to the estate tax feature. Similar generalizations can be drawn for the other five flower bonds. While the six flower bonds shown in the table have somewhat different yields, the market prices are virtually the same, $86 to $86\frac{22}{32}$. This phenomenon again attests to the fact that they are bought almost entirely for purposes of settling federal estate taxes and not for other reasons.[23]

As flower bonds are used to pay federal estate taxes, they are retired by the Treasury. As a result, the supply of flower bonds constantly diminishes over time. Table 10-3 shows amounts outstanding for the six flower bonds with maturities of 1990 or later. With the rise in interest rates that began in 1965, these bonds sold at increasing discounts and became increasingly attractive as vehicles by which to reduce the estate tax burden. As a result, increasing numbers were so used and their supply diminished accordingly. Diminishing supply exerts upward pressure on prices and downward pressure on yields, all other things the same. As no new flower bonds will be issued and none have been issued since 1963, existing flower bonds will be in decreasing supply in the years to come.

REFLECTIONS ON DISCOUNT BONDS

In Chapters 6 and 8 and in this chapter, we considered several things that bear on the valuation of discount bonds. It is useful now to review them prior to looking at some related issues. With respect to the mathematics of finance, we saw in Chapter 6 that the deeper the discount, the longer the duration of a bond. To the extent that the term structure of interest rates is upward-sloping with respect to duration, this proposition implies a higher yield for the discount bond than for a bond with the same

[23] For a further analysis of the valuation of flower bonds, see Timothy Q. Cook, "Changing Yield Spreads in the U. S. Government Bond Market," *Economic Review of the Federal Reserve Bank of Richmond,* 63 (March/April 1977): 3–8.

maturity but with a current coupon rate. The opposite would occur in the case of a downward-sloping yield curve. Another factor influencing the valuation of discount bonds is callability.

Discount bonds are particularly attractive in times of falling interest rates, because of the protection they afford the investor against being called. While this influence is most applicable to corporate bonds, it applies also to other fixed-income securities that are subject to call. For sinking fund purposes, corporations will buy back their bonds in the market when interest rates rise significantly above the coupon rate so that the bond sells at a discount. This adds liquidity to the market, and investors can either sell bonds or continue to hold them. In contrast, when the bonds trade at par or above, the trustee will call them by serial number in order to satisfy the sinking-fund requirement. Here investors may have bonds called, which may be viewed as unfavorable. We saw in this chaper that discount bonds are also attractive because of the favorable tax treatment of capital gains relative to that of interest income. Finally, estate tax bonds that sell at a discount have a special demand.

With the exception of the duration argument,[24] all these factors work to make taxable bonds selling at a discount more attractive in the market than comparable bonds selling at par. In general, the deeper the discount, the greater the attraction of a discount bond and the lower its yield relative to comparable bonds selling at par. However, beyond a point, the discount affords little incremental call protection to the investor. Put another way, if interest rates on corporate bonds are never expected to fall below 9 percent, it makes little difference from the standpoint of call protection whether an investor holds a bond with a $7\frac{1}{2}$ percent coupon rate or one with a 5 percent coupon rate. While sorting out the separate influences on the value of discount bonds is difficult, we know that the capital gains tax influence and the estate tax consideration, when applicable, are the most important. The duration factor is relatively unimportant and the callability and sinking fund factors are important primarily in times of falling interest rates.

TAX EFFECTS AND THE TERM STRUCTURE

Bonds selling at a discount can distort the drawing of the yield curve, a subject considered in Chapter 5. For example, if a particular maturity range consisted only of discount bonds, while observations for other ranges consisted of bonds selling around par, the yield curve would be pulled downward in the former range. This type of distortion is illustrated in Fig. 10-6, where the observations in the long-term area are low

[24]Even here the term *structure* with respect to duration must be upward-sloping for discount bonds to provide higher yields than bonds selling at par, all other things remaining the same.

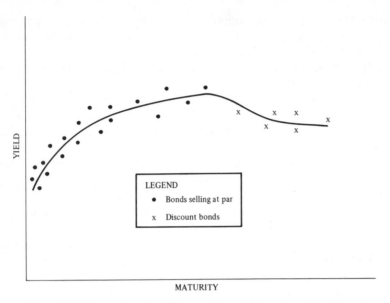

Figure 10-6. Illustration of yield-curve distortion introduced by discount bonds.

coupon bonds, which bend the yield curve downward. With rising interest rates, bonds issued in the past sell at increasing discounts, and such distortions of the yield curve become even more of a problem. Due to the mathematics of interest rates, the longer the duration, the greater the yield effect of discount bonds versus par bonds. As a result, when the "true" term structure is upward-sloping, yield-to-maturity curves understate the term structure.[25] The steeper the term structure, the more the understatement.

Several approaches to reducing the problem have been advanced. If a sizable portion of total observations is represented by current coupon bonds, one can simply ignore the low coupon bonds in the drawing of the yield curve. For example, the Treasury ignores deep discount bonds in fitting yield curves to the observations shown in the *Treasury Bulletin.* However, there remains a problem if there are maturity areas where no bonds are selling near par. This occurred from the mid-1960s to the early 1970s, when the Treasury was precluded from issuing bonds by the $4\frac{1}{4}$ percent interest-rate ceiling imposed by Congress. As interest rates rose, long-term bonds with coupon rates of $4\frac{1}{4}$ percent or less sold at increasing discounts. As there were no higher coupon bonds being issued, the lower coupon levels had to be used in drawing the yield curve.

[25]For an analysis of the relationship between yield curves for coupon bonds and zero coupon bonds with differential taxes on interest income and capital gains, see Miles Livingston, "Bond Taxation and the Shape of the Yield-to-Maturity Curve," *Journal of Finance,* 34 (March 1979): 189–96.

Another method of adjustment is to assume tax rates on ordinary income and on capital gains for investors at the margin. These rates then are inserted into Eq. (10-6), or a variation thereof, and after-tax rates of return or adjusted before-tax returns are estimated. The yield curve can then be drawn on the basis of the adjusted data. Alexander A. Robichek and W. David Niebuhr used various pairs of Treasury bonds with different coupons, but roughly the same maturity, to derive implied tax rates.[26] These estimates varied widely, but the median was roughly 44 percent for ordinary income taxes. One half of this, or 22 percent, was assumed as the capital gains tax rate. These tax rates then were used to derive adjusted before-tax yields for all Treasury bonds on two dates. Although yield curves were not drawn, the results were still rather striking. Because prevailing yields in the market on the two dates were above the coupon rates on all of the bonds (maximum of $4\frac{1}{4}$ percent), tax-adjusted yields were higher than observed yields. The greatest adjustments occurred for the deep discount bonds. Overall, the adjustment process considerably smoothed differences in yield observed for bonds of like maturity.

While the adjustment of yields for taxes using a variation of Eq. (10-6) goes a long way toward making yield observations more consistent, some problems still remain. For one thing, tax rates for the marginal investor must be estimated and these estimates are subject to error. In addition, effective tax rates of marginal investors change over time. Moreover, the tax-adjustment process ignores other factors, which affect the valuation of discount bonds. These include duration, the call protection afforded, and the use of certain Treasury bonds for the settlement of federal estate taxes. The last bias was particularly evident in the Robichek and Niebuhr results.

J. Huston McCulloch used a more sophisticated variation of Eq. (10-6) to adjust for taxes for discount bonds.[27] He also made adjustments for bonds selling above par and for Treasury bills, where all of the appreciation is treated as ordinary income for tax purposes. Estate tax, or flower, bonds were analyzed after tax adjustments were made. As in the case of Robichek and Niebuhr, McCulloch endeavored to estimate the coupon rate necessary to issue new debt at par. Using Treasury security data from 1965 to 1973, he estimated the discount function with respect to maturity using an instrumental variables approach. Given estimates of the discount rates, the value of a specific security was estimated on the same basis as other securities in the regression study. The largest errors in estimate were found for the two longest-term flower bonds, and these errors were attributed to the estate tax effect. McCulloch fitted yield curves to the coupon rates which the bonds would need to have had in order to sell at par. He also

[26]Alexander A. Robichek and W. David Niebuhr, "Tax-Induced Bias in Reporting Treasury Yields," *Journal of Finance*, 25 (December 1970): 1081–90.

[27]J. Huston McCulloch, "The Tax-Adjusted Yield Curve," *Journal of Finance*, 30 (June 1975): 811–30.

used the data to fit forward rate curves under the assumption that the bonds were pure discount ones, with appreciation taxed at the ordinary income tax rate. In this regard he used a cubic spline approximation technique to smooth yield and forward rate curves, a technique for which he is famous. Finally, McCulloch estimated an implied tax rate for investors in Treasury securities and concluded that it fell somewhere in the range of 22 to 30 percent.

Stephen M. Schaefer developed a different approximation method for measuring the term structure in the face of coupon bonds and diverse investor tax brackets.[28] Instead of a single set of yields, which equates the present value of after-tax cash flows with price for all bonds in the market, he used an inequality in which present value is less than or equal to price under the assumption of no short selling. Finding the bonds that were optimally held at a particular tax bracket, the term structure was calculated as the solution to a linear program. Schaefer concluded that taxation has a strong effect on choice of bonds and that the term structure for different tax brackets may differ significantly in shape. As a result, empirical studies using yield-to-maturity curves not adjusted for taxes are suspect, particularly when discount bonds strongly influence the drawing of the curves.

In summary, there are several ways for adjusting yield observations for the differential impact of taxes on interest income and capital gains. All of the approaches have their difficulties, so estimates are subject to error. However, the goal is more nearly to compare "apples" with "apples," as opposed to "apples" with "oranges." The yield curves that are fitted to the adjusted data give a more accurate and consistent picture of the relationship between yield and maturity than is the case when raw yield observations are used.

SUMMARY

Taxes affect yields in a variety of ways. Because interest income on municipal securities is tax exempt, yields are lower than they are on other fixed-income securities. Moreover, the higher the level of interest rates, the wider the differential should be between yields on the two types of bonds. The tax-exempt feature has caused the municipal market to be relatively segmented on the demand side, consisting primarily of commercial banks, fire and casualty companies, and high income individuals. This segmentation, together with the fluctuating participation by the institutions, causes municipal yields to be somewhat more volatile than Treasury or corportate yields and causes the yield curve almost always to be upward-sloping. The value of the tax exemption feature is shared be-

[28]Stephen M. Schaefer, "Measuring a Tax-Specific Term Structure of Interest Rates in the Market for British Government Securities," *Economic Journal*, 91 (June 1981): 415–38.

tween the municipality and the investors. The portion realized by the municipality tends to vary inversely with the level of interest rates and with the degree of monetary restriction.

A differential tax on interest income and on capital gains affects the valuation of discount bonds. Because part of the yield-to-maturity is comprised of a capital gain, discount bonds are attractive and accordingly provide lower yields than do bonds with coupon rates which result in their selling at par. The attractiveness of discount bonds can be studied by comparing yields on bonds having low coupon rates with those having current coupon rates. The yield differential moves in keeping with changes in the level of interest rates. While discount bonds are attractive relative to bonds selling at par for taxable issues, the opposite is true for municipal securities. Here capital gains are taxed, whereas interest income is not. Certain Treasury bonds can be used in the settlement of federal estate taxes, where they count for their full value. As a result of this feature these bonds, known as flower bonds, are in special demand when they are selling at a discount.

Because of the tax consequences, discount bonds are attractive to only a limited number of investors. In a sense the market is segmented in much the same way as the municipal market is segmented. The supply varies directly with the level of interest rates and is volatile if interest rates are volatile. Empirical evidence was examined and it was found to be consistent with the important effect that the differential taxation of interest income and capital gains has on the valuation of discount bonds. The presence of a number of discount bonds in a particular maturity range can distort downward the drawing of the yield curve. Several methods were explored for adjusting yields for the capital gains effect so that the yield observations were more consistent with each other. In addition to the capital gains and estate tax effects, we endeavored to integrate considerations of call protection, sinking funds, and duration into our examination of the valuation of discount bonds.

SELECTED REFERENCES

Caks, John, "The Coupon Effect on Yield to Maturity," *Journal of Finance,* 32 (March 1977): 103–16.

Colin, J. W., and Richard S. Bayer, "Calculation of Tax Effective Yields for Discount Instruments," *Journal of Financial and Quantitative Analysis,* 5 (June 1970): 265–73.

Cook, Timothy Q., "Changing Yield Spreads in the U.S. Government Bond Market," *Economic Review of the Federal Reserve Bank of Richmond,* 63 (March–April, 1977): 3–8.

Cramer, Robert H., and Stephen L. Hawk, "The Consideration of Coupon Levels, Taxes, Reinvestment Rates and Maturity in the Investment Management of Financial Institutions," *Journal of Financial and Quantitative Analysis,* 10 (March 1975): 67–84.

Livingston, Miles, "The Pricing of Municipal Bonds," *Journal of Financial and Quantitative Analysis,* 17 (June 1982): 179–93.

——, "The Pricing of Premium Bonds," *Journal of Financial and Quantitative Analysis,* 14 (September 1979): 517–27.

——, "Bond Taxation and the Shape of the Yield-to-Maturity Curve," *Journal of Finance,* 34 (March 1979): 189–96.

McCollum, John S., "The Impact of the Capital Gains Tax on Bond Yields," *National Tax Journal,* 26 (December 1973): 575–83.

McCulloch, J. Huston, "The Tax-Adjusted Yield Curve," *Journal of Finance,* 30 (June 1975): 811–30.

Mussa, Michael L., and Roger C. Kormendi, *The Taxation of Municipal Bonds,* Chapter 4. Washington, D.C.: American Enterprise Institute, 1979.

Peterson, John, *Changing Conditions in the Market for State and Local Government Debt,* a study for the Joint Economic Committee, 94th Congress, 2d Session. Washington, D.C.: U.S. Government Printing Office, April 16, 1976.

Pye, Gordon, "On the Tax Structure of Interest Rates," *Quarterly Journal of Economics,* LXXXIII (November 1969): 562–79.

Robichek, Alexander A., and W. David Niebuhr, "Tax-Induced Bias in Reporting Treasury Yields," *Journal of Finance,* 25 (December 1970): 1081–90.

Schaefer, Stephen M., "Measuring a Tax-Specific Term Structure of Interest Rates in the Market for British Government Securities," *Economic Journal,* 91 (June 1981): 415–38.

——, "Taxes and Security Market Equilibrium," in William F. Sharpe and Cathryn M. Cootner, *Financial Economics: Essays in Honor of Paul Cootner,* pp. 159–78. Englewood Cliffs, N.J.: Prentice-Hall, 1982.

——, "Tax Induced Clientele Effects in the Market for British Government Securities," *Journal of Financial Economics,* 10 (July 1982): 121–60.

Shiller, Robert J., and Franco Modigliani, "Coupon and Tax Effects on New and Seasoned Bond Yields and the Measurement of the Cost of Debt Capital," *Journal of Financial Economics,* 7 (1979): 297–318.

Skelton, Jeffrey L., "The Relative Pricing of Tax-Exempt and Taxable Debt," Research Paper, University of California, Berkeley, 1979.

Van Horne, James C., "Implied Tax Rates and the Valuation of Discount Bonds," *Journal of Banking and Finance,* 6 (June 1982): 145–60.

——, and Samuel S. Stewart, "A Simultaneous Equations Analysis of the Bond Markets," *The Southern Economic Journal,* XXXVIII (April 1972): 538–46.

11

CONVERTIBLE SECURITIES

We have purposely postponed the consideration of convertible securities until now, because they resemble common stock more closely than they do fixed-income securities. The instrument itself is a corporate bond or preferred stock that can be converted at the option of the holder into common stock of the same corporation. The value of this type of security to an investor depends on (1) its value as a bond or preferred stock, and (2) its potential value as common stock. Because the latter tends to be the distinctive characteristic of the security and because it usually is dominant in the valuation of convertibles, the instrument is generally treated as delayed equity financing by corporations. Companies that issue convertible securities expect them to be converted in the future.

In this chapter, we first explore the features of the conversion privilege. This is followed by an exploration of the value of the security and the return to investors. The security itself is an option to its holder. As a result, the option pricing theory is relevant, and we present this theory in the appendix to the chapter. Also in the appendix, we analyze the value of convertible securities in an option pricing context in which there is volatility in the value of the corporation, default risk on the instrument, and fluctuating interest rates.

FEATURES OF THE INSTRUMENT

As the features and valuation principles for a convertible preferred stock are nearly the same as those for a convertible bond, our subsequent discussion will focus only on bonds. Perhaps the most important feature is *the ratio of exchange* between the convertible bond and the common stock. This ratio can be stated in terms of either a *conversion price* or a *conversion ratio*. Foremost-McKesson's $9\frac{3}{4}$ percent convertible subordinated debentures ($1,000 face value), issued in June, 1981, have a conversion price of $43.75, meaning that each debenture is convertible into 22.86 shares of common stock. We simply divide the face value of the security by the conversion price to obtain the conversion ratio, $1,000/$43.75 = 22.86 shares. The conversion privilege can be stated in terms of either the conversion price or the conversion ratio.

The conversion terms are not necessarily constant over time. Many convertible issues provide for increases, or "step-ups," in the conversion price at periodic intervals. A $1,000 face value bond might have a conversion price of $100 a share for the first 5 years, $110 a share for the second 5 years, $120 for the third 5, and so on. In this way, the bond converts into fewer shares of common stock as time goes by. Usually, the conversion price is adjusted for any stock splits or stock dividends that occur after the securities are sold. If the common stock were split two for one, the conversion price would be halved. This provision protects the convertible bondholders and is known as an antidilution clause.

The *conversion value* of a convertible security is the conversion ratio of the security times the market price per share of the common stock. If Foremost-McKesson stock were selling for $50, the conversion value of one convertible subordinated debenture would be 22.86 × $50, or $1,143.

The convertible security provides the investor with a fixed return from a bond or with a specified dividend from preferred stock. In addition, the investor receives an option to convert the security into common stock, and thereby participates in the possibility of capital gains associated with being a residual owner of the corporation. Because of this option, the company usually is able to sell the convertible security at a lower yield than it would have to pay on a straight bond or preferred-stock issue. At the time of issuance, the convertible security will be priced higher than its conversion value. The differential is known as the *conversion premium*. The Foremost-McKesson convertible subordinated debentures were sold to the public for $1,000 a bond. The market price of the common stock at the time of issuance of the convertibles was approximately $38\frac{1}{2}$ per share. Therefore the conversion value of each bond was 22.86 × $38\frac{1}{2}$ = $880, and the differential of $120 between this value and the issuing price represented the conversion premium.

Frequently, this premium is expressed as a percentage; in our example the conversion premium is $120/$880 = 13.6 percent. For most issues of convertibles, the conversion premium ranges from 10 to 20 percent. For a growth company, it is likely to be in the upper part of the range, whereas for a company with only moderate growth potential, it will be in the lower part. The range itself is established mainly by market tradition, in keeping with the idea that the stock should be expected to rise in price so that it exceeds the conversion price within a reasonable period of time, such as 3 years.

Practically without exception, convertible securities provide for a *call price*. As was true with the straight bond, the call feature enables the corporation to call the security for redemption. Few convertible securities, however, are ever redeemed. Instead, the purpose of the call is to force conversion when the conversion value of the security is above its call price. Almost all convertible bond issues are subordinated to other creditors. That fact permits the lender to treat convertible subordinated debt or convertible preferred stock as a part of the equity base when evaluating the financial condition of the issuer. In the event of liquidation, it makes no difference to the lender if the issue is actually converted; in either case, the lender has a prior claim.

VALUE OF CONVERTIBLE SECURITIES

The value of a convertible security to an investor is twofold: its value as a bond or preferred stock and its potential value as common stock. Investors obtain a hedge when they purchase convertible bonds. If the market price of the stock rises, the value of the convertible is determined largely by its conversion value. If the market for the stock turns down, the investor still holds a bond whose value provides a floor below which the price of the convertible is unlikely to fall.

Bond Value

The bond value of a convertible security is the price at which a straight bond of the same company would sell in the open market. It can be determined by solving the following equation for B in the case of a bond with semiannual interest payments:

$$B = \sum_{t=1}^{2n} \frac{I}{\left(1+\frac{i}{2}\right)^t} + \frac{F}{\left(1+\frac{i}{2}\right)^{2n}} \tag{11-1}$$

where B = straight bond value of the convertible
I = semiannual interest payments determined by the coupon rate
F = face value of the bond
n = years to final maturity
i = market yield to maturity on a straight bond of the same company

In the equation, we assume semiannual interest payments, which are typical with corporate bonds, so the total number of interest payments is two times the years to maturity, n, and the semiannual interest rate on a straight bond is i divided by 2.

Suppose a company has outstanding a 9 percent convertible debenture with a final maturity 20 years hence. If the company is to sell a straight 20-year debenture in the current market, the yield will have to be 11 percent to be attractive to investors. For a 20-year bond with a 9 percent coupon to yield 11 percent to maturity, the bond has to sell at a discount. Using the above equation and rounding, we have

$$B = \sum_{t=1}^{40} \frac{\$4.50}{(1.055)^t} + \frac{\$1,000}{(1.055)^{40}} = \$840$$

Thus the bond-value floor of the company's convertible bonds is $840. This floor suggests that if the price of the common stock were to fall sharply, the price of the convertible would fall only to $840. At that price, the security would sell as a straight bond in keeping with prevailing bond yields for that grade of security.

The bond-value floor of a convertible is not constant over time. It varies with (1) interest-rate movements in the capital markets and (2) changes in the financial risk of the company involved. If interest rates in general rise, the bond value of a convertible will decline. If the yield to maturity on a straight bond in our example increases from 11 to 12 percent, the bond value of the convertible will drop from $840 to $774. Moreover, the company's credit rating can either improve or deteriorate over time. If it improves and the company is able to sell a straight bond at a lower yield to maturity, the bond value of the convertible security will increase, all other things held constant. If the company's credit standing deteriorates and the yield on a straight bond increases, the bond-value floor will decline. Unfortunately for investors, when the market price of the stock falls because of poor earnings, the company may have financial difficulty, in which case its credit standing will suffer. As a result, the straight bond value of the convertible may decline along with the decline in its conversion value, giving investors less downside protection than they might have expected originally.[1]

Premiums

Convertible securities usually sell at premiums over both their bond value and their conversion value. Recall that the conversion value

---

[1] Mathematically, the straight bond value of a convertible security will rise over time, all other things held constant, if the face value of the convertible is above the straight bond value at the time of issuance. At final maturity, the straight bond value will equal the face value of the convertible, assuming the company is not in default.

of a convertible is simply the current market price per share of the company's common stock times the number of shares into which the security is convertible. The fact that the convertible bond provides the investor with a degree of downside protection, given the qualifications mentioned above, often results in its selling at a market price somewhat higher than its conversion value. How much higher will depend largely upon the probability that the conversion value of the security will fall below its bond value. In general, the more volatile the price movements of the stock, the more valuable is the downside protection afforded by the bond-value floor. For this reason as well as for additional reasons discussed later, the market price of a convertible security frequently is above its conversion value. The difference is known as the *premium-over-conversion value.*

Moreover, a convertible bond typically will sell at a *premium-over-bond value*, primarily because of the conversion feature. Unless the market price of the stock is very low relative to the conversion price, the conversion feature usually will have value, in that investors may eventually find it profitable to convert the securities. To the extent that the conversion feature does have value, the convertible will sell at a premium over its straight bond value. The higher the market price of the common relative to the conversion price, the greater this premium.

Relation Between Premiums

The tradeoff between the two premiums depicts the value of the option to investors and is illustrated in Fig. 11-1. The market price of the common is on the horizontal axis; the value of the convertible security is on the vertical. It should be pointed out that the two axes are on different scales. If the conversion ratio were 20 to 1, the horizontal axis might be in units of $10, while the vertical axis would be in units of $200. The diagonal line, which starts at the origin, represents the conversion value of the bond. It is linear, as the conversion ratio is invariant with respect to the market price of the stock. The bond-value line, however, is related to the market price of the common. If a company is doing badly financially, the prices of both its common stock and its bonds are likely to be low. At the extreme, if the total value of the company were zero, both the bonds and the stock would have a value of zero. As the company becomes sounder financially and the common stock increases in price, bond value increases but at a decreasing rate. After a point, the bond-value line becomes flat, and further increases in common stock price are unrelated to it. At this point, the bond-value floor is determined by what other high-grade bonds sell for in the market. The upper curved line represents the market price of the convertible security. The distance between this line and the bond-value line is the premium-over-bond value, while the distance between the market-value line and the conversion-value line represents the premium-over-conversion value.

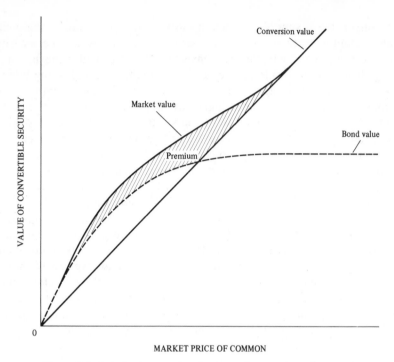

VALUE OF CONVERTIBLE SECURITY

Conversion value

Market value

Bond value

Premium

0

MARKET PRICE OF COMMON

Figure 11-1. Relation between bond-value and conversion-value premiums.

We see that at relatively high common-stock price levels, the value of the convertible as a bond is insignificant. Consequently, its premium-over-bond value is high, whereas its premium-over-conversion value is negligible. The security sells mainly for its stock equivalent. Investors are unwilling to pay a significant premium-over-conversion value for the following reasons. First, the greater the premium of market price of the convertible over its bond value, the less valuable the bond-value protection is to the investor. Second, when the conversion value is high, the convertible may be called; if it is, investors will want to convert rather than redeem the bond for the call price. Upon conversion, of course, the bond is worth only its conversion value.

On the other hand, when the market value of the convertible is close to its straight bond value, the conversion feature has little value. At this level, the convertible security is valued primarily as a straight bond. Under these circumstances, the market price of the convertible is likely to exceed its conversion value by a significant premium.

The principal reason for premiums in market price over both conversion value and bond value is the unusual appeal of a convertible as both a bond and a common stock. It offers the holder partial protection on the downside, together with participation in upward movements in stock price. Thus the distribution of possible outcomes is skewed to the right, and this characteristic finds favor with investors. Because of the skewed nature of the distribution of possible outcomes, the convertible security, like any option, should have more value the greater the volatility in the market price of the common. Investors have the downside protection of the bond-value floor shown in Fig. 11-1 coupled with unlimited upside potential; thus, the greater the dispersion of the probability distribution of possible common-stock market prices, the higher the expected value of return. In turn, this leads to a higher value for the option, which in this case is a convertible security. In the appendix to this chapter, we explore in more detail the valuation of convertible bonds in an option pricing model framework.

Other Reasons for Premiums

Although we have concentrated on the main reasons for premiums, other factors appear to have at least a modest influence. Some of the influence stems from the presence of certain impediments to the perfect market assumptions implied earlier in our discussion. For one thing, lower transaction costs on convertible bonds relative to those on common stocks enhance the attractiveness of these bonds. By purchasing convertible bonds and converting them into common stock, investors incur lower transaction costs than they would by purchasing the stock outright. This attraction should exert upward pressure on the premiums-over-conversion value and over-bond value. Yet another influence that may raise premiums is that certain institutional investors, such as life insurance companies, are restricted with respect to investing in common stock. By investing in convertible bonds, they gain the benefits of a common-stock investment without actually investing in common stock.

The duration of the convertible option also should affect the premiums. In general, the longer the duration, the more valuable the option. Unlike other options, the time to expiration is uncertain, owing to the fact that the company can force conversion if the price of the common stock is high enough. The longest time is the maturity of the security, but the actual duration typically is much shorter. Another factor is the dividend on the common. The greater the dividend, the greater the attraction of the common vis-à-vis the convertible security and the lower the premiums, all other things the same. All these influences affect the premiums at which convertible securities sell. Although they tend to carry less weight than the influences discussed in the previous section, they need to be considered nonetheless in determining the value of a convertible security.

RETURN ON CONVERTIBLES

The return on a convertible security is complicated in that it derives its value from being both a bond and a common stock. If prospective investors have a fixed investment horizon, the expected return might be found by solving the following equation for k_c.

$$P_0 = \sum_{t=1}^{2n} \frac{I}{\left(1+\dfrac{k_c}{2}\right)^t} + \frac{P_n}{\left(1+\dfrac{k_c}{2}\right)^{2n}} \tag{11-2}$$

where P_0 = market price of security at time 0
$\quad\ I$ = contractual semiannual interest payment
$\quad\ n$ = investor's horizon period
$\quad P_n$ = expected market price of the convertible at the end of period n

For simplicity, we assume that there is no risk of default on the contractual payment of interest.

The expected market value at the end of the horizon period, P_n, represents the mean of a subjective probability distribution. This distribution usually is skewed to the right because of the bond-value floor of the security. To illustrate, suppose that the investor at time 0 formulated the probability distribution of possible conversion values at the end of period n shown in Fig. 11-2. However, investors know that if the conversion value falls below the bond-value floor of the security, the market price of the security will not drop below that. If a bond value of $900 is assumed, the modified probability distribution can be shown in Fig. 11-3. Over most of the probability distribution, however, the market price of the convertible security is likely to sell at a premium over both its bond value and its conversion value. Consequently, the probability distribution of conversion values in Fig. 11-3 must be modified to take account of these premiums. By comparing the two premiums for a sample of convertible securities of similar companies, an investor can gauge the size of the premiums. On the

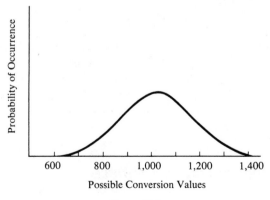

Figure 11-2.

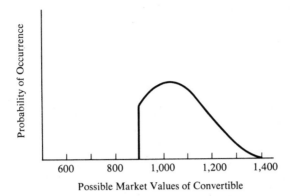

Figure 11-3.

basis of this information, the probability distribution in Fig. 11-3 can be modified to reflect the addition of the premiums. An example of the modification appears in Fig. 11-4.

Given a probability distribution of possible market prices at the end of period n similar to Fig. 11-4, the expected value of the distribution can be determined. With P_n in Eq. (11-2) thus determined, the expected return to the investor can be found by solving the equation for k_c.[2] Whether the expected return is attractive to the prospective investors will depend upon their opportunity rates of return for investment in other securities of the same risk. The perceived risk of the convertible to the investor is determined importantly by the shape and dispersion of the probability distribution of possible market values at time n; this distribution was illustrated in Fig. 11-4.[3] If the computed expected return is higher than the investors' opportunity rate, they will purchase the convertible security; if it is lower, no purchase will occur.

The realized return on investment in a convertible security can be determined in the same manner as that for fixed-income investments. For a given holding period, it would be the rate of discount that equates the present value of interest payments plus terminal value with the initial market price of the security. This realized rate then could be used for comparative purposes with rates of return on common stocks and returns on other financial instruments. Unfortunately, average rates of return for holding convertible securities are not available. Consequently, the analysis

[2]For a similar approach to determining returns, see William J. Baumol, Burton G. Malkiel, and Richard E. Quandt, "The Valuation of Convertible Securities," *Quarterly Journal of Economics*, LXXX (February 1966): 48–59.

[3]If the interest payments and bond value are assumed to be subjective random variables, the opportunity rate, or required return, of the investor also would depend upon these distributions. Figure 11-4 would have to be modified further to allow for possible variations in the straight bond value of the convertible. See the appendix to this chapter for a treatment of this problem.

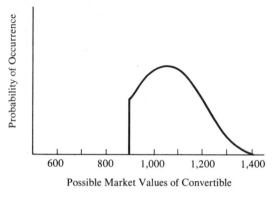

Figure 11-4.

of returns tends to be confined to the evaluation of individual convertible securities.

SUMMARY

A convertible security is an option under which the holder can obtain common stock. The conversion price is the face value of the instrument divided by the number of shares into which the security can be converted. The latter is known as the conversion ratio. Almost all convertible bonds are subordinated to other creditors and carry a call provision. The value of the convertible security in the marketplace is determined primarily by its value as a straight bond or preferred stock and its conversion value as common stock.

The market price of a convertible security is typically above both its conversion value and its bond value. These premiums are due primarily to the security's partial downside protection as a bond and its upside potential as stock, resulting in an overall distribution of possible returns that is skewed to the right. Other factors affecting the premiums are the volatility of the common stock (explored in the appendix), the dividend on the common stock, the expiration of the convertible option, and certain institutional imperfections that affect investors.

The return on a convertible security can be measured as the discount rate that equates the present value at the end of a horizon period with the current market price of the security. The estimation of possible terminal values is complicated because the security is both a fixed-income security and common stock. We treat this complication in the appendix, where we analyze the valuation of convertibles in an option pricing model framework where there are many variables.

APPENDIX:
VALUING CONVERTIBLE SECURITIES
IN AN OPTION PRICING
MODEL CONTEXT

Because a convertible security is an option to the holder either to convert the security into common stock or to continue to hold it, a rich body of theory can be brought to bear on the problem. In this appendix, we first present the option pricing theory and then apply it conceptually to convertible security valuation. This allows us to come to grips with the volatility of common stock, default risk, and changing interest rates.

An option is simply a contract that gives the holder the right to buy or sell the common stock of a company at some specified price. Among a variety of option contracts, the most prevalent are the *call option* and the *put option*. The call option gives the holder the right to buy a share of stock at a specified price, known as the *exercise price*. We might have a call option to buy one share of ABC Corporation's common stock at $10 through December 31, which is the expiration date. The party who provides the option is known as the *writer*. In the case of a call option, the writer must deliver stock to the optionholder when the latter exercises the option.

Suppose that we were concerned with the value of a call option, (hereafter simply called an option) on its expiration date. The value of the option is simply

$$V_O = \text{Max}(V_s - E, O) \qquad (11\text{A-}1)$$

where V_x is the market price of one share of stock, E is the exercise price of the option, and Max means the maximum value of $V_s - E$ or zero, whichever is greater. To illustrate the formula, suppose one share of Selby Corporation's stock is $25 at the expiration date and that the exercise price of an option is $15. The value of the option would be $25 - $15 = $10. Note that the value of the option is determined solely by the value of the stock less the exercise price; however, the option cannot have a negative value. When the exercise price exceeds the value of the stock, the value of the option becomes zero.

This notion is illustrated graphically in Fig. 11A-1. The theoretical value of the option is represented by the solid line in the figure, and the actual market value is shown by the dashed line. When the market value of the associated stock is less than the exercise price, the theoretical value of the option is zero. When the value of the associated common stock is greater than the exercise price, the theoretical value of the option is positive, as depicted by the solid diagonal line. One might think of the line showing theoretical value as representing the value an option might take at the moment of expiration.

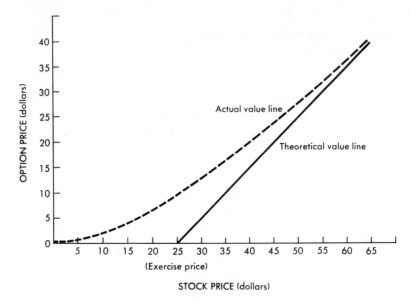

Figure 11A-1. Relation between the option price and the stock price for XYZ Corporation.

Valuation Prior to Expiration

Consider now the value of an option with one period to expiration. For simplicity, let us assume that it can be exercised only on the expiration date. The value of stock at the expiration date is not known, but instead is subject to probabilistic beliefs. As long as there is some time to expiration, it is possible for the market value of the option to be greater than its theoretical value. The reason is that the option *may* have value in the future. This was discussed for the warrant, so further discussion is not necessary. The actual value of the option might be described by the dashed line in Fig. 11A-1.

In general, the longer the period of time to expiration, the greater the value of the option relative to its theoretical value. This makes sense in that there is more time in which the option may have value. Moreover, the further in the future one pays the exercise price, the lower its present value, and this too enhances the option's value. As the expiration date of an option approaches, the relationship between the option value and the stock value becomes more convex. This is illustrated in Fig. 11A-2. Line 1 represents an option with a shorter time to expiration than that for line 2, and line 2 represents an option with a shorter time to expiration than that for line 3.

Usually, the most important factor in the valuation of options is the price volatility of the associated stock. More specifically, the greater the

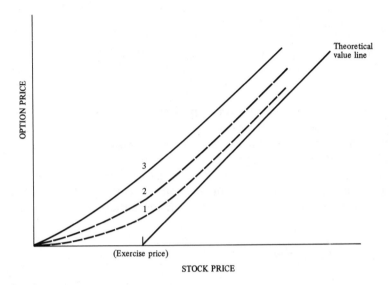

Figure 11A-2. Relation between stock price and option price for various expiration dates.

possibility of extreme outcomes, the greater the value of the option to the holder, all other things the same. We may, at the beginning of a period, be considering options on two stocks that have the following probability distributions of possible values at the expiration of the option:

Probability of Occurrence	Price of Stock A	Price of Stock B
.10	$30	$20
.25	36	30
.30	40	40
.25	44	50
.10	50	60

The expected stock price at the end of the period is the same for both stocks: $40. For stock B, however, there is a much larger dispersion of possible outcomes. Suppose that the exercise prices of options to purchase stock A and stock B at the end of the period are also the same, for example, $38. Thus, the two stocks have the same expected values at the end of the period, and the options have the same exercise price. The expected value of the option for stock A at the end of the period, however, is

$$\text{Option A} = 0(.10) + 0(.25) + (\$40 - \$38)(.30)$$
$$+ (\$44 - \$38)(.25) + (\$50 - \$38)(.10) = \$3.30$$

whereas that for stock B is

$$\text{Option B} = 0(.10) + 0(.25) + (\$40 - \$38)(.30)$$
$$+ (\$50 - \$38)(.25) + (\$60 - \$38)(.10) = \$5.80$$

Thus, the greater dispersion of possible outcomes for stock B leads to a greater expected value of option price on the expiration date. The reason is that values for the option cannot be negative. As a result, the greater the dispersion, the greater the magnitude of favorable outcomes as measured by the stock price minus the exercise price. Increases in the volatility of the stock therefore increase the magnitude of favorable outcomes for the option buyer and, hence, increase the value of the option.

Hedging with Options

Having two related financial assets—a stock and an option on that stock—we can set up a risk-free hedged position. Price movements in one of the financial assets will be offset by opposite price movements in the other. A hedged position can be established by buying the stock (holding it long) and by writing options. If the stock goes up in price, we gain in our long position; that is, in the stock we hold. We lose in the options we have written, because the price we must pay for the stock in order to deliver to the person exercising the option is higher than it was when the option was written. If the stock goes down in price, the opposite occurs. We lose on our long position, but gain on the options we have written.

Thus, when one holds a combination of stock and options written, movements upward or downward in the price of the stock are offset by opposite movements in the value of the option position written. If one does this properly, the overall position (long in stock, options written) can be made approximately risk-free. In market equilibrium, one would expect to earn only the risk-free rate on a perfectly hedged position.

Black-Scholes Option Model

In a seminal paper, Fischer Black and Myron Scholes developed a precise model for determining the equilibrium value of an option.[4] This model is based on the hedging notion discussed above. Black and Scholes assume an option that can be exercised only at maturity, no

[4]Fischer Black and Myron Scholes, "The Pricing of Options and Corporate Liabilities," *Journal of Political Economy*, 81 (May-June 1973): 637–54.

transaction costs or market imperfections, a stock that pays no dividend, a known short-term interest rate at which market participants can both borrow and lend, and, finally, stock price movements that follow a random pattern.

Given these assumptions, we can determine the equilibrium value of an option. Should the actual price of the option differ from that given by the model, we could establish a riskless hedged position and earn a return in excess of the short-term interest rate. As arbitragers entered the scene, the excess return would eventually be driven out and the price of the option would equal that value given by the model.

To illustrate a hedged position, suppose that the appropriate relationship between the option and the stock of XYZ Corporation is as shown in Fig. 11A-1. Suppose further that the current market price of the stock is $20 and the price of the option $7. At $20 a share, the slope of the line in Fig. 11A-1 is one-half. A hedged position can be undertaken by buying a share of stock for $20 and writing two options at $7 each. The *net money* invested in this position is $20 − 2($7) = $6.

This combination of holding one share of stock long and two options short leaves us essentially hedged with respect to risk. If the stock drops slightly in value, the value of the short position goes up by approximately an equal amount. We say *approximately* because with changes in the price of the common and with changes in time, the ideal hedge ratio changes. With a stock price increase, for example, the slope of the line in Fig. 11A-1 increases. Therefore, fewer options would need to be written. If the stock price declines, the slope decreases and more options would need to be written to maintain a hedge. In addition, the line itself will shift downward as time goes on and the expiration date approaches. This was illustrated in Fig. 11A-2.

Thus, one's short position in options must be continually adjusted for changes in the stock price and for changes in time if a riskless hedged position is to be maintained. The assumptions of the model make this possible; but in the real world, transaction costs make it impractical to adjust one's short position continuously. Even here, however, the risk that will appear as a result of moderate changes in stock price or of the passage of time will be small. Moreover, it can be diversified away. For practical purposes, then, it is possible to maintain a hedged position that is approximately risk-free. Arbitrage will assure that the return on this position is approximately the short-term, risk-free rate.

If the price of the option got out of line with that of the stock, it would be possible for a person to earn more than the short-term rate on a hedged position. In the example above, the net money invested in the position was $6 [$20 − 2($7)]. As the total hedged position is riskless, the net money invested should provide a return equal only to the short-term rate. If, for some reason, the prices on the two instruments got out of line with each other, it would be possible to earn a return on the total position in excess of the short-term rate times the net money invested. In other words, excess returns would be possible on a position perfectly hedged for risk.

As a result, arbitragers would enter the picture and would borrow large sums of money, establish hedged positions, and reap the excess returns available. This action would continue until the buying or selling pressure on the prices of the stock and the option drove such prices into equilibrium with each other. At such time, the return on the net money invested in a fully hedged position would once again be the short-term rate. Thus, there are equilibrating forces that cause a riskless hedge to provide a return equal to the short-term rate.

In this context, the equilibrium value of an option that entitles the holder to buy one share of stock is shown by Black and Scholes to be

$$V_0 = V_s N(d_1) - \left(\frac{E}{e^{rt}}\right) N(d_2) \tag{11A-2}$$

where
V_s = the current price of the stock
E = the exercise price of the option
e = 2.71828
r = the short-term interest rate continuously compounded
t = the length of time in years to the expiration of the option
$N(d)$ = the value of the cumulative normal density function
$$d_1 = \frac{\ln(V_s/E + (r + 1/2\sigma^2)t}{\sigma\sqrt{t}}$$
$$d_2 = \frac{\ln(V_s/E) + (r - 1/2\sigma^2)t}{\sigma\sqrt{t}}$$
$\ln$ = the natural logarithm
σ = the standard deviation of the annual rate of return on the stock continuously compounded

The important implication of this formula is that the value of the option is a function of the short-term interest rate, of the time to expiration, and of the variance rate of return on the stock, but it is not a function of the expected return on the stock. The value of the option in Eq. (11A-2) increases with the increase of the time to expiration, the standard deviation, and the short-term interest rate.

The reason for the first two relationships with option values is obvious from our earlier discussion. The last is not so obvious. Recall that a person is able to take a position in options that will provide the same dollar movements as the associated stock, but with a lower net investment. The difference in net money in the option relative to the stock may be invested in short-term market instruments. The greater the return on these investments, therefore, the greater the attraction of the option relative to the stock, and the greater its value. Another way to look at the matter is that the greater the interest rate, the lower the present value of exercise price that will need to be paid in the future if the option is exercised, and the greater the value of the option. Of the three factors affecting the value of the option, however, the short-term interest rate has the least impact.

In solving the formula, we know the current stock price, the time to expiration, the exercise price, and the short-term interest rate. The key unknown, then, is the standard deviation. This must be estimated. The usual approach is to use the past volatility of the stock's return as a proxy for the future. Black and Scholes, as well as others, have tested the model using standard deviations estimated from past data with some degree of success. Given the valuation equation for options, Black and Scholes derive the ratio of shares of stock to options necessary to maintain a fully hedged position. It is shown to be $N(d_1)$, which was defined earlier. Thus, the Black-Scholes model permits the quantification of the various factors that affect the value of an option. As we saw, the key factor is estimating the future volatility of the stock.

Option Pricing—A Summing Up

In summary, it is possible to establish a riskless hedged position by buying a stock and by writing options. The hedge ratio determines the portion of stock held long in relation to the options that are written. In efficient financial markets, the rate of return on a perfectly hedged position would be the risk-free rate. If this is the case, it is possible to determine the appropriate value of the option at the beginning of the period. If the actual value is above or below this value, arbitrage should drive the price of the option toward the correct price.

The Black-Scholes option pricing model provides an exact formula for determining the value of an option based on the volatility of the stock, the price of the stock, the exercise price of the option, the time to expiration of the option, and the short-term interest rate. The model is based on the notion that investors are able to maintain reasonably hedged positions over time and that arbitrage will drive the return on such positions to the risk-free rate. As a result, the option price will bear a precise relationship to the stock price. The Black-Scholes model provides considerable insight into the valuation of contingent claims.

Application of Option Pricing Concepts to Valuing
Convertible Securities

As we know, a convertible security is an option to obtain common stock in a corporation. As with any option, the greater the volatility of the stock and the underlying volatility of firm value, the greater the value of the option to the convertible security holder.

In a conceptual sense, the debtholders of a corporation can be viewed as option writers, and equityholders can be viewed as holding an option on the firm's total value. At the maturity of the debt, the equityholders have the option of buying back the firm from the debtholders at a specified price, which is the face value of the debt instrument. In this context, the greater the volatility of the value of the total firm, the greater the value of the option to the equityholders. On the other hand, the greater the volatility, the greater the default risk in the sense that the firm will be worth less than the debt's face value. If default occurs, equityholders will not exercise their option, bankruptcy by definition will occur, and debtholders will suffer a loss. In Chapter 9, we explored the valuation of the call option on straight debt. Here we found that the greater the volatility of future interest rates, the greater the value of the call option to the equityholders and the greater the value loss to the debtholders. If such interest-rate volatility is anticipated at the time of the loan, lenders will demand a higher interest rate to compensate them for the call risk.

All three factors influence the valuation of convertible bonds, and it is useful to explore the interrelationships. What will emerge is not a precise model, if indeed one were possible, but a general overview of the valuation underpinnings. To begin, let us assume that financial markets are perfect, that a firm has no debt other than convertible bonds, and that bondholders and the firm follow optimal strategies. Under these circumstances, optimal strategies consist of: (1) bondholders converting their bonds into stock if the value of the convertible is less than its conversion value; (2) bondholders forcing the firm into bankruptcy and seizing its value if the value of the firm falls below the debt's face value, assuming that the ability to do so is written into the contract; and (3) the firm calling the bonds when their value equals the call price.

Given these actions, the boundaries for the valuation of convertible bonds are shown in Fig. 11A-3. If the value of the bonds should exceed the call price, they will be called so their value is bounded on the upside by the call price. On the downside, bondholders will force bankruptcy, should the value of the firm fall below the total face value of the bonds outstanding.[5] Moreover, bondholders will convert if the value of their

---

[5]This assumes that at the time of the loan, the firm's value exceeds the face value of the bonds.

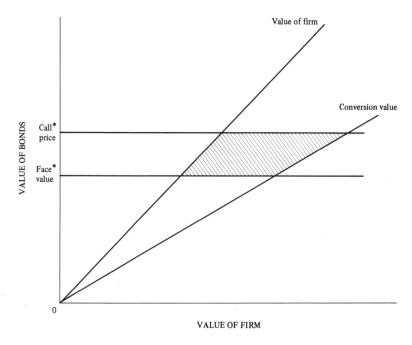

*Represents the total value of all bonds at the call price and at face value.

Figure 11A-3. Boundaries of convertible bond valuation.

bonds falls below the conversion value, so we have another lower boundary. Finally, the total value of the bonds cannot exceed the total value of the firm. As a result of these constraints, the value of the bonds must fall within the shaded area in the figure.

Within these boundaries, certain relationships are likely to hold. For one, we would expect an inverse relationship between the risk of default and the value of the firm. That is, increases in firm value would be associated with decreases in default risk up to a point. As a result, we might expect the relationship shown in the upper panel of Fig. 11A-4. Here we see that the value of the bonds increases at a decreasing rate until the curve eventually turns up, in keeping with the change in conversion value. This phenomenon was discussed in the chapter, and we know that it embraces both default risk and firm value volatility.

For a given firm value, companies can have different business-risk strategies, which result in different default risks. Therefore, the relationship between bond value and firm value will differ, depending on the risk strategy chosen by the firm. In the bottom panel of Fig. 11A-4, risk strategy 1 is safer than strategies 2 and 3, in the sense of less volatility of firm value. Accordingly, the risk of default is less for any level of firm value, and the value of the convertible bonds is higher.

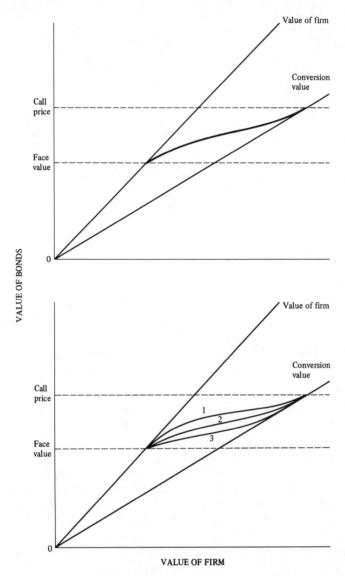

Figure 11A-4. Convertible bond valuation with default risk.

   Having considered default risk, we turn now to interest-rate risk. For given levels of firm value and default risk, the greater the interest rate, the lower the value of the outstanding convertible bonds. The relationship is depicted by the upper panel of Fig. 11A-5. For a hypothetical interest rate of 6 percent, the bond-value line is higher than it is for interest rates of 10 percent and 14 percent, respectively. This follows, of course, from the valuation of any fixed-income security. Apart from the expected level

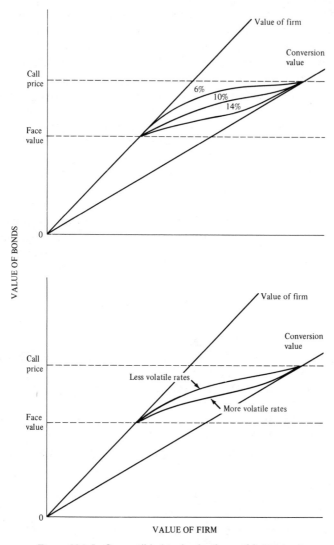

Figure 11A-5. Convertible bond valuation and interest rates.

of interest rates, the greater the volatility of future interest rates, the greater the value of the call option to the company and the lower the value of the convertible security to the holder. This situation is depicted in the lower panel of Fig. 11A-5. Bear in mind that if the bond is called, the holder has the option to convert it into common stock; therefore, the impact of the call is far less than it is in the case of straight debt. Finally, we should point out that in determining whether a convertible security is called, stock-price volatility usually dominates interest-rate volatility.

We have described the more important two-way relationships affecting the valuation of convertible bonds, but there are others that complicate the picture. For one thing, there is likely to be an association among the level of interest rates, default risk, and the value of the firm. High interest rates often are associated with periods of high and uncertain inflation. Consequently, the value of the firm will be less, all other things the same, than it is in times of low inflation, moderate uncertainty, and low interest rates. Similarly, periods of high inflation, great uncertainty, and high interest rates may be characterized by greater default risk. Thus, the volatility of firm value and of interest rates are not independent, and this makes the valuation of the hybrid convertible security very complicated indeed.

Our purpose is not to present a formal model, but to point out the direction of bond value changes that are likely to accompany parameter changes.[6] This discussion, which draws on concepts of option pricing theory, gives us a richer understanding of the valuation of convertible securities, a topic that will see increasing research in the vein taken up in this appendix.

SELECTED REFERENCES

Alexander, Gordon J., and Roger D. Stover, "The Effect of Forced Conversion on Common Stock Prices," *Financial Management*, 9 (Spring 1980): 39–45.

Baumol, William J., Burton G. Malkiel, and Richard E. Quandt, "The Valuation of Convertible Securities," *Quarterly Journal of Economics*, 65 (February 1966): 48–59.

Black, Fischer, and Myron Scholes, "The Pricing of Options and Corporate Liabilities," *Journal of Political Economy*, 81 (May-June 1973): 637–54.

_____ , "The Valuation of Option Contracts and a Test of Market Efficiency," *Journal of Finance*, 27 (May 1972): 339–417.

Brennan, M. J., and E. S. Schwartz, "Convertible Bonds: Valuation and Optimal Strategies for Call and Conversion," *Journal of Finance*, 32 (December 1977): 1699–1715.

_____ , "Analyzing Convertible Bonds," *Journal of Financial and Quantitative Analysis*, 15 (November 1980): 907–29.

Brigham, Eugene F., "An Analysis of Convertible Debentures: Theory and Some Empirical Evidence," *Journal of Finance*, 21 (March 1966): 35–54.

Frankle, A. W., and C. A. Hawkins, "Beta Coefficients for Convertible Bonds," *Journal of Finance*, 30 (March 1975): 207–10.

Ingersoll, Jonathan E., Jr., "A Contingent-Claims Valuation of Convertible Securities," *Journal of Financial Economics*, 4 (January 1977): 289–321.

---

[6]For one approach to modeling the relationships, see Michael J. Brennan and Eduardo S. Schwartz, "Analyzing Convertible Bonds," *Journal of Financial and Quantitative Analysis*, 15 (November 1980): 907–29.

———— , "An Examination of Corporate Call Policies on Convertible Securities," *Journal of Finance*, 32 (May 1977): 463–78.

Jennings, Edward H., "An Estimate of Convertible Bond Premiums," *Journal of Financial and Quantitative Analysis*, 9 (January 1974): 33–56.

Mikkelson, Wayne H., "Convertible Calls and Security Returns," *Journal of Financial Economics*, 9 (September 1981): 237–64.

Piper, Thomas R., and Jaspar H. Arnold III, "Warrants and Convertible Debt as Financing Vehicles in the Private Placement Market," *Explorations in Economic Research of the National Bureau of Economic Research*, 4 (Spring 1977): 277–302.

Rubinstein, Mark, and John C. Cox, *Options Markets*, Englewood Cliffs, N.J.: Prentice-Hall, Inc., 1982.

Walter, James E., and Agustin V. Que, "The Valuation of Convertible Bonds," *Journal of Finance*, 28 (June 1973): 713–32.

Weil, Roman L., Jr., Joel E. Segall, and David Green, Jr., "Premiums on Convertible Bonds," *Journal of Finance*, 23 (June 1968): 445–63.

———— , "Reply," *Journal of Finance*, 25 (September 1970): 931–3.

12

THE SOCIAL ALLOCATION
OF CAPITAL

Stated early in this book was the proposition that funds flow
from savings-surplus economic units to savings-deficit ones *primarily* on
the basis of expected return and risk. We then looked at various factors
affecting risk and return and analyzed their impact on the yields we observe
in the marketplace. Factors considered included maturity, duration, inflationary expectations, default risk, callability, sinking funds, taxability, and
market imperfections. We also saw that the more efficient the financial
markets of a society, the less the cost and inconvenience with which funds
flow from ultimate savers to ultimate investors in real assets. The efficient
channeling of savings requires competition among financial intermediaries
and continual financial innovation. When profit opportunities arise, new
intermediaries, financial instruments, or methods come into being to exploit these opportunities and, ultimately, to drive out the excess profits
previously available. Thus, competition leads to financial innovation, which
in turn leads to a reduction in the cost of financial intermediation and,
from an economic standpoint, to a more efficient allocation of savings in
society.

Market imperfections impede the efficiency with which financial markets operate. In Chapters 5 through 10, we investigated some of the more
important imperfections. Such things as institutional restrictions on investor
and borrower behavior, transaction costs, and taxes were examined. Where
empirical evidence *was* available, these imperfections were found to have
only a modest effect in hampering market efficiency. Still, in certain instances, significant effects were found over what would have been the case
if interest rates were allowed to seek their own levels in free and competitive
financial markets.

In this chapter we examine another influence on the flow of funds and on interest rates—the influence of the government. This influence is one apart from its taxing power and certain other government restrictions already discussed. Our focus will be on attempts by the government to direct the flow of funds in our society toward socially desirable goals or to lower the interest-rate cost to socially desirable borrowers. These attempts fall under a broad heading that we will call the *social allocation of capital*. Because of the nature of the topic, our consideration of it will be somewhat more conceptual in orientation than was true of former topics.

THE ISSUES INVOLVED

By social allocation of capital, we mean any action by the government that attempts to direct the flow of savings in our society toward some specific objective. This objective might be housing (through mortgages), inner cities, low-income families, pollution and environmental control, minority enterprises, consumer cooperatives, small businesses, farmers, a failing corporation, or what have you. The essential thing is that savings flows are directed in ways that would not occur if market forces alone were allowed to prevail. In other words, the "socially desirable" project does not attract the financing that the government would like it to attract at an interest rate that is sufficiently low from a social standpoint. To remedy the perceived deficiency, the government steps into the savings allocation process to redirect flows toward socially desirable projects at appropriate interest rates (presumably low).

At the time the program is initiated, the perceived social benefits exceed the social costs in the eyes of the initiators—Congress, the executive branch, state legislatures, or others. The benefits are readily apparent; one category or group in our society is able to borrow at favorable interest rates where before credit was either unavailable or available only at a higher interest cost. As a result of a program to socially allocate capital they move to the head, or nearly to the head, of the credit line. However, seldom are the social and economic costs of a program evaluated in their totality. These costs involve not only the *out-of-pocket cost* to the government in administering the subsidy, but also the *opportunity cost* of the restrictions imposed on the efficiency of financial markets, the opportunity cost of lessened economic growth which in turn results from directing savings toward projects on the basis of social return as opposed to economic return, and, in certain cases, the redistributional effects which work to the detriment of low-income families. As this chapter unfolds, we identify these costs as we explore various methods for socially allocating capital in our society.

Our purpose is not to suggest that the social allocation of capital is bad per se. Rather we suggest the need for a more encompassing cost-benefit-type of analysis before a plan is undertaken. Too often the costs of a method to socially allocate capital are not considered in their entirety, or they are ignored altogether because of their "hidden" nature. It is not surprising then that proposals to socially allocate capital are so popular. The political appeal is irresistible. The benefits to a disadvantaged constituency are perceived to be abundant and the costs negligible. Is it any wonder that proposals to socially allocate capital are so popularly received? In this chapter we hope to make a case for a more objective appraisal of such plans so that the need, the benefits, and the costs can be realistically appraised, and, when a decision to go ahead is made, the most efficient and equitable method can be chosen.

A number of methods have been used to socially allocate capital to a desired cause and/or to lower the interest rate that otherwise would be paid. We endeavor to evaluate these methods with respect to their conceptual underpinnings. The methods examined include: (1) a ceiling rate of interest on loans; (2) the use of a government guarantee or "moral obligation" to enhance a borrower's appeal in the market; (3) a government interest subsidy to the borrower or lender; (4) the government borrowing in the financial markets and relending to the socially desirable project; (5) the imposition of various government regulations, such as deposit rate ceilings, to divert the flow of savings to a social project; and (6) the federal government deciding who and what qualify for tax exempt financing. We investigate each of these in turn.

CEILINGS ON BORROWING COSTS

A number of states have usury laws, which govern the maximum interest rate a lender can charge. The intent of these laws is to lower the cost of borrowing, particularly to lower-income families, and to protect those less educated in the mathematics of compound interest. Whereas once usury laws were religious in conception, this has not been the case since Martin Luther caused lending to be tolerable, if not respected. The greatest concentration of usury laws occurs in the areas of consumer credit and, up to 1983, residential mortgages. The question we wish to address is: What is the effect of interest-rate ceilings on the supply of loans and on noninterest costs?

The Effect of Usury Laws

When the equilibrium market rate of interest is below the interest-rate ceiling imposed under a usury law, there is no effect on either the supply of loans or on noninterest costs. Borrowing and lending occur in free and competitive markets. However, when the ceiling is below what

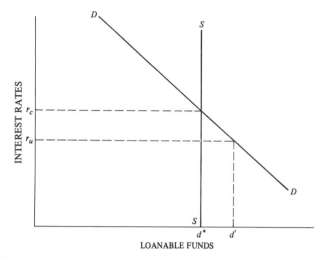

Figure 12-1. Illustration of interest-rate ceiling with an inelastic supply curve.

otherwise would be a market clearing rate, there usually is an effect. The notion that interest rates can be held down by government mandate without an adverse effect on loan flows rests on a proposition of complete segmentation, or unsubstitutability, between markets. In other words, the supply of loans is interest inelastic. The situation is illustrated in Fig. 12-1. At the market clearing rate of r_c, the supply of loans is d^*, while at the lower rate determined by usury laws, r_u, the supply is still d^*. However, at a rate of interest of r_u, desired demand is d', so there is excess demand of $d' - d^*$. In the face of this excess demand, lenders would be expected to: (1) increase the quality of their loan portfolios by raising credit standards and screening out riskier borrowers, frequently low-income families; and/ or (2) seek additional compensation through various noninterest devices such as closing fees, servicing fees, and discounts from the face value of the debt instrument, (known as *points*).[1] Thus, even with completely segmented markets and an inelastic supply curve, the presence of excess demand results in some side effects which are adverse from the standpoint of the framers of usury law legislation.

In the case of an interest elastic supply curve, the amount of loanable funds available will be less if the usury rate is below what would otherwise be the market clearing rate of interest. From all that we know about the competitive nature of financial markets, we would have to say that an assumption of an elastic supply curve is reasonable. The situation is illustrated in Fig. 12-2.

[1]A discount from face value enables the lender to obtain a higher effective yield. If the face value were $1,000, the usury rate ceiling were 10 percent and the lender advanced only $940, the yield would be higher than 10 percent because the borrower would need to repay the full $1,000 plus compound interest of 10 percent.

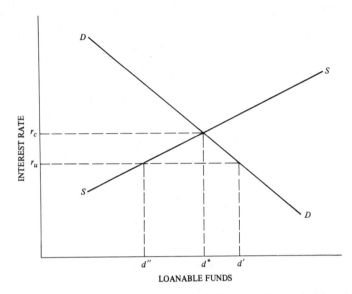

Figure 12-2. Illustration of interest-rate ceiling with an elastic supply curve.

We see that at a ceiling rate of interest of r_u, lenders will supply loans in the amount of d'', which of course is less than would occur with a market clearing rate of r_c. The presence of excess loan demand, $d' - d''$, will result in the same incentives as before—namely, for lenders to upgrade the quality of their loans and to seek other compensation that falls outside the usury law. To the extent this occurs, the supply of loans at r_u may be greater than d''. What we have done then is to introduce dimensions other than interest payments to the supply of loanable funds. As a result, the supply curve in Fig. 12-2 would no longer hold, but in some measure would shift to the right. It is conceivable the shift might be sufficient to provide d^* or even more loanable funds at the lower than market clearing rate, r_u. However, this does not mean that the usury law is working for its intended purpose—only that it is being circumvented and the lender is receiving payment by other means.

Are usury laws harmful then? For the most part the answer is yes. For one thing, they affect the efficiency with which financial markets operate. Inherently, the mechanisms for circumventing usury laws are less efficient than the simple use of interest rates to allocate credit. To the extent that a financial market is less efficient, there is greater cost and/or inconvenience associated with the channeling of savings in our society. Moreover, circumvention around usury laws results in less truth in lending. Borrowers may not fully recognize the true cost of a loan. To the extent they are deceived relative to what they would be if interest charges alone were the only cost, this too is counter to the intentions of those advocating social measures to allocate capital.

Finally, and perhaps most importantly, usury rates below market clearing rates of interest usually result in credit being rationed. The larger the gap of excess demand in Fig. 12-2, the more lenders will try to increase the quality of their loans and seek alternative forms of compensation. In upgrading quality, riskier loan applicants will be increasingly rejected. To the extent that these applicants are low-income people or the poor, their ability to borrow is foreclosed. As the formulation of most usury laws is with a concern for the cost of borrowing by the poor, ironically the end result may be that there is no cost for them because they are unable to obtain credit at the ceiling rate. Thus, there should be concern not only with the impact of usury laws on the total amount of credit extended but on the composition of borrowers as well.

Empirical Studies of Usury Laws

In general, various empirical studies on consumer credit and mortgages support the idea that when interest-rate ceilings are binding, the volume of loans declines, lenders try to upgrade quality to the detriment of lower income individuals, and noninterest methods of compensation increasingly are employed. Studies of consumer credit have shown that risk acceptance by finance companies is directly related to the level of the interest-rate ceiling. These studies suggest that in those states with high interest-rate ceilings, finance companies are less stringent in their credit standards, as evidenced by loan rejection rates. This also is manifested in higher losses from bad debts.[2] In addition, there is some evidence that the supply of personal loans is adversely affected by binding interest-rate ceilings. However, the empirical evidence here is mixed, owing to certain data problems. In one of the more comprehensive studies, which was based on an extensive sample survey, Greer found that the supply of personal loans was directly related to the legal rate ceiling.[3] As the ceiling decreased, small personal loans in particular were curtailed.

For mortgage loans, empirical studies have shown that binding interest-rate ceilings cause lenders to upgrade credit standards and to increase closing fees and discounts. Increased credit standards are reflected in such things as a higher percentage of downpayment required, a higher ratio of family income to debt, and a shorter maturity of that debt. As explained in footnote 1, a discount is the amount by which the loan advanced is less

---

[2]See Douglas F. Greer, "Rate Ceilings and Loan Turndowns," *Journal of Finance,* 30 (December 1975): 1376–83; Greer, "Rate Ceilings, Market Structure, and the Supply of Finance Company Personal Loans," *Journal of Finance,* 29 (December 1974): 1363–82; Robert P. Shay, "Factors Affecting Price, Volume and Credit Risk in the Consumer Finance Industry," *Journal of Finance,* 25 (May 1970): 503–15; and Daniel J. Villegas, "An Analysis of the Impact of Interest Rate Ceilings," *Journal of Finance,* 37 (September 1982): 941–54.

[3]Greer, "Rate Ceilings, Market Structure, and the Supply of Finance Company Personal Loans."

than the face value of the instrument: the lower the discount, the higher the effective yield on the loan. These studies also have shown that the volume of mortgage loans decreases as the market clearing rate rises above the interest-rate ceiling, and that the level of economic activity in the area is reduced because of the impact on construction expenditures.[4]

On the whole, then, the empirical evidence on usury laws suggests that they can result in reductions in the supply of loans and increases in the number and types of loan applicants rejected. Also, there is indication that noninterest forms of compensation are employed. All of this is in accord with our previous conceptual discussion of usury laws in financial markets characterized by elastic supply curves. Under the *Depository Institutions Deregulation Act of 1980,* usury laws on residential mortgages and business and agricultural loans were voided (in 1983) unless voters in a state specifically approved them. However, consumer credit is still subject to usury laws.

GOVERNMENT GUARANTEES, INSURANCE, AND MORAL OBLIGATIONS

The government also can socially allocate capital through a guarantee of a borrower's obligations to private lenders or through insurance, where the government insures a loan against default. Virtually every department of the federal government has guaranteed and insured loan programs, several hundred in all. With such a program, of course, the default risk of the loan is reduced to zero. With this risk reduction, the debt obligation is made more attractive to investors. The potential borrower may now be able to attract lenders where before there were none, or it may simply pay a lower interest cost. In all cases, the debt instrument becomes a more desirable substitute relative to other financial instruments in the marketplace. As the guarantee and insurance are identical with respect to risk reduction, we analyze only the guarantee.[5]

The situation is illustrated in Fig. 12-3. In this case, the demand curves represent those of a single borrower. Without a guarantee, the demand curve DD and supply curve SS intersect at point X, which results in a market clearing rate of interest of r_c. With the guarantee, however, the supply curve shifts to the right—to $S'-S'$. This occurs because the financial

---

[4]See James R. Ostas, "Effects of Usury Ceilings in the Mortgage Market," *Journal of Finance,* 31 (June 1976): 821–34; and Steven M. Crafton, "An Empirical Test of the Effect of Usury Laws," *Journal of Law and Economics,* 23 (April 1980): 135–45.

[5]The cost of insurance may be borne by the government, by the borrower, or by all borrowers in a category based on the default experience of the category. In the first two instances, insurance and the guarantee are very similar; in the last they are not, with respect to cost. As exploration of this topic is a digression from the central focus of this chapter, we do not do so.

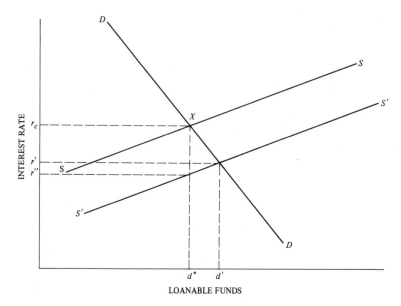

Figure 12-3. Illustration of the effect of a government guarantee.

instrument now is more attractive due to the reduction in risk. If the borrower is unrestricted by the government in the amount it is able to borrow, it will seek d' in financing at an interest rate of r'. Thus, the interest rate will decline and the amount borrowed will increase. If, however, the government restricts the amount that can be borrowed, the effective supply curve shortens. Suppose for purposes of illustration the restriction were set at the amount borrowed before the guarantee, d^*. Instead of a supply curve of $S'-S'$, the supply curve would be $S'-d^*$ in Fig. 12-3. As a result, the interest rate would be r''. Thus, the entire effect of the guarantee would be on interest cost and not on the amount of financing.

Use of Guarantees and Moral Obligations

There are a number of instances where loan guarantees have been used. The Veterans Administration guarantees mortgages for qualified veterans. During World War II and on occasion thereafter, the federal government guaranteed bank loans of certain defense manufacturers. This program was called the Victory Loan, or V-Loan, program and it endeavored to assure credit being available to essential defense contractors. Larger and more recent examples include guarantees of the loans of Lockheed Corporation (later eliminated because they were no longer needed), Chrysler Corporation, and Wheeling-Pittsburgh Steel Corporation. While national security considerations may have been a motivating factor in these guarantees, most of the debate in Congress was over the preservation of jobs. There are numerous other instances of government guarantees and insurance. For example, the Export-Import Bank guarantees certain financing incurred in the export of U.S. goods and services. We will not try to list all guarantees, if indeed that were possible, because our concern is with the principle and not the specifics.

In recent years, various state governments have set up special corporations to borrow money with the "moral obligation" of the state. While this backing is not legally enforceable, there nonetheless is an implied backing, and this works to make the debt instruments of the borrower more attractive than otherwise would be the case. The most controversial example of the use of moral obligations was by New York State with their housing authority corporations. These were set up to finance low-to-moderate-income housing. When many of the authorities experienced financial difficulty in 1975 and 1976, this unfortunately coincided with the difficulty experienced by New York City. It became clear to investors that the state would not necessarily honor the housing authority's obligations. As a result, the "value" of New York State's moral obligation declined appreciably in the minds of investors. The original purpose was to find a way socially to allocate capital to urban development and low-income housing at favorable interest costs without taking on a contingent legal obligation. It worked— if you could call it that—for a while, until the moral obligation was put to the test and found lacking.

The Transfer of Underlying Risk

The use of a guarantee, insurance, or moral obligation obviously has great appeal. Borrowers are able to avail themselves of financing that otherwise might not be available or available only at a significantly higher interest cost. In many instances, the government receives a guarantee, or insurance, fee. Proponents of this method of socially allocating capital will argue that everyone gains and no one loses. The apparent implication is *pareto* optimality with no boundaries. However, when one analyzes the situation a little more closely one finds that there is a cost and that someone must bear this cost.

The crux of this issue is that underlying risk does not go away with a government guarantee or insurance. Borrowers can still default, particularly if there is a limit to the amount of government assistance. The underlying risk is simply shifted from the investor to the federal government and to taxpayers at large. If default occurs, the federal government will need to make good on the obligation. In final analysis, this will result in forgoing federal programs, increasing taxes, or increasing the federal debt. Therefore, there is a cost to the guarantee or insurance program, though admittedly it is largely a hidden one. It is the contingent or potential cost to present and future taxpayers. As discussed in Chapter 8, which dealt with default risk, the cost is represented by the left-hand side of the probability distribution of possible returns where actual returns are less than the promised return. This probabilistic cost is absorbed by the government in order to make credit available at a lower cost to a socially desirable project.

Thus, the government supplants the marketplace in judging the risk-return tradeoff, and return is broadened to include not only the project's economic return but its social return as well. More will be said about this supplanting later in the chapter once we have considered other methods for socially allocating capital. Unfortunately, there has been little empirical work done on the effect of government guarantees and moral obligations on yields and risk. An exception is Howard B. Sossin who used the option pricing model to analyze the value to the corporation and cost to the government of a guarantee.[6] (See the appendix to Chapter 11 for a presentation of this model.) He investigated the cost to the government if it were to buy the guarantee in competitive financial markets, using historical market averages for return, variance, and ratios of debt to total value. Sossin finds that for the average corporation the value/cost of a guarantee is relatively small. However, as the market variance of a company increases beyond the average of all firms, the value/cost of the guarantee and the interest cost savings to the company increases dramatically.

INTEREST-RATE SUBSIDIES

A third method for socially allocating capital is for the government to pay an interest-rate subsidy to either the lender or to the borrower. When it goes to the lender, the government typically subsidizes a category of loans—such as mortgages or loans to cities. This approach tends to be "shotgun," in that it benefits all borrowers in a particular category. While this may be appropriate if one is trying to stimulate housing or construction overall, it is not effective if the purpose is to enable low-income families to purchase housing. Here a subsidy to the borrower, or to the lender where the subsidy is tied to a loan to a specific borrower, is better. Note that in either case the lender receives the market clearing rate of interest on the loan. The borrower pays this rate minus the subsidy. For

[6]Howard B. Sossin, "On the Valuation of Federal Loan Guarantees to Corporations," Research Paper, Columbia University, 1980. For similar, but theoretical, applications of the model, see Robert Merton, "An Analytical Derivation of the Cost of Deposit Insurance and Loan Guarantees," *Journal of Banking and Finance*, 1 (June 1977): 3–12; and E. Philips Jones and Scott P. Mason, "Valuation of Loan Guarantees," *Journal of Banking and Finance*, 4 (March 1980): 89–107.

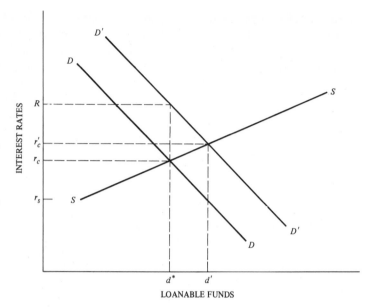

Figure 12-4. Interest-rate subsidy with an elastic supply curve.

the most part, interest-rate subsidies have been used to subsidize the mortgage payments of low income families. If the market clearing rate on a mortgage were 14 percent and the subsidy were 6 percent, the effective interest cost would be 8 percent.

The Effect of the Subsidy

With an interest-rate subsidy, the demand for that type of financing presumably will increase. Whether or not the supply of financing increases, however, depends on the elasticity of supply. In turn, this depends on the substitutability between the type of debt instrument or market involved and other financial instruments.[7] If the supply curve is reasonably interest elastic, the amount of financing will increase. The situation is illustrated in Fig. 12-4. Before the subsidy, the demand for financing is depicted by DD. With a supply curve of SS, financing in the amount of d^* will occur at a market clearing rate of r_c. With a subsidy of $R - r_c$, the demand curve shifts to $D'D'$. In turn, this causes the amount of financing to increase to d', and the market clearing rate to increase to r'_c. However,

---

[7]For an analysis of this point, see Rudolph G. Penner and William L. Silber, "The Interaction between Federal Credit Programs and the Impact on the Allocation of Credit," *American Economic Review*, LXIII (December 1973): 839–42.

the interest rate the borrower pays is the new market clearing rate minus the subsidy, or $r_c' - (R - r_c) = r_s$. Thus, the amount of financing increases, and the effective interest rate paid by the borrower declines.

If the supply curve were inelastic, however, there would be no increase in the amount of financing. This situation is illustrated in Fig. 12-5. Here a subsidy of $R - r_c$ shifts the demand curve to $D'D'$. However, because of the inelastic supply curve, the amount of financing does not increase. The shift in the demand curve is reflected entirely in an increase in the market clearing rate, namely from r_c to R. Thus, this increase exactly offsets the subsidy, so the effective rate of interest to the borrower is the same as before. Put another way, all the subsidy goes to the lender.

Thus, the degree of substitutability between the financial instrument or market involved in the subsidy arrangement and other financial instruments and markets determines the success of the arrangement. With an inelastic supply curve, neither the amount of financing is raised, nor is the effective rate paid by the borrower lowered. Given all we know about financial markets, however, the case for a completely inelastic supply curve of loanable funds for a particular financial instrument seems weak. We would expect supply curves to be reasonably elastic and the situation to resemble that depicted in Fig. 12-4.

One important feature of the interest-rate subsidy approach to socially allocate capital is that the government does not intercede directly into the marketplace. It pays a subsidy, but financial markets then equilibrate on

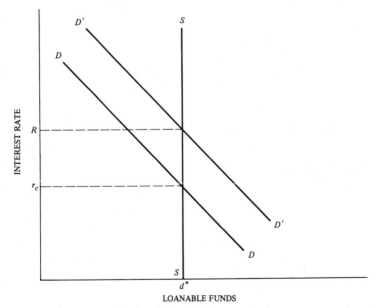

Figure 12-5. Interest-rate subsidy with an inelastic supply curve.

the basis of expected return and risk. Therefore there is a minimum of interference in the workings of financial markets. However, indirect pressure on financial markets can result if the subsidy is raised by increasing the amount of government debt. By issuing securities in the Treasury or municipal markets, the supply curve for the particular market to which the government is trying to socially allocate capital would be adversely affected if there were substitutability between the markets. Put another way, it is final general equilibrium in financial markets which is important in judging the success of a plan to socially allocate capital. If the secondary effects offset the initial action, this must be considered before a decision can be made. Instead of an increase in government debt to pay for the subsidy, the capital may be raised by an increase in general taxes. In this case, there is little effect on other financial markets and this offsetting factor can be safely ignored when judging the merits of the subsidy arrangement.[8] More will be said about the relative merits of an interest-rate subsidy approach once we have considered all of the methods for socially allocating capital.

FINANCIAL INTERMEDIATION THROUGH BORROWING AND RELENDING

Another means for socially allocating capital is for the government, or an agency thereof, to borrow in the financial markets and then to relend to a savings and loan association, a corporation, a housing authority, a municipality, or what have you, at either the same rate at which it borrows or at a higher rate. In either case, the rate charged is lower than what the ultimate borrower would pay in the market. Examples of this type of arrangement include the federal government's revolving credit to New York City (1976), where the ultimate source of these funds was an increase on the federal debt; the Export-Import Bank, which borrows from the Treasury at the government bond rate and then relends to foreigners purchasing U.S. products; and government sponsored enterprises—such as the three agencies of the Farm Credit Administration, and the Federal Home Loan Bank—which borrow funds in the capital markets and relend them in support of various specified activities. Whether it be exports, farmers, or home buyers, a subsidy is involved because financing is at below market rates.

The Situation Illustrated

In all of these cases the government becomes a financial intermediary for purposes of redirecting the flow of savings toward socially desirable projects. In so doing, the credit worthiness of the government

[8]*Ibid.*

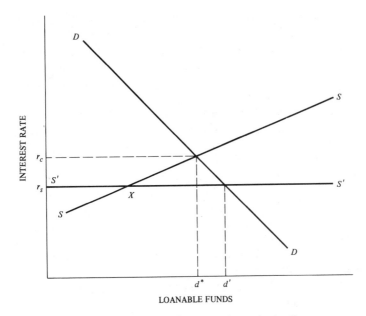

Figure 12-6. The effect of borrowing and relending.

or agency thereof is substituted for that of the party involved. Because of the credit worthiness of the government, the rate the borrower pays is lower. The situation is illustrated in Fig. 12-6. Before the government program to borrow and relend to the socially desirable project, the intersection of the supply, *SS*, and demand, *DD*, curves results in a market clearing rate of r_c and in a total amount borrowed of d^*. When the government steps in, it replaces the previous supply curve with a new supply curve, $S'S'$. We assume that the interest rate charged, r_s, is the same regardless of the amount borrowed, although this need not be the case.

It is possible that part of the funding of the project will be fulfilled by private sources if a discriminating auction takes place. In the case of Fig. 12-6, this would result in a kinked supply curve of SXS', with the former portion coming from private sources. If the subsidy rate charged is low enough, however, the government will end up displacing entirely the financing of the project through private sources. Another qualification to Fig. 12-6 is that the government may not wish to provide unlimited amounts of financing at a rate of r_s. Rather, it may simply agree to provide up to so much financing, in which case the supply curve $S'S'$ in Fig. 12-6 would be a horizontal line which would stop abruptly at some point.

The Effect of Government Intermediation

The effect of this form of socially allocating capital is somewhat the same as that which occurs in the case of a government guarantee or insurance. In whole or in part, the government absorbs the risk of default. As before, the underlying risk of the project does not go away but it is merely shifted from private investors to the government and, ultimately, to taxpayers at large. In addition, the amount borrowed will be larger than would occur under free market conditions, unless the government limits the amount it is willing to lend. In Fig. 12-6, equilibrium borrowings occur at d' where before they were at the lower d^*.

What happens, of course, is that the government borrows at a favorable interest rate and then relends to the project involved. Again the equilibrating mechanism in financial markets is distorted. Funds no longer flow on the basis of expected return and risk. One set of potential borrowers moves to the head of the credit line and capital is allocated to those borrowers on the basis of government decree, not by the marketplace. To the extent that substitutability exists between the financial instrument or market involved in the social allocation process and other financial markets and, to the extent that the amount of financing for the social project is larger than would otherwise be the case, the supply function for the other markets is adversely affected from the standpoint of borrowers. In other words, the supply curves for the other markets would shift to the left. In general equilibrium, then, other borrowers may pay somewhat higher interest rates as a result of the government's borrowing and relending for the social project. This would also affect the government in its borrowing, so part of the expected advantage would be offset. However, if the amount of capital socially allocated is relatively small, there will be little offset.

Another way of looking at the matter is that as long as a project is able to obtain a social allocation of capital from the government and relatively few others are able to do so, significant advantage accrues to it. However, if a large number of other borrowers have similar access to the government, the advantage diminishes. Beyond a point, essentially all financial flows would be determined by social criteria as opposed to economic criteria, and there would be no private financial markets as we know them. Savings would not flow to investment projects that appear to be most productive from an economic standpoint. They would flow on the basis of government determined priorities. To the extent that these priorities differed significantly from economic priorities, the economic growth of the country would lessen and the wherewithal to address social problems would be reduced. The point of all this is simply to show that while some borrowing and relending by the government for social purposes may be beneficial to the favored parties and not significantly detrimental to other borrowers, as more and more action takes place the advantage quickly disappears. In an era of economic scarcity, it takes a relatively rich nation to deal effectively with its social problems. The tradeoffs are ever present and must be recognized. This issue will be discussed further in the closing section of the chapter.

REGULATIONS AFFECTING INVESTOR AND BORROWER BEHAVIOR

The fifth method for socially allocating capital is the use of government regulations to divert the flow of savings toward socially desirable projects. In this case, artificial restraints are established to affect the flows. The best known and most important example of this method has to do with mortgage financing. By establishing ceiling rates of interest that mortgage lending institutions may pay to attract savings and by creating certain barriers to the saver with respect to investing elsewhere—i.e., by restricting competition—the hope is to increase mortgage financing at rates of interest lower than what would otherwise be the market clearing rates. Unlike other approaches for socially allocating capital, the government's role is indirect, sometimes bordering on the obscure, but nonetheless may be powerful.

The Effectiveness of this Approach

The success of this approach depends on the degree of substitutability between markets. The more isolated the mortgage market is relative to other markets and the less the substitutability between mortgages and other financial instruments, the greater will be the flow of savings to mortgages and the lower the rate of interest, all other things remaining the same. However, if mortgages and other financial instruments are perfect substitutes, lenders who are unrestricted by the government will simply substitute other securities for mortgages whenever the risk-adjusted rate of return falls below that which is available in other financial markets. The actions of these unrestricted investors will offset actions by financial institutions, which are restricted in their investment behavior to mortgages. Therefore, within limits, government efforts to lower mortgage rates and increase the supply of mortgage funds will be for naught.[9] Increases in mortgage purchases by restricted lenders will merely replace the exit of unrestricted lenders. However, if there are no unrestricted investors and only restricted lenders make mortgage loans, the government's efforts to increase the flow of savings to these institutions will be successful in increasing the amount of mortgage loans.

Let us turn now to the situation where mortgages and other securities are less than perfect substitutes and there are unrestricted lenders present in the mortgage market. Here there would be a less than one-for-one offset by unrestricted lenders in selling mortgages for other securities when the risk-adjusted return was forced below that available in other markets. In

[9]*Ibid.,* pp. 841–3.

the extreme case of zero substitutability between markets, there would be no offset. As long as the degree of substitutability is less than perfect, there will be a "stickiness" on the part of unrestricted lenders in selling mortgages, even though risk-adjusted rates may be more attractive elsewhere. As a result, this approach to socially allocate capital will be only partially successful. In summary, this approach is essentially one which advances the government imposing restrictions to thwart competition so that the flow of savings to mortgage lending institutions can be enhanced.

On Whom the Costs Fall

With this approach there is no direct cost to the government and to taxpayers, with the exception of the costs associated with initiating the restrictions and with enforcing them. Therefore, the approach is viewed by some as costless. However, there are costs, although admittedly they are largely hidden. For one thing, artificial restrictions result in a less efficient functioning of the financial markets of society. They impede the effectiveness with which financial markets channel savings from savings-surplus economic units to savings-deficit ones. Moreover, there is a cost to savers who must accept lower interest rates on their savings than otherwise would prevail.

The cost falls unevenly on different savers. Higher-income individuals with larger amounts of savings typically are able to take advantage of alternative investment opportunities, such as money-market instruments, which pay higher rates of interest. Because of minimum denomination problems and transaction, information, and inconvenience costs, low- to moderate-income families in the past were unable to take advantage of these alternatives. Even here, however, the forces of competition and financial innovation were not long shackled. In the 1974–1975 era of high interest rates, money-market funds developed that enabled individuals to invest in money-market instruments in smaller denominations than is possible with a direct purchase of Treasury bills, commercial paper, bank certificates of deposit, or bankers' acceptances. This financial innovation has given the traditional saver alternatives.

With the *Depository Institutions Deregulation Act of 1980,* ceilings on savings deposits gradually were increased in the early 1980s and eventually will be removed altogether. At the end of 1982, deposit institutions were allowed to offer fully-competitive rates on accounts of $2,500 or more. For time certificates of deposit, the minimum denomination was reduced and competitive rates were allowed to be paid here as well. As a result, individuals are able to avail themselves of these investment vehicles. Low-to-moderate-income families benefit in receiving a more competitive rate of interest on their savings than in the 1960s and 1970s. In those earlier times, they had to accept lower savings rates than would have been possible in competitive markets unhampered by ceiling deposit rates and other restrictions. The beneficiaries of this social allocation of capital were home buyers, residential building buyers, and, to a much lesser extent, commercial building buyers. These owners typically were medium-to-high-income individuals. Very few low-income families own homes. Therefore, we had an equity or income redistribution problem. Those individuals who benefited most from available mortgages at favorable interest rates usually were able to avail themselves of alternative investments for their savings when money-market rates rose significantly above deposit rates. Those who were least able to take advantage of such alternatives were not home buyers, so they did not benefit directly from the social allocation of capital to mortgages. In this sense, there was discrimination against the small saver.

Empirical Studies of Mortgages and Housing

Of all the areas involving the social allocation of capital, mortgage financing has received the most attention empirically. In a comprehensive study of federal credit programs designed to spur housing, Penner and Silber categorized the various programs as to the approach used.[10] Also, the interrelationships between programs were studied to determine if they were reinforcing, negatively correlated, or neutral. A key factor for both subsidy-type programs and regulatory-type programs is the degree of substitutability between mortgages and other financial instruments. Penner and Silber suggested that actions undertaken to increase the attractiveness of mortgages and their substitutability with other financial instruments are compatible with subsidy-type programs, but not with regulatory-type programs. This point was examined in previous sections. While Penner and Silber do not analyze actual mortgage data, their contribution lies in carefully synthesizing the various programs for socially allocating capital to mortgages.

There have been several studies dealing with the effectiveness and cost of past government efforts to protect the flow of savings to savings and loan associations, as well as to mutual savings banks, during periods of sharply rising interest rates. During these times, interest rates on money-market instruments rose significantly above deposit rates. Given attractive yields elsewhere, thrift institutions experienced a slowdown, and sometimes even a decline, in their deposit growth. Called *disintermediation*, this phenomenon caused concern for many in government, due to the important role these institutions play in mortgage lending. In studying the 1966 period, Peter Fortune developed an econometric model of the household sector

[10]*Ibid.*

with particular emphasis on their allocation of liquid assets, including savings deposits.[11] Among other things, Fortune found that flows of new savings were more sensitive to interest rates than were existing savings deposits. This held for both commercial banks and thrift institutions. In studying the effect of commercial bank competition on thrift deposit flows during 1966, Fortune discovered that only about 20 percent of the decrease in such flows could be attributed to commercial bank competition. Most of the disintermediation was attributable to competition from money-market instruments. Fortune also studied the effect of the $10,000 minimum denomination purchase of Treasury bills, which was initiated in 1970, as a means for protecting thrift deposit flows. In contrast to the previous results, he found that this action was highly effective in protecting such flows during 1970.

Another question regarding the use of regulations to redirect savings flows to mortgages is that of income redistribution. As we studied earlier, the cost of socially allocating capital in this way falls primarily on low-to-moderate-income families, who are forced to accept lower than market clearing rates on their savings. David H. Pyle endeavored to estimate the overall size of the opportunity loss to savers.[12] In so doing, he devised a model to estimate the deposit rates that would have been paid during 1968–1970 in the absence of these restrictions. Separate estimates were made for savings and loan associations, for commercial banks, and for mutual savings banks, based on 1952–1967 data. The parameters derived then were used to predict deposit rates for 1968, 1969, and 1970. Comparisons of predicted rates with actual rates for each of the years were as follows:

Year	SAVINGS AND LOAN ASSOCIATIONS		COMMERCIAL BANKS		MUTUAL SAVINGS BANKS	
	Predicted	Actual	Predicted	Actual	Predicted	Actual
1968	4.88%	4.68%	4.46%	4.25%	4.88%	4.76%
1969	5.22	4.80	4.96	4.34	5.17	4.89
1970	5.61	5.06	5.49	4.72	5.53	5.01

In all three years, predicted rates were above actual rates, and Pyle attributes this to binding interest-rate ceilings. Using the differential between predicted and actual rates as an estimate of the interest income lost by savers due to restrictions, he multiplied these differentials times the stocks of savings deposits at each institution for each of the years. For the three years, his overall estimate of the interest income loss was in excess of $5 billion. This represents an opportunity loss in the sense of what savers

[11]Peter Fortune, "The Effectiveness of Recent Policies to Maintain Thrift-Deposit Flows," *Journal of Money, Banking and Credit,* 7 (August 1975): 297–315.
[12]David H. Pyle, "The Losses on Savings Deposits from Interest Rate Regulation," *Bell Journal of Economics and Management Science,* 5 (Autumn 1974): 614–22.

would have received if market clearing savings rates had been paid and what they actually were paid. As discussed earlier, the burden of this opportunity loss would be expected to fall heavily on low-to-medium-income families.

Charles Clotfelder and Charles Lieberman also studied the dollar amount of interest income not received by various income groups as a result of deposit rate restrictions.[13] Using Pyle's estimation procedure, they calculated a measure of the rate of interest forgone for each deposit asset, based on the distribution of households' asset holdings. The authors found interest losses to be quite substantial and the restrictions to have a regressive income distributional effect. The implicit "tax" of interest income forgone was higher for lower income groups than for higher ones. Edward C. Lawrence and Gregory E. Elliehausen updated the Clotfelder-Lieberman estimates using data on 1977 asset holdings.[14] In general, the findings were similar—deposit rate ceilings were regressive. However, the authors found less regressivity in 1977 than in 1970. They attribute this difference to the fact that consumers adjusted better to inflation's adverse effect on fixed-interest savings accounts by shifting to assets which are better protected from inflation. Moreover, financial innovations are said to result in the difference. Thomas Mayer and Harold Nathan also estimated the costs of time deposit rate ceilings for various income and socioeconomic groups.[15] The authors found the ceilings to be regressive with respect to income but not according to occupation, where professionals, managers and the self-employed suffered the worst. When households were classified by age, the heaviest burden fell on the 60 and over group.

In summary, empirical evidence of the 1960s and 1970s indicates that deposit rate ceilings and other restrictions were effective in diverting savings flows to mortgage lending institutions. Moreover, the principle burden of this method for socially allocating capital fell on low-to-moderate-income families in receiving less than competitive rates of interest on their savings. As these restrictions were largely removed in the 1980s, such evidence no longer exists.

QUALIFICATION FOR TAX-EXEMPT FINANCING

The last means for socially allocating capital that we examine is the designation of certain projects for tax-exempt financing. The advantage to the borrower is obvious—the interest cost is significantly less than

[13]Charles Clotfelder and Charles Lieberman, "On the Distributional Impact of Federal Interest Rate Restrictions," *Journal of Finance,* 33 (March 1978): 199–213.

[14]Edward C. Lawrence and Gregory E. Elliehausen, "The Impact of Federal Interest Rate Regulations on the Small Saver: Further Evidence," *Journal of Finance,* 36 (June 1981): 677–84.

[15]Thomas Mayer and Harold Nathan, "The Distributional Effects of Interest Rate Ceilings on Time and Savings Deposits," Staff Paper, Comptroller of the Currency, 1982.

it would be if taxable bonds were issued. While we usually think of municipal debt financing schools, sewers, public buildings, parks, and highways, this no longer is the case. At present, less than one-half of all tax-exempt financing goes to such projects, the rest being used to finance essentially private projects. Corporations issue industrial revenue bonds to finance plants, as well as commercial structures (limited to $10 million per project). While industrial development bonds were begun in Mississippi in the 1930s to attract industry, they now finance fast-food outlets, retail car dealers, department stores, bank branches, racquet clubs, and many other private projects. With mortgage revenue bonds, home buyers borrow from housing authorities at lower than prevailing mortgage rates because the authority issues tax-exempt bonds. (This use was greatly restricted by the Congress in 1980.) Pollution-control bonds finance the installation of pollution-control devices on industrial plants at the tax-exempt rate. Student loans and farmer loans are other examples of the use of tax-exempt debt to finance private projects. Such financing is burgeoning and dominates the municipal securities market.

If we ignore second-order effects for the moment, the situation is illustrated in Fig. 12-7. In the absence of financing "qualified" private projects on a tax-exempt basis, the intersection of the supply, SS, and demand, DD, curves results in a market clearing rate of r_c and in a total amount borrowed of d^*. The availability of lower-cost tax-exempt financing shifts the supply curve to the right in the figure. Qualified borrowers now

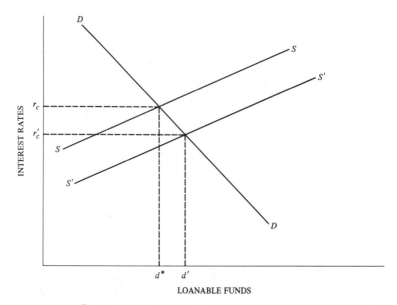

Figure 12-7. Tax-exempt financing of private projects.

seek d' in financing at the lower market clearing rate of r_c'. Thus, additional less-productive projects are undertaken, which would not be the case if they had to be financed in the taxable bond market. The magnitude is depicted by $d' - d^*$ on the horizontal axis in Fig. 12-7. There obviously are great incentives to get one's project qualified for tax-exempt financing. Given rational behavior, it is little wonder that such financing of essentially private projects has flourished. The limiting factors are only the demand for such projects and the legality of whether or not a project qualifies.

However, there are second-order effects that considerably cloud the picture presented in Fig. 12-7. Certainly society gains with some of the projects: Employment in a depressed area is stimulated; pollution is reduced; housing may be enhanced; hospitals are built or improved; or energy production is somehow increased. These benefits are an inducement to those in government to continue to allow the municipal interest subsidy to go for these purposes. However, there are obvious issues of equity and redistribution of income, regarding who qualifies and who does not. This phenomenon is particularly acute with industrial revenue bonds. Moreover, there are costs. For one thing, there is a revenue loss to the federal government, as tax-exempt bonds are substituted for taxable bonds. In essence, the government subsidizes those private projects that qualify. Owing to certain offsets, the revenue loss is less than one-for-one. Still, the loss to the government is significant, and this loss results in either federal programs being forgone, higher taxes for others, or increases in the federal debt.

As discussed before for other methods, at the margin less-productive projects are favored over those that can be financed only with taxable bonds. Consequently, there is an opportunity cost to society in lower productivity than is possible if all private projects competed for capital on the same basis. Another consideration is that the market for municipal securities may be partially segmented on the demand side, as discussed in Chapter 10. That is, only a limited number of investors are able to take full advantage of the tax exemption of interest income. As the overall supply of municipal securities increases, municipalities must appeal for funds to investors in lower and lower tax brackets. As this occurs, interest rates in the municipal market rise, all other things the same. As a result, municipalities financing public projects must pay a higher interest cost than would be true if there were no tax-exempt financing of private projects. Thus, the capital costs associated with providing such traditional facilities as schools, sewers, recreational areas, and highways increases.[16]

---

[16]For an excellent presentation of the issues involved in the tax-exempt financing of private projects as well as empirical studies of the magnitude of the problem and the costs, see George G. Kaufman, ed., *Efficiency in the Municipal Bond Market: The Use of Tax Exempt Financing for "Private" Purposes* (Greenwich, Connecticut: JAI Press, 1981).

POLICY IMPLICATIONS

In this chapter we have examined a number of means by which the government can influence the flow of savings to a desired cause and/or reduce the rate of interest paid by a designated borrower. In all cases, there is intervention into the marketplace; hence we have in whole or in part a social allocation of capital as opposed to a pure market allocation. There is little question that the social allocation of capital has become increasingly popular in recent years. Special interest groups and politicians see it as a means for improving the condition of a particular sector of society, enabling it to borrow funds which might not otherwise be available or might be available only at a significantly higher interest cost. The political appeal is irresistible—there appear to be enormous benefits and, on the surface at least, few costs. However, we know from our previous discussion that there are costs. For one thing, the function of financial markets is altered. This function is to channel savings in our society efficiently to the most productive investment opportunities. These opportunities may be private sector investments, where there are private rates of return, or public sector investments with social rates of return. The mechanism by which funds are channeled is the tradeoff between expected return and risk. When the government explicitly directs funds to certain investments which would either not be able to attract funds on their own or would attract them only at a higher rate of interest, it tampers with the workings of the marketplace. This tampering can lead to less efficient financial markets with the result that savings are allocated at higher costs and/or with greater inconvenience. This has adverse implications for us all.

Funds no longer flow on the basis of expected return and risk. Certain borrowers—namely, those whom the government decides are socially deserving—no longer must justify their investment's private or social rate of return in relation to a market determined standard of efficiency. The result is that some investments are undertaken that would be rejected if the borrower had to compete directly in the financial markets for funds. Put another way, in society as a whole investments are undertaken which are not optimal in the sense of economic efficiency. As a result, there may be an adverse effect on real economic growth. Moreover, if distortions in risk-return relationships lead to less efficient financial markets, this also may have an adverse effect on economic growth. Financial markets simply become less efficient in channeling savings to investment opportunities on a risk-adjusted return basis. For these reasons, economic growth and want satisfaction in society may be less than otherwise would be the case.

What we have is the social allocation of capital to selected projects, some by choice and others by default. As we have discussed repeatedly, there is a serious question of equity in who is to benefit from the social allocation of capital. In a number of instances, there is income redistribution, not always with the intended or desired results. Moreover, the loss of tax revenue to the Federal Government that is associated with certain of the methods requires new taxes, expenditure reductions, or more Treasury borrowings. These second-order effects are seldom considered, but are factors of concern nonetheless.

This is not to say that savings flows should be allocated on the basis of economic considerations alone. Without question, there are unmet social needs, and some of these needs may be satisfied by the social allocation of capital. The probem is that methods for socially allocating capital are seldom evaluated in their totality. Usually the benefits are readily apparent and always cited. However, the "true costs" are seldom considered. As a result, the idea is often given that the social allocation of capital is either without cost or that the costs are unimportant. As we have shown, however, there is a cost, not only to the government and to taxpayers, but to society as a whole, in having less efficient financial markets and lower than possible economic growth. Unfortunately, the more hidden the cost, the more tempting it is to allocate capital socially. More disturbing is the fact that usually the more hidden the cost of a method, the less efficient the process by which capital is allocated socially.

These problems, as well as others that we have discussed throughout this chapter, are sufficient to give insight into the costs of socially allocating capital. It is extremely important that these costs be recognized and evaluated before a decision is made. The benefits of a plan to allocate capital socially must be judged in relation to the opportunity cost to taxpayers, to other borrowers, to savers, to the efficiency of financial markets, and to the economic and/or social contribution forgone by the rejection of other projects. While there is little question that the decision-making process is easier if these costs can somehow be ignored, they represent the very crux of the issue. As they ultimately must be borne by society in one way or another, these costs should be analyzed at the time of a decision.

In those cases where Congress or some other part of government deems it appropriate on the basis of a cost-benefit-type of analysis to allocate capital socially, a strong case can be made that it be in the form of an interest-rate subsidy to the borrower. Assuming a high degree of substitutability and competition between various financial instruments— and most evidence seems to confirm this—the subsidy is likely to be the most effective way to allocate capital socially, provided it comes from general tax revenues. With an interest-rate subsidy, financial markets are able to perform their function in terms of market clearing rates of interest as opposed to some artificial ceiling rate of interest imposed by government. With an absence of such restrictions, we would expect financial markets to perform as efficiently as possible under the circumstances. The subsidy would come from the federal government at the expense of taxpayers in general rather than a subset of them as now occurs. The advantage of such an arrangement would be that savings would be more efficiently channeled in society. While there still exists the question of social priorities versus economic priorities,[17] once these are resolved a free market mechanism would allocate savings in a competitive environment on the basis of risk and return.

SUMMARY

The social allocation of capital involves efforts by the government to direct the flow of savings in our society toward socially desirable projects and/or to lower the interest cost for these projects. A number of methods for allocating capital socially were analyzed. These include: (1) a ceiling or usury rate of interest on loans; (2) the use of a government guarantee, or "moral obligation"; (3) an interest-rate subsidy; (4) government's borrowing in the financial markets and relending to the socially desirable project; (5) the use of regulations to divert the flow of savings toward socially desirable projects; and (6) specification of who and what projects qualify for tax-exempt financing. Each of these methods was examined in regard to its effect in increasing the flow of financing and in lowering interest costs. A key ingredient was found to be the substitutability of the financial instrument in question with other financial instruments. In our analysis, available empirical evidence was examined and examples were presented.

In most cases, the costs of allocating capital socially are not understood. These costs include such things as the probabilistic cost of making good on a guarantee or insurance by the government, the less-efficient functioning of financial markets, the lessened allocative efficiency of real resources, the loss of tax revenue to the federal government and the consequences of how it is made up; it is critical that these costs be considered in relation to their benefits before a decision to socially allocate capital is made. Too often this does not occur, due to the "hidden" nature of many of the costs. When it is deemed appropriate to socially allocate capital, a strong case can be made for the use of an interest-rate subsidy, because it has the least disruptive influence on the functioning of financial markets. Use of this method implicitly assumes a reasonably high degree of substitutability among financial instruments.

---

[17]The use of a subsidy may result in overconsumption of certain commodities relative to others. Consideration of this issue in an overall framework of public choice is beyond the scope of this book.

SELECTED REFERENCES

Crafton, Steven M., "An Empirical Test of the Effect of Usury Laws," *Journal of Law and Economics,* 23 (April 1980): 135–45.

Fortune, Peter, "The Effectiveness of Recent Policies to Maintain Thrift-Deposit Flows," *Journal of Money, Credit and Banking,* 7 (August 1975): 297–315.

Greer, Douglas F., "Rate Ceilings, Market Structure, and the Supply of Finance Company Personal Loans," *Journal of Finance,* 29 (December 1974): 1363–82.

Kane, Edward J., "Good Intentions and Unintended Evil: The Case against Selective Credit Allocation," *Journal of Money, Credit and Banking,* 9 (February 1977): 55–69.

Kaufman, George G., *Efficiency of the Municipal Bond Market: The Use of Tax Exempt Financing for "Private" Purposes.* Greenwich, Conn.: JAI Press, 1981.

Penner, Rudolph G., and William L. Silber, "The Interaction between Federal Credit Programs and the Impact on the Allocation of Credit," *American Economic Review,* LXII (December 1973): 838–52.

Pyle, David H., "The Losses on Savings Deposits from Interest Rate Regulation," *Bell Journal of Economic and Management Science,* 5 (Autumn 1974): 614–22.

Sossin, Howard B., "On the Valuation of Federal Loan Guarantees to Corporations," Research Paper, Columbia University, 1980.

Van Horne, James C., "The Withering of Capital," *Journal of the Midwest Finance Association,* 10 (1981): 83–91.

Villegas, Daniel J., "An Analysis of the Impact of Interest Rate Ceilings," *Journal of Finance,* 37 (September 1982): 941–54.

INDEX